WAR OF THE GODFATHERS

WAR OF THE GODFATHERS

THE BLOODY CONFRONTATION BETWEEN
THE CHICAGO AND NEW YORK FAMILIES
FOR CONTROL OF LAS VEGAS

by

William F. Roemer, Jr.

DONALD I. FINE, INC.
New York

Library of Congress Cataloging-in-Publication Data
Roemer, William F., 1926-
War of the godfathers : the bloody confrontation of the Chicago and New York
families for Las Vegas / by William F. Roemer, Jr.
p.   cm.
ISBN 1-55611-193-2 :
1. Organized crime—Nevada—Las Vegas. 2. Casinos—Nevada—Las
Vegas—Finance. 3. Mafia—Illinois—Chicago. 4. Mafia—New York
(N.Y.) I. Title.
HV6452.N3R64 1990
364.1′06′09793135—dc20   90-55089
                                                     CIP

Manufactured in the United States of America

10   9   8   7   6   5   4   3   2   1

Designed by Irving Perkins Associates

Many of the characters in this book are alive and active in La Cosa Nostra today.
Certain of the events involving them as presented herein are fictitious though
informed by the author's knowledge and expertise.

God spent the Seventh Day creating Jeannie.
I dedicate this book to her.

Acknowledgments

THERE are many people I would like to thank for their help and support in writing this. First, all of the fine people from Donald I. Fine, Inc., my publisher. They include Don Fine himself, and David Gibbons, my editor.

I would also like to acknowledge those who unwittingly are the prime characters in this work; those who gave me great insight into their personas and their activities as I investigated them through the decades. They include Tony Accardo, Joe Bonanno, Moe Dalitz, Gus Alex, Murray Humphreys, Joe Ferriola, Tony Spilotro, and Donald Angelini—guys I have personally confronted cumulatively on over a hundred occasions.

Although they were unaware that they were to be characters in my book, I express appreciation to old pals like Pete Wacks, Art Pfizenmayer, and "Buck" Revell from the FBI, Jeff Johnson and Gary Shapiro from the United States Attorney's office in Chicago, and Bill Ouseley, formerly of the FBI in Kansas City.

From the Las Vegas casinos, I thank Jim Powers, Warren Salisbury, Chuck Thomas, John Schreiber, Dave Gulliand, Larry Whelan, and Emmett Michaels. Also Herb "Speedy" Newman, the Las Vegas "professional sports investor."

From the Chicago Crime Commission, my gratitude to John Jemilo, Jerry Gladden, Jeanette Callaway, and Pat Healey.

From the fourth estate, I value the assistance I have received from Sandy Smith, John Drummond, Chuck Goudie, Al Tobin, Steve Neal, Phil LaVelle, Kup, John O'Brien, Art Petacque, Wes Smith, Roy Leonard, Clark Webber, Ron Koziol, Patricia King, Lorenzo Carcaterra, David Dawson, Jerry Seper, John Winters, J. C. Martin, John Rawlinson, Art Rotstein, Bill Brashler, Jill Boughton, Diane Stephen, Rick Shaughnessy, Mike Sneed, Jim Simon, Don Jaye, Bob Grant, Larry King, Geraldo, Heather Richards, Mike Flannery, Ted Laudenbach, Stacey Taylor, Bruce Dumont, Sally Sherman, Joe Donlon, Ted Machamer, Toni Stanton, Dean Bacquet, Judith Brown, Roy Laos, Bill Bowler, John Milewski, Luke Michaels, Richard Urey, Bruce Frankel, Sam Meddis, Bob Slatzer, Angela Aiello, George Haas, Belinda Rosser, Connie Powell, Preston Westmoreland, Jeff Gerth, Alex Alexander, George Rush, Jim McGee, John Hubner, Rich Serrano, Bob Weidrich, Ralph Bloomenthal, Denny Walsh, Georgie Ann Geyer, Jack and Pat Brickhouse, Hal Higdon, Jim Duffy, Lou Mucciollo, Jim Gillis, Ben Bentley, Ray Coffee, Jess Kane, Mark Belling and Kristina Rebolo.

I can't forget Jim Mansfield and Ralph Salerno, the congressional investigators; Miles Cooperman, Deputy Chief of the Internal Investigations Division of the Cook County Sheriff's Office; Tom Carrigan, former Chief of Investigations and Intelligence for the Nevada Gaming Control Board; Larry Bagley and Eddy Hall of the Tucson FBI; Joe Yablonski, former Special Agent in Charge of the FBI in Las Vegas; John Bassett and Ray Shryock, my old partners in the FBI in Chicago; Bill Duffy, former Deputy Superintendent of the Chicago Police Department; Bill Hartnett of "Here's Chicago"; Bill Lambie of the FBI, Chicago Crime Commission and the office of the Attorney General of Illinois; Greg Kowalick of the New Jersey Casino Control Commission, Division of Gaming Enforcement; and Gino Lazzeri of the Philadelphia Crime Commission.

Last, but far from least, the support of my sons, Bill and Bob; my daughter-in-law, Earlene; and my three outstanding grandkids, Chris, Matt, and Tim.

Introduction

MURRAY Kempton has said that "the novelist can always teach us
more than the political scientist because the realm called fiction is ruled
by what is real and the territory called fact has to make do with the
dubieties of the fancied." In *War of the Godfathers,* I have limited
myself, especially in Book I, to the playing field of acknowledged histor-
ical fact in dealing with the major characters. I've filled in a few gaps
by inventing a handful of minor characters as well as by dramatizing
conversations or events where I was not present or was not privy to
direct testimony. In other words, I have indulged in presenting some
hearsay as evidence. Of course this method would not be admissible in
a court of law, but, claiming poetic license, I maintain that it is certainly
bona fide information between the covers of this book.

A number of the important episodes in *War of the Godfathers* have
been fictionalized for several reasons, including protecting the sensitive
nature of ongoing investigations and prosecutions and respecting the
privacy of certain living characters. A few of the actions are composites

of one or more episodes that have occurred within my knowledge and experience during my many years of combating organized crime; I have introduced some speculation and at times I have extrapolated on actual events. But at all times I have based all the characters and incidents on real events, on fully believable and/or probable scenarios. In other words, this is a work consisting mostly of fact. In those limited portions that are fictionalized, the underlying basis is either fact or an inferential projection thereof. Where I deemed it necessary, events or conversations were dramatized because no official law enforcement version of the real events exists and because the myths of the underworld would otherwise prevail.

I have also changed, on just a few occasions, while keeping most identities real, the names of some of the active characters. I have done this so as not to prejudice ongoing prosecutions of these mobsters. Many readers who are familiar with organized crime figures or who have read my first book, *Roemer: Man Against the Mob,* will easily recognize who these hoods are in real life; all readers will, I expect, sense that these are authentic, real-life mobsters.

I have attached as Appendix A the testimony I gave before the U.S. Senate on behalf of the Chicago Crime Commission and as Appendix B a current list of the sixty most prominent mob members in Chicago today. I originally prepared the testimony from FBI files while I was still with the Bureau and later updated it for the Chicago Crime Commission. It is included in order that the reader may review that factual history, all of which is very relevant to the story at hand. The same rationale applies to the "Hoods Who," the list of Who's Who in Organized Crime in Metropolitan Chicago. I extend my deep appreciation to the Chicago Crime Commission, with whom I work as a consultant, for permitting me the only authorized publication of this product of their fine efforts.

In view of my unique perspective on the characters portrayed herein, the vast majority of whom I have investigated, monitored, confronted personally, arrested and interviewed during the past forty years, there seems little doubt that this book could not have been authored by anyone else. I know both of the godfathers very well from personal encounters with each of them on several occasions. I spent decades of intense investigation into the activities of Tony Accardo, aka "Joe Batters," while I was an FBI agent in Chicago. I also worked as an FBI agent in New York City for two years. I was one of the agents assigned exclusively to the FBI's intensive investigation of Joe Bonanno in Tucson for two years after having previously interviewed him in Chicago. For the past ten years, my private investigations have taken me to Las Vegas on dozens of occasions and have been focused on the major character of this work, Moe Dalitz, and on the casinos which have been "mobbed up" there. Additionally, while in the Chicago FBI, I was the case agent on investigations entitled "Nevada Gaming Industry," VEGMON (the acronym for "Vegas Money") and "Skimming Activities in Nevada Casinos." Therefore, in addition to the characters portrayed here, I came to know the four principal locales for this story very well: Las Vegas, Chicago, New York City and Tucson. I don't need a guide in any of those spots, that's for sure!

It has been said that I have had "more confrontations with mobsters than any other lawman in history, including Eliot Ness." I believe that is true. I believe it is also true that I have spent more time than any other lawman monitoring the conversations of mobsters on the hidden microphones I have helped place in their secret meeting places. I reemphasize all this not to boast but to insure for the reader total credibility when digesting the story told in *War of the Godfathers.* I have learned what mobsters talk about and how they say it. Therefore, the dialogue I create is altogether realistic and credible.

WAR of the Godfathers is not a sequel to my first book, *Roemer: Man Against the Mob,* although many of the characters are the same. "Bill Richards" is an invention, yet any reader of my first effort—and many others as well—will easily recognize him. At the risk of seeming immodest, I decided not to adopt the technique used by Norman Mailer, for instance, in his book *Miami and the Siege of Chicago,* in which he refers to himself in the third person. Instead I created the character of Richards who is, as those who know me well will attest, mostly yours truly—faults and all.

Accardo and Bonanno, the protagonists in this book, were also leading characters in my first book. Moe Dalitz, Frank Sinatra, Bugsy Siegel, Sam Giancana, Gus Alex and Tony Spilotro are also prominently mentioned in both books. Although it is in no way a necessity that *Man Against the Mob* be read to enjoy the present book, I presume to recommend it. I also am at work on a third book, tentatively entitled *Four Pals (The Priest, the Mob Boss, the FBI Agent and the Senator).*

IN my first book I maintained that we now see the light at the end of the tunnel, that law enforcement—and particularly the FBI—is making great progress in winning the war against the mob. Now, a year later, I continue to identify this progress. I congratulate my former colleagues in the FBI all over the country for their successful effort in the battle against what is generally known as "traditional organized crime." I especially congratulate the Chicago FBI for the indictments which have been brought against many of the top leaders of the Chicago mob in the major RICO case against the likes of "Rocky" Infelice, Sal DeLaurentis, Lou Marino and others, a case that parallels the one I depict near the end of this present work. I salute the FBI perhaps even more for the "Kaffee Klatsch" investigation, which is particularly focused on the corruption in the First Ward of Chicago. Whereas I was instrumental in installing a hidden microphone in the headquarters of the Regular Democratic Organization of the First Ward in Chicago a quarter of a century ago—as detailed in *Man Against the Mob*—my successors in the Chicago FBI have carried that work forward. Although the bug I helped plant defined the extent of the widespread corruption produced in the First Ward, "Kaffee Klatsch" has the potential of being even more productive in this regard, especially since the information obtained from my bug was inadmissible in court whereas the "Kaffee Klatsch" bugs are fully admissible. I believe "Kaffee Klatsch" has the promise of destroying the Chicago mob, since no mob can function at anywhere near its potential without widespread corruption of public officials, political leaders, law enforcement people, labor leaders and anybody in a position to extend favored treatment. Since the Regular Democratic Organization of the First Ward in Chicago is the conduit through which the orders of the mob are relayed to corrupted public officials, and since the focus of "Kaffee Klatsch" is on the First Ward, we should soon see the mob's key interests there wiped out. To the FBI, particularly in Chicago, I say: "Keep Punchin' and Keep the Faith!" This book is testimony to their efforts and to the efforts of all those who fight the pestilence of organized crime.

WFR, Jr.
Tucson
August, 1990

Book I

THE RISE OF THE GODFATHERS

ACCARDO AND BONANNO CONSOLIDATE THEIR POWER BASES

CHAPTER

1

The Agenda of the New York Godfather

IT was a typical January day in Tucson in 1986. Warm, in the seventies, and the skies were not cloudy all day.

Instead of cowboys in the corrals at the Bar Bon Ranch, however, it was an entirely different kind of crew. Instead of Stetsons, this bunch wore fedoras. Rather than sun-tanned, this crowd was swarthy. Instead of Levis, this group wore $250 custom-made dress slacks.

The lazy breeze blew through that spot in the mountains where the Santa Catalinas join the Rincons, just enough to dissipate the car emissions in the valley which contains the city of Tucson with the result that the air refreshed itself continuously.

Joe Bonanno had called a sit-down. Not only had he commanded the attendance of his underboss, his son Salvatore, who they call Bill, but also of his other son, Joe, Jr., a capo in his crime family. He had brought a number of trusty soldiers with him to Tucson, including Charlie "Bats" Battaglia, Pete Notaro, and Tony "Short Pants" Cacioppo. This was not unusual. Bill and Joe practically lived at the Bar Bon; Bats,

Notaro, and Short Pants attended their boss there regularly.

But it was a first visit for the other three conferees; Michael "The Clean One" Immaculata, Paulie Primosa, and Angelo "The Ape" Annunciata were much more familiar with the mean streets of Brooklyn than the cactus canyons of Arizona. Not that these three thugs were unfamiliar with ropes and six-shooters. The Ape prided himself on his ability to garrote his victims; six of his adversaries had departed their vale of tears roped from behind by this trademark of his style of execution. And all those present were no strangers to firearms. Most had notches on their weapons; not so much the younger Bonannos, probably the other Tucson attendees and most definitely the visitors from New York. For these three were the "heavies," the Bonanno family capos who had made their bones in the internecine warfare that characterizes the five New York La Cosa Nostra families and who had ascended to the current leadership of three Bonanno family street crews.

Catherine Bonanno, Joe's daughter, came into the ramada with some Vernaccia and antipasto for the conferees. She immediately went on her way after she deposited her trays, knowing that she was no part of what was to be discussed on this day.

"Fellas, let us get down to basics," the cultured, refined, and articulate elder Bonanno commanded in his heavy Sicilian accent. "What we discuss here this afternoon, in the greatest of confidence, is perhaps the most serious business this family has discussed in our history."

This caused a stir among the attendees. The young Bonannos knew what their father intended and the Tucson trio had some idea. But the visitors from Brooklyn had been kept in the dark until now. They had been busy back in Bensonhurst and Greenpoint tending to the important but mundane Bonanno family rackets: bookmaking, loan sharking, labor racketeering, prostitution, as well as running the legitimate family businesses such as bars and restaurants. Little did they know that the godfather had big plans for them now; little did they realize what a quantum leap the wily old Sicilian fox was about to make.

"My compadres, we are boxed-in back in Brooklyn. I have known this for a long time and you know it. New York is a great city for those of us in our tradition. There are many opportunities for us there. And we have taken advantage of them; we have made a fine living there. But, as we would say here in Arizona, we are corralled in there. The Gambinos, the Luccheses, the Genoveses, the Columbos, they all must make their living in the Volcano. [Bonanno frequently used this word to describe New York City.] As you know, we have had our problems with these families. And the new fathers of these families are hostile to us. They continually test us."

So far, Bonanno was not telling his subordinates anything new. They were all aware of the turmoil, the battles which had decimated their ranks and those of their foes. All present had been deeply involved. They had killed, they had been wounded, and they had lost comrades.

Now the father of his family stood. He was a slender 5'11", and at the age of eighty his gray hair was going white, he wore glasses that rested on his rather impressive Roman nose, allowing him to cultivate a very flamboyant and theatrical manner. Bonanno spoke with a very thick Sicilian accent, the heaviest accent of any mobster this author has ever encountered. He got down to business. "Now, my friends we are going to do something which will necessitate going back to the mattresses. But it won't be the New York families we will be fighting on this occasion. It will be the Chicago family."

Immaculata, Primosa, and Annunciata were perplexed. They knew the reputation of the Chicago family, since the days of Capone, was that of fierce fighters. Anything which might bring the Bonannos into conflict with Chicago was not to be taken lightly. What could possibly be important enough to this Brooklyn-based family that they would be willing to risk warfare with Chicago? They all glanced nervously at one another.

Bonanno quickly sensed their anxiety. "Hear me out. If what I propose is not to your liking, I will excuse you. You can leave here as you came and go back to Bensonhurst and Williamsburg and Green Point and the rest of that small part of the Volcano which we have and you can continue to live the comfortable life you now live; eating and drinking in our small, dark restaurants and leading your small, dark lives. But if you are men of vision—if you are the men I believe you to be—men who I felt when I picked you to lead your regimes to have a sense of conquest—then I believe you will give me your enthusiastic support. When I studied at the university in Sicily, I studied the men of vision, of conquest. I learned that the great men of our tradition, like my father, were unsatisfied with simple accomplishments. Men like Garibaldi looked far ahead and saw the fields which were ripe for picking. They were not content to languish in Sicily when America was ripe for picking. They reached out to make themselves great. And they did not recoil because they also saw the danger that such conquest entailed. They were truly men of honor. And they were not satisfied with mediocrity. So, in the tradition of those of us who left Sicily's barren fields for the ripe fields of America, I ask you to follow me in the fight for the ripest field in America today. Instead of suffocating in the small piece of the Volcano we hold today, we will fight our way out, men of vision, seeing the vast new world outside the Volcano, which, if we can use the resources which are available to us, can make us the proudest family of all; the greatest family in all of the history of our tradition. Can we seize the prize which can be ours if we have the courage to fight for it?"

Now the Volcano visitors were really mystified. What was the godfather talking about? They had grown comfortable in Brooklyn. After all, they had had to fight for what they had accomplished along the banks of the Gowanus. It hadn't been easy. And why was the godfather diminishing their glory? And why should they be dissatisfied with their lot as it existed? What could be so important as to jeopardize what they now held? Where was the great Bonanno intending to lead them?

Bonanno continued. "My friends, we have been one of the few families which has not benefited from the great source of wealth which has been available to other families of La Cosa Nostra. While other families have plucked from the vines of this great plant, we have been content to go our own way. Now our weak brothers have allowed the Chicago family to reap the harvest from this field, have allowed themselves to be deceived into believing that the bargain we have all made has been a just one. We have been deluded into believing that what we traded for this great prize was ample consideration for this agreement. It is not. Salerno and Castellano and the rest were idiots. While I was involved in other matters they made this *infamia,* this contract with Chicago. And now, even though we now realize how deceived we are, they live up to it. They have no spine, there is no red blood running through their veins. They allow Chicago to keep their ill-gotten prize. I have sat with Tony Accardo on so many occasions. I can see him smiling at his home in Palm Springs; I can see him counting his money as he gloats over the deception he played on all of us in the eastern families."

Now Immaculata, Primosa, and Annunciata began to glean what it was their godfather was getting at. They were very much aware of the pact which had been made in 1977 when the Chicago family had proposed to their brothers on The Commission, the national ruling body of La Cosa Nostra, that Chicago take Las Vegas, with the exception of those hotel-casinos that were already under New York control. In return the eastern families were given a free hand in Atlantic City. It was a bum deal for the easterners since they were unable to make in Atlantic City anywhere near what Chicago had made in Nevada.

"I can see you now realize what I am proposing," Bonanno said. "Yes, Las Vegas! And then the rest of Nevada!"

Bonanno speared some antipasto as he let this sink in, then picked up his glass of wine and enjoyed a leisurely sip. A murmur arose among those assembled. Las Vegas! For years Vegas had been an "open city." Any and all families had been free to make their way there. In fact, it was the New York families, under the direction of Meyer Lansky and his operative, Bugsy Siegel, who had paved the way for Las Vegas to become the gaming capital of the world, and thus the source of the greatest income for several LCN families. This tradition continued for many years, until the treaty under which The Commission had given Nevada to Chicago. They knew that any incursion into Nevada now would bring them into immediate conflict with Chicago, that powerful and well-armed family.

Bonanno set his glass down. He wiped his mouth with his cloth napkin. He looked directly into the eyes of each of his capos. "I know what you must immediately be thinking. Number one, why should we reach out for this when we got such a good thing in Brooklyn? Number two, why bother when it might be disaster for us to go against Chicago as we must? And number three, is it wise to defy the orders of The Commission which has decreed Nevada for Chicago?"

Each of the capos gazed back at their leader.

"I'll address each of these concerns," the articulate, well-educated godfather announced. "Number one. I can't conceive that any of you is satisfied with the small turf we have in Brooklyn. To be *one* of just five New York families. Or to be just *one* of twenty-four Cosa Nostra families. To be drinking Riunite instead of Dom Perignon. We love our pasta, but isn't it nice to have chateaubriand whenever we want it? Why should we be men of such little sense of accomplishment to be satisfied with half a loaf when we could have it all? Did I pick you men to lead our people with me because I felt you were capable of maintaining our status quo in Brooklyn? Or because I felt you were men of destiny who could help me lead our people into a field where the crop is bountiful, where our reward, though hard fought, would be many times what we have now?"

Bonanno could see the chests puff up. He could see that his dramatic presentation appealed to their egos, their manliness.

He continued, holding up his two forefingers. "Number two. Chicago is fat. Accardo is old and weak and sick. He is no longer the young man who fought with Capone, the young man who took out the Moran gang in that garage on St. Valentine's Day. And his whole family has gotten fat with him. They are no longer the family of Capone or Nitti or Giancana. They have a new leadership there, a young man who has never been one of the best in their tradition. The FBI in Chicago has put all of their top people away. Accardo's protégé, Cerone, is gone and even this Aiuppa, who was weak, is in prison. This new man, Ferriola, is nothing compared to me. I have been the father of my family since 1931. He has been nothing. I have picked you wisely. You are the best. Compared to them you are men, they are boys. We have as many rifles as they and we are better."

The egos were being stroked. The chests puffed and the capos nodded to each other in assent.

"Now, number three," Bonanno went on, obviously satisfied with the progress of his presentation so far. "Don't worry about The Commission. I have spoken to those who count. They don't like it that they have been deceived. They know the *infamia* which has been cast on them for making such a bad bargain. I have their word that they will not interfere. This new Chicago boss, Ferriola, will come before them. He will seek their intervention, guided by Accardo. But they will sit on their hands. They will secretly be with us. It will cost us for this when we win. We will bring them in for some of the spoils. But it will be worth it. When Hitler moved on Czechoslovakia, he had already had the understanding with Chamberlain in Munich. I have read my history, I studied it well. I have made our Munich. We will have no interference from the other families. It will be us against Chicago. And when we have shown the other families our courage and our strength we will get some *picciotti* from them. They will want to be on the side of the winner."

Bonanno paused once again to let the scenario he was creating sink in. Once again he partook of his wine and his antipasto as he watched his subordinates murmur to themselves and to each other.

"Now there is one last thing before I ask you for your enthusiasm and for your support. If you have been following the situation in Las Vegas you will know that Chicago has lost so much of what they had there. No longer do they have the many casinos they once had. No longer do they have great income from the skim. They no longer have a war chest of great proportions with which to fight us. They are no longer stronger than us. No longer do they have the politicians in the number they once had. No longer are they strong with Metro [the police department]. No longer do they have the influence in the Gaming Control Commission they had. And their man there, this Spilotro, he has no vision. He has perverted our tradition there. His key men have become informers. He is under prosecution in Las Vegas, Chicago, and Kansas City. He is sick, he has had a bypass from the doctor in Houston. He has been dealing narcotics in violation of the law of the Chicago family. Chicago is therefore poorly represented in Las Vegas; he has many enemies there. They are as vulnerable there as never before. The time right now is ripe for us. And if we need any more help we got it. 'The G' is now after Accardo. They have now given Accardo immunity, just like they did Giancana before him. Accardo, who, as I say, is weak and old, is now concerning himself with this problem. He will not have the energy to deal with this. If we don't move now, we never will."

Bonanno had concluded his presentation. Again, he paused to sip his Vernaccia and eat his antipasto. He allowed his capos time to confer with each other.

Then he made his request for support. It was Bonanno's way. A firm ruler, he also knew that a good leader does not get too far ahead of his constituency. If Bonanno felt he did not have the absolute assurance that his capos were with him all the way, he would not make this move, more drastic than any he had contemplated in all his years as the godfather of his family. He knew he had the support of his underboss, his number one man, his son, Bill, and he knew also that Joe, Jr., one of his capos, would be right alongside. He had already discussed his plans in broad strokes with them. And he felt strongly that Bats Battaglia's firm support would be with him. Notaro and Cacioppo mattered somewhat but little compared to The Ape, Paul Primosa, and The Clean One. Immaculata and Annunciata were the prime *picciotti,* the hitters, whose enthusiasm must be gained if this bold plan was to be brought to fruition.

As the underboss, it was Bill Bonanno's right to speak first. As expected, he fully supported his father. "It's the right move at the right time," was the essence of his remarks.

Battaglia, short on articulation, assented. Joe, Jr., Notaro, and Cacioppo had little to say except to indicate they would follow the leader.

"Clean" Immaculata then stood up. Now the nitty gritty would
commence. "This I got to say," he stated. "I hear what my godfather
is saying. I see no reason why it can't be worked out. I respect my
godfather. If he feels it can be worked out, then I'll follow him to the
end. Here's what I think. I think my crew in Brooklyn is up to this.
I've heard some rumblings there which tell me that they're ready for
this because they're not happy with what we got in Brooklyn. I've got
some eighty guys there. I could cut loose fifty to send them to Las Vegas
if we had to and keep the other thirty to run the store in Brooklyn. I'm
for it."

When Immaculata sat down, Paulie Primosa stood up. "I feel the
same way. I've got more guys than 'Clean' and we could use half of
them in Vegas. I'm with you."

Then it was the turn of The Ape. "I'm ready! This is right up my
alley. I've been trainin' my crew for years and nothin' like this has come
up. I've got my soldiers all ready. I'm all for it, you can count on me
and my crew!"

As Annunciata sat down, Paulie stood up again. Bonanno considered
The Ape and Clean to be his warriors, Primosa to be his strategist. "One
thing I'm not clear on," Paulie said. "Knowing you, Joe, I know you've
given this a lot of thought. You must have a plan. Before I go back to
Brooklyn and get my crew sorted out, I'd like to have some idea of what
your plan is."

Bonanno stood. "That's fair, that's what you have coming. I want to
give you an idea but I wanted to see if you were with me first. What
we have discussed to this point I want you to discuss with your *regimes*.
I assume any member of your *regimes* must be trusted or you wouldn't
have them. This is the time for loyalty. If there is anybody you have
any doubt about, this is the time to rid yourself of them. It is essential
we don't have anybody getting the word to Chicago, or to anybody
outside our family. It is essential that we keep this tight inside our
family. No one with a loose mouth should be in our family. I assume
your discipline is now at a point where we have no such problem. What
has been discussed here so far today can be, and should be, discussed
with your *regimes*. But what we now discuss will not be. Is that fully
understood?"

The ramada was filled with nodding heads.

Bonanno then assumed an air of extreme dignity, a posture at which he was adept. "You all know who Moe Dalitz is." It was not a question. Even the lowest soldier would know of the legendary Moe Dalitz. In the early days he had been a front for the New York families in the gaming capital. Later he switched allegiance to Chicago. Nobody at the Bar Bon had to be reminded of Dalitz's stature.

Bonanno then made a startling statement: "Dalitz is ours!"

Primosa was the first to react. "He's been Chicago's man in some of the best joints out there. For years!"

"Dalitz is ours! He's with us!" Bonanno forcefully repeated his statement.

The godfather let this sink in. He was not certain that Immaculata and Annunciata caught the full impact of this. These two were noted foremost for their fighting abilities, not for their intelligence. Primosa had the smarts, the other two the muscle, although each had enough of the opposite traits to survive quite well. "Dalitz is with us. And he will bring enough of his best people along so that the experience and the capability we need will be ours. With Dalitz and his people, we will have the brains. Chicago will be left with the residue. And Dalitz will recruit more for us. Not only people inside the casinos but the politicians. And law enforcement and regulatory people, what they call 'gamers.' Maybe not the FBI, but Metro. With Dalitz and his people we will have the knowledge. With the people in your *regimes,* the muscle."

Primosa still thirsted for knowledge. "How did you bring Dalitz onto our side? Doesn't he have a good thing going, especially at his age, with Chicago?"

Bonanno smiled. "That's a good question, Paulie." He obviously was pleased that his capo was thinking. "Before Meyer Lansky died in 1983, I met with him in Acapulco, not far from here. I told him what I was thinking. I've been planning this ever since I got out of prison, in Springfield. Started there, actually. Meyer told me Dalitz is the key. I was discouraged at this because, like you, Paulie, I knew Dalitz was tied up with Chicago. But Lansky told me that Dalitz was not happy. You might know Dalitz was with Lansky before he was with Chicago. They were as close as brothers even after Dalitz went with Chicago. Lansky told me Dalitz hates this little person they call 'The Ant', Spilotro, who is running things for Chicago in Vegas. Lansky told me that if I solidified my plans so that there was no backing out, he would go to Dalitz and feel him out. He did. Three years ago, just before he died. Then Dalitz came here, right here where we're sitting in this ramada. Three times. We hammered it out. We have to supply the soldiers, make sure we protect him and his properties. It will take a hundred of our people to settle in there, at least at first. And we have to make it right for Dalitz, better than he has now. And for his key people. But we can do that. If what I envision works out, there will be plenty for all of us. Paulie, I been working on this for five years. I didn't want to bring it on the floor in front of you before it was ready. Now it is. Now it's time for you people to become involved. Trust me, I've never led you astray before. I know what I'm doing."

With the assurance that Dalitz and his key people were involved with his family, Primosa seemed assuaged; whatever doubts he may tentatively have entertained faded. Not only did he gain faith by the realization that Dalitz was on their side but by the revelation that the godfather had been planning this move for all of five years and that he had consulted with "the chairman of the board" of organized crime, the legendary Meyer Lansky, the financial wizard of the New York families since the 1930s, who had at least tacitly endorsed the project by being the intermediary with Dalitz.

Bonanno had one more ace in the hole he had been waiting to play. "There is one more thing. Sinatra. You all know that he was brought up by Willie Moretti in New Jersey. And then he got close to Chicago; first Fischetti, the cousin of Capone, and then finally Giancana. But they had a falling out—before Giancana was disposed of they were no longer friendly. However, he has continued to perform in the Chicago hotels in Las Vegas. He is doing so these days only out of respect for Dalitz. With Dalitz we get Sinatra. And with Sinatra we get Dean Martin and Sammy Davis and Liza Minnelli and Don Rickles and who knows who else. They will sign exclusive contracts to perform only at our hotel, Camelot. At our Vegas Star we will have the young crowd for the low rollers, rock and roll and the like. But when we open Camelot for the high roller we will have the best, Sinatra. And Dalitz tells me he might be able to get Wayne Newton also. You know he has been close to our friend, Guido Penosi, who was the cousin of the capo of the Gambinos in Bridgeport, the guy who was clipped in the phone booth there, ah, Frank Piccolo. Although Newton is in no way beholden to any of us, we may be able to work something out with the Gambinos through this Penosi for Newton to give us an exclusive also.

I have not gone into our plans for our hotels there, but at our next meeting I will tell you of our plans for the Star and then to build the biggest hotel in the world, to be called Camelot. The world has heard of the plans for the new Mirage and Excalibur and the plans of this Kerkorian fellow from the movie studio, MGM, to build big and fancy hotels. Wait until they see Camelot! My friends, I will explain to you our plans for this when we next meet. You will share the vision. Many think I am old and you are soft and fat. They will soon find out how old and fat and soft *we* are! The time has come for us to rise above what we have in the Volcano! The time has come for this family to show its heels to all the rest! They will see."

This outburst of enthusiasm on the part of the godfather excited his capos. They seemed enraptured, completely caught up in his fervor. Their reverence for their leader had been chiseled in stone due to their many successful experiences with him through so many years—so many decades. Now a fire had been ignited which spread quickly through the ramada. The thrill of raising their family high above its current existence in Brooklyn into the neon lights of Las Vegas generated an excitement never before experienced. If Bonanno had had any concern that his capos might not line up solidly and enthusiastically behind him, his mind was now completely eased. His confidence that his objective could be met was solid as a rock. It was a go! Full speed ahead!

CHAPTER

2

The Agenda of the Chicago Godfather

CHICAGO was experiencing an all-too-common January blizzard, the white stuff blowing almost diagonally across the frozen ground, the turf of the successors to Al Capone.

It was early 1986 and the Chicago mob had just lost its proven, longtime chiefs, Joey Aiuppa and Jackie Cerone, along with some mid-level leaders, after the successful federal prosecution of the "Strawman Case" in Kansas City. The FBI there had documented the involvement of the Chicago mob bosses with the leaders in K.C. in illegal skimming of millions from Las Vegas casinos. Aiuppa, Cerone, and many of their associates were in federal prison, with long sentences that could very well extend for the rest of their natural lives.

A new crew of leaders had just been installed in Chicago. They were meeting together in a private room which they had swept for bugs, the electronic kind, in the Czech Lodge Restaurant in Riverside, a western suburb of Chicago. It was their first meeting as a group and the purpose was to put together an agenda. Their plans were to have far-reaching consequences, not only in the Windy City but in Las Vegas—and in New York City and Arizona.

Presiding at the "sit-down" was the dinosaur of the dynasty of Capone, Tony Accardo, the guy called "Joe Batters" by Capone himself after Accardo had battered to death one of Capone's foes with a baseball bat. Accardo is the *consigliere* of the Chicago family of La Cosa Nostra, is the elder statesman who must approve every major decision of his family. To Accardo's right sat Joe Ferriola—Joe Negall to his associates. Joe had just been named the new boss by Accardo, Cerone, and Aiuppa after having been a capo, a captain, for years.

Next to Ferriola sat the new underboss, Rocky Infelice. Around the table were holdover capos Albert Caesar Tocco and Vince Solano, also two newly appointed capos, Donald Angelini, aka Don Angel, and Dominic "Large" Cortina. Angelini and Cortina had been with Ferriola for decades, and had just received important promotions.

At the end of the table sat Dominic "Butch" Blasi, the administrative arm of each leader since Accardo took over and especially of Sam Giancana and Aiuppa—their bodyguard, driver, and appointments secretary.

Outside the room, at the door, stood John "No Nose" DiFronzo and Sam "Wings" Carlisi, two up-and-coming soldiers of the mob. Outside in the parking lot serving as lookouts and keeping the cars of the conferees warm were Frankie "The German" Schweihs and Wayne Bock, the mob hit men. Loyal hit men they were, but not of Italian descent and therefore not eligible to be "made" into a family of La Cosa Nostra.

As the wind howled through the cemetery across the road from the restaurant—a setting not incongruous for the nature of this meet, as it was to turn into—Accardo called the "sit-down" to order. His first order of business was to formally welcome Ferriola as the new boss and to formally "make" him as the boss. Then Infelice, Angelini, and Cortina were "made" capos. The ceremony consisted of a short speech by the godfather acknowledging the contributions and accomplishments of each man in broad, general terms, then welcoming them as official leaders of the family. Simple as that.

Following this ceremony Accardo instructed Blasi to go out into the public dining area of the Czech Lodge and escort Gussie Alex into the meeting. Gussie is Greek, so he cannot be "made" into a family member. As head of the "connection guys," or what the FBI calls "the corruption squad," it is Gussie's job to insure that there is always available a corps of public officials, law enforcement officers, political leaders, judges, labor leaders, and legitimate businessmen who will provide favorable treatment to the Chicago family. Obviously, in this important capacity, Gussie is a major player in the affairs of the Chicago mob, more important even than the underboss or the capos.

With Gussie seated at the table, Accardo began to explain to the assembled leadership of the Chicago mob his thoughts about what their agenda should be at this time as they assumed their command. Although nobody's dummy by any stretch of the imagination, in fact perhaps the most respected leader of any mob in history, Accardo does not possess the polished and refined air of Joe Bonanno. Bonanno had a college education in Sicily and had the advantages of upbringing as the son of a Mafia Don there. He is well read—he is even an author. Accardo, by contrast, was born and raised in a poor Chicago neighborhood, of a near-impoverished family. He had none of the advantages of Bonanno in his youth. But that is not to say that he does not have Bonanno's native intelligence; in fact, he has at least as much.

"Fellas," Accardo began, "we start this new regime today at a critical time in the existence of our outfit. Some real problems face us right from the beginning. A couple are minor and easily solved but have to be dealt with if you are to gain the respect of our outfit.

"First of all, you have to deal with this kid, DePrizio, the construction guy. We got him all those contracts from the city, thanks to Gussie, Pat Marcy,[1] and John D'Arco. Now he's got caught, he's thinking of making a deal. And we find he's been holding out on us. I say hit him and hit him fast before he can cut any deals with 'the G'. That's absolute.

"Then you got John Fecarotta. He was a good man under Angelo[2] but when Angelo went away he thought he should be the capo. Well, we decided otherwise and he's got to live with it. He's now making a lot of trouble, trying to line up people to support him. If you don't stop that, it can be a festering problem. We've found out in the past that in this outfit you do what you're told or we take you out. Talk to Feca-

1. Pat Marcy is a "made" man who is responsible for running the Regular Democratic Organization of the First Ward in Chicago. John D'Arco, Sr., is the former alderman and the current Democratic ward committeeman in the First Ward. Marcy and D'Arco are closely associated with the Chicago mob.
2. Angelo LaPietro, formerly a capo in the Chicago family, now imprisoned after conviction for conspiracy to skim from Las Vegas casinos.

rotta, explain the situation. Give him a chance to straighten out, he's been a good man for many years but if he don't come around, then you got to think about clipping him."

Accardo looked down from his seat at the head of the table. All heads nodded. They understood his meaning. The nods also indicated assent. It would be done.

"Now we got this guy, Bill Richards. He's the guy who was always out front with 'the G'. He's the guy came to us with the deal on the families. I know the kid well. Of course, he ain't a kid no more, none of us are. He come to me one time at midnight. We made a deal over Bernie Glickman when we had Glickman out front for us with the prize-fighters, Liston and a few other champs. I know you all know Richards."

Angelini spoke up for the first time. "He arrested me twice." Gussie chimed in. "He chased me from when 'the G' first got involved. And he tried to make a deal with me too. He come to me through my first wife, tried to get me to be a fink, said he'd find a nice spot for me in Texas. And my wife went for it."

Ferriola and Cortina smiled and looked at each other. They had met Richards also.

Blasi stammered and then spoke up. "Let me say this. The guy is not all bad, you know. 'The G' had me nailed one time because of a rat they had. This guy testified to the grand jury I was involved in a burglary. But Richards knew that couldn't be true and it wasn't. Richards went to that grand jury and straightened them out. He didn't do it for me but because he was a stand-up guy. So I wasn't indicted."

Accardo spoke again. "I know that, he never framed nobody. He was a worker but he was straight. But here's my point. When he left here and went to Arizona he should have left us alone. When he retired from the FBI, what, six, seven years ago, then he's got no more right to come after us. I think you know why I'm hot at him. When he left the FBI he goes to work for some newspaper in California which had put a blast on the guy in Palm Springs, that Rolls-Royce dealer who was close to us and Sinatra. Richards comes to me, and you too, Gussie, and gives us word that if we don't get this car dealer to drop his suit against his client, the newspaper, he's going to bring us in for depositions. He's a fuckin' lawyer too, for Christ's sake. He's gonna poke around, ask us some tough questions. Stuff he knew from when he was with 'the G' here. Then he goes to work for *Penthouse,* when Dalitz and them guys brought the libel suit against them over what they wrote about the LaCosta resort in San Diego. Same thing; he goes to see Lansky in Miami and tells him he's going to bring him into the suit because Lansky is with Dalitz. Then he goes to work for the Chicago Crime Commission here and gets up in front of the Rackets Committee and gives them some fuckin' chart of us guys and says 'Here's Accardo, he's been a member of the mob here for seventy years.' I had to count it out. How could I be in it for seventy years? I'm only eighty. But our lawyers show how he twisted that by saying *parts of seven decades.* He tells them, Accardo is the big man, always has been, always will be. So those jackoff senators subpoena me, they give me immunity just like they did Giancana. Only this time, I con them, I ain't about to spend no years in jail for some bullshit thing like this. And, Gussie, it took us a lot to smooth that over. I thought I was going down for the first time in my life. And he showed them pictures of all you guys, you, Gussie, especially.

"Now that ain't right. When he left he shoulda left. When he was with 'the G', okay, we got to deal with him. But when he hands in his badge, what the fuck right has he got to keep comin' after us? And he's been in Vegas, fuckin' us up there twenty times! What right has he got? Who gave it to him?

"Now I ain't sayin' we hit him. From Al's days we don't take out cops or prosecutors or reporters or politicians or none of them kinda guys unless they take our money and then fuck us. And Richards ain't done that. He's never taken nothin'. If we hit him, he's still 'the G' in everybody's mind. He's worked for every newspaper in the country, for Christ's sake. He's with the Crime Commission, he's big in that association for ex-FBI guys, he's on the radio and television all the fuckin' time.

"But here's what I suggest. Throw some fear at him. Put some God damn fear in him to slow him down, make him think about what he's doin'. Make him believe we're serious about hitting him. Kneecap him maybe. Back him down. Get him to go up there in the mountains where he lives out there in Arizona and piss down all he wants, but not on us."

Accardo stopped again. "Think about it, plan it out." He leaned on his cane, the one with the replica of a tuna for a handle, as he stood. Nobody ever calls Accardo "Big Tuna" except the media, but he is amused by that moniker and makes good use of the gift, the cane with the tuna for a handle.

"Okay, now we got another problem which is worse than those three. Gussie is gonna tell you about it."

With that, Gussie Alex, leader of the connection guys in the Chicago outfit, stood up.

"I've been getting some bad vibes about what we got going in Las Vegas," Gussie began, getting right to the heart of the matter. "As you know, we got Sidney Korshak working with us out there, not only in Vegas but in Hollywood. Now you all know, Sid's been with us for years. He was a lawyer here when Nitti was boss in the thirties and he's been with us ever since. He's been very good for us. As you also know, I've been close to him for forty years, even when I was under Jake Guzik and then under Hump. I just got back from Palm Springs where Korshak lives. He's smelling something rotten in Vegas. He's been our guy with Dalitz for years and years. Ever since we made our deal with Dalitz to bring him with us instead of with New York like he was when he first went out there from Cleveland. Now there's nothing Sid can put his finger on, but he's been getting the run around from Dalitz the last couple months. He don't like it."

Gussie paused, took a sip of water, and continued. "I'm sure you know that the action isn't so good in Vegas for us like it used to be. We used to have the Stardust, the Fremont, the Desert Inn, the Riviera, and the Hacienda. Now we don't have none of them. But we still got a lot of our guys in those casinos. Guys we put there and guys we still got control of. That's what Spilotro does out there for us. I'll get to him in a minute. Pit bosses, stickmen, dealers, floor bosses, shift managers, guys like that. They're able to keep some skim comin' into us. Not like before but still very worthwhile for us.

"So that's one problem. We got to figure out if what Sid thinks about Dalitz might be true. Got to keep our finger on that situation. But here's another thing. I am recommending to you new guys that we step up our action in Vegas. Or elsewhere in Nevada. Maybe we can't regain what we had there in the good old days, but we should be able to do a lot more than we are now. Now, in the last years of the regime of Jackie and O'Brien [Aiuppa], they made a decision to let things go out there because of all the heat and the legal problems they had. They watched things go sour out there for us but didn't want to do nothing about it because they were already in so deep. But now you guys come in, fresh. I have talked this over with Joe [Batters, i.e. Tony Accardo] and we are making the recommendation to you that you beef up our interests out there. We think you should look for opportunities out

there, what I call 'pockets of potential.' Christ, Nevada is booming.
And what we were a big part of for so long, we got little of now.

"We are suggesting to you," Gussie said, "that you pick one of you
to be out front on this. We've got a lotta guys out there who have
worked with us in the past. Guys like Babe Baron, Yale Cohen, Al
Sachs, Herb Tobman, Joey Cuzamano, Joe Pignatello. Sit down with
them. Find out where they think we might get something going. And
not just in Vegas itself. There's Lake Tahoe, Reno, Sparks, Carson City,
Elko, Minden, and Laughlin, this new place on the Arizona border
which is booming. Maybe go sit down with Lefty [Rosenthal, longtime
front man for the Chicago family at the Stardust]. You guys were close
to him for years. He ain't there no more, but he sure knows the territory. And, of course, talk to Spilotro. I know he's muscle, not much
else. But for Christ's sake, he's been out there for twenty years! He's
got to have a handle on somethin'. I know he's done a lotta things we
don't like—burglars and dope and lettin' some of his people fink. But
let's milk what he knows. Let's use whatever talents the guy might have,
let's not cut our nose off to spite our face."

Gussie paused. He looked around the room to gauge the attentiveness
of his audience. He liked what he saw. Gussie Alex, though ineligible
for actual membership in La Cosa Nostra, was deeply respected by his
peers in the outfit. He had come up the hard way, as a hit man for the
mob and then as the chief lieutenant for Jake "Greasy Thumb" Guzik
and then for Murray "The Camel" Humphreys, when those two wise
men were the leaders of the connection guys. Alex had been both the
brawn *and* the brains; a mobster couldn't have better underpinnings.

Alex continued with his presentation. "We have one more recommendation to you in this regard. Whoever you send out there to be in
charge of our operations should keep his head down. When you put our
new man out there to run things, keep him what the lawyers call sub
rosa. Low profile. Let Spilotro stay out front. He likes that anyway and
he's known there, too well known. Let the world think he's the main
man. We need him for his muscle out there anyway. He's goofy, he's
fucked some things up, but he serves a purpose. On balance he's good
for us. The people out there have a fear of him. That's good for us. But
don't let him run things like he's done for the last *regime*. Pick one of
you guys, keep him sub rosa like I say and make him the man. But keep
Spilotro up front, like he's the man."

Gussie sat down. Accardo stood up again, leaning on his cane. "Okay, that's about all we got. Unless there is something somebody don't understand, that's it."

Nobody was about to say they didn't understand Accardo's pronouncements.

Joe Ferriola took it upon himself as boss to speak up. "Joe," he said, "we understand what you say. I know I speak for all of us here when I say you are our man of respect. Nobody has earned respect like you. I know you want to go back to your place in Palm Springs tomorrow but we would appreciate it if you will stay in touch with us close and that you will be available to us at all times. If it's okay with you, I'm gonna designate Donald to be the man who stays in touch with you. He will be back and forth. And Gussie, you too, we thank. I know you want to go back to your spot in Florida, but we have listened to what you have had to say, with Joe's backing, and we will take it up. I'm gonna designate Donald to be the man in touch with you also. Thank you both."

With that the wizened, stooped, battered old backbreaker stood. So did Gussie. With the help of the tuna cane, Accardo and his old comrade departed the room together.

"Okay, that's it," Ferriola announced. The group drifted off—into the storm before the storm—in ones and twos so as not to attract undue attention.

ON January 27, 1986, Richard DePrizio, 36, president of the DePrizio Construction Company, was gunned down in Westchester, Illinois, not all that far from the Czech Lodge.

On September 14, 1986, apparently unheeding the advice given him, John Fecarotta was slain outside a North Side Chicago bingo hall.

On September 21, 1987, Bill Richards received a phone call at his home in Tucson. He was asked to meet with Accardo in Santa Monica, California. When he demurred, he was told that he "had a marker out" due to the fact that Accardo had met with Richards when Richards had requested a sit-down with him in Chicago years before to negotiate for the life of a federal witness who had testified against mob members in Chicago and New York. When Richards arrived at the designated meeting place, the Municipal Pier in Santa Monica, he immediately recognized a dead end, out over the Pacific Ocean. He changed the location to a less dangerous spot. Accardo never showed but two gunsels did. Richards eluded the confrontation. He was warned, some "fear was thrown."

3

Battling for Turf in Chicago and New York

IT was 1903. Francesco and Maria Accardo, along with their son, Martin, emigrated from their difficult life in Palermo, Sicily, to the new world. Francesco was a shoemaker's helper. They settled in the Little Sicily area of Chicago, at 1353 West Grand Avenue, near Ogdon Avenue, on the Near West Side. Three years later, on April 28, 1906, another son was born to Francesco and Maria, now known in their adopted country as Frank and Mary. He was named Antonio Leonardo and was soon baptized at Holy Name Cathedral several blocks away from the Accardo domicile.

As the nineteenth century became the twentieth, there was another family in Sicily that would soon develop connections in the new world. This was the Bonanno family, headed by Giuseppe. They resided in Castellammare del Golfo, which means "castle by the sea by the gulf," and it is tucked into a beautiful gulf on the far western tip of Sicily. The Accardos and the Bonannos were a far cry from each other—not just geographically, but sociologically and economically. For the House of

Bonanno was the social ruler in the western part of Sicily while the Accardos were poor in almost every way. Giuseppe Bonanno had a son who had been a seminarian, studying to be a priest, but after some difficulty over a stolen gold candelabrum, he left the seminary and eventually became a member of the Mafia band headed by Stefano Magaddino, an uncle. This son, named Salvatore, married Catherine Bonventre in 1903 and on January 8, 1905, a son was born: Giuseppe Bonanno. He was to be the only son of the union. Soon Salvatore became known as Don Turridru to the peasants and landlords alike, and he became the leading Mafioso in western Sicily as young Giuseppe grew.

In 1908, Salvatore and Catherine Bonanno emigrated with Giuseppe to the United States where they also settled, like the Accardos, in Little Sicily. Except that their Little Sicily was located in the Williamsburg section of Brooklyn. Their home was at the corner of Roebling and North Fifth Street near the East River. Giuseppe's name was soon Americanized to Joe.

In 1912, when Joe was twelve, Don Turridru was called back to Sicily, where his family's interests were being jeopardized by a rival Mafia gang, the Buccellatos. After dealing with this problem, Don Turridru was called into the service of his country during World War I and was fatally wounded.

Joe was then sent to the Joeni Trabia Nautical Institute, a college specializing in tutoring its students for life as merchant marine officers. He was not to graduate, however, because in his third year there, Benito Mussolini and his Fascists came to power in Italy and purged the country of the Mafia. Joe Bonanno returned to Brooklyn at this point. Tony Accardo was residing in his Little Sicily in Chicago; Joe Bonanno in his Little Sicily in Brooklyn.

TONY Accardo dropped out of Holy Name Cathedral School in the middle of the fifth grade. He and a buddy, another Tony, this one named Capezio, found that the thrills and the income from petty thievery was much more to their liking than the three Rs. They engaged in street crime, mostly petty larceny in the Loop, the center of downtown Chicago, located about fifteen blocks from their homes. After a couple of years of this, the pair came to the attention of Vincenzo de Mora. He was a leader of the Circus Gang, sometimes known as the Circus

Cafe Gang after the name of its headquarters, an establishment located on North Avenue. Accardo and Capezio were recruited into the Circus Gang by de Mora. At first they were merely "gofers," going for coffee, beer, and other such errands. But soon they graduated into lookouts for the gang during burglaries, mostly invasions of homes on the West Side of Chicago.

In 1923, de Mora left the Circus Gang to join the big time. He was soon to become known as "Machine Gun" Jack McGurn. It was the era of the "Noble Experiment." Prohibition had come to America, outlawing all liquors with more than one-half of one percent of alcohol, effective at midnight on January 16, 1920. Accardo was fourteen at the time. The mob boss had been "Big Jim" Colosimo, but by 1923 when de Mora joined up, the mob was under the control of two new leaders.

Big Jim simply had not been visionary enough. He had not realized the potential that Prohibition represented to his mob. His right-hand man did, however. Johnny Torrio became most anxious when he realized that his boss did not share his insight. He travelled to New York where he contacted his old mentor, Francisco Uahe, better known as Frankie Yale. He discussed the problem with Yale. Yale suggested he "chop" Big Jim. When Torrio complained that he had no comrade in Chicago he could trust to kill the boss, Yale put him in touch with a young gunsel in Brooklyn who had done some "heavy work" for the New York mob. His name was Alphonse Caponi. It was a propitious situation for this young man since he was "hot" in Brooklyn, being sought by the police for his crimes. He readily agreed to accompany Torrio to Chicago where Torrio stashed him at The Four Deuces, a night spot at 2222 South Wabash. Caponi's job was to supply towels to the prostitutes at the Four Deuces. Up the street, at 2126 South Wabash, was Colosimo's Cafe, Big Jim's headquarters. On May 11, 1920, just a few months after the advent of the Noble Experiment, Caponi and Frankie Yale "chopped" Big Jim. They caught him in the vestibule of his restaurant and cut him down in a hail of gunfire. Torrio was now the boss, Caponi was his right-hand, and Yale returned to Brooklyn to rule his own domain there.

While these developments occurred, Tony Accardo was making his way up the ranks of the minor leagues of organized crime in Chicago. Soon he was commissioned by the Circus Gang to handle a festering problem. The Hanlon Hellcats, headquartered in the Shamrock Inn, were infringing on the Circus Gang's territory. Accardo, Capezio, and two others caught the Hanlons at midnight in January of 1923 coming out of the Shamrock Inn. They blasted them to kingdom come. But in fleeing they were chased by officers of the Austin District of the Chicago Police Department. Just before they were apprehended, Accardo commanded that the guns be tossed away. Although booked, Accardo and his crew were immediately released on bail and were never convicted. There was no evidence. No eyewitnesses and no weapons.

Accardo obviously was making his way up the ladder of success in the minors just as the new kid in the majors, Alphonse Caponi, was knocking them dead, in more ways than one, in his league. Caponi even changed his name. He was now known as Al Capone.

Torrio and Capone now set out to organize a hard-hitting mob and to rule their Prohibition-era Chicago turf with an iron hand. They put together an organization of the most capable Sicilian-Italian mobsters in Chicago. They recruited families in the Little Sicily area and in "the Patch," the area where most of the Italians had settled, on the Near Southwest Side of Chicago, around Taylor and Halsted streets. Then they got hold of Alex Louis Greenberg. They made him their "front," putting up money for Greenberg to buy the Malt-Maid Company at 3901 South Emerald Avenue on the Near South Side. They changed the name to the Manhattan Brewing Company and built it into the biggest brewery in Chicago. They bought several others. They arranged for stills to distill whiskey all over the Chicago area and its suburbs. They bought bars and taverns and made them into speakeasies. Capone sent back to Brooklyn and brought in his brothers and his cousins, the Fischettis. They recruited Italian mobsters such as McGurn.

SUCH was the situation when Joe Bonanno returned to Brooklyn from Sicily. Bootlegging was flourishing in Brooklyn as it was in Chicago. Joe moved in with his uncle, Peter Bonventre, who wanted to train him in his trade, as a barber. But Joe was the proud son of Don Turridru. Barbering was beneath him. Instead, at the age of nineteen, he hooked up with two shirttail relatives, Gaspar DiGregorio and Giovanni Romano, whom he had known in Castellammare. They had preceded Joe to America and were operating a very profitable bootlegging still in Brooklyn. Due to his stature as a Bonanno, Joe was invited in as a full partner. The year was 1925.

Later that year an event occurred which was to change Joe

Bonanno's life. Salvatore Maranzano came to America. Maranzano was a well-respected Mafia capo in Sicily. He had worked for Don Turridru and had earned a glorious reputation in the old country. When he came to America he settled in Little Italy on the Lower East Side of Manhattan. Maranzano invited the son of his Don to visit. Young Joe Bonanno was enthralled with the stories of Maranzano's adventures in Sicily. Maranzano became his icon, his mentor.

Maranzano soon made his move in America. He built his own boot-legging venture all over New York City, upstate New York, and even in Pennsylvania. He invited Joe Bonanno to join his *regime,* not as a partner but as a soldier. He appointed the youngster as overseer of all his whiskey stills. Joe demonstrated his worth very early. He found the highjackers who had pillaged a Maranzano warehouse in Wappingers Falls in upstate New York. After a deadly gunfight, Bonanno and his men recovered the stolen whiskey.

While earning his stripes in the Maranzano mob, known as the Castellammarese since all of its members came from that section of Sicily, Joe fell in love. The recipient of his affections was Fay Labruzzo, sometimes called Fanny by her friends. They became engaged but it would be some time before they could be married since Joe was so caught up in the turmoil of Prohibition.

AT the precise time that Bonanno was succeeding in New York, Tony Accardo was about to make his advent into the big time. Torrio and Capone were up to their ears in competition in Chicago. The rival gang, the O'Banion-Weiss-Moran Gang, was a worthy foe. Dion O'Banion had been killed in 1924 in his floral shop on State Street but Hymie Weiss and Bugs Moran had taken up where he left off and now, in 1926, Torrio and Capone needed new talent. Machine Gun Jack McGurn had become one of their top enforcers. One day Capone called him into his suite at the Lexington Hotel on the northeast corner of Michigan and Twenty-second Street just south of the Loop.

"Jack, we need some new shooters," he told McGurn. "Go out and bring some in. You used to be with that Circus Gang and then there's that 42 Gang in 'the Patch.' Go find out who their best men are and bring them with us. We'll 'make' them into our thing and use them to fight these Irishers."

McGurn was well aware of the reputation Tony Accardo was gaining in McGurn's old bunch, the Circus Gang. He heard about Accardo and Capezio's work in the Hanlon Hellcat shootout. He brought them both to Capone at the Lexington Hotel. There was no ceremony. Capone simply told them: "McGurn likes you guys. So I 'make' you. You are now one of us. If you fuck up, we take it out on McGurn. He is your sponsor. Fuck up and it's his ass. You work in his crew, he is your capo." It was as simple and quick as that. Nothing fancy. Accardo had arrived! He was now in the big leagues.

At the same time that Accardo and Capezio were "made," several others joined up: A young Welshman from the South Side, Murray Humphreys; a young Italian from the West Side, Paul DeLucia, who years later would be known as Paul "The Waiter" Ricca; Louis "Little New York" Campagna, who had come from New York where he had done some work for Frankie Yale; Frankie Rio, who was closest to Capone. A tough named Frank Nitti; a financial genius named Jake Guzik; another "heavy guy," Phil Andrea, and many others, were already aboard.

It was at this time that Hymie Weiss made a big mistake. He tried to take out Johnny Torrio. But he only wounded him. It gave Torrio food for thought. "This is a tough business. This Chicago is a bloody place. Too much competition and they are all a little nuts, ready to pull out the guns and blast away." Torrio told Capone from his hospital bed, "Al, I've had enough. I want to get out and go back to New York where I grew up. I can pick and choose what I want there. Here's my deal. Send me ten per cent of everything you take in, every month, and I'll turn it over to you."

Capone immediately recognized what a nice deal it was for him and accepted it.

Torrio called a meeting to announce his decision. Al Capone became the boss, and the Chicago family was thereafter to be known as the Capone Mob.

Tony Accardo was assigned to be one of Capone's personal bodyguards. When Capone held court in his suite on the fourth floor of the Lexington Hotel, it was Accardo's job to sit in the lobby of the hotel with a machine gun in his lap to discourage any unwelcome visitors. When Capone moved about the city, Accardo was one of the bodyguards who went with him. When he left Chicago, Capone usually went out to Cicero where he ruled. Capone had two prime spots in that western suburb of Chicago, which at the time was actually the sixth-largest town in Illinois: The Town Hotel, where he had a suite and where he held court in the Turf Lounge, and at the Hawthorne Inn, both on Twenty-second Street. He would travel due west from the Lexington at Michigan and Twenty-second to Cicero Avenue and Twenty-second, forty-nine blocks. The entourage would be led by the special bulletproof armor-plated Cadillac Capone had had manufactured for him. Capone owned Cicero. He had stuffed the ballot boxes, then slapped around the mayor he had thereby elected on the steps of City Hall in full view of the public. There was no doubt who the boss of Cicero was. But one day a convoy of the Weiss-Moran troops drove down Twenty-second Street in Cicero and shot up the Hawthorne Inn while Capone hugged the floor with Accardo on top of him as his shield. Weiss had become too much.

Accardo and Capezio were assigned a new task. Take out this bedbug, Weiss. It was a sign of ascendancy in the Capone Mob. They were obviously rising stars. They did the deed. Ironically, by a quirk of fate, they did it right in front of Holy Name Cathedral where Weiss had been an altar boy under his true name, Earl Wajciechowski, where Accardo and Capezio had gone to school and where Accardo had been baptized. Accardo had been trained by McGurn in the use of the Capone gang's trademark, the Chicago chopper, the Thompson submachine gun, which was what he used to kill Weiss. To this date, there are chips in the masonry at Holy Name from errant bullets fired on the day Accardo and Capezio clipped Weiss.

Now that Weiss was down, it was Bugs Moran who was the prime enemy. Accardo was just twenty-three. After his successful encounter with Hymie Weiss, however, he was recognized for what he was, a tough man who performed well in tight situations. Capone picked him and Capezio to get Moran. It was also at this time that Tony Accardo acquired a mob moniker. He had battered a Capone foe to death with a baseball bat. When Capone called him in to congratulate him in front of his peers, he clapped Accardo on the back and shouted for all to hear: "Hey, that's my boy, that's Joe Batters!" Not only was his reputation enhanced for expertise with the .45 and the Chicago chopper but now with almost any weapon at hand, even a baseball bat! Joe Batters, indeed! The name given him by Capone would cling to Accardo throughout his long career, even to this day.

McGurn sat down with his crew: Joe Batters, Tony Capezio, and Louie Campagna. They asked Jake Guzik, who was known as "Greasy

Thumb" because of his facility in counting money, and Murray Humphreys, known as "The Camel" or "Hump," to sit with them. They followed Bugs Moran. They found that Moran's headquarters was in a garage owned by a member of his gang, Adam Heyer, called the S.M.C. Cartage Company at 2122 North Clark Street on the North Side of Chicago. It was also used as a warehouse for Moran's whiskey.

Murray Humphreys found that the Genna brothers on the West Side were selling whiskey to Moran. Hump went to Angelo Genna, whom he knew and had worked with, and got Angelo to call Bugs Moran and make arrangements for a delivery on February 14, 1929, at 10:30 in the morning. Hump instructed Genna to make sure Moran and his entire gang would be present by arranging for an extralarge load, which would require many hands, and a large C.O.D. payment from Moran himself. Hump borrowed a police department squadrol from the captain of the police auto pound. He then obtained two uniforms from one of the police officers on the Capone pad.

McGurn and Campagna were outfitted in the uniforms of the police. Accardo and Capezio joined them in the squadrol. At precisely 10:30 on February 14, the foursome arrived at the Moran garage. The two "coppers" entered the building in the lead, Accardo and Capezio behind. Inside they found seven members of the gang.

"Up against the wall, this is a raid!" they shouted.

Believing it to be a legitimate police raid and knowing that it would be handled under the arrangements made with the police captain on the Moran pad, the seven members of the Moran gang docilely did as directed. It was almost too easy. When the uniformed "policemen" had the gang lined up, Accardo and Capezio stepped forward. From under their overcoats, they withdrew their trademark Chicago choppers. The shooting lasted just a few seconds. The victims could have drowned in their blood it ran so deep.

Then the rest of the scheme was put in place. Accardo and Capezio replaced their Tommy guns under their overcoats. Then they stretched their hands high in the air. The "coppers," McGurn and Campagna, pointed their .38 police specials at them and marched them out of the garage and into the rear of the squadrol. Away they roared, and nobody moved a muscle to stop them. Not even three onlookers down the block. For Bugs Moran and two of his men, Teddy Newberry and Willie Marks, had been late arrivals at the garage. They watched as the "police" made their raid. They were unaware that seven-tenths of their mob had been rubbed out as they watched the killers calmly escape.

As part of the strategy, Big Al Capone made himself very visible at his home in Palm Island, Florida. It was a perfect alibi for him.

When the press caught up with Moran and threw questions at him, he uttered: "Nobody but Capone kills like that!"

The St. Valentine's Day Massacre appeared initially not to be a total success since Moran himself was not a victim. But it didn't make much difference. Moran decided he had had enough. He fled to Wisconsin, never to cross Capone again. Joe Batters and his accomplices had done their job. Capone couldn't have been more pleased.

The audacity and the terrible bloodletting of the attack created an impact which was to have a far-reaching effect in Chicago. The St. Valentine's Day Massacre was the *coup de grace*—the final act. There would be many, many gangland killings in Chicago after 1929. But none of them would be for the purpose of muscling in on the Chicago Outfit. Accardo and his colleagues had cast it in iron. What Capone had put together in 1929 would last into the 1990s, at least.

All rivals since then have been cowed by their recollection of what Tony Accardo, truly Joe Batters, and his men did on Valentine's Day of 1929. No one has risen to try to take Chicago from Capone and his successors since.

THAT same year, 1929, in Brooklyn, Joe Bonanno was about to become a "boy from the first day." A mob war was about to begin there, one even more terrible and widespread than the one in Chicago. And just as Joe Batters was a major force in the Chicago battle, Joe Bonanno was a big part of what was transpiring in New York, the Volcano.

At this time there were five mob groups involved in bootlegging and the other rackets in New York City. The major one was led by Joe Masseria, who was called "The Boss" because of his supremacy among all the bosses. The Castellammarese family, led by Cola Schiro, was second, followed by Al Mineo's group, including such heavyweights as Albert Anastasia and Vincent Mangano. Then there was Tom Reina's family, which included rising stars such as Tommy Lucchese and Gaetano Gagliano, and finally the fifth family, headed by Joe Profaci.

The Volcano began to blow in January of 1930 when Gaspar Milazzo, the leader of the Castellammarese in Detroit, was murdered in a fish market. The Castellammarese called a council of war in Brooklyn. Salvatore Maranzano was chosen to replace Schiro due to his proven qualities in battle as demonstrated in Sicily. He selected Joe Bonanno as his chief of staff.

Masseria ordered the killing of Vito Bonventre, one of the most affluent of the Castellammarese bootleggers. It was accomplished. Then Maranzano ordered the killing of Peter "The Clutch Hand" Morello, Masseria's top man. It was done.

In September of 1930, Bonanno suffered his first arrest. He was caught by the NYPD in a car near City Hall in lower Manhattan with a handful of Chicago choppers, i.e. Thompson submachine guns. Since this weapon was a trademark of the Capone Mob in Chicago, the police mistakenly identified Bonanno as a "gun runner for Al Capone" and so informed the press. This characterization has clung to Bonanno to this day, although nothing could have been further from the truth, since Capone supported Joe Masseria in what would become known as the "Castellammarese War." The label would haunt Bonanno for the rest of his life and would even be used to his detriment in presentence and probation reports.

A major break in the Castellammarese War occurred in October of 1930. Joe Valachi, who years later would become the first major defector from the mob ranks, was assigned to be a lookout at an apartment building in the Bronx which Masseria was known to frequent. One day Valachi spotted Masseria. Bonanno and his men hustled to the scene. When a group emerged, Bonanno's crew opened fire. Although Masseria escaped unharmed, two of his top men were killed. It had somewhat the same effect on Masseria as the St. Valentine's Day Massacre had had on Bugs Moran. It was too close for comfort and Masseria backed off. After a couple more killings on each side, Maranzano sent word to the man who had succeeded The Clutch Hand as the top aide of Masseria. "Come over and you will be rewarded." The recipient of this message was Charles Lucanio. He would later become better known as "Lucky" Luciano.

Luciano got the message. He met with Maranzano who was accompanied by Bonanno. With Luciano was Vito Genovese, who would become a well-known figure in mob history.

The deed was done in April of 1931, following the Maranzano-Luciano conference. Luciano lured Masseria to lunch, just between the two of them, at the Nuova Villa Tammaro restaurant in Coney Island. When Luciano excused himself to go to the bathroom, Genovese, Joe

Adonis, Albert Anastasia, and Bugsy Siegel burst into the restaurant and killed Masseria. The Castellammarese War was over.

Maranzano, with Bonanno at his side "from the first day" to the final deed, was the victor. The Castellammarese were the winners. You might come from Corleone, another Sicilian breeding ground for the best of the Mafiosi, but you now had lost your bragging rights. The Castellamarese now wore the garland. They were now in position to claim the spoils.

Maranzano, however, was magnanimous. Soon thereafter he called together all of the leaders of what he now called La Cosa Nostra. The meeting was held in a large banquet hall on the Grand Concourse of the Bronx. If you didn't get an invitation to what was to be the grand coronation of the *Capo di Tutti Capi,* the boss of all bosses, you didn't belong.

Bonanno's bubble burst upon arrival at the hall. Maranzano had arranged the seating in order of importance. Luciano was placed at his right hand. Bonanno, his right-hand "from the first day," was honored by being at the table but not alongside the boss. The proud Castellammarese swallowed hard. He had to accept it.

The *Capo di Tutti Capi,* a close student of the old Romans, decreed who was to be the boss of each "family of La Cosa Nostra," as he called it. He gave one such family to Joe Bonanno. He gave another to Lucky Luciano, another to Joe Profaci, another to Gaetano Gagliano, another to himself. In Chicago, he named Al Capone, of course. He gave Cleveland to Francisco Milano. He gave Buffalo to Stefano Magaddino, the cousin of Joe Bonanno. Down the line he went. None were surprises; they were the leaders who had established themselves in their respective territories. But by putting his imprimatur on each family, Maranzano made it official.

He then decreed that each family would be headed by a boss who would appoint a *sotto capo,* an underboss. Each family would have a *consigliere,* the advisor and counselor to the family and the buffer between the men and the leader. Each family was to have several capos, depending on the number of soldiers, which were the last rung in each family.

As Lucky Luciano left the hall that evening he felt very good about things. Whereas Maranzano had split his family by giving many of his men to Joe Bonanno for the latter's family, Luciano had a strong number of proven men. His *sotto capo* was Vito Genovese, a proven gunman of the first order. Tommy Lucchese, the underboss of another family, was one of his closest friends. The underboss in another family was Albert Anastasia, another close ally. In addition he had very close ties to men he had grown up with but who were Jewish, not La Cosa Nostra members. However, they were every bit as good, in his estimation, as his Italian people. They were Meyer Lansky and Benny "Bugsy" Siegel, trusted and proven "workers." Luciano also knew he could trust Arthur Flegenheimer, better known as "Dutch" Shultz, Abner "Longy" Zwillman, and Louis Buchalter, better known as "Lepke," to side with him in any dispute.

In addition Luciano knew he could count on alliances he had made all over the country. Capone was no friend of Maranzano. He had backed Masseria in the War. Through Capone, Luciano had gotten to know Frank Nitti, Murray Humphreys, and Jake Guzik. In fact, he had gotten to know the young bodyguard of Capone, the guy who had had a hand in the St. Valentine's Day Massacre, Tony Accardo—the guy they called Joe Batters because he was so handy with weapons of any description. Even a baseball bat.

Luciano knew he could count on the man who had taken over Cleveland with his Mayfield Road Gang, a young Jew named Moe Dalitz. This Dalitz had earned a widespread reputation as a bootlegger, not only in Cleveland but in Detroit where he had been the admiral in "The Little Jewish Navy" of rum runners from Canada.

Knowing that it was Luciano who had double-crossed his boss, Masseria, and set him up for the kill, Maranzano did not trust Luciano. He gave him a family because that was his deal with Luciano. Now he plotted to kill him. Luciano, however, learned of the plot. Maranzano retained a man outside his family to clip Luciano, Vincent "Mad Dog" Coll. Luciano did likewise. He hired "Red" Levine.

Maranzano ruled his domain from a swanky suite of offices in mid-Manhattan in the Grand Central Building at Park Avenue and Forty-sixth Street, high above Grand Central Station. The time came on September 19, 1931, just months after Maranzano had proclaimed himself *Capo di Tutti Capi.* Into his suite burst four men, obviously not Italian, posing as IRS agents. They were led by Levine. They cornered Maranzano in his private office and killed him. They then fled down the stairway. On the way down they met "Mad Dog" Coll, on the way up to receive his final instructions from Maranzano on killing Luciano. The perfidious Luciano had acted just in time!

Now Luciano moved to consolidate his power. He had everything going for him in Manhattan, where he felt he was supreme and he did not want to alienate anybody. His buzzword was appeasement. He felt no need to grab somebody else's territory or interests. To this end he called a meeting, emulating Maranzano. But he asked Al Capone to host this one in Chicago. Again, anybody who was anybody was invited. The meeting was held in the grand ballroom of the Congress Hotel in the extreme southern end of Chicago's Loop.

It was at this meeting that the stately Bonanno met the rough-hewn Accardo. Accardo was part of Al Capone's entourage. He was introduced to Bonanno in the lobby of the Congress Hotel on the first evening of the conclave. Regal by nature, Joe Bonanno took little notice of Joe Batters. "Just another of the young toughs of this uncouth Capone," he thought.

At the Congress Hotel meeting, there was no head table. The arrangements were crafted for democracy. Each family sat together— Bonanno with his *sotto capo*, Gasparino DiGregario. Capone sat with his underboss, Frank Nitti. Accardo sat outside in the lobby, on guard.

The most notable difference in the Congress Hotel and the Grand Concourse meetings, however, was in the nationalities of the participants. Among the attendees in Chicago were such luminaries as Dutch Shultz, Jake Guzik, Longr Zwillman, Murray Humphreys, Meyer Lansky, Bugsy Siegel, Lepke Buchalter, and Moe Dalitz. Maranzano never would have invited these non-Italians. Nor would have Bonanno had he been the one to make such a decision. But all were to play important roles in the affairs of organized crime in years to come. As a matter of fact, Moe Dalitz's star would rise many years later in a territory none of the conferees in 1931 had ever heard of. In fact, at that very moment, events that would totally escape the attention of the assembled mobsters were taking place in that faraway place, events that would some day be almost their sole focus. If New York was considered the Volcano for its fierce warfare and if Chicago was an equally violent scene of combat, the mob hadn't seen nothin' yet compared to what was brewing out West!

CHAPTER

4

Glitter Gulch and the Strip

IF ever there was something made from nothing, it is the state of Nevada. Statehood was granted in 1864 but about all there was sun, trees, hills, valleys—and desert. In 1913 gambling had been outlawed by the legislature, but still there were plenty of poker, blackjack, roulette, and even crap games set up in the dance halls and saloons. In 1930 "Pappy" Smith arrived and started to build a place he called Harold's Club even though his first name was Raymond.

Then in 1931 Nevada legalized all forms of gambling, creating a local control authority. That same year legislation was passed authorizing divorce based on a mere six-week residency, by far the least amount of time any state allowed. Many alienated women flocked to Reno and lost their alimony after spending a couple of months there. The city erected an arch over Virginia Street, its main thoroughfare, proclaiming it "The Biggest Little City in the World." It stands to this day. The *Chicago Tribune* cried "Cancel Nevada's statehood." The *Los Angeles Times* called Nevada "a vicious Babylon." Reno, Elko, Winnemucca, Ely,

Ruth, Carson City, Minden, Sparks, and little Las Vegas geared up for gambling.

The first spike in the tracks of the Union Pacific had been driven linking a hick town named Las Vegas to the site of the Hoover Dam, some twenty-two miles away, giving this burg a boost in tourism. The population of Las Vegas was less than 8000.

The stock market crash and the start of the Depression in the early 1930s dampened any discretionary spending and Nevada was no exception. Franklin Delano Roosevelt was elected President of the United States; Adolf Hitler was assuming power in Germany; Al Capone was going to prison; Prohibition would be ending soon. It was an era of change.

When gaming was legalized in Nevada in 1931, the town situated to benefit by far the most was Reno. There already were dozens of small casinos set up for crap games, "21," and poker. In 1931 the first big casino was erected there. It was called the Bank Club and it was run by Bill Graham, Nevada's pioneer casino operator. It featured the usual games as well as chuck-a-luck and faro and soon would add a huge parimutuel wheel. Virginia Street, Commercial Row, and Center Street in Reno were to become loaded with small and medium-sized casinos. Even Douglas Alley would have a couple. As such, during the early years of legalized gambling in Nevada, Reno was the major locale. The Union Pacific ran its "City of San Francisco" and its "City of Los Angeles" trains to "The Biggest Little City in the World," and hundreds flocked to sample its wares. Prostitution, also legal in Nevada, added to the attraction.

Nevada has another town 450 miles south of Reno. The downtown section of Las Vegas, on Fremont Street, saw sparse action in the 1930s. In fact, there was a big banner over Fremont Street in the 1930s which read "Las Vegas, Gateway to the Boulder Dam." This served as appropriate commentary on the state of mind of the citizens of Las Vegas and their concept of tourism.

On Boulder Highway south of Las Vegas, the Cornero brothers— Frank, Louis, and Tony—had built a small casino called, appropriately, the Meadows. Again, a commentary on the state of entrepreneurship in Las Vegas. In order to travel by train from Las Vegas, it was necessary to take the Union Pacific through Salt Lake City.

During 1936, Harold's Club finally opened and soon Bill Harrah, destined to remain a major name in Nevada to this day, built a bingo parlor in Reno, only to go bust and then open the Tango Club the next year. It wouldn't be until 1942 that he built Harrah's Club, but he was in Nevada to stay and he eventually was enshrined in Nevada's Gaming Hall of Fame.

One of the big boosts to tourism in Las Vegas came in 1939 when Clark Gable's wife, Rhea, came for a divorce. The Chamber of Commerce, moving out of the dark ages, focused on her visit and took photos of Mrs. Gable riding horseback, playing golf, swimming in Lake Mead, and climbing Mt. Charleston. Together with quotes from Rhea about the sun, warmth, and fresh air, these photos went to hundreds of the leading newspapers around the world as advertisements for Las Vegas. Vegas, as it was getting to be known, had begun its challenge to Reno as a tourist attraction. If you wanted to get laid, gamble, and/or get a quick divorce, come to Las Vegas. It was all legal.

Then Tom Hull, a Sacramento hotel man, came through Las Vegas on his way to build a hotel in, of all places, Deming, New Mexico. Hull got an idea. Instead of Deming, he would build his hotel in Las Vegas with its added attraction of legalized gambling. If you have visited Deming, New Mexico, lately, you will realize his wisdom. Deming is a quaint, dusty, lazy retirement community; a very pleasant place to lie in the sun. The largest hotel or motel there today is a Best Western. What Hull did was revolutionary; he put his hotel south of downtown although all the other casinos were located downtown. He put his place south of the city limits, out on Highway 91. It was called the El Rancho Vegas and it was to become the first hotel on what is now Las Vegas Boulevard, and is often called the Strip.

El Rancho was a large complex, consisting of a main hotel and casino and sixty-three bungalows with a large pool on seven acres of trees and shrubs. It sat on top of an underground artesian lake—the complex needed all the water it could get, consuming, as it did, ten million gallons of water a month.

Then Moe Sedway came to Las Vegas. He ran the Trans-America Wire Service. The wire services were a necessity for all bookmakers who depended on race results. In the late thirties, Trans-America was the only competitor to the Continental Press Service. Trans-America was run by the New York mobsters; Continental by James Ragen, an independent from Chicago. Continental serviced all bookmakers from Chicago west, and Continental had had a monopoly in Nevada. Now Sedway, representing Luciano, Lansky, and Siegel, was posing a challenge, and this challenge would be a precursor of things to come.

Sedway would eventually win. Why not—with the backing he had, and with the fact that Ragen's Continental Press was a loner? Ragen not only didn't have the mob as his partners, he didn't want them. He'd rather lose business than gain such partners. He didn't know he would someday lose more than business when he opted not to take in the Chicago mob as his partners.

About that time, in the late 1930s, a skinny little kid from Hoboken, New Jersey, began singing in road houses and little night spots in the Garden State. Soon he came to the attention of Willie Moretti, the mob boss there. Thanks to Moretti, he also came to the attention of Tommy Dorsey, one of the era's top band leaders. He became the "boy singer" with the Tommy Dorsey band. But he wanted more than that. Soon Willy put up $50,000 to promote this kid, get the attention of the public, get him some clothes, grease the palms of anyone who could help his career. This skinny little kid from Hoboken soon had the bobby soxers swooning from coast to coast. From his appearances at the Paramount and the Roxy in New York, to the Chicago Theatre and the Aragon and Trianon ballrooms in Chicago, to the Coconut Grove in Los Angeles—from coast to coast this skinny little kid blossomed into stardom. As his career blossomed so did Nevada—and Las Vegas in particular. They were on an identical course. It was inevitable that one day their ascending destinies would coalesce at the same time at the same spot. They were made for each other.

When America was thrust into World War II on December 7, 1941, it was a boon to Las Vegas and for the rest of Nevada! Thousands upon thousands of soldiers and airmen from the corn fields of Iowa, from the mean streets of Queens, from the black belt of Chicago, and from the iron range of the northern plains discovered Las Vegas. What a life style! Girls galore, some for a few bucks, many others there for a quickie divorce, just looking for a quick jump in the hay. All the excitement of the gaming tables. A great climate, sunny days, and clean air. Great entertainment!

And right smack in the middle of World War II came Bugsy Siegel, in 1943 to be precise. He was sent by Meyer Lansky and Frank Costello, then major players in the New York family of Lucky Luciano.

Las Vegas would never again be a cow town, a second cousin to Reno. Dusty old Highway 91 was about to become arguably the most famous boulevard in the world. The street of a million, maybe a billion, neon lights. High rollers and low rollers. Skims and scams. Wheelers and dealers. Show girls and hole girls. Prime joints and grind joints. Even a showplace Catholic cathedral reflecting the glare of the nearby casino lights where the Risen Christ in the sanctuary looks more like a disco dancer than the divine deus. And it would be the mob, La Cosa Nostra, that would supply the prime impetus, that would catapult that lovely valley in sun into the sin capital of the world. As General Douglas MacArthur was accepting the surrender of the Japanese empire, Bugsy Siegel was building what was to become an empire all its own.

5

The Mob Learns the Casino Business

MEYER Lansky, the financial genius of Lucky Luciano's mob in New York, in 1933 had gone to Havana, Cuba, where he had been set up with Fulgencio Batista, the president of Cuba. After the requisite negotiations, all under the table of course, Lansky perfected arrangements to take over the Hotel Nacional in Havana and to operate a major gaming casino there to cater to the high rollers, the wealthy tourists from the United States. It became a major income producer for the Luciano organization. It would be a prelude to what the mob would later do in Las Vegas. The experience gained in the casinos in Cuba would stand the mob in great stead later in gaming ventures in Las Vegas and the rest of Nevada. The tricks of the trade, the ability to skim, would be learned in Havana beginning in the 1930s so that when the mob landed in Las Vegas they would be experienced pros in the art of how to operate casinos.

When Joe Bonanno learned about Luciano's good fortune, he approached his friend. "Charles," he said, always calling Lucky by his given name, "you have opened up this door to Cuba. Now I understand it was your man, Lansky, who made the arrangements and that makes it understandable that you should reap the major share in Havana. But do you not think I should have been included in these arrangements? Is it not right that, as your fellow member of The Commission, I am entitled to some small portion? Is that how one friend treats another?"

Luciano gave Bonanno one small concession. He allowed a member of the Bonanno family to work as a shift manager at the Hotel Nacional. Controlling such a position, it was possible to skim enough from the tables and from the slots to bring Bonanno a very nice monthly stipend.

Skim is the reason the mob is interested in obtaining a hidden interest in a casino—anywhere. Although gaming stocks are excellent business investments and although ownership of a hotel-casino is profitable, it is the skim that makes it so rewarding for the mob. Skim is the method by which the proceeds of the gaming tables, the roulette wheels, the keno, the slot machines, and baccarat are intercepted before the official count. Somewhere between the tables and the counting room, they are siphoned off. Sometimes it is done right in the counting room before the official count is made. Once obtained, the skim is surreptitiously couriered to those who have hidden interests, called points, in the hotel-casino. Obviously, this is a very nice bonus, not only because of the vast amounts of money involved, but because no tax is paid. The skim can total in the millions annually from a decent-sized casino. The mob developed its ability to skim in Havana and later perfected it in Las Vegas.

On February 9, 1946, Lucky Luciano had been exiled to Italy by the U. S. government. He hated his homeland, however, and secretly left there in October 1946 to travel to Havana where he hoped that Meyer Lansky's relationship with Fulgencio Batista would serve to make him welcome. It would have to be a surreptitious residence, however, since it was an obvious and blatant violation of his parole which called for his deportation to Italy and nowhere else.

Other than comfort, Luciano had another reason for wanting to settle in Havana. A more important one. He wanted to regain his unofficial title of *Capo di Tutti Capi,* which he had lost when he was exiled by the U. S. government. He couldn't do this in Rome. He might do it in Havana, just miles from Miami. And under certain conditions, from there he might be able to sneak into the United States often enough to resume control of his Cosa Nostra family. Although Miami had been decreed "open territory" by The Commission, obviously, if he could reinstitute his power there, this decree was not carved in stone.

Just as obviously, since he was most envious of the esteem in which Luciano was held, Joe Bonanno had severe reservations when he learned of this agenda. He learned about it directly, when he was informed that a meeting of The Commission and of some associate members, was scheduled for December 22, 1946, in Havana, just in time for Christmas. Bonanno was piqued. After all, he now chaired The Commission meetings. Who was Luciano to call a meeting? But rather than revive old animosities, now approaching his fortieth birthday, Bonanno accepted the invitation in his usual urbane manner.

The president of Cuba was now Ramón Grau San Martín. But he was the puppet of Fulgencio Batista, then living in Florida, and it was Batista, even in absentia, who still had the power in Cuba. A share of the skim from the Nacional made its way to Batista—not to San Martín.

The delegates arrived as scheduled. In addition to Bonanno, the New York delegation included Joe Profaci and his underboss, "Fat Joe" Magliocco; Frank Costello, who had succeeded Luciano as the boss of that New York family; Joe Adonis, now living in New Jersey but maintaining his interests in New York City; Albert Anastasia, the boss of Murder, Inc., who someday would head his own family; Tommy Lucchese, also a future family boss; Willie Moretti, who one day would be murdered by his own when his mental condition caused him to open his mouth too often; "Little Augie" Pisano, who one day would be murdered necking in a car with a girlfriend; and Mike Miranda, also someday to be on a hit list. Tony Accardo represented Chicago—it was 1946 and Paul Ricca had not yet been sprung from the federal pen at Leavenworth. Accardo was the acting boss in Chicago and he brought the Fischetti brothers—the cousins of Al Capone and the close friends, as was Moretti, of a certain celebrity guest who would make a cameo appearance at the gangland enclave. Steve Magaddino came from Buffalo. Carlos Marcello flew in from his domain in New Orleans. And Santo Trafficante, Jr., the son of the elder Trafficante who had assisted Lansky in his original infiltration of the island in 1933, came in from Tampa. And, in addition to these "made" members of La Costa Nostra came two more guests, one of them the most important, perhaps, of all the invitees—Meyer Lansky. The other was "Dandy" Phil Kastel, the man Luciano had sent to open up Louisiana for the mob and whom Costello had retained there as his man.

The celebrity guest, one who was invited but who would not be privy to any of the mob discussions, was the skinny little kid from Hoboken. He was the cover for the meet. Ostensibly, this large gathering of such ominous types was there to celebrate the holidays with their pal, Frank Sinatra. In fact, he had flown into Cuba with the Fischetti brothers, although it was another Fischetti brother, Joe, who was his closer friend and who was not invited to this shindig.

The first order of business was for each of the arrivals to present themselves at the mansion Luciano had leased in Miramar and drop an envelope on him. The $150,000 Luciano thereby acquired was then given to Lansky who made a matter of record of it when he transferred a major interest in the Hotel Nacional to Luciano, thereby giving him an official reason to participate in the profits as well as the skim which he was already receiving and to be in Cuba.

The first item on the agenda was one that Joe Bonanno and Joe Batters were in firm agreement about. Both had strong opinions about dope dealing, but some of the attendees were becoming involved in this area. Particularly, Vito Genovese. But also Albert Anastasia. It was something Salvatore Maranzano had decreed was strictly off limits, but now his decree was more honored in the breach than the observance.

That first night Joe Bonnano, in his usual courtly fashion, would invite Joe Batters to join him at his table for dinner. Accardo bluntly refused the invitation to join Bonanno and instead invited him to join the Chicago table with the Fischetti brothers. Bonanno accepted but soon gained a lasting impression that this family from Chicago was a crude, unmannerly faction. Why, they even ordered pasta when the occasion called for chateaubriand. "Peasants," thought Bonanno. "But what can you expect from a native of Palermo? He wouldn't have the class of one from Castellammare. And those Fischettis, they have the class of their cousin, that Neapolitan, Capone."

But before the dinner, while the meeting was still in progress, "the Siegel Situation" became the main topic of discussion. And it was a very serious Meyer Lansky who introduced it.

Although all in attendance were aware of what Benjamin "Bugsy" Siegel was doing in the desert oasis of Las Vegas, that sleeping little cow town which was undergoing a remarkable transformation—some were much more aware than others. The two Joes, for instance, were nominally aware, but had not been asked for financial assistance and therefore had no idea of the specifics. On the other hand, Murray Humphreys of Chicago had flown out to Las Vegas and had taken a good look at the situation after Johnny Roselli, who was representing the Chicago Mob out West, had alerted the Chicago bunch as to what Siegel and his backers, Lansky and Costello, were building in Nevada. Humphreys had made a cursory report to Accardo, but Accardo, with so much else on his mind, paid it little heed. Now, however, Accardo gave his attention to Lansky. He became fully aware that Luciano, while still confined in state prison at Great Meadow, had received Lansky and Costello as visitors. (Luciano was cooperating with the government in its war effort on the waterfront so he had great leeway at Great Meadow.) Lucky agreed with them that Bugsy's idea was worth throwing some money at. It had promise. The year was 1943. Bugsy's idea was to build a grand hotel-cum-casino on Highway 91. There was just one casino there at the time, the one at the very top of the highway. Bugsy's place would be about a mile south and it would be the grandest of the grand. He would name it the Flamingo after the flock of pink flamingos at the Hialeah race track in Florida—the Luciano-Lansky-Siegel combine had once owned a piece of Hialeah—and it had been a very lucky spot for Benny.

Now into Siegel's life had come Virginia Hill. Virginia was a hillbilly from Kentucky. In 1933 she had come to Chicago as a beautiful but countrified teen-ager. She turned some tricks at "A Century of Progress," the World's Fair on the Chicago lake front, where she had come to the attention of Joe Epstein. Epstein was one of Chicago's top bookmakers, an ace at handicapping the races. A short, unattractive man in his thirties at the time, he immediately fell in love with the pretty hooker and took her under his wing. He gave her fancy clothes, took her to the best hair dresser, put her up at the Seneca Hotel on the Near North Side, took her to the best restaurants, introduced her to his fairly sophisticated circle of cohorts, and, in general, taught her to be a lady who could move in smart circles. It was a long way from the hills of Kentucky.

But one day in 1940, Epstein took his young protégé to enjoy the theater and the nightclubs in New York City. At the Copacabana, they ran into Bugsy Siegel in the company of Frank Costello, who had a piece of that famous New York night spot. Mutual friends in the underworld introduced Epstein to Siegel, two good Jewish boys, and as his good manners would dictate, Epstein, in turn, introduced his "niece" to Siegel. It wasn't long before Virginia Hill was spending more time in the Big Apple than in the Windy City.

In 1943, Virginia decided to move to yet another town. This time, Las Vegas, to be with Benny full time. She would be his hotel consultant, his decorator and all around ex officio vice-president.

It was Benny's dream to make the Flamingo the apex of the entertainment world. Gambling, entertainment, girls, opulence of the first order. The best food, the best drink, the best surroundings—an ambiance fit for kings and queens. So he gave Virginia a free hand. Spend whatever she needed to make it the best. Money would be no object. What a heady spot for the young girl just down from the hills of Kentucky.

Soon Bugsy began to outrun his budget. Not a great problem. Lansky and Costello just dug into their pockets and sent some more cash out West. His initial budget was $1,000,000—a nice hunk of change in 1943. But here we were in 1946; he and Virginia had already spent over $6,000,000, with more to come if the Flamingo was to be finished. When he began to receive complaints, Siegel decided to open the casino even before it was quite finished. December 26, the day after Christmas, was to be opening day. As anybody familiar with Las Vegas these days would tell you, he could hardly have picked a worse day. But that is hindsight, based on knowledge acquired up into the 1990s.

Humphreys had learned of all this during his visits to Siegel and had reported it to Accardo in cursory fashion. The other conferees were also vaguely aware of the history of the Flamingo.

Now the demeanor of Lansky darkened. "You all know that Benny and Lucky and I grew up together. We were kids on the Lower East Side and we made our bones together. We've been close as brothers ever since. So it hurts me as much as anything in my life to have to tell you here today that we have put a tail on Virginia Hill and what we have found is most disturbing. We have tailed her from Los Angeles—where she lives in Beverly Hills, for Christ's sake, when she is supposed to be handling things in Vegas—and she has gone to Zurich, Switzerland. She headed right to a bank and I've learned that she has one of those numbered accounts there and on the occasion that we tailed her she deposited $300,000 into it. Now, obviously, that ain't her money. And it ain't Benny's. It's ours. Now, worse than that, while we was watching her she goes to a real estate guy in Switzerland and they go looking at houses, in the suburbs of Zurich on the way to a place called Lucerne. She picks out quite a nice place and we now learn she has rented it—on a long term lease, for Christ's sake. I would have to say, Benny has skimmed from us pretty deep and he's getting ready to skip in case things don't work out."

Lansky paused. "Now I get to the worst part. What I got to recommend to you. Benny has been my brother since we were born. I love the guy. He'd do anything for you. And he's the best shooter I've ever known. The guy is fearless. He's made moves none of us would ever think of. I could tell you stories about guys he's clipped that I would never have been able to get done. All in all, Benny Siegel has been one of the best men ever in our business. No question about that. So we owe him. But when a man steals from his best friends, that ain't right. That's a death sentence. Now here's what I'm gonna suggest. See what you think. I've got a guy out there in Vegas, close to Benny, he knows nothing about. For our protection. Benny is gonna open his place this week. After he opens it, my guy is gonna call me. If it's what Benny has told us it will be, a great success, if he gets all the high rollers to come in there from California and all those fucking movie stars who say they will show up to add to the glitz and it therefore looks like he's making it, that there is the potential there he has told us there is, then we sit back and give Benny a shot at it. But if it is a flop, what I think is that Ben will know he hasn't got a chance and that we're gonna come after him. That's when he'll skip. And we can't let him get away with that. Let him set an example like that and every fucking person in the world will know it and try the same fucking thing. So we gotta down him if it don't work when he opens. I hate like hell to say it, but that is my opinion. I don't come at it easy, you all know I love that fruitcake, but that is my recommendation to you today."

Lansky sat down. The room was quiet.

Luciano finally broke the silence. "I got to go for what Meyer says. You all know I've been as close to this guy as Meyer and for as long. But what he says makes sense. Even if it's your brother, if he cheats you, steals from you, you got to go after him. I say we do just what Meyer says. Wait till we see what happens when he opens and then go from there."

Nobody disagreed. After all, the real money in the place was that of Lansky and Luciano. If they agreed on this course of action, so be it.

On Christmas eve, the wives and girlfriends of the conferees arrived as prearranged. A gala was held in the ballroom of the Nacional. Frank Sinatra was at his best as he entertained and a great time was had by all. The skinny kid from Hoboken preened at the attention lavished on him by mobsters. He loved every moment of it. The guy who had helped him in his early stages was there, looking proudly on, and Willie Moretti was happy that he had been in a position to be of such assistance.

On December 26, the gangsters gathered again to await the results of the opening of Benny Siegel's Flamingo. As he had promised, Bugsy had brought in some top entertainers. Georgie Jessel was master of ceremonies. Xavier Cugat and his bombshell singer and wife, Abbe Lane, provided the music for dancing. Jimmy Durante paid a debt or two by starring in the floor show. George Raft also worked off a marker by being there to greet the customers. It should have been a great attraction.

But it wasn't. The call from Lansky's pal came at three o'clock in the morning in Havana. It was a flop. Nobody came, not to the gaming tables and not even to watch Jessel or Durante. Nobody cared that they could shake hands with the likes of George Raft. But Lansky went softhearted. He couldn't bear to carry out his recommendation that his pal be murdered. "Let's give him one more chance. I'll take it on myself he don't run. I'll go out there and we'll give it everything we got to make it work. Give me one more shot at it."

In spite of everything, the mob agreed. They would give Benny Siegel his final chance. Their patience was not far from being exhausted, however. It was tissue thin—touch and go—for Bugsy.

The tissue broke several months later, however, when it became obvious that Bugsy Siegel had no intention of cleaning up his act.

SIX months later, on the afternoon of June 20, 1947, Bugsy Siegel had just had his regular manicure at Harry Drucker's barbershop in Beverly Hills. He was alone. Virginia was once again in Switzerland doing her thing, and Bugsy's two daughters were to arrive early the next week.

The Flamingo, at long last, had been completed and business was improving somewhat after a shaky start. Things were pretty good for Benny Siegel. Or so he thought.

From the barbershop he went home to the mansion which he shared with Virginia on North Linden Drive in Beverly Hills. He took a long nap. Then Chick Hill, Virginia's brother from Kentucky who was staying at Bugsy's place came back with a girlfriend, a young blonde named Jerri Mason. They exchanged some small talk and then the couple went upstairs. About nine, Allen Smiley came over. Smiley was a mid-echelon Los Angeles hood—no hood in Los Angeles has ever been top echelon—but he and Bugs were good friends and frequent companions both in L.A. and Las Vegas.

Bugsy made a phone call to Vegas at about ten. The tables were pretty well filled, the gray-haired old ladies were pulling the levers on the slot machines, and although it wasn't a gala night compared to what action on the Strip would become in later years, it was a good night for the summer of 1947.

When Siegel completed the call, he settled down on the couch in the living room and continued some small talk with Smiley. Then it happened. Through the large picture window in the living room came a fusillade of bullets from a .30–.30 carbine. One bullet ripped out Bugsy's left eye. Four more caught him in his torso. Three more ripped into the wall behind him.

The agenda set at the party in Havana for the skinny little kid from Hoboken was now completed. The deed was done.

That same evening, just after Bugsy's last call—which was the signal—three men walked into the general offices of the Flamingo Hotel. Benny wasn't even dead yet. They advised the office staff that they were now in charge. By the time the office personnel called Bugsy's home in Beverly Hills to confirm, there was no answer.

Gus Greenbaum and Morrie Rosen, two of Lansky's top men who had been his key people in Havana at the Hotel Nacional, were put in charge. Greenbaum should have gone to school on what happened to Bugsy—being in charge of the Flamingo was not good for one's health. He would later be murdered in Phoenix. A third guy who walked into the Flamingo that night was Moe Sidwirtz, who would become well known on the Strip as Moe Sedway.

Most mob experts believe that Jack Dragna, another mid-level Los Angeles hood, was the guy who fired the carbine. Dragna would one day become the boss of what derisively would come to be known as "The Mickey Mouse Mafia" in Los Angeles. In fact, Dragna would revel in such history. It was his biggest claim to fame.

However, Dragna was nowhere near Beverly Hills on the night of June 20, 1947.

The Los Angeles family of La Cosa Nostra is under the complete domination of the Chicago family. In fact, Chicago controls everything west of Chicago to the Pacific Ocean. It did in 1947 and it does today. Kansas City, Denver, Los Angeles, San Diego, San Francisco—they all have LCN families. But all those families are subservient to Chicago. Therefore, any hit in the western part of the United States has to be sanctioned by Chicago. In June of 1947, the acting boss of the Chicago family was none other than Tony "Joe Batters" Accardo.

In 1947, Joe Batters had two up-and-coming young stars on his hands. These two guys were made from the same mold as Accardo and Tony Capezio three decades before. They were boyhood pals who had grown up in the same neighborhood, went to grade school together—though not to high school since neither finished grade school—and then had gone on to bigger and better things, not in Little Sicily as had Accardo and Capezio, but in "The Patch," that area where the Italian immigrants had migrated in the early part of the century. Actually, they came from just a little bit east of "The Patch," at Twenty-sixth and Wentworth, where one of their dads had operated a small family restaurant which had become a favorite of Al Capone. These two pals worked as busboys, then short-order cooks in the restaurant and came to revere the Capone mobsters who frequented the restaurant. Soon they came to the attention of the mobsters, Tony Accardo in particular, and it was just a matter of time.

They had done some jobs around Chicago. For instance, they were in a trail car to assist in the getaway when Lenny Patrick, Willie Block, and Marshall Caifano hit James Ragen, the wire service operator, a year before.

Their names were Gus Alex and Frank Ferraro. They called Gus "Slim" and they called Frank "Strongy." They were about to make their first move, the first step up the ladder, and they showed the promise of great futures in the Chicago mob.

In 1947, Tony Accardo's headquarters was an alcove in a restaurant named Meo's Norwood House in the western suburb of Chicago, Norwood. This is the restaurant to which Accardo summoned the two young hitters.

"I got a special job for you two guys. You ain't done nothin' like this yet, but I think you can do it. The New York mob wants to hit Bugsy Siegel. He spends part of his time in Las Vegas where he's got the Flamingo Hotel and part of his time in Beverly Hills where he lives with his broad. If the broad is there, take her out too, but Siegel is the important one. This is our responsibility since L.A. is ours. And Las Vegas is an 'open city.' New York wants it done and I agreed we would do it. This is early May, there is no great rush, go out there, set it up, take your time, but do it right. I don't want those fucking New Yorkers to think we don't do things right."

So Gussie Alex and Strongy Ferraro had travelled to Las Vegas, thinking it would be easier to do the job there. But then they got a call from Accardo. "We don't want the hit in Vegas. It looks like we might make something out of it and we don't want no blood there. The Commission has decided no hits there. It's bad for the tourist business. Set up the hit in L.A."

Alex and Ferraro travelled to L.A., their first trip there, and set it up, slowly but surely. When the opportunity came, the deed was done. Mob "experts" might blame Jack Dragna for the killing, but back in Chicago, those few in the know—and none of them were investigators on the side of the law—knew that the stars of Gussie Alex and Frankie Strongy had just lifted off the horizon and that the two young pals would be forces to be reckoned with for years to come in the affairs of organized crime.

6

Moe Dalitz Arrives in Las Vegas

WITHIN a matter of months after Bugsy went down, his dream began to materialize without him. It became quite evident that what he had envisioned not only was becoming reality but that it had even more potential than he had imagined.

Soon a guy named Wilbur Clark started the Desert Inn, about a half mile north of the Flamingo on the same side of Highway 91. And soon thereafter came the Thunderbird.

Then Wilbur Clark faltered. That opened the way for Morris Barney "Moe" Dalitz, who was destined to be known as "the godfather of Las Vegas." Even in 1949 when he came to the desert, he was a well-known hood.

Moe Dalitz started his criminal career way back in the Prohibition Era. He had been one of the admirals in "the Little Jewish Navy" in Detroit when, as a rum runner, he ferried booze across the Detroit River from Canada to quench the thirst of the many Motor City citizens who were eager to taste the whiskey, wine, and beer forbidden by the "Noble Experiment."

Dalitz had teamed up with members of the Purple Gang in Detroit in the 1920s, the Bernstein brothers, Joe and Ben. But then the Zerellis were run out of St. Louis and landed in Detroit. So things got too hot for Dalitz in Detroit and he ran to nearby Cleveland. There he found his niche. While Prohibition was still the law of the land he confined himself to bootlegging, the trade he had learned in Detroit. When Prohibition ended, he used his cunning to become the leader of what was to be known as the Mayfield Road Gang. That gang soon existed side by side with La Cosa Nostra in Cleveland and became heavily involved in all kinds of gambling: bookmaking, pinball machines, slot machines, and the lottery. The gang was soon doing what all mobs had to do to survive in any town: sow the seeds of corruption. Before long many of Cleveland's public officials, political leaders, and law enforcement officers were "on the pad" of Moe Dalitz and such fellow Mayfield Road Gang members as Morris Kleinman, Sam Tucker, and Louis Rothkopf, aka Lou Rody. They made their headquarters in Suite 281 of the Hollenden Hotel in Cleveland.

Dalitz and his gang were careful to form strong alliances with mobsters throughout the country. One of the first things Lucky Luciano did when he became the *Capo di Tutti Capi* after the killing of Salvatore Maranzano was to travel to Cleveland to meet with Dalitz.

Luciano, however, was not the only top gun in the outfit to meet with Dalitz and become his ally. In 1952, Dalitz would testify before the New York State Crime Commission hearings on the New York waterfront that he owned a yacht, the *South Wind,* and that Abner "Longy" Zwillman, the New York and New Jersey mob leader, was a frequent guest on the yacht, as was Eddie McGrath, the prominent numbers racketeer. At the waterfront hearings, Dalitz would admit being close to Joe Adonis, Frank Costello, Meyer Lansky, Bugsy Siegel, Dandy Phil Kastel, Frank Erickson, and other major mob figures.

In fact, as far back as 1929, Dalitz had been present at a gangland meeting in Atlantic City which was attended by the major mob leaders of the day including Capone, Costello, Luciano, Johnny Torrio, Adonis, Lepke Buchalter, Erickson, Dutch Shultz, Albert Anastasia, Vincent Mangano, Jake Guzik, Rothkopf, Waxey Gordon, Zwillman, and Willie Moretti.

In 1934 Dalitz attended another meeting at the Waldorf-Astoria of such top guys as Lansky, Torrio, Costello, Adonis, Kastel, Zwillman, Paul Ricca, and Isadore Blumenfield, the notorious Kid Cann, who controlled Minneapolis for the mob.

When Luciano was deported from the United States on February 9, 1946, Dalitz attended Luciano's going-away party on the *Laura Keene,* the ship that took Luciano to Italy. Also present on that auspicious occasion were Costello, Anastasia, Lansky, Moretti, Siegel, Zwillman, Tommy Lucchese, our pal Joe Bonanno, Carlo Gambino, Steve Magaddino, Kastel, and Owney Madden, in from Hot Springs.

In Chicago, Dalitz's pals included Tony Accardo, Murray Humphreys, Jake Guzik, and Frank Nitti.

After the end of Prohibition, Dalitz, Kleinman, Tucker, and Rothkopf spread their wings not only into gambling in Cleveland but into northern Kentucky where they built the Beverly Hills Country Club in Fort Thomas and the Lookout House in Newport. They existed there side by side with another guy who would later become a major force in Las Vegas, Eddy Levenson, and his brother, "Sleepout Louie." Dalitz also built a dog track in Dayton, Ohio.

From 1942 to 1945, Dalitz served his country in the U. S. Army but continued to receive his share of the proceeds garnered in his absence by his cohorts in the Mayfield Road Gang. When the war ended, Dalitz met with Meyer Lansky and Frank Costello in Costello's suite at the Waldorf.

Lansky told Dalitz: "Moe, the boys here have a problem. We have put Siegel out in Nevada where he is building us the Flamingo. But he is having problems getting it on track and we are having problems with him. He's got this broad from Kentucky that Joe Epstein of Chicago took under his wing and we think there are things going on there which are not kosher. Now you are expert on casino gambling from your days in northern Kentucky. Frank and I would like you to go out to Vegas and take a peek at what's going on. You know Murray Humphreys from Chicago, stop there first and get a report from him. He's been out there with Chicago's man, Johnny Roselli, and Hump has got a good idea of what's going on with Benny in Vegas."

Dalitz took the trip. When he reported back shortly to Lansky and Costello, he had two major observations:

"Number one, I like what I see out there. I can see why Siegel got this idea. I think it's a good one. Now Hump thinks he's robbin' you guys. Hump thinks that the broad is the nigger in the woodpile, that she has got the ear of Benny, that he has become pussy whipped and will do anything for her. Hump thinks he's scamming, mostly from the contractors who are doing the work on the Flamingo, getting kickbacks from them with them inflating their invoices for goods and services. But he hasn't checked into that, I think he just has a hunch on it. Chicago knows the broad, she was a hooker there when she came to the World's Fair from Kentucky and Epstein, that big bookie, took a shine to her and brought her up. That's what got Hump interested when he found out Siegel was hooked up with her—it's more a gut reaction than anything else, I think."

Lansky chimed in at this point. "Hump has good instincts though, I think. He usually knows where he's coming from."

"I agree," said Dalitz. "But all he's got at this point is smoke and little fire."

"Here's what Frank and I would like you to do," Lansky said, referring to his partner, Costello. "I know you're busy in Cleveland and so forth but we'd like you to take some of your guys who know casino gambling and go out there on the sly. We've got a guy out there who is our watchdog, keeping an eye out, but he needs expert help. His name is Moe Sedway. We'll put you in touch and you look into it and give us a report."

Dalitz did as instructed. An idea had flashed into his head. If Siegel was to fail, if the New York mob were to take him off the project, they'd need somebody to replace him. He'd take a good look at the prospects up and down Highway 91 and if his initial hunch from his first trip out there proved out as he devoted more attention to it, he'd be in on the ground floor. Let Siegel iron out whatever bugs—no pun intended— there might be and go to school on those problems.

So Moe Dalitz went to Vegas in 1946 as requested and looked into the affairs of Bugsy Siegel and Virginia Hill. He was the main contributor to the growing opinion that everything was not on the up and up. His report was the major reason why Lansky, Costello, et al., made their report to the assembly in Havana in December 1946 and later in June when it was finally decided to chop Bugsy.

But Dalitz and his Mayfield Road Gang were not quite ready for Vegas in June 1947, which was the reason Gus Greenbaum and Moe Sedway were moved in. There were too many things popping back East. They bided their time, filling their bellies with what they had in the Buckeye and Bluegrass States. It wasn't until 1949 that they were squared away in Ohio and Kentucky and ready to go west.

First they met with Lansky and Costello again in New York. Dalitz and Kleinman represented the gang at the meet and Costello spoke to them. "Guys, we got a problem. We agree with you that Vegas can be big. But our problem is that if we send the millions it will take to do it right out there, the IRS will be all over us. Because we can't show any kind of money like that."

What Costello meant was that he and his associates had never reported on their income tax returns anywhere near the amount of income needed to support the kind of investments they planned to make. If they did, IRS would conduct routine "net worth" and "net expenditures" cases on them and immediately realize that their reported income could not support such expenditures.

"Now how about you guys? Could you get away with it if you front for us out there? Can you show the kind of money it will take?"

Dalitz and Kleinman thought about it. They had the foresight after their first trip to Vegas to realize what a gold mine it could be. They realized that if they put themselves in position to show sufficient money, they would be the natural fronts for the mob when it came time for the mob to expand.

So they allowed to Costello and Lansky that their IRS records, showing the receipt of millions from their casinos, dog tracks, and other legit investments in Ohio and Kentucky, would support vast expenditures in Las Vegas.

In 1949, they made their way to Vegas in what was to be, perhaps, the most historic arrival in the West since the homesteaders exactly 100 years before. These were the 1949ers, not the 1849ers. One migration came to reap; Dalitz and *his* homesteaders came to rape. Their first conquest was the Desert Inn. Wilbur Clark ran into financial troubles and the Mayfield Road Gang took over to complete the construction and open the hotel, although at first they kept Wilbur's name on the marquee.

It was 1950, the same year the Kefauver Committee began its hearings, which for some reason neglected Joe Bonanno. But they sure did focus in on Frank Costello, Moe Dalitz, and Tony Accardo.

CHAPTER

7

The Godfathers Move West

PAUL "The Waiter" Ricca came out of prison in August of 1947. He immediately sat down with Tony Accardo and told him that he did not want any further action as the boss of the Chicago mob. He turned the position over to Accardo and agreed to become Accardo's *consigliere,* his advisor. Whenever the forty-one-year-old Accardo found himself in a tough spot, it would be Ricca who would advise him. But the day-to-day operations of the Chicago family would be left to Joe Batters. When the official elevation of Accardo was announced to the rest of the outfit, it was accepted without reservations. They had the greatest respect for Joe and it showed. After all, as Ricca had said years before, "Joe Batters has more brains at breakfast than Al Capone had all day." Ricca should know. He had been a close associate of both for years.

Joe had married a young professional dancer, Clarise Porter. At about the same time he took over the reins of the mob, his fourth child was born, giving him two sons and two daughters. (One would eventually give Tony a grandson who would become a professional football player.)

Befitting his stature in the mob, Accardo now moved into one of the most luxurious homes in the Chicago area. This mansion was located at 915 Franklin in the affluent and prestigious suburb of River Forest. It had twenty-two rooms, occupied one-quarter of a large block, and was surrounded by a seven-foot-high wrought-iron fence with two electrically controlled gates. The baths were fitted with gold-plated fixtures. It had a swimming pool and two bowling alleys in the basement. Also in the basement was a large gun and trophy room which doubled as the mob conference room in those days when no law enforcement agency was watching. In the rear of this palatial estate was a large guest house and another house which served as the servants' quarters. There was also a greenhouse where Joe Batters tended his flowers. Although he might be FBI Number 1 410 106 and Chicago Police Department Number D-83436 after having been arrested on such charges as General Principles, Investigation, Carrying a Concealed Weapon, Disorderly Conduct, Material Witness, and Conspiracy to Defraud, the home of Tony Accardo took a back seat to none.

It was at this point that the Chicago mob, under the direction of its new boss, made its first move on the long road ahead.

First, however, there would be a slight glitch. The Chicago Crime Commission had been founded in 1919 by a group of public-spirited private citizens who were concerned with the wave of violence in Chicago, the inefficiency of the local and federal law enforcement agencies with regard to the crime wave, and the corruption which seemed to be so pervasive in Chicago, particularly in the courts and in the ward organizations. The Chicago Crime Commission has been a most positive force for good in Chicago for the past seventy-two years. First of all, the CCC obtained the good will of most responsible citizens and the media in Chicago and became very vocal about the Colosimo, Torrio, and Capone mob in the 1920s. In fact, it was the famous Secret Six, strongly supported by the CCC, which aroused the public and the government to do something about Capone. Headed by Col. Robert Isham Randolph, one of Chicago's most prolific patriots, this group of six of Chicago's richest and most prominent citizens put together a war chest to hire the brother-in-law of Eliot Ness to lead ten private detectives in the fight against the mob. Colonel Randolph subscribed to the belief that "the end justifies the means" and "we will try anything to put the gangster behind bars." "Anything" included tapping the phones of mobsters and even engaging in shootouts with them. If official law enforcement couldn't, or wouldn't, do the job, by God, the Chicago Crime Commission-backed Secret Six would. Their efforts materially assisted in finally getting the job done. One of the members of the Secret Six, Frank L. Loesch, went on to become president of the Chicago Crime Commission.

Early in January 1953, Virgil Peterson, the former FBI agent who had become the Operating Director of the Chicago Crime Commission, learned through his sources that Tony Accardo and his mob were negotiating to take over the Golden Hotel-Bank Club casino in Reno, perhaps the biggest gambling operation there—not to mention the Chicago mob's first incursion into the Nevada gambling industry. Perhaps a forerunner of bigger and better things to come in Nevada. The Crime Commission learned that a conference was scheduled to take place in Nevada within a few days. In future years, the course of action of the Crime Commission would be to furnish this information to the FBI which, with its nationwide resources, would have been the ideal agency to deal with the situation. In 1953, however, J. Edgar Hoover continued to insist that there was no such thing as a national crime syndicate and that he had no jurisdiction with which to combat such an organization even if there was one. As a result, Peterson could only confide in the Los Angeles Police Department and the Nevada State Police. But that was enough.

On January 15, 1953, Tony Accardo boarded an airplane in Chicago bound for Los Angeles, preparing thereafter to drive to Reno and further his plans to take over the Golden Hotel-Bank Club casino, giving him an entry into gaming in Nevada. He took Sam Giancana, the rising young mobster, as well as Dr. E. J. Chesrow, superintendent of the Oak Forest old people's home in suburban Chicago, a good friend who would enjoy the gambling in Nevada. At the Los Angeles International Airport they were met by Tony Pinelli, a Chicago mob representative in Los Angeles, and by the young mob hitter, Frank "Strongy" Ferraro who, after he teamed up with Gussie Alex when Bugsy Siegel was chopped, had remained on the coast to assist with the Chicago mob's domination of organized crime activities in L.A.

As Ferraro and Pinelli walked up to greet the entourage of Accardo at the airline gate, however, so did detectives of the Intelligence Unit of the Los Angeles Police Department led by Captain Jim Hamilton and Lieutenant Marion Phillips. Accardo and his group were taken by the arm, informed their presence in Los Angeles was undesirable, and escorted to another plane out. The group circuitously arrived in Las Vegas the next day. Again they were met by the authorities, who had been alerted by the Chicago Crime Commission, and again they were told to board the next plane out.

Although that trip didn't work out as planned, the Bank Club casino in Reno was soon thereafter taken over by Johnny Drew, a man who would become known as Chicago's man in Nevada. Many of the key employees were fired and replaced by bookmakers from Chicago. It was soon found that the Bank Club's records contained two cancelled checks totaling $103,000 made out to Tony Accardo who cashed them at a Chicago bank. Although not without problems, Tony Accardo had initiated the Chicago mob into Nevada.

IN 1949, an event had occurred which meant nothing to Accardo at the time but would be a major landmark in the incursion of the Chicago mob into Nevada. The International Brotherhood of the Teamsters union instituted its Central States Pension and Welfare Fund. In years to come it would serve as the bank for the Chicago mob, among other mobs, to finance the move into Nevada gaming. But for the moment, it had no particular significance to the mob.

At about the very same time a related happenstance which would be of extreme importance to Accardo and Chicago's outfit would begin to shape up. In Chicago there was a labor hack, an official of the Waste Handlers union, who was close to Murray Humphreys. His name was Paul Dorfman and they called him "Red." Red Dorfman had developed a friendship with a Detroit labor leader of potential named James Riddle Hoffa. They called him Jimmy. Now Red Dorfman, having been on Humphrey's pad for years, recognized potential when he saw it. Potential for capability in heading unions but also potential for corruption. He introduced his mentor, "The Camel," to Jimmy Hoffa. Soon Hump recognized the same characteristics in Hoffa. In years to come, the Chicago mob would boost the career of Hoffa right into the presidency of the Teamsters union, into a position where Hoffa could insure that the funds of the Central States Pension Fund were channeled where they could do the most good for the Chicago crime syndicate. In fact, he would maneuver the son of Red Dorfman into the spot where he had the greatest influence over the Central States Pension Fund and could determine who the recipients of loans from the pension fund would be. In many cases, the recipients would be the Chicago Cosa Nostra.

By this time, the Chicago mob had been badly beaten by the New York mob, which had invaded Las Vegas with a small army of gaming operatives. First they opened the Flamingo, Bugsy Siegel's dream. Then in 1948 it was the Thunderbird, with Meyer Lansky and his brother, Jake, behind it. Then in 1952 the Sands opened on the Strip; "Doc" Stacher, an associate of Lansky and Frank Costello, was "the man" there. In fact, he was the man of record there. It would not be until most of the hoods were already firmly entrenched in Nevada and in Las Vegas in particular before the mentality of cow town politics would begin to shift. It would not be until several years later, in 1955, when the Nevada Gaming Control Commission and its enforcement and investigative arm, the Gaming Control Board, would be established and not until 1959 when its powers would be fortified, when Governor Grant Sawyer would begin to staff it and give instructions, however hollow and belated, to "keep organized crime out of Nevada." Talk about closing the barn door after the cows had escaped. Or in this case, after the animals had come in!

IN the early fifties, a Los Angeles gambler, Tony Cornero, who had operated a large gambling ship out alongside Catalina Island, began building the Stardust Hotel and Casino on the Strip across from the Desert Inn. But in 1955 Cornero died.

Tony Accardo called Johnny Roselli in from Las Vegas, where his duties as Chicago mob rep in Los Angeles had recently been expanded to include Las Vegas and the rest of Nevada. He called Murray Humphreys and Jake Guzik into the conference with Roselli at Meo's Norwood House, in the private alcove, his headquarters. While Butch Blasi sat at the entrance to warn against any interlopers, the four mobsters conferred.

Accardo initiated the conversation, getting right to the point: "Fellas, Johnny has brought us something interesting. He called me the other day about a situation which might be just what we're looking for. I'll let John tell you about it."

Roselli then took center stage. "You guys know that a friend of ours, Tony Cornero, was building a new joint on the Strip in Vegas. And you know he just dropped dead. Now Joe, here, has been after me to find a good opportunity for us in Vegas. I think this might be it. Cornero spent a lot of money there, he has got it almost complete, and I've looked it over. It's in a great spot, across from the D. I., where Moe Dalitz has made a great thing, right in a great place on the Strip, which is becoming the hot spot in Vegas—it's gonna outshine downtown, Fremont Street, in no time. I think if we could make the right maneuvers here, we could get this Stardust and make a great thing of it."

Joe Batters spoke up. "How could we get it?"

"The best way would be to do what those New York guys are doing. Get some straight guy to front for us, somebody who could 'show the money.' Then we skim the hell out of the place. Obviously, we'd like to make some money on the investment. But the real money's in the skim. Steal the hell out of the place before the money gets counted. No taxes, nobody knows from nothin'. But the key is to get a guy to front it, a guy with a good reputation but a guy we got control over, a guy who will do what the hell we tell him to do and keep his nose outta our business. What the hell, it's a good deal for him too. He gets a nice office, pretty secretaries, lotta perks, and a nice income. To do nothin'. Just sit in the fucking office, dress nice, and walk around the casino once in a while as if he's in charge."

Accardo turned to Guzik and Hump. "Who could we get?" Humphreys had an idea. Years before, in the thirties, he had been close to "Jake the Barber" Factor of the Factor cosmetics family. He had used Jake the Barber as a victim to phony up a kidnapping implicating Roger Tuohy, a gangland rival in the thirties. The ploy had eliminated Tuohy as a competitor. In fact, Tuohy would not return to Chicago from prison until 1959 when he would immediately be murdered on the front steps of his West Side home, right in front of his bodyguard.

Hump chimed in. "You guys know I have stayed close to Jake Factor. I think he'd be just right for this. He's clean, comes from a society family, got all the credentials. Nobody knows he's close to me. I think he'd be the guy."

"Go talk to him, feel him out. What do you think, Jake?"

"Sounds good to me," Guzik replied.

"Okay, that's it. I want to talk to Paul about this too. He's at his farm in Indiana. Couldn't make the meet today. But I think he'll go along. Okay, everybody get started."

When Hump sat down with Jake the Barber, he found Factor to be enthusiastic about the prospect of being the "owner" of a large Las

Vegas gaming establishment. Hump reported back to Joe Batters, who, after conferring with Ricca, gave his approval to do the deal.

The Chicago mob had arrived in Las Vegas. They owned the Stardust, one of the largest hotel-casinos on the Strip, which was rapidly becoming the center of the world's hottest gambling mecca. It was no longer known as Highway 91. It was the Strip, Las Vegas Boulevard. Millions of neon lights were going up to replace the old light posts. And the blue and lavender neon lights of the Stardust, flashing on and off, took a back seat to no other hotel-casino.

But the Chicago mob had an immediate problem. Factor knew nothing about the gaming industry. He didn't even know that the other name for blackjack was "21." They would need to call in somebody capable of running the day-to-day operation of the Stardust. It necessitated another sit-down. This time, the Chicago group, including Ricca, journeyed to Las Vegas for the meeting. They wanted to get a look at what they owned. Factor escorted them to the best suite in the Stardust and left them to their confab.

One other guy had been invited to this conference. He was Johnny Drew, the same guy who had been running Chicago's first venture in Nevada—the Bank Club in Reno.

Accardo again instituted the proceedings. He got right down to business, not being one to waste time on the niceties. "Drew, we brought you down here today from Reno to discuss a move for you. We got this place about to open but we need somebody who knows gaming. We've talked about it with Roselli here and we think you are our man. How about it?"

Drew was somewhat hesitant. "I could do it. It would be a big move up for me, but I could do it. I'll tell you what I would suggest though. I would need to staff this place with a hundred guys. To get that many right away would be a job. Here's what I suggest. Put me in charge as the general manager. But go see Moe Dalitz. Hire him to operate the place with his men. He's got a crew across the street at the D. I. He could milk twenty-five or so to come over here and he could bring in another twenty-five or so from his joints in Ohio and Kentucky. Then we could bring in about fifty guys from Chicago from your Big Game there, experienced guys. I'm talking about a casino manager, shift managers, pit bosses, floor men, dealers, stick men. I'll be the boss but let Dalitz put his own casino manager in and we'll alternate shift managers and pit bosses between his guys and our guys from Chicago."

The group agreed that this would be a good plan. Accardo put in a call to Dalitz at the Desert Inn and asked him to come across the street to the Stardust. When he did, he brought Morris Kleinman, his associate, with him. The outcome of the ensuing conference was that Dalitz and his United Hotels Corporation would be hired to run the Stardust pursuant, more or less, to the arrangement outlined by Drew. But Dalitz had another idea.

"Let me suggest one thing to you," he said. "Morris here and I have been thinking for the past few months or so about this. The Desert Inn is a high-class place, designed for the upscale betters, the high rollers. We've built up a clientele of V.I.P.'s who regularly come into town. We let them run up markers, on credit, no checks. Sometimes they pay the marker before they leave town, sometimes afterwards when they feel like it. But our customers are high-class, rich guys. We've been thinkin' we need a spot for the average Joe. The guy who takes his wife on a vacation once a year or once every couple years. The guy who can't afford to blow $10,000 over a weekend. He might come in here pulling a trailer behind his car. He can't play at a ten-dollar minimum table of blackjack, he wants a dollar minimum. The low roller. Now, before you say anything, think about it. For every high roller, you got fifteen low rollers. You make up in volume what you lack in the few high-priced guys. Quantity instead of, or alongside, quality. The high rollers go across the street to the D. I. The low rollers here to the Stardust. We get the best of both worlds. And one other thing, with a high roller you got to wine and dine them. Give them a lot of attention. Pick them up at the airport in limos, give them first-class suites. Pick up their dinner bills, give them free drinks. It's called 'comping.' But with the low roller, fuck 'em. We call this operation, as I propose it, a 'grind joint.' Grind them in and grind them out. No perks. No 'comps', or at least, very few 'comps.' Get them in, get their money, get them out, get somebody else in. The bottom line is, you get about the same amount of money, you got much less overhead, and you got at least as much to skim. And there is one additional benefit. The D.I. and the Stardust won't be in direct competition with each other. We'll be across the street from each other, but we won't be tryin' to steal each other's best customers. Ours won't want to come over here and your's won't be able to afford to come over there. It seems simplistic but somewhat true. Think it over. Tell you what. We got a great gourmet restaurant at the D.I., the Monte Carlo Room. Jimmy Durante is entertaining in the showroom. Come on over after you discuss this and Morris and I will 'comp' *you* guys. We specialize in steak *marchand de vin* in the Monte Carlo Room. Be our guest and we can discuss this further."

The Chicago group took up Dalitz's suggestion. Or most of it. They agreed to hire his United Hotels Corporation to help Drew run the Stardust. They agreed it would be fashioned into a low-roller, "grind joint," although they would reserve a few tables for the big spenders. And they joined Dalitz and Kleinman in dining on the steak *marchand de vin,* with escargot and spinach salad yet. All but Joe Batters. He had the kitchen cook up some good old spaghetti with Italian sausage. It seemed Accardo found the Stardust would be more to his liking than this Desert Inn. Joe Bonanno wouldn't have been surprised.

AT about the same time as Tony Accardo had moved his family into interests in the West, so did Joe Bonanno. It may have been subconscious, but Bonanno was putting himself into a geographical position which would serve his interests in years to come. His move to Arizona would serve as a springboard to its neighbor, Nevada.

Joe had married Fay in 1931. A year later their first son, Salvatore, named after Joe's mentor, Salvatore Maranzano, was born. To Joe's great disappointment, however, his son would Americanize his name to Bill. As Bill grew, he became allergic to different elements in the atmosphere in the East and his doctors advised Joe to take him to Arizona where the air would be more conducive to his health. After a brief time in Phoenix, Joe settled his family in Tucson although he continued to spend most of his time in Brooklyn, where he tended his LCN family's affairs, and at his large farm in upstate New York. He used the Abraham Lincoln Political Club on Metropolitan Avenue in Brooklyn as his headquarters. His *sotto capo,* Gasparino DiGregorio, was capable and efficient so Joe was able to put things on automatic pilot most of the time.

Both godfathers had firmly placed one foot in the West.

8

The Chicago Godfather Steps Aside

IN early 1957 Joe and Fay Bonanno travelled to Miami and then to Havana for a little R&R. They then took off for Europe, travelling in grand style and visiting Joe's boyhood haunts in Castellammare. He was received there in grand style, the current leader of the Bonannos, the stately son of Don Turridru, a great success in America, returning to his ancestral home. It was a hero's welcome and Joe preened at the reception. He was at the peak of his powers, the grand master of his domain. All was well in his world.

Tony Accardo was also feeling very good about things as 1957 dawned. The Stardust deal in Las Vegas was going very well and soon he would use his connections with Jimmy Hoffa and the Dorfmans, father and son, to obtain a million-dollar loan from the Teamster Pension Fund for improvements at the Stardust Hotel.

As a matter of fact, Accardo was so serene about life in general, he decided to live it. To the hilt. He decided he'd had enough—enough money, enough power, and enough headaches. He was fifty years old now and it had been a tough fifty years—from street bandit to member of the Circus Gang, from the early days of violence with Al Capone peaking on St. Valentine's Day in 1929, to his status as a capo under Frank Nitti, from his term as the underboss under Paul Ricca (although he was actually the boss then in everything but the formal title) to his service for the past dozen years as *the* boss. During his reign Accardo had brought the Chicago family of La Cosa Nostra unprecedented power—he had established firm control and dominance from the streets of Chicago to the Riviera Hotel in Havana, to the Stardust in Las Vegas and throughout the western part of the United States. He had escalated the Chicago outfit to unprecedented heights. He had proved the tale that he "had more brains at breakfast than Capone had all day." He had undoubtedly done more for the Chicago mob than *any* of his predecessors. He was, like Bonanno, at the peak of his powers. But, unlike the J. B. from Brooklyn, he had had enough. He was ready to step down.

So Joe Batters called a sit-down of his top people. It was early 1957 and they closed Meo's to the general public that night, for it was an illustrious crowd. There was Paul Ricca, his *consigliere,* in whom he had already confided of his plans; Frankie La Porte, who controlled the southern suburbs of Chicago as the capo there; Ross Prio, the capo in charge of the North Side of Chicago; Fiore "Fifi" Buccieri, the capo on the West Side; "Nigger Joe" Amato, the capo in DuPage and McHenry counties to the west of the city; Lenny Patrick, in charge of gambling in Rogers Park on the Northeast Side; Ralph Pierce, the South Side boss; Gussie Alex, who now had the Loop, and Frankie Ferraro, who worked the Loop with his boyhood pal, Gussie; Murray Humphreys, the master fixer; Sam Giancana, the all-around trouble-shooter; Johnny Roselli, who had come in from the Coast; Charley and Rocco Fischetti, also trouble-shooters extraordinaires; Eddy Vogel, in charge of the mob's slot machines and other coin-operated machines; Jimmy Allegretti, in charge of the night clubs on Rush Street; Les Kruse, the boss in Lake County, Illinois; Tony Pinelli and Johnny Formosa, who ran Chicago's interests in Gary and Hammond, Indiana; and Marshall Caifano, who ran with Giancana. Not present were two of Accardo's closest pals and confidants, both of whom had recently died of natural causes: his old pal from boyhood, "Tough Tony" Capezio, one of his capos, and Jake "Greasy Thumb" Guzik, a guy who had worked with him since he first joined the Capone Mob in the mid-twenties. He missed them both. Tony Accardo never had any qualms about associating with Jews, non-Sicilians, or non-Italians. He needed their expertise and he enjoyed their company.

Accardo opened the meeting. "Fellas," he said, as usual foregoing the amenities, "we're here today to do two things. Say goodbye to me as a boss and get a new one."

No surprise there. Rumors in the outfit had long been that he wanted out.

Paul Ricca spoke for them all. "Joe, we respect your wishes. But this is a sad day for all of us. I want all to know that I have tried to talk you out of this. You have done wonderful things for this family and I speak again for all of us when I express my appreciation to you for what you have made of our thing. We are grateful, more than you know. One last time, will you reconsider?"

Accardo firmly shook his head. His mind was made up. He stood. "Now, the next order of business is to select a replacement for me. Paul and I have also discussed this. It is our recommendation to you that the man to succeed me is Sam Giancana. He has done everything he has been assigned to do and done it well. It was Sam who brought us into the numbers and policy, which has been so good for us. Whenever there was any rough stuff to do, he did it and did it well. He's made his bones many times. We recommend this. Any objections?"

Murray Humphreys looked up. "No, I don't have any objection. If you and Paul decided on Sam, I go along with it. But let me say, he would not have been my choice. He is still quite a young man for that spot. I agree he is a good man in this business. I don't object, I just speak out to see if anyone feels like I do. If not, I'm in agreement."

No one spoke out. After a few seconds, when it became obvious that there would be no further comments, Hump again spoke out. "I have one other suggestion then. Who will be the *consigliere* here and who will be the underboss? The reason I ask is that in view of the limited experience of Sam, we need somebody experienced, who has been in it for a long time, to counsel with Sam. I think that is very important. You, Paul, are you willing to stay on as *consigliere?*"

Ricca spoke. "I think we got a much better choice here. We got the guy, still a young guy, who has been through all this. Who could we get better than J. B.? Not me, I'm ready for the farm."

Accardo immediately shook his head. Vigorously. "No, fellas, I've just had enough."

At this point, Giancana spoke up for the first time. "Joe, I will take over on one condition. That you be my *consigliere*. You know the law anyway—nobody quits. So I ask you to be available when we need you, when I need you. That don't mean you have to be around all the time. I'll run it and I look forward to it. I want it. In the worst way. I been livin' for this day. But if I know I can reach out for you when it's needed, not every day, not every week, for Christ's sake, but when I really need you, then I'll be more comfortable. Joe, I want you."

What could Accardo say? "Okay, if that's what you all want. But Clarise and I want to travel. I want to go to Bimini and fish, I want to get a place out West—Clarise likes Palm Springs. I'll do all that, but when you need me, send somebody out, or if it's extra important, I'll come in, I'll keep a place here too, or, Sam, you come out to see me yourself. Okay, I'll do it; I'll be *consigliere.*"

Ricca spoke again. "Now about underboss. That's Sam's decision. The boss picks his own underboss. But let me suggest something to you, Sam. Joe and I have talked about this. You have been a West Sider all your life, at least after you left The Patch. Your people, guys like Fifi and Joey Amato, your pals, Chuckie English, Milwaukee Phil, Marshall, are all West Side guys. We think if you would appoint a guy who bridges all the territories represented here today, it would be a good thing for harmony. Make the underboss a guy who is close to the rest of the guys. I'm talking about Frankie Strongy. He's done all the things that need to be done and he would work well with everybody. It's your decision, but it's the suggestion Joe and I make to you."

Sam Giancana had no objection. He would have chosen Buccieri, but he could see the wisdom of choosing Strongy, and he liked Strongy and respected the work he had done. "If it's okay with you it's okay with me," he said.

It was done. When the group walked out of the meeting, Joe Batters walked over to Butch Blasi, his driver, bodyguard, and appointments secretary, and pointed to Giancana. "You're with him now." The changing of the guard was complete.

9

Apalachin!

WHILE Gaspar DiGregorio, Bonanno's *sotto capo,* was running things during Bonanno's long vacation with his wife in Florida, Cuba, and around Europe, an indication of how well his family functioned on automatic pilot, things were blowing up in the Volcano.

The Tropicana had opened on the Strip on April 3, 1957. It is a beautiful hotel, located on the bottom of the Strip, at the time the last establishment at the southern end.

On May 2, 1957, Frank Costello, the "prime minister of organized crime," according to the newspapers (but not to Bonanno), dined with Generoso Pope, the publisher of *Il Progresso,* an Italian-language newspaper, and Phil Kennedy, the owner of a modeling agency, at L'Aiglon, a high-class East Side Manhattan restaurant. When the dinner was over, it was suggested that they have a drink at Monsignore, another fine dining establishment in Manhattan. Costello begged off, however, saying he had to make some phone calls from his apartment at 115 Central Park West, in one of New York's finest neighborhoods, overlooking the park between the Sheep Meadow and Columbus Circle.

As Kennedy was saying good night to Costello in front of Costello's apartment building, a long black Cadillac pulled up. Out of the car walked Vincent "Chin" Gigante, a soldier in another New York family. He preceded Costello into the lobby. Kennedy continued down the street, Costello entered his lobby, and Gigante stepped out of the shadows and fired point blank at Costello's head. As blood streamed from the fallen mob boss, Gigante ran from the building and jumped into the getaway car and made his escape.

Bleeding profusely, Costello was placed in a cab hailed by the doorman (who would thereafter claim he had seen nothing) and rushed to Roosevelt Hospital where he reached the emergency room at 11:08 P.M. Freakishly, the bullet had entered behind the left ear, burrowed under the scalp, continued around the back of Costello's head, and emerged close to the other ear. The path of the bullet, virtually a miracle, had saved his life. Under almost any condition, a bullet shot into a victim's head at point blank range will travel straight through the head, from one ear to the other, and if it doesn't kill it will certainly do incalculable damage. As it was, at 12:15 A.M. the same night, Costello, bandaged and somewhat shaken, walked out of Roosevelt Hospital, took a cab home and presumably spent a peaceful night, or what was left of it, in his own bed.

When Gigante was arrested, or, to be specific, when he surrendered, on July 17, 1957, he, of course, maintained his innocence. At his trial Costello turned out to be an excellent witness—for Gigante. He claimed he saw nothing, just like the doorman who turned out to be blind in one eye, with his vision impaired in the other eye. Gigante was quickly acquitted. At a dinner party Costello gave soon thereafter, Gigante was one of the guests. Only in the Volcano!

In an interesting twist, it turned out that when the twenty-five detectives who were assigned to the investigation of the attempted murder analyzed the contents of Costello's pockets on the night of the assault, they found that contained therein was a note which read: "Gross casino wins as of 4-26-57: $651,284." There were other significant notations on the piece of paper as well. Analysis subsequently determined that the note had been handwritten in part by one Michael J. Tanico, a cashier at the Tropicana in Las Vegas, and that the other part had been written by Louie Lederer. Tanico had been an employee of Costello's in the Beverly Club near New Orleans and Lederer was a close associate of

Accardo, Humphreys, and others in the Chicago mob and an owner of record of the Trop. The Gaming Control Board in Las Vegas confirmed that $651,284 was the exact casino win for the Tropicana the week ending 4-26-57. Ironclad proof that the New York mob—and probably Chicago as well—was involved in Vegas.

Violence in the Volcano continued. On June 17, 1957, Frank "Don Cheech" Scalise, a capo in the family of Albert Anastasia, was killed by two gunmen in the Bronx outside a fruit and vegetable store. Then, on September 19, 1957, Scalise's brother disappeared, never to be seen again.

But the Volcano had not belched its final eruption yet—not by a long shot—now perhaps the most dramatic killing in mob history was about to take place.

On October 25, 1957, Albert Anastasia, the boss of one of the five New York families of La Cosa Nostra, was shot down in the barbershop of the Park Sheraton Hotel in New York where he had gone to get a shave and a haircut.

The sensational Anastasia murder took place in the same hotel where another famous gangland killing had been committed. Arnold Rothstein, the major gambler of his day, the man who engineered the Black Sox Scandal of 1919 wherein members of the Chicago White Sox threw the World Series, had been killed twenty-nine years before in his suite at the Park Sheraton. It was November 4, 1928, and the hotel was then called the Park Central; it is now an Omni hotel.

The Rothstein slaying had caused a political upheaval that rocked New York in 1928. The 1957 killing of Anastasia in the same hotel would have even more serious repercussions.

THE series of shootings of four of the top bosses—Costello, the two Scalise brothers, and Anastasia—all within the space of just several months, caused great concern on the part of The Commission members. Joe Bonanno, who was spending most of 1957 travelling, got reports in Europe of the Volcano violence. He hurried home. In Chicago, Tony Accardo, settling into unaccustomed leisure for the first time in his life, had also been travelling, first to Bimini where he loved to fish—he would be nicknamed "The Big Tuna" by the press for his love of angling—and then to Palm Springs, California, where he leased a lovely home on a mountainside. Both mobsters would be summoned to the biggest mob sit-down in history. The subject of the conference was what to do about the outbreak of the violence in the Volcano.

Just three weeks after the Anastasia murder at the Park Sheraton, some seventy top mobsters from all over the country gathered in the upstate New York village of Apalachin, not far from the Pennsylvania border. The date was November 14, 1957, and the site of the meet was Joe Barbara's estate, which contained a large picnic area with a huge barbecue pit.

Like Bonanno, Barbara was a native of Castellammare. He was the president of the Canada Dry Bottling Company of Endicott, New York. He had been involved in the rackets in Pittston, Pennsylvania, and had been picked up there on two occasions during investigations of gangland murders. But in New York State, he had risen to prominence in his community and had been named Man of the Year by his local Chamber of Commerce.

Just a year before, Sgt. Edgar D. Croswell had begun to keep his eye on Barbara after he had discovered him registered at the Arlington Hotel in Binghamton on October 16 and 17, 1956, in the company of Joe Bonanno. The hotel bill had been paid by Barbara. The two Castellammarese were obviously good friends.

The old adage that "luck is the residue of design" would come into play. On November 13, 1957, Sergeant Croswell and his partner, Trooper Vince Vasisko, were investigating a bad check case at a motel on their patrol. While there they observed Joe Barbara's son come into the motel and reserve three rooms for two nights for out-of-towners. Knowing the history of Joe Barbara, the state troopers became suspicious. Croswell notified the only federal agency which he felt might be interested, the Alcohol, Tobacco, and Firearms Unit of the Treasury Department. He knew that the FBI had no interest; J. Edgar Hoover was still clinging to his belief that there was no such thing as a national network of organized crime and that the "Mafia" was just a myth. The FBI could find no jurisdiction to base any investigation of organized crime under any name, and Croswell well knew that to go to them would be a waste of time.

On the next day, November 14, 1957—a date that would become a landmark in mob history—Sergeant Croswell, his partner, and two ATF agents drove into the driveway of the Barbara estate. As soon as they were spotted, pandemonium broke loose. Scores of men started running all over the place like kindergarten kids. A road block was thrown up and reinforcements from the New York State Police were called. Some of the conferees attempted to escape by car, others by running helter skelter, not knowing which was north or south, east or west, in a panic, just trying to get out of there. Some did, some didn't. Those who didn't were all taken to the state police barracks at Vestal for questioning. They were identified by their driver's licenses.

Two of the escapees were Tony Accardo and Sam Giancana. They were never officially identified as having been at Apalachin. But some seventy other top men in La Cosa Nostra—including Joe Bonanno— were. Some of the most important mobsters from across the country were caught including Vito Genovese, Joe Profaci, Joe Magliocco, Carlo Gambino, Santo Trafficante, Geraldo Catena, Carmine Lombardozzi, and Paul Castellano. Bonanno would later claim he had not been there, that he had been there the week before for a friendly visit but had left before the sit-down and that someone else was carrying his driver's license. A likely story.

In addition to the many mobsters from New York, the leading mobsters from downstate Illinois, upstate New York, Philadelphia, Boston, Cleveland, Kansas City, New Jersey, Texas, Colorado, California, and even Cuba, were caught in attendance. Twenty would be convicted for obstruction of justice when they refused to testify before properly convened hearings but years later those convictions would be overturned on appeal.

And there would be hearings, congressional hearings. And J. Edgar Hoover would be called to explain who these men were, what they represented, and why they were conferring. What an embarrassment! Because Mr. Hoover himself simply had no answers. There was no such thing as a body of organized crime which extended over state lines. Or so he thought. At least until Apalachin.

To add insult to injury, the press would trumpet the occasion. "The largest gathering of crime breakers in one place at any one time in history! And the FBI knows nothing about it!" "J. Edgar Hoover says 'the Mafia is a myth!' " "Another Edgar Outshines the FBI's Edgar!" "Edgar Number Two is Named Hoover!" They spotlighted the fact that some seventy of the top mobsters in the country could meet together without the knowledge of law enforcement and except for the fluke that a state trooper happened onto them would have escaped without detection.

Apalachin may have been a sad day for the mob, and it would have even sadder repercussions before the passage of many weeks, but it was also a very sad day for law enforcement which was caught with its pants down, with no intelligence which would have alerted it to the sit-down. And it was the FBI and J. Edgar Hoover who bore the brunt of the criticism. For days the media trumpeted the story. When it finally began to die down, it would become front page news again and again as the hearings got under way and produced fresh news of Apalachin— and fresh assaults on the reputation of J. Edgar Hoover and his beloved FBI. Hearings were held by the U. S. Senate Select Committee on Improper Activities in the Labor or Management Field, popularly known as the Senate Rackets Committee and headed by Sen. John L. McClellan; by the New York State Commission of Investigation and the State Joint Legislative Committee on Government Operations. The attorney general of the United States set up a Special Unit of Organized Crime investigations. He appointed Milton Ralph Wessel as a special assistant to the attorney general to spearhead a drive against organized crime. Under Wessel's direction, the Apalachin conference was thoroughly investigated and was the subject of a federal grand jury in New York City. In Chicago, Richard Beale Ogilvie would be appointed chief of the Midwest unit of the attorney general's organized crime unit. What a great name he was to make for himself in years to come!

All of this as the result of the violence in the Volcano which caused the Apalachin sit-down. It was to be the line of demarcation between the old and the new in law enforcement. Almost like "Before Christ" and "After Christ."

At almost the precise time that Sam Giancana succeeded Tony Accardo as the boss of La Cosa Nostra in Chicago, times would change so drastically that it would seem a guardian angel must have been sitting on Accardo's shoulder—he got out, more or less, just as his world would change forever. The low profile that he and his mob had kept for decades after Capone would now be escalated into the glare of the klieg lights. Although the low-key approach of Accardo would degenerate into what was to become the high-profile personality of Sam Giancana, it would be a lot worse than that because the public was now aroused.

It was not just Accardo and Giancana who would be magnified. Joe Bonanno would soon become a household name. His activity in Brooklyn would be scrutinized as never before. No longer would he be able to squirrel himself away in the back room of the Abraham Lincoln

Political Club and conduct his "business." And it was all because of Apalachin. From little acorns big oaks grow. Who could have guessed as both Bonanno and Batters were enjoying their leisure and relaxation in the fall of 1957 that times would change so drastically and so quickly? Who could have guessed when they set out on the trip from their homes to a lazy, hazy little village in central New York that their lives would forever be changed? The name of that little village would forever after be the buzzword for the new era of law enforcement, especially inside the FBI. The great divide would be crossed and, in the annals of law enforcement, November 14, 1957, would be the date of its New Year. If Columbus had discovered America on October 12, 1492, J. Edgar Hoover discovered the Mafia on November 14, 1957. But it was another explorer named Edgar, not Edgar Hoover, who had forged into the new frontier and had gotten there first. What he found would initially embarrass his namesake and eventually alter the entire thrust of Hoover's investigative organization. His first priority would now become organized crime, not Communism.

10

J. Edgar Hoover Finally Leads
His FBI into the Fight

On November 14, 1957, Bill Richards was in many ways a typical young FBI agent assigned to the Chicago office, then located at 212 West Monroe in Chicago's Loop. He was assigned to "security work," the investigation of the Communist Party-USA. Specifically to those Communist Party members who had gone underground, who had "colonized" by relocating to a new town where they were awaiting instructions from their leaders to undermine and sabotage the key institutions in which they had obtained jobs.

When Director Hoover finally brought his troops into the battle against organized crime for the first time, however, Bill Richards was assigned to the new program. It was named the Top Hoodlum Program (THP). Every FBI office across the country was ordered to create a THP squad, and to assign an appropriate number of agents to it, depending on the strength and number of mobsters in the territory covered by each office. In Chicago, Hoover decreed that there would be ten such agents, each to be assigned to one target hoodlum. The number one target in Chicago was Tony Accardo. The FBI had no way of knowing that he had been succeeded by Sam Giancana. In fact, Giancana was way down the list of targets. Actually, the FBI had little knowledge of who should be targeted. It was hit or miss, and many of the top mobsters across the country were not even on the original list of subjects. It would be months and even years before the FBI would be successful enough in penetrating the mobs to develop accurate information.

Bill Richards was assigned Gus Alex, Bugsy Siegel's nemesis, as his target. Alex's partner, Frank Ferraro, was not targeted. It would be a couple of years before his stature as Chicago underboss would be uncovered by the FBI, making him a subject of intense investigation. Typical of the extent of the FBI's knowledge—or lack thereof—in 1957.

But the battle between the FBI and La Cosa Nostra had finally been joined.

The FBI, and especially Bill Richards, stumbled and bumbled during its early months, but eventually got up to speed. Richards worked with several partners such as Marshall "Maz" Rutland, Ralph Hill, John Bassett, and Joe Shea. All were good young hard hitters who enjoyed mixing it up with the hoods.

Richards, especially, enjoyed mixing it up with Sam Giancana. He looked forward to every opportunity to thwart the man and his plans. First time they met, they engaged in a shouting match at O'Hare Airport in Chicago when Giancana arrived there one evening with his mistress, Phyllis McGuire of the singing McGuire Sisters. Richards called Giancana "slime, garbage, and a jerk" in front of hundreds of airline passengers in the American Airlines concourse, and Giancana retaliated by shouting at him: "You lit a fire tonight that will never go out! I'll get you if it's the last thing I do!" Their battle became really personal when Richards put a "lock-step" surveillance on Giancana, dogging his every footstep wherever he went. Giancana fought back by bringing the FBI, and Richards in particular, into court to obtain an injunction against the lock-step tail. Giancana prevailed.

But eventually the FBI won the battle against Giancana when Judge William Campbell of the U. S. District Court for the Northern District of Illinois granted the Chicago chieftain immunity for all his crimes. This took away his right to invoke the Fifth Amendment, so when he refused to answer questions put to him before a grand jury he was found in contempt by Judge Campbell and sent to jail for almost a year. When he got out, Giancana was confronted by Tony Accardo, still "the man" in Chicago no matter who the boss might be. It was decided that Giancana's reign as boss was over. He fled to Mexico where he was to remain for eight years. In 1975, a year after he was thrown out of Mexico, he was murdered by his own people at home in Chicago.

Giancana was succeeded by Sam Battaglia, Felix "Milwaukee Phil" Alderisio, and Jackie Cerone. None lasted long. "The G" got them all. In short order.

So, by 1971, Tony Accardo was brought back by his men to be the boss once again. This time as part of a "triumvirate." Gus Alex, the first non-Italian ever to be so positioned, and Joey "O'Brien" Aiuppa were the other members of the Triple A Committee at the top of the Chicago outfit.

When Jackie Cerone came back from prison in the mid-1970s, he and Aiuppa shared the top spot, and Tony Accardo retired one more time. Gus Alex stepped down and resumed his role as the chief of the connection guys, the fixers, the corruption squad. Accardo resumed his spot as the *consigliere* one more time, still the "man" in Chicago.

IN the meantime, Joe Bonanno was living a good life. Still on remote control under the supervision of underlings such as Gaspar DiGregorio, Joe Notaro, Paulie Primosa, Angelo "The Ape" Annunciata, Michael "The Clean One" Immaculata, Bill Bonanno, and John Morales, his Brooklyn family was doing well, if not great. Joe spent most of his time in Tucson, enjoying the warmth, fresh air, and sunshine. He was soaking it up, but things were about to change. The FBI decided to institute an intensified investigation of Bonanno in Tucson, designed to find out once and for all what this godfather was involved in.

As fate would have it, Bill Richards, when he found out that the FBI was about to come down with both feet on Bonanno, successfully requested a transfer from Chicago to Tucson. He and his wife Jeannie had visited their son, Bill, a Tucson television sportscaster, on six occasions and had fallen in love with the Old Pueblo. When he arrived in Tucson, he was assigned to help the three other agents who were working on Bonanno: Donn Sickles, Bill Christiansen, and "Skip" George. Together with agents of the Arizona Drug Control District, they picked up Bonanno's garbage twice a week. It was Bonanno's habit to make notes of his agenda for the day and when it was all over to throw the notes in his garbage. The agents also tailed Bonanno endlessly, twenty-four hours a day, in order to locate the public phones he used to call Brooklyn and elsewhere to give his orders to his men. Once they were located, the agents obtained court orders and wiretapped those phones and recorded his conversations. Then they conducted an all-day raid of his home on St. Patrick's Day in 1979 and executed a search warrant there.

At this point, their evidence was taken to the assistant United States attorneys working under Mike Hawkins, the United States attorney in Arizona. Bonanno was indicted for obstruction of a grand jury in San Jose, California, where his sons, Bill and Joe, Jr., were being investigated. He was tried, convicted, and sent away for four years in the federal penitentiary in Springfield, Illinois.

MEANWHILE, in Chicago, Tony Accardo instructed his two bosses, Joey Aiuppa and Jackie Cerone, to concentrate on Las Vegas. Their interests there, especially in the Stardust, the Fremont, and the Hacienda, were their paramount source of income. The skim amounted to millions per year beginning in the early 1970s. The Chicago mob also worked very closely with Moe Dalitz at the Desert Inn and at the Riviera. It was obvious that what Chicago had in Las Vegas was the most important thing they had going for them.

To oversee their interests in the desert gaming capital, Tony Accardo selected a new capo. His name was Joe Lombardo. They called him "The Clown." At least the press did. But he was no clown; he was a deadly killer and a tough hood.

Lombardo had worked closely with another young tough named Tony Spilotro. Spilotro had become involved in crime as a "juice" collector for loan shark "Mad Sam" DeStefano, the worst torture-murderer in the history of Chicago. This Sam, however, was completely demented and he became a liability for the mob. One Saturday morning Lombardo and Spilotro caught him in his garage—with two barrels each from their shotguns. DeStefano was dead before he hit the pavement, one arm completely severed from his body.

In 1971 Accardo instructed that Spilotro be sent to Las Vegas to become the Chicago representative there. Spilotro was to replace Marshall Caifano who in turn had replaced Johnny Roselli there in the late 1950s.

Accardo also assigned Lombardo another task: to be the Chicago outfit liaison with the Teamsters union. The Teamsters had established their Central States Pension and Welfare Fund. It was the mob bank. Loans to racket-connected enterprises, especially in Las Vegas, were made indiscriminately by the fund. Indiscriminate perhaps, but motivated by the control the mob had over the Teamsters and its fund through Allen Dorfman, the son of Paul "Red" Dorfman. Dorfman had been put in place by Jimmy Hoffa, a close friend of the elder Dorfman, when the Chicago mob informed Hoffa they needed one of their own in such position.

Lombardo was given the task of staying very, very close to Allen Dorfman. And to Roy Williams, then the president of the Teamsters. Williams was on the pad of Nick Civella, the boss of the Kansas City LCN, a family subservient to Chicago.

At this time, which brings us up to the mid-seventies, Joe Batters "made" a new capo. His name was Joe Ferriola. They called him Joe Negall. He was a short, pudgy, balding guy. A guy with a lot of potential. He was tough and aggressive and Accardo had him tabbed for bigger and better things. First, however, he assigned him to be the capo in charge of gambling throughout the Chicago area. From the Wisconsin state line to Kankakee and from Lake Michigan through DuPage and McHenry counties, the far western suburbs of Chicago. Ferriola had become the most important capo in Chicago.

THE FBI had entered the battle in 1957 when J. Edgar Hoover had finally officially acknowledged that there was, in fact, such a thing as a national crime organization, and from that time on the mobs would never be the same. Their income would be drastically reduced, their power to corrupt diminished, and their leaders and members sent to prison as never before in history. In spite of that general trend, however, organized crime in Chicago had seen somewhat of a rebirth as of the late seventies. Joe Batters had come back and pounded the thing into shape again. And got away with it. He had still not spent a night of his entire life in jail. Now *there* was an accomplishment of which a mob boss could boast. More than half a century in the mob and the government had never seriously laid a finger on him.

The FBI would not lie down, however. After Bill Richards left Chicago for Tucson to work on Joe Bonanno, he left behind a cadre of good, experienced FBI agents. Two of these had worked with Richards for several years. One was Pete Wacks, who would become one of the greatest street agents of all time, and the other was Art Pfizenmayer, who might have challenged Wacks for that honor if he hadn't become a supervisor.

Wacks and Pfizenmayer began to follow the trail of Allen Dorfman as a hidden owner of Las Vegas establishments. Their investigation, called "Pendorf"—for penetration of Dorfman—commenced in the fall of 1978. Dorfman was the son of Red Dorfman, the Chicago labor hack who had put Jimmy Hoffa in touch with Murray "The Camel" Humphreys in the late 1950s or early 1960s. Allen Dorfman had been convicted in 1972 of illegally arranging a kickback on a Central States Teamster loan, and Wacks and Pfizenmayer knew that he was the key figure in the relationship between the mob and the Central States Pension and Welfare Fund.

Wacks and Pfizenmayer also knew that Dorfman was controlled by the Chicago family of La Cosa Nostra and that he had strong ties with other crime families, particularly with Nick Civella, the boss in Kansas City. He owned and operated the Amalgamated Insurance Co., located in the International Tower on Bryn Mawr Avenue near O'Hare Airport in Chicago. Amalgamated was heavily dependent on the Teamsters and its pension fund for business. And they got it. Lots of it.

Wacks and Pfizenmayer went to the Organized Crime Strike Force of the Justice Department, located just several floors above the FBI office in the federal building and through Doug Roller, the chief, and Jeff Johnson, Roller's assistant, were able to obtain court authority to bug several locations in Chicago, particularly the Amalgamated Insurance Co. They expected to uncover information about Tony Accardo's hidden interests in Vegas casinos. They were looking for evidence of the skim which the Chicago mob was taking from those casinos. Years earlier, in the 1960s, Richards and his partners had developed the VEGMON case wherein they followed the prime courier, a woman named Ida Devine, as she travelled from Vegas all around the country dispensing the skim to Accardo, Lansky, and the others who had hidden "points" in the casinos, namely the Stardust, the Fremont, the Desert Inn, and the Riviera.

Fortuitously, Wacks and Pfizenmayer began to overhear Allen Dorfman conferring with Joey "The Clown" Lombardo. Readers will recall that Lombardo was the guy who oversaw the Vegas overseer, Spilotro, and who was the mob liaison to Dorfman and the Teamsters. The agents began to pick up what was an apparent bribery plot on the hidden microphones they had installed. The scheme involved seven acres of land owned by the Teamsters Pension and Welfare Fund near the Las Vegas Hilton. They found that United States Sen. Howard Cannon, Democrat from Nevada, was attempting to purchase the land as part of a group of investors. There was a rival group competing for the land, however. The intercepts monitored Cannon's son-in-law as he discussed with Dorfman the possibility that the competing bid be withdrawn which would open the way for Senator Cannon's group.

What Lombardo, Dorfman, and the leaders of the Teamsters, including their president, Roy Williams, wanted was for Senator Cannon and his Commerce Committee of the Senate to quash trucking deregulation legislation. The Teamsters were waging a fierce fight against the legislation. As it turned out, Senator Cannon was able to wage a successful jurisdictional battle with Sen. Ted Kennedy, who headed the Senate Judiciary Committee, and was able to get control of the legislation. The plotters planned to influence Senator Cannon to shelve the deregulation bill with the *quid pro quo* that Senator Cannon's group would gain the right to buy the property near the Vegas Hilton. As charged in the indictment that followed, Williams and his cronies did influence the other bidders to withdraw bids on the land and then attempted to give Senator Cannon's group an exclusive to purchase the property at a specified price. There was no evidence, however, that Senator Cannon had any part in the machinations nor that he knew anything about them. He was not charged and he testified for the government at the subsequent trial.

The indictment was returned by a federal grand jury in Chicago in May of 1981. After a jury trial the defendants—Roy Williams, Allen Dorfman, Joey Lombardo, Thomas O'Malley, a Chicago trucking company executive who was on the board of the pension fund, and Andrew Massa, who directed labor relations for the fund—were all convicted. Williams agreed to step down as Teamster president after receiving a long prison term. Lombardo is currently serving his fifteen-year sentence.

In December 1981, Tony Accardo met with his key men in the Chicago mob. They had agreed to chop Dorfman but they needed

Tony's sanction to do the job. It was not expected that this guy, not a hard core "made" guy, would be able to do "hard time." It was expected he might decide to make a deal with the government in return for leniency on all his troubles with the law.

In January 1983, Allen Dorfman was walking with his pal, bondsman Irv Weiner. They were going to lunch in a Northwest Chicago suburb, but Allen never made it. He was chopped by two unknown assailants wielding revolvers, and Dorfman became just another of the roughly one thousand victims of gangland slaying in Chicago alone since 1919.

TONY Accardo had lost a lot. He lost Roy Williams, his man in the Teamsters, the guy the mob depended upon for oh, so many things. Williams had been right out of the mold of Jimmy Hoffa and Frank Fitzsimmons, other presidents of the Teamsters who were beholden, lock, stock, and barrel to the mob. A great loss. He had lost his capo, Joey Lombardo, the guy who ran Tony Spilotro, the mob's man in Las Vegas, and a very capable guy. And, one way or another, he had lost Allen Dorfman, who for so many years had been depended on by Accardo to facilitate and expedite the high-risk loans the Teamsters Pension Fund was doling out to the mob. Chicago's crime syndicate would not have had the handle on Las Vegas had it not been for Dorfman and his entrée to the Teamsters Pension Fund.

Things were to get much blacker, however. The "Pendorf Case" was a major effort by the Chicago office of the FBI and would rank as one of the very best investigations ever conducted anywhere at any time by the Bureau. What was to come would certainly rival it in the all-time annals of the FBI.

WHAT followed was the "Strawman Cases" in Kansas City. What Kansas City had in 1978 was the classic example of what is needed to fight organized crime. They had one of the greatest street agents in the FBI, Bill Ouseley; one of the finest FBI supervisors in Gary Hart; and an extremely competent and aggressive Strike Force chief, Dave Helfrey. A street agent is by far the most important of the three-pronged attack since it all starts with him. If he doesn't uncover and develop the evidence then a case against any mobster would never get off the ground. He is comparable to the prizefighter. If he doesn't get into the arena and spill the blood then no matter what anyone else does, the fight will never be won. But the fighter needs support. The FBI field supervisor is like the fighter's manager, who knows his needs, allocates his time, arranges his matches, and keeps extraneous concerns out of his way while he is doing his business. The United States Attorney's office, or in the Strawman Case, the Justice Department's Organized Crime Strike Force, is like the fighter's owner. He gives the fighter and the manager the resources to do the battle and then takes the product they have produced and invests it. In Kansas City, the Ouseley-Hart-Helfrey team was just the right personnel at just the right time. Joe Batters was up against the best.

In April of 1978, Bill Ouseley discovered that the Kansas City family of La Cosa Nostra, headed by Nick Civella but under the sanction of the Chicago family where Accardo was "the man," had marked a victim for murder. Civella's family was actively stalking its prey. Ouseley discussed this situation with his supervisor, Hart, and then went to Helfrey. It was determined that Ouseley would prepare an affidavit to support an application for a court-authorized electronic surveillance. Such authority is granted under Title III of the 1968 Omnibus Crime Act and is therefore called, in the trade, "Title III Authority" or sometimes just "T-3." Sufficient evidence to support probable cause in the affidavit was shown by Ouseley and in May 1978, the U. S. District Court in Kansas City authorized the "elsur," or electronic surveillance. There was not enough time to prevent the killing, though. The victim was murdered in a tavern by three hit men before the "elsur" was operational. Ouseley learned, however, that this was just one in a string of hits planned by Civella and his mob in K.C. and prepared another Title III affidavit. This time he hit pay dirt. When the bug was placed, lo and behold, Ouseley almost immediately overheard a conversation between the acting boss of the Kansas City mob, Carl "Cork" Civella (Nick was in prison at the time, and Cork, his brother, was minding the store) with the Kansas City underboss, Carl "Tuffy" DeLuna. The conversation, serendipitously, concerned the mob's interests in Las Vegas. Since Ouseley was an experienced agent, most knowledgeable not only about his targets in Kansas City but of the situation in Las Vegas, he was able to grasp the full significance of what he was hearing immediately and take it to Hart and then to Helfrey for proper handling.

This tap led to another in a hotel located in the eastern industrial section of Kansas City where DeLuna was set up to receive incoming calls from Kansas City's representative in Las Vegas, Joe Agosto. Joe Agosto, true name Vincenzo Pianetti, at the time (1978) was the entertainment director at the Tropicana Hotel (before it was sold to Ramada and cleaned up). When Ouseley obtained Title III authority to tap the public pay phone at the hotel where DeLuna was receiving Agosto's calls, the pay dirt became a gold mine. For Agosto was continuously giving DeLuna a blow-by-blow account of the moves being made in Las Vegas, not only by him on behalf of Kansas City but by Tony Accardo's Chicago mob! At the time, Chicago was behind Allen Glick, who was fronting for them in the Argent Corporation which owned, among other hotel-casinos, the flagship hotel of Chicago, the Stardust. Agosto talked in code, calling Glick "Baldy" and "Genius" and Chicago's chief operator in the Stardust, Frank "Lefty" Rosenthal, "Crazy."

More than anything, however, Agosto's calls clearly gave evidence that the K.C. mob was skimming the Tropicana.

The first two taps led to more Title IIIs. Ouseley placed taps on DeLuna's home phone; he got coverage at a law firm Nick Civella utilized (Civella was by then paroled due to poor health). Ouseley tapped the phone of mob member Peter Tamburello, Civella's driver, and the phone of mob member Charley Moretina, an enforcer for the K.C. mob. In November of 1978, Ouseley made a bold move. He heard that Agosto and Carl Thomas, the master of skim in Las Vegas who headed crews at several casinos, were coming in to report to DeLuna and to Nick Civella himself in the basement of one of Civella's neighbors. Knowing it was a one-time shot, Ouseley moved quickly to obtain Title III authority and then to plant the bug. What he heard was extraordinary. First, Carl Civella showed up unexpectedly, just for a short time, to get approval from his brother, the boss, to murder a mob rival who was causing problems. Then he left and the business of the day was handled. Agosto and Thomas explained to Nick Civella and Carl DeLuna the methods and techniques of skimming. Thomas said there were "twenty-one holes in the bucket," and he explained many of them. It was a continuing education for Ouseley, who listened and studied intently and then passed his information on to the agents in Las Vegas who were attempting to stem the tide there.

The first phase of "Strawman" culminated on St. Valentine's Day, 1979, the fiftieth anniversary of Joe Batters's participation in the killing of the Bugs Moran Gang. That had been a mob success. This was to be a mob calamity! The first part of the holiday celebration took place at the airport in Kansas City when Ouseley and other agents intercepted the courier who was bringing the weekly skim to the Kansas City mob, to be shared with Tony Accardo and his Chicago family. Ouseley relieved the courier of $80,000. Then Ouseley and his agents went to the home of Carl DeLuna. It turned out that DeLuna kept meticulous records of everything he and the Kansas City mob did! The records represented the closest thing to what might be called "the books" of a mob's operation. They were seized and would play a key role in the two major trials, Strawman I and Strawman II, which would follow. Among other things, they showed that the "Rancher," Roy Williams, the president of the Teamsters, was on the pad.

When Nick Civella went back to prison at Leavenworth, a bug was placed, with Title III authority, in the visiting room of the penitentiary there. This coverage continued into 1980.

With reams of evidence thereby developed, Ouseley, Hart, and Helfrey sat down to make sense of it. As a result of their conference, the top leadership of the Kansas City mob was indicted in November 1981. Included were DeLuna, Nick and Carl Civella, Moretina, Tamburello, and Carl Caruso. Tony Chiavola, a Chicago policeman in whose home another Title III had been activated, was also indicted as were Carl Thomas, Joe Agosto, and two members of their "skim team" in Las Vegas, Don Shepard and Billy Caldwell.

Ouseley then began to build a rapport with Joe Agosto. Ouseley, the son of an Italian mother, and Agosto, who had been born in Italy, soon became very friendly. Eventually, Agosto became a full-fledged informant for Ouseley and agreed to testify against his co-conspirators. He was a super witness, in spite of his heavily accented English.

Prior to the trial in mid-1983, Nick Civella died after having led the Kansas City mob for some thirty years. The stress had finally caught up to him. When all the defendants with the exception of Tamburello were convicted, a crippling blow was dealt to the Kansas City family, a blow which also battered Batters since it cut off a substantial part of the flow of skim from Vegas and decimated the leadership of the Kansas City family which was a subsidiary of his.

Now "Strawman II" commenced. The Tropicana phase was successfully completed, and the Ouseley-Hart-Helfrey team turned to the Argent phase. This phase concerned the hidden interests of Tony Accardo and his Chicago mob, and their allies, in the hotels owned by the Argent Corporation which had been run for them by Glick and Rosenthal. It mainly targeted the star of the Chicago show, the Stardust. It also concerned mob control of the Teamsters and the Central States Pension and Welfare Fund.

Indicted were DeLuna, Civella, and Tamburello from Kansas City; Frank Peter Balistrieri, the LCN boss in Milwaukee and his two key men there, sons Joe and John; Milton J. Rockman, a key to the Pension Fund in Cleveland; Tony Spilotro and Carl Thomas of Las Vegas, *and*—hold on to your hats—Joey Aiuppa, Accardo's hand-picked boss; Jackie Cerone, Accardo's underboss, and Joe Lombardo, Accardo's capo in charge of Spilotro and his activity in Vegas as well as being the liaison to Allen Dorfman and the Teamsters Pension Fund, the mob's bank. Also indicted, once again, were Tony Chiavola, Civella's nephew and his son, Tony, Jr., who had allowed the Kansas City mob leaders to come into Chicago and meet in their home with the Chicago mob leaders. The story of how the FBI bugged that meeting is typical of the excitement of the chase, especially when placing bugs.

The FBI had entered the home of the Chiavolas on the West Side of Chicago late at night as the family slept! They made the necessary moves to install the device and departed, without waking any of the family members. The information obtained as a result, completely admissible due to the court-ordered Title III authority and therefore unlike the bug planted by Richards before such authority was made possible by legislation, was essential to tie Aiuppa, Cerone, and Lombardo into the case.

After a trial lasting more than four months most of the defendants were convicted. The most important ones from Accardo's viewpoint; Aiuppa, Cerone, and Lombardo were no exception. They were each to receive twenty-five-year sentences and, with the possible exception of Lombardo, will probably spend the rest of their lives in jail. Cerone, for instance, is seventy-six years old as of this writing and he is in just the fourth year of his twenty-five-year sentence. Aiuppa is eighty-four. Spilotro was severed from the trial before it began due to ill health. The two Chiavolas pled guilty, as did DeLuna midway during the trial. Carl Thomas was granted immunity and testified for the government. Allen Glick testified for the government also. Joe Agosto died before he could. The judge directed verdicts in favor of Joe and John Balistrieri as part of their father's plea of guilty.

Strawman I and Strawman II gave the FBI, the Justice Department, and the public graphic evidence of how the mob operated in Las Vegas. First a mob found a clean businessman, one who could withstand close scrutiny of his character and past, to use as a "front"; to act as the owner of record. Then this man applied for a multi-million-dollar loan from the Teamsters Pension and Welfare Fund. Then the mob used their influence over the fund, formerly through Allen Dorfman, to grant the loan. When the scheme was fully in operation, the mob set up the mechanics of skim, usually through such characters as Agosto and Thomas, and then skimmed millions annually from the casino. A small portion of this was then kicked back to those who were corrupted to make the loan from the Teamsters Fund and to the mob(s) who controlled the vote of the Teamsters board members who voted for the loan.

Strawman I and Strawman II are classic examples of the great work the FBI has done in combating organized crime. They completely crippled the strong Kansas City mob and did the same to the vital Milwaukee mob. And Joe Batters certainly felt great pain in Chicago when his top leadership was sent away. For good. It was precisely at this time that he held his meeting with his new leaders and that coincidentally Joe Bonanno did the same with his New York mob in Tucson as described in Chapters One and Two.

Book II

THE BATTLE

**ACCARDO AND BONANNO EACH GRAB FOR
THEIR PIECE OF THE STRIP**

CHAPTER

11

Janet Comes to Las Vegas

SHE was sweet sixteen. And although she had been kissed, she hadn't gone much further than that. Her name was Janet Zaleski. The world would never come to know her by that name, but South Bend, Indiana, where she grew up, did.

Janet grew up in the Harder Heights neighborhood of South Bend adjacent to University Heights, which borders the University of Notre Dame golf course and is next to the university itself. Harder Heights is a very nice upper-middle class neighborhood. Folks like "Moose" Krause, the legendary Notre Dame star athlete, coach, and athletic director, and "Digger" and Terry Phelps, the Irish basketball coach and his wife, live in Harder Heights, as do many Notre Dame professors and their families.

Janet had been your typical "girl next door," the gal every boy would want living next door! She attended parochial school in her parish, St. Joseph's, at Hill and Colfax, where she was an altar girl for Father Van, the beloved pastor there. When she graduated from grade school, she made a 180-degree turn, but only in a geographical sense. Instead of trodding southward each morning, she went north to another St. Joseph's, this one the high school located about ten blocks away on Highway 31, known as Dixie Highway, which borders the west side of the Notre Dame golf course.

At St. Joseph's High School, renowned for its athletic teams, Janet was truly the all-American girl. In her mother's generation she would have been the captain of the cheerleaders, rooting on the boys' football and basketball teams. In her generation, she was the captain of the girls' basketball team and the girls' tennis team. Her unusual height—she was 5'8" and growing—was a big asset to her athletic career. As a matter of fact, she became well known in South Bend when she won the city girls' tennis title at Leeper Park, then went on to lasting fame as the state champ when she won in Indianapolis, the state capital.

That was not the only fame she won in South Bend at St. Joe's. She was the Homecoming Queen in her senior year and then entered the Miss America contest. She easily won Miss St. Joseph County (St. Joseph seems to be the patron saint in that area even though Notre Dame—"Our Mother"—is the dominant influence). Her string of successes ended, however, after she became a finalist in the state Miss America contest but was not crowned Miss Indiana. This minor setback didn't destroy her, however; her vanity wasn't that fragile. She had everything going for her in her young life and when she graduated from St. Joe's it even looked like she was headed for marriage to her counterpart, South Bend's male student-athlete of the era.

The couple took off for Bloomington, the site of Indiana University, "The Big Red." It caused a furor in her family.

"Glory and Praise!" her mother raved. (It was Mrs. Zaleski's favorite phrase.) "Glory and Praise to God! You spend your first years devoted to Our Lord and His Mother and then you go off to a heathen college! And only because you are infatuated with another heathen who went to John Adams High School and didn't have the religious upbringing you did. Glory and Praise!"

Head over heels in love, however, Janet took off to travel way to the other end of Indiana, down to beautiful Brown County where "the gleaming candlelight still shines bright, through the sycamores for me" and "the new mown hay sends all its fragrance." Back home in Indiana. It wasn't long, however, before Janet and her true love, Bobby Doran—another famous name in South Bend—had problems. Bobby had become the darling of the coeds. While still a freshman, he won the starting tailback spot on the Hoosier football team and his sparkling blue eyes and blond hair captured the attention and passion of the many pretty young coeds. Soon Bob and Janet, the ideally matched pair—at least up to this point—had it out. "Bobby, I've had enough of this," Janet cried. "All of this attention has gone to your head. You're not the same boy I knew back in South Bend. I heard you were at the Student Union last night with Ginger Jones! That's not right! I was in my dorm waiting for you and you're out with that hussy from Kokomo!"

"Listen, Janet, get off my back!" Bobby shot back. "You'd think we were married or something! I'm eighteen years old! I want to have fun in this life. I sweat my ass off on the football field and in between the season and spring practice I deserve a little recreation."

"So, I'm not 'recreation,' is that what you're saying?" Janet began to cry. It was probably the first real reversal of her life and, after all the good things that had happened to her, she was totally unprepared to handle it. "Robert Doran, you do what you want. If you think I'm going to sit in my room waiting for you while you make eyes—or whatever else—with girls like Ginger Jones, you've got another think coming!" She turned her back and flew away. Bobby Doran let her go. It was the end of a beautiful relationship.

It had no further consequences than that, however. Janet's upbringing at home and at the St. Joseph's schools, by her parents and by the good priests, sisters, and brothers of the Holy Cross had prevented her from losing any of the flower of her maidenhood. She was still the fresh and lovely teen-ager, the beautiful and athletic girl, undamaged, at least in body, by her bad experience. Her body was still wrapped in cellophane.

In mind, however, it was a different story. Try as she might, Janet could not cope emotionally with the first major setback of her young life. Her tennis game suffered and soon she was no longer on the Indiana team. The tennis scholarship she had won was still intact, since NCAA rules are such that performance, or lack thereof, is not a qualification for retaining a grant-in-aid once received. But this additional frustration added to her mental and emotional problems. The fact that she was considered "Bobby Doran's girl," even though she no longer was, kept the boys from flocking to her dorm door. As the final straw, the stress rattled the concentration needed to devote to her studies. Janet was not

a poor student, but the extracurricular activities all through her forma-
tive years had been her focus, not academics. When her final grades
came out in May, Janet had flunked two mandatory courses, calculus
and her foreign language, French. She was placed on academic probation.

When Janet found that her marks had been so poor and that her
status at I. U. was so shaky, she was almost afraid to travel home. It
was all so hard to deal with after years of nothing but acclaim. Back
in South Bend, presumably for the summer, and after she informed her
parents of her situation, her mother could do nothing but repeat, time
and again, "Glory and Praise to God! Glory and Praise!"

It got so bad that Janet felt compelled to move out. She made the first
of several bad decisions she was to make in her life.

Janet had gotten to know a fellow student at I.U. He was a shoulder
to cry on, but their friendship had not developed into a romance. When
she decided that life in Harder Heights was too uncomfortable she
called her friend, Steve North. As it turned out, Steve had been planning a trip. He had gotten a "package deal" from the Tropicana Resort
and Casino, "the Island of Las Vegas," and was planning a long week-
end there.

"Jan, join me!" he shouted. Steve exalted in the thought. If he could
get the beautiful, statuesque Janet Zaleski to join him on a trip to Las
Vegas, it would be the highlight of his life. He thought he just might
get lucky in Vegas.

"Las Vegas?" Janet responded. "Las Vegas? I've never thought of
going there. I've heard all kinds of things about what goes on out
there!" It was out of the question. But was it? In her rebellious state
of mind, might it not be just the thing? On impulse, she decided to go.

Steve and Janet arrived at McCarran Airport in mid-afternoon on a
June day. Even Janet got a charge as she and Steve exited from the gate
area towards the baggage claim area on the moving walkway. The
recorded voices of such stars as Frank Sinatra, Dean Martin, and
Wayne Newton were exhorting in singsong: "Stay to the right, be
courteous, let others pass you on the left." The tickle of the coins
dropping into the metal catchboxes on the slot machines in the airport
was music to the first-time visitor's ears. The large advertisements
lining the walls of the concourse corridor highlighting the top entertainers at the luxurious hotels added an air of excitement. She had heard
about and read about Las Vegas all her nineteen years, now she was

going to experience it! She hadn't been so excited since Bobby Doran left her. It was a big surprise to her. Although she had known about all the fun to be had in Las Vegas, it had never been high on her agenda of places to visit. Janet had always felt that New York City, with a visit to Central Park, St. Patrick's Cathedral, and Rockefeller Center would be more entertaining and more in keeping with her background. But here she was in Las Vegas. And she was plenty excited before she had even left the airport. How could this be? As Steve and Janet followed the signs to "ground transportation," Steve enthusiastically pointed to a large sign and shouted, "That's where we're going! Look at that, how does that strike you?"

It was an advertisement for the Tropicana. It showed the South Seas waterpark which had just been added to the resort, in between the two high-rise towers. The Trop had just been made over to the tune of seventy million dollars and the "Island of Las Vegas" looked to the two young Hoosiers like something out of this world. Janet began to feel her skin tighten. "If you don't watch out, young girl," she said to herself, "you'll be getting goosebumps!" Rather than pay for a cab, although the resort is as close to the airport as you can get, the pair waited for a Gray Line bus and were soon dropped off at the entry way to the Tropicana. It was amazing. Registering at the counter to the left of the doors as they entered, they found that they had been assigned to the new tower, the rear one with 806 rooms, behind the original one, with a thousand rooms. As they walked between the two towers, Janet was amazed to see the 110-foot waterslide, the five spas, whirlpools, the waterfalls, the lagoons, the outdoor bar, and the snack bar. She saw that the pool was the length of the football field at I. U. Probably what amazed her the most was the sight of two swim-up "21" tables in the pool with a dropbox system which included a heater for drying paper money! She watched the flamingos, the cranes, the penguins, and other birds walking freely on "the island." She was intrigued by the palm trees, scores of them, the exotic flowers and other tropical flora. She enjoyed the several types of tropical fish swimming in two of the lagoons.

When they entered the new tower, they took the elevator up to their adjacent rooms. "Hurry, Jan," Steve called. "We'll go down and have a drink at the Java Java Coffee House and I'll get in touch with Mel Greenberg." Greenberg was a "host" at the Tropicana who Steve had met on his last trip. Greenberg was a friend of Steve's dad, who enjoyed

V.I.P. status there. "He's the guy who set this 'package' up for me. Usually, you have to show money before they set you up like this, but my dad is special here. They don't 'comp' me, but they sure make it nice."

Janet continued to be amazed as the couple walked through the lobbies of the vast resort. So many lounges and restaurants! The Rhapsody, El Gaucho, Mizuno's, the Island Buffet, and even the Fairway Room out on the plush golf course adjoining the hotel. They looked into the lounge area of the Tropics Room which consisted of a full bar enclosed in rock formations, waterfalls, and an eighty-seat entertainment floor. They noticed that The Treniers would be performing there that night. Then they walked to the Atrium, another restaurant-lounge, and saw that The Coasters were on the bill for that evening.

Now the youngster, fresh from the "new mown hay and the sycamores" of Indiana, did get goosebumps. This was totally unexpected. She never would have believed, even yesterday when she anticipated what Las Vegas might be like, that it would be as grand as this. She had expected a certain amount of flash, a somewhat gaudy atmosphere. There certainly was all of that. But this place was something more than that. There was a certain, well, grandeur here. Totally unexpected.

Then Mel Greenberg arrived as the two sat drinking coffee and munching on pastry at the Java Java Coffee House in the hotel.

"Good to see you, kid," Greenberg announced. "How's your dad? Tell him to get back here soon, he's one of our best customers! Say, what do we have here? Are you here to audition for the Folies?"

Janet blushed. She didn't know what the "Folies" were, but she felt it must be a compliment.

Greenberg, as a host, had the job of attracting and entertaining a clientele of high rollers to the Tropicana. He was one of several and each had the function of developing and maintaining contact with those V.I.P.'s from all over the country. Most of his clients were from the Midwest and West since Atlantic City had opened and siphoned off some of the best customers from major cities like New York and Philadelphia and even Boston and Washington. Others kept coming back because, in at least one respect, Vegas has a big advantage over Atlantic City. New Jersey does not allow "sports books." Betting on football, baseball, basketball, and the races is a major attraction in the Las Vegas resort-casinos, so much so that it would not be long before almost every major casino would have a large area with mammoth TV screens where a "player" could watch—and bet on—three or four events at one time! Football, baseball, basketball, prize fights, horse races, golf, and tennis! With the advent of the satellite dish, almost any event being televised any place in the country could be brought onto the big screens in the "sports books" of most of the major Vegas casinos. Many the sports enthusiast from Chicago, Denver, Phoenix, Los Angeles, San Francisco, etc., would come to Las Vegas, especially on weekends, to bet and follow the action on the big screens.

Janet wasn't interested in any of that. To her surprise, however, she was interested in trying her hand at blackjack or "21." "Would you teach me?" she asked Steve. He taught her how to stand on 15 or over, double down only on 11, never buy "insurance," and watch what the dealer had *up* before she took any chances. When the roving cocktail waitress came around and offered her a drink—overlooking the fact that she was just nineteen—she started to reach into her purse. "No, no," Steve whispered to her, "you don't pay as long as you play. They want you to drink, gets you loose, takes away your inhibitions."

That night, Janet found out what the "Folies" are. The famous Folies Bergère, the floor show at the Tropicana. First they dined with Greenberg at the three-tiered Tropics Restaurant, in the new tower, with fountains, streams, and waterfalls running under, through, and around it. Janet dined on Polynesian food while Steve had Oriental. Then, thanks to Greenberg, they joined the throng to watch the Folies Bergère in the Trop showroom. They caught the eleven o'clock cocktail show for $12.95 each.

Janet's goosebumps turned to shivers. What beautiful girls! Not that she was turned on sexually, but she was astounded at the pulchritude of these showgirls! "Glory and Praise," as her mother would have said had she been there. Of course, the boy dancers looked like any other boy dancers. Not like Bobby Doran, that's for sure! But the girls! Not one under 5'10", some probably 6'2". Probably 37"–25"–36", all of them. Wow! Even the reserved, laid-back Janet was awed by their beauty.

Greenberg came over to their table. "You like it?" Steve and Janet did. For some reason she could not describe, even to herself, Janet found that all this excitement got under her skin. First there were the costumes. Not much to them, but what there was, was breathtaking—particularly the hats, which used much more material than any other piece of the costume. Then there was the music and the dancing itself.

It was an all-American extravaganza. First a blues number, then the '40s boogie-woogie, and finally the famed ten-minute finale, the cancan with its acrobatics, climaxing with the kick-line. Wow!

That night, as they retired to their rooms on an upper floor of what they discovered was called "The New Island Tower," Steve suggested they order room service, "just a nightcap," in his room. "Steve, it's been such a long day, I am so worn out," Janet firmly stated. They went to their separate rooms.

Janet and Steve slept until noon the next day. After all, it had been a long day and they didn't get to their rooms until the wee hours. After a big lunch at the Island Buffet, they walked out to Las Vegas Boulevard, the Strip, and walked over to the Hacienda. "This is a starter for our tour," Steve told her. "It's not one of the best by any means, but we'll start here." Going up the Strip from the Hacienda, they walked past the vacant property where, in 1990, the fabulous Excalibur would be built. It was to become the world's largest hotel, built with two castle towers like something out of Disneyland. Then up the street past the small Marina, then the Aladdin and they crossed over to the Dunes.

The great Caesars Palace was across from the Dunes. What an outstanding place! Then kitty-corner, back across the street, to Bally's. On the way back onto the Strip—while still a part of it, Bally's sat far back off the Strip—they walked through the quaint little Barbary Coast, a very nice, small hotel-casino, one Janet took an immediate liking to. By this time, Janet was getting tired. There was so much walking and the titillation was tiring. So they hopped a bus going back towards the Trop and returned.

"What I need before dinner," Janet said, "is a nap." Quickly, she gave Steve a peck on the forehead and closed her door behind her.

At eight it was back to the "21" tables. They hunted down one of the few $2 minimum tables and gambled for an hour or so.

"Steve," Janet said, "I had so much of that buffet for lunch, why don't we skip dinner and catch that Folies Bergère show again at eleven?"

"Again? We caught that last night. Why don't we catch a cab? I see Ray Stevens and Louise Mandrell are at the Desert Inn. Remember 'Everything is Beautiful'? That was Ray Stevens. I like him."

"Steve, I really would like to see the Folies again. I thought they were great," Janet pled.

"Well, all right, if they really turn you on." Steve got Greenberg on the house phone and arrangements were made for him and Janet to enter through the V. I. P. line, rather than wait with the masses. Steve then "toked" the maitre d' with a fiver, not all that much and certainly not what the maitre d' was accustomed to, but they got a nice booth, up above the tables, with a nicer vantage point than the night before. Again, Janet was taken with the showgirl dancers. This time, one in particular. A girl in her mid-thirties, about the shortest of the line at 5'10". When Greenberg showed up during the finale, the cancan, Janet pointed to the girl. Greenberg told her, "She should be good. That's Debbie Lee, not her real name, of course, but she's a 'principal', she's been here about fifteen years. She's one of the few from here, she grew up here. She's married and has two kids."

"What's a 'principal'?" Janet inquired.

"That's a lead role, that's why you noticed her," Greenberg answered.

That night, Steve put more of a move on Janet. After all, he had honored her request to see the Folies one more time when he would rather have gone to see Ray Stevens. This time, Janet gave Steve a long, somewhat fervent kiss at her door, but again swung on through it and evaded any further action.

By prearrangement, the duo slept again into the afternoon hours. The next day they took a Gray Line bus to that portion of the Strip where the Flamingo, Bugsy Siegel's old place, now a Hilton, is located. Then they traversed the rest of the Strip. They saw the Sands, the Frontier, the Stardust, Circus-Circus, the Desert Inn, the Riviera, and the El Rancho before they wound up at the Sahara. While at the Riviera they stopped for their buffet on the second floor above the pool. "Best buffet in town," Greenberg had told them, quietly, since it was a conflict of interest.

"Are you game to walk over to the Landmark and the Las Vegas Hilton off the Strip, or should we go downtown and catch the Golden Nugget, the Four Queens, the Fremont, or the new Sundance?" Steve asked.

"I'm bushed, Steve," Janet replied. "Let's take a cab back and get a nap before we decide what we do tonight." They did.

That night Steve insisted they get out of the hotel for the evening. He had Greenberg make reservations, not that they really needed them, but just in case, at the Alpine Village. He liked the Old World food and the authentic German music he had experienced there on his last trip.

Janet enjoyed it too. But about 10:30, she said: "I know you're going to think I'm nuts, Steve, but one last favor. Let's go back to the Tropicana and catch the Folies one more time."

"Oh, Janet! There's so much else to do here! We've Bill Cosby at the Hilton, Tony Bennett at Bally's, Lou Rawls at the Nugget, Redd Foxx at the Sahara."

"I wouldn't see that obscene Redd Foxx in a million years and that Sahara was dirty," Janet said.

"Well then, how about one of the other showgirl extravaganzas? They got 'Jubilee' at Bally's and they got 'Lido' at the Stardust. Or we could see Siegfried and Roy, with all those lions and tigers and their magic show, at the Frontier. We've already seen the Folies and this is our last night! We've seen them both nights, enough is enough already!"

"Please, Steve, if *you* won't take me I'll go myself."

Steve thought about it. No wonder she and Bobby Doran split up, he thought. She really has a mind of her own.

So they went, for the third straight night, back to the Trop and to the Folies Bergère.

When Steve hastily called Greenberg one more time with his request to get them into the V.I.P. line, Greenberg expressed his surprise. Steve told him "It's all my girl's idea. She is really taken with those showgirls. It's amazing."

Greenberg got an idea. Janet had expressed an interest in Debbie Lee. Wouldn't it be nice if this kid, Steve, went back to Indiana and told his high-roller dad how good Greenberg had been to them when they came to the Trop?

That evening, while Janet was once again enthralled watching the kick-line of the Folies, Greenberg stopped by their table. "Hold on a few minutes after the show. I got two people want to say hello."

When the finale, the cancan, climaxed the show and the curtain came down, Greenberg came up to Steve and Janet's table. "Come on," he said.

He took Steve and Janet into the dressing room adjacent to the showroom. There, in a private cubicle of her own, befitting her status as a "principal," was Debbie Lee. Having removed her headpiece, she was starting to take off her makeup. She was very friendly even though it was obviously an imposition. But Mel Greenberg had asked her to do this favor so that he could ingratiate himself with Steve's father and she was used to such things. It went with the territory. Janet was visibly impressed, not only with Debbie, but with the entire ambience of the backstage of the Folies.

"Now, I got another person wants to meet you," Greenberg said. He took them into the executive offices of the Tropicana. Into the offices behind a door marked "Entertainment Director." Inside the plush offices, decorated lavishly, mostly with all kinds of palm fronds, sat a swarthy, beefy, middle-aged man.

Greenberg did the introductions. "This is the guy who runs this joint," he said. "This is Joe Agosto."

Joe Agosto arose. He shook Steve's hand and then looked at Janet. Now it truly *was* Joe Agosto's job to "run the joint." His title as "Entertainment Director" of the Tropicana was pretty much a sham. As the "Strawman I" case would reveal, he did the bidding of the Kansas City mob in running the Trop. Of course, Kansas City reported to Chicago. In effect, Joe Agosto was Tony Accardo's man at the Trop just as Lou Lederer had been Frank Costello's man at the Trop when Costello was shot in the lobby of his apartment building at 115 Central Park South in 1957. That, of course, was the prelude to the Albert Anastasia murder the same year, which led to the meeting of Apalachin and resulted in the advent of the FBI into organized crime investigation.

If Janet Zaleski had been enthralled with Debbie Lee, Joe Agosto was enthralled with Janet Zaleski. It was not just her statuesque beauty. Sure, she was 5'10", 135 pounds, 37"–25"–36", with beautiful blonde hair and a lovely face to go with the figure. But what got to Joe more than even that was the wholesomeness in Janet. It was as if her virginity flowed through her skin and created a sensuousness that even a man as warped as Joe Agosto could discern—or perhaps *especially* a man as warped as Joe Agosto could discern.

He took her hand and held it. "Let's see your legs," he stated, matter of factly.

"What?" the startled Janet gulped. Steve started forward.

"No, I'm not gettin' afresh," Agosto stated in his broken English. "I'm not insultin' ya. I'm complimentin' ya. I think you'd be great for the Folies."

Janet gaped at him for a moment. What a wild idea! But way down deep she was intrigued. Just as she had been intrigued by the Folies she was subconsciously intrigued by the idea of becoming a member of the Folies. After a few moments, she slowly lifted her skirt high above her knees. Steve could see she was wearing pink panties.

Agosto liked what he saw. The many years of basketball and tennis had made Janet very shapely in that area. "You look pretty good, kid," he said. "I'll tell you what, come here tomorrow at three and we'll give you an audition. I gotta another kid from Minnesota coming by and we catch the two of ya."

"Wait just a minute," Steve interrupted. "We didn't come here to be insulted!"

"Steve, please," Janet waved him back, "give me a chance to think about it."

Silence reigned for a full minute as Janet looked at Joe Agosto and Joe looked at Janet. Finally she said, "I'll be here at three."

Steve was flabbergasted. Janet Zaleski? No, not her! Of all the people he knew, he would have wagered a large sum of money in the sports book that Janet Zaleski, the pride of South Bend, the virginal princess of South Bend, would not be interested in becoming a Las Vegas showgirl! Not Janet Zaleski!

Janet's kiss to Steve that night was as perfunctory as it had been the first night. A peck and off to bed, only to spend the whole night sleepless, pondering her future. Did she dare? What would her mother say? Janet knew: "Glory and Praise to the Lord!"

Steve and Janet were scheduled to fly out the next day at noon. Steve, bewildered, shocked, did. Who would have guessed it when they arrived Friday that he would be leaving on Monday without Janet? Or that Janet was entertaining the idea of becoming one of "those girls" in Las Vegas. Wait until he told the folks back in South Bend!

At three o'clock that afternoon, Janet presented herself in the showroom at the Tropicana. There was another girl about her age, and her size, and just about as pretty, waiting there.

The girl introduced herself. "I'm Betty Bjornson from St. Paul."

Janet returned the pleasantry and asked the obvious. "Are you here to audition?" She was.

Joe Agosto arrived. He was brusque. He apparently had other things on his mind. "Let's get goin'," he said. Somebody turned on the piped-in music, and Janet and Betty were waved onto the stage. Betty went first. She was pretty good. She could dance and she looked great. Then Janet took her turn. She looked terrific. She was athletic, she had a natural grace and rhythm. She didn't move Joe Agosto much with her dance technique, "but, what the hell, she looks great, there's a certain charm about this broad that shines out, let's take a chance.

"Okay, I seen enough, I gotta get someplace. Both report to Debbie Lee here tomorrow night. She'll put you through the ropes, get you inta the hang of it."

It would be a couple of weeks before Janet would be ready. In the meantime, Debbie told Janet and Betty, "You two have got to come up with some stage names. Janet Zaleski and Betty Bjornson? What kind of names are those for a Las Vegas showgirl?" What kind of names, indeed . . .

Janet called her mother. This was the dreaded moment. Mrs. Zaleski listened for a moment and uttered her usual phrase: "Glory and Praise to the Lord!" Then Mrs. Zaleski dropped the phone.

At that moment, Janet Zaleski ceased to exist. A new Las Vegas showgirl had been born. Her name was Glory Praise.

12

The Fat Gets in the Fire!

FOLLOWING his sit-down with his top men in Tucson, as described in Chapter One, Joe Bonanno moved to further his plans to move his family into Las Vegas.

In late January of 1986, a lousy time to leave Tucson for any reason, he had "Short Pants" drive him out to the Tucson International Airport, then he took an American Airlines flight to O'Hare Airport in Chicago, and then on to Detroit where he landed at City Airport.

Joe was met at the airport by one of the Toccos, a relative of "Black Joe," and taken to Grosse Pointe where he met with Joe Zerelli. He had always gotten along with the boss of the Detroit family, a fellow Commission member. Zerelli had originally become active in La Cosa Nostra in St. Louis but had moved to Detroit during the violent twenties. He had made an accord with Gaspar Millazo, Bonanno's fellow Castellammarese at that time, and together the two families had gotten a hold on bootleggers in the Motor City. So much so that Moe Dalitz, the admiral of "the Little Jewish Navy," had been forced to move his base of operations to the other side of Lake Erie, to Cleveland, where he established his Mayfield Road Gang. It had worked out well for both. Zerelli was able to make his family in Detroit a powerful one and we already know that Dalitz did the same in Cleveland and elsewhere. Actually, it had been a noncontentious move on the part of Dalitz, one that worked out so well for him that he never had any animosity towards Zerelli and had worked very well with him on matters of mutual interest.

Furthermore, Joe Bonanno had a pleasant accord with Zerelli based on their long association together on The Commission. He had already discussed his plans, his generalities, with the New York members of The Commission, as he had informed his men at the ranch in Tucson, and he had requested Zerelli to attend that meeting also, as the only non-New York Commission member invited. Therefore, he had already sounded Zerelli out before he travelled to Detroit for this meeting.

After the usual amenities, Bonanno got right down to business. "Joe," he said to Zerelli, "you know I am planning to move on Las Vegas. That's why I come to you today. I want your help."

"You know you have my support, Joe, but what is it exactly?" Zerelli replied.

"First of all, I need my back protected from Chicago. I know that when Tony Accardo finds out what my plans are, he will come first to you. I need to insure that, primarily, you will give him no help. I have that accord with the New York families. They will insure that no family east of Chicago fights me. You are the only family in the Midwest who can hurt me if you were to throw in with the other side. Nick Civella is dead in Kansas City and the rest of his top men are in jail. I have no fears there. Frank Balistrieri in Milwaukee is in prison and his two top men, his sons, have been scared off with their prosecution in Kansas City, the 'Strawman Case,' as they call it. They are free only because their father pled guilty in return for the severance of their case. There is no other threat I fear. There is no more Cleveland family to speak of. The Smaldone family in Denver is too weak, Carlos Marcello is in prison and there is nothing left in New Orleans. I can't worry about Los Angeles and San Diego because they belong to Chicago, but they are not forces to be contended with anyway. In Phoenix and Tucson, of course, I have no fears. There is only one family I must be concerned with and that is your family here in Detroit."

"What do you propose?" Zerelli asked, getting right to the point.

"I propose that you send twenty or so of your men to Las Vegas to stand beside the one hundred or so I will bring there," Joe responded.

"Twenty is too many, I can't spare twenty. But, first of all, we must discuss what I would be standing to gain from throwing in with you."

Bonanno had certainly anticipated that response. "You will gain exactly in proportion to how you support me. I am taking over the Star immediately. If I send one hundred men and you send twenty, you will get twenty percent of the action. Then as I build Camelot, you will gain the exact percentage of the money you invest in its construction and the number of men you send to help me. I feel twenty is just right. You would have twenty percent of the 'key employees', twenty percent of the profits, and twenty percent of the skim."

"Joe, before we go any further, let me ask you this. You told The Commission that you had Moe Dalitz. Can I really believe that is true? He had been so close to Chicago for so many years. If I could really believe that, I would be much more able to make up my mind." Zerelli had leaned forward in his chair to press this point.

"I'll make a deal with you, Joe. Talk to Moe Dalitz himself. Go out there and discuss it with him. I am so certain of his participation with us, I will present this proposition to you. After you talk with Dalitz, if you are not completely satisfied, I will not press you any further. As a matter of fact, when you leave Las Vegas, come to my ranch in Tucson and we will settle this there. Now you have an idea of our proposition. Consider it and we will finalize it in Tucson after you check with Dalitz." Bonanno seemed satisfied that when Zerelli sat down with Dalitz, his concerns would be alleviated. He left Detroit feeling very good about himself and his situation.

When Joe Bonanno left Detroit, he flew to Kennedy Airport where he was met by Paulie Primosa and John Morales, two of his top men. They drove into Manhattan over the Triborough Bridge and into a suite at the Sheraton Centre Towers on Seventh Avenue, just a couple of blocks from the old Park Sheraton where Albert Anastasia and Arnold Rothstein had been killed. Joe had not wanted to meet in Brooklyn where his presence would be a beacon.

They were soon joined by Michael Immaculata and Angelo Annunciata.

Joe opened the meeting by asking how his capos had progressed in following his instructions given them at the Bar Bon Ranch in January. Had they decided which of their soldiers would join them in Las Vegas and which would be left in Brooklyn to carry on the mundane rackets of the Bonanno family there? Joe knew that some of the soldiers would be just what was ordered to carry out his agenda in Nevada whereas others were better suited to continue the gambling, loan sharking, labor racketeering and the other mob business in Brooklyn. He would not know which would be which but his capos would, which is why he left the specific choices to his top deputies.

When he was satisfied that his capos had given the decisions appropriate consideration and that their choices seemed to have been made with all due deliberation, he then confided in them as to his plans for the Bonanno family invasion of Las Vegas.

First of all he turned to Morales, his underboss. "John, I have decided you are to remain in Brooklyn where you will be in charge of all our affairs there. I know you will have a reduced number of *soldati,* but I am sure you can run things while most of us are involved in Las Vegas. If things get tight for you here, I give you the authority to 'make' some new members, bring in some new *soldati* to assist you with the routine things here. Things have been going smoothly here for the last couple years and I have the assurance from The Commission that they will keep their hands off our family here while we make our move into Nevada."

After Morales had assented—he was getting on in years and did not have the desire to move his base of operations—particularly when he did not have a fire in his gut to become involved in what would undoubtedly transpire in Vegas—Bonanno moved on.

"Paulie, Michael, and Angelo, I want you to move there now. Take those *soldati* with you who you have decided on and get them out there now. We will soon have to guard Moe Dalitz and his key people and the Vegas Star. I expect you all to be in place by February 15."

Joe paused and looked at his capos.

"Now here is our plan. Years ago I got to know a lawyer here named John Walsh. He did a few things for me and I got to trust him. He is a partner of William Herlands who was one of the key people under Thomas E. Dewey when Dewey was a special prosecutor here in New York in the mid-thirties and when he prosecuted Lucky Luciano and sent him away. Then when Herlands left the prosecutor's office, he hooked up with Walsh in the practice of law just a couple of blocks from here over in Rockefeller Center. So Walsh has the connections. And he is just as clean as he can be. I have sat down with him. He is willing to 'front' the Vegas Star for us as the president of a holding company which his law firm will set up for us. It will be called CamStar, Inc. As the president of this company he will oversee the operation of the Star. But even more important than that, he will oversee the construction of a new hotel we will call Camelot. It will be the ultimate hotel in Las Vegas. Bigger than Caesars Palace, Bally's, the Vegas Hilton, or anything else there now. Even bigger than this new Mirage which will be built, and Excalibur, an even bigger hotel which is to be constructed across from the Tropicana way down on the Strip. Camelot will be the grandest hotel ever built anywhere. There will be nothing like it. Now Walsh has a close friend, a man named Ford in Detroit who also has been a prosecutor and who is a distant relative of the Henry Ford family. He has talked to Ford and Ford is willing to be involved with us also. They will be our fronts. Men who can withstand any scrutiny the gaming authorities may give them. They are both in a position to show the amount of money they will make as our primary investors in CamStar. So we should have no trouble hiding behind them. Now, of course, we move Moe Dalitz in. He and his people will run the casino at the Star and later at Camelot. We will hire a general manager who has expertise to run the hotel side of the operation without knowledge that we are the principals in his hotels. One who can be licensed without undue trouble."

Bonanno paused. It was his general strategy when addressing his troops to pause, not only for effect, but to gauge his audience. Were they with him steadfastly; were they paying attention; did they understand? On this occasion, he felt they were with him in all respects.

He continued. "Of course, the main purpose for being in Vegas is the skim. That is where the money is for us. We let Walsh and Ford take a big percentage of the legitimate profit—that is why they are willing to go with us. But we take all of the skim. That's what we have Dalitz for. He and his crew, they're the grandfathers of skim. What they learned in Cuba and in their casinos in Ohio and Kentucky they brought with them decades ago to Las Vegas. Even with the tight security these days they know how to get the skim out. That is why we need Moe Dalitz and his people.

"So what we have is two very clean fronts—Walsh and Ford. They can withstand any investigation. Dalitz is already licensed, so are his key people. We will need a general manager who can be kept in the dark on the hotel side and who can be easily licensed. We will find one. Now it will be the job of you people to protect them. When Chicago finds out just what we are up to there is going to be trouble. Big trouble. We must protect Dalitz and his key people from them. We must protect the Star now and Camelot later. That is why we need you and your *soldati* out there now. To get in place to do that. As soon as Chicago learns that the Star has been sold they will investigate to find who has purchased it. They won't get too far finding out who Walsh and Ford represent, but when they find out that Dalitz will be operating the casino, then is when the trouble will start. We must demonstrate to Chicago that it is a done deal and that we are so strong that we can protect Dalitz and his people from them. Now, are there any questions?"

Paulie Primosa had one. "What about Walsh and Ford, do they need protection?"

"We will gauge that as we go along," Bonanno replied. "Not now, there does not seem to be any reason to believe they will be in any physical danger now."

When there did not seem to be any further discussion necessary, Joe handed envelopes to the three capos who would be moving to Las Vegas. "Here's some cash to move yourselves and your men out there," he said. "Now there is one more thing I want to discuss with you each. John, you stay here but your responsibilities will be greater and your job harder. We will increase your percentage of what you have been receiving five per cent. Angelo, Michael, and Paul, you will be under great pressure. I understand that. I increase your percentage fifteen per cent. And each of the *soldati* who go west will be increased ten per cent. With the understanding that all of you will have so much more that those percentages will represent large amounts. My son, Bill, will move to Las Vegas also and he will be in charge of our finances. What you need he will have right on the spot."

Joe paused again. "Now one more thing. Paulie, arrange for the transportation of our weapons and ammunition out there. Truck it out, it cannot be taken through airline detection equipment. Assign three or four *soldati* to truck it out. When you get to Vegas, Bill will have a large suite where we will keep it at the Star. To equip our men. So you get what you need from Bill. Money and guns. Also, Bill has gotten in touch with a real estate agent there who has begun to line up homes for all of you, mostly in North Vegas in the same neighborhood. So the wives will have each other for support and so it will not be a difficult problem to make such a move."

Having outlined his agenda to his people as he had promised he would during the sit-down at the Bar Bon Ranch, Joe Bonanno then took them all across Seventh Avenue to the Stage Delicatessen where he had made arrangements for a large corner table. The gigantic pastrami and corned beef sandwiches on rye were not what this group usually feasted on, but Joe felt that if they were to move on Las Vegas they should get used to changing the stilted habits and try something new for a change—even in their dining habits. The famous New York cheesecake featured at the Stage Delicatessen capped the meal perfectly.

The broad strokes of his agenda which had been set at the Bar Bon Ranch in January were now sketched in in more detail for his men. They would now have a clearer idea of what they intended to do in Vegas. Joe was satisfied he had the continued support of all his troops. He then flew back to Tucson, this time connecting through the Dallas/Fort Worth Airport. (There are no direct flights from New York to Tucson.) He did not care to connect through O'Hare. The less contact he had with Chicago the better!

Bonanno now awaited further contact with Joe Zerelli following Zerelli's meeting with Dalitz. Within ten days, Zerelli had completed his talk with Dalitz and flown into Tucson to confer with Bonanno. It was decided that, since Dalitz had left no doubt with Zerelli of his intentions, that Zerelli would come in for fifteen per cent of the action. He would supply fifteen soldiers to be led by one of his capos who would move to Las Vegas but spend some of his time back home in Detroit. This would be Pete Scarfatti, one of Zerelli's "warriors." He had had a hand in the killing of Jimmy Hoffa in 1975 and had been rewarded with his own crew as a result. He had been convicted of a gambling violation in Judge Gus Cifelli's courtroom in the late 1970s but spent just a few years in prison and was now out and ready for the type of action the foray into Las Vegas would entail. Things were coming together for the Bonanno plans for Las Vegas.

MEANWHILE, back in Chicago, Tony Spilotro brought some news to his boss, Joe Ferriola. He had begun to hear of some suspicious activity in Las Vegas. Ferriola summoned Gus Alex from his home on Galt Ocean Mile in Fort Lauderdale, where he had been spending some time during the winter season, and told him to get out to Los Angeles where he was to meet with Sidney Korshak. If anything was moving out in

Las Vegas, Korshak and/or Spilotro should know about it. Korshak was living in the prestigious Bel-Air section of Los Angeles, right in the shadow of the famous Hotel Bel-Air, and also had a home in Palm Springs. This well-established attorney had powerful connections throughout the world, but especially in Los Angeles and Las Vegas. He was expected to be on top of all developments there and to keep the Chicago mob advised of all of them.

Ferriola also sent word out to Joe Batters through Donald Angelini, the capo who had been designated by Ferriola to be the liaison with Accardo and to be their man in Las Vegas.

Once Alex and Angelini had made contact with Korshak and Accardo at their respective homes in Palm Springs, they sat down with Ferriola. Alex reported first. "First of all, I talked to Sidney. He hasn't gotten anything more definite but he will get into Vegas and talk to his people there. Then I went over to the country club and talked to Joe Batters. He told me he had just talked to Donald, and he knew what was going on. He told me that he had told you, Joe, to make this your number one priority. He has a strong instinct here that something is wrong. He has a real dislike for this fucking Joe Bananas. He tells me he wants you in Vegas too, Donald. We got to find out what's up there, it's the most important thing we got going now. We can't lose what we got in Vegas!"

Angelini affirmed that those were his instructions to the boss, Ferriola, from the "man," the *consigliere* Tony Accardo.

The first hard-core information came from Korshak. Through one of his sources at the Nevada Gaming Control Commission in Las Vegas, Korshak learned that John Holmes had resigned as general manager of the Four Aces, a mid-sized downtown hotel-casino, and had applied for a license to become the general manager of the Vegas Star. Looking further, Korshak had discovered that the Vegas Star was about to change hands and that the Gaming Control Board had recently reported its investigation to the Gaming Control Commission, favorably recommending that the new ownership be approved by the commission. The new owners had impeccable backgrounds as bankers, lawyers, and businessmen from New York and Detroit. None of them had ever been associated, as far as the Gaming Control Board could determine, with any organized crime figure or activity. The primary investor, who would own twenty-six per cent, was one John Walsh. He had been a successful attorney in midtown Manhattan for years and, in fact, was a partner in Herlands and Walsh, a major New York law firm. Furthermore, William Herlands also had an outstanding reputation. Why, he had even been associated with Thomas E. Dewey, the New York prosecutor, when Dewey et al., successfully prosecuted the famous Lucky Luciano and sent him away—for good. How could you suspect a man like John Walsh? Another prime investor, for fifteen per cent, was a banker from Detroit named Donald Ford, who also had been a prosecutor at one time, and was distantly related to the Ford family of Detroit. Those were pretty good credentials.

Sidney Korshak, however, had been in this business a long time. After all, he was the man who sat in on some of the sessions at the Bismarck Hotel in Chicago in 1940, when Frank Nitti and Paul Ricca, with Tony Accardo in the shadows, were dealing with Willie Bioff and George Browne of the Stage Employees Union in the Hollywood Extortion Case. He was also the attorney who had approved the contract in 1956 between Tony Accardo and Fox Head Brewing Company when they put Accardo on the payroll. He went way back with the mob. He knew something was up now. What it was, however, he knew not.

The rat came out of the woodpile, however, when Paulie Primosa, Michael "The Clean One" Immaculata, and Angelo "The Ape" Annunciata and dozens of their men moved into Las Vegas on February 15. When Tony Spilotro got wind of this he put in an emergency call to Donald Angelini, his capo. Angelini hurried to the home of Joe Ferriola in Oak Brook, a suburb of Chicago which now rivaled River Forest in opulence, and in mob leaders, since Joey Aiuppa also lived there before he was sent away in the "Strawman" case.

Ferriola immediately realized they were in trouble. "Donald, get your ass out to Palm Springs and fill Joe Batters in. As a matter of fact, I'll go with you. This is the most important thing we've got. Call him and tell him we're coming in tomorrow. Where will we stay?"

The call was made and the two Chicago mobsters moved into Gene Autry's beautiful hotel, on Palm Canyon Drive just down the road from Bob Hope's spectacular home up on the hill and not too far from Frank Sinatra Drive and the home of that skinny kid from Hoboken who was not skinny in any way anymore.

They met Joe Batters in the dining room of the Indian Wells Country Club overlooking the golf course. When Joe heard the story he had one immediate reaction. "We've got to protect what we got. The first thing," he said to Ferriola, "is for you and me to get to The Commission. I'll call those assholes today and line us up to come in there. Let's see who I know there now? There's this Nicky Scarfo, from Angelo Bruno's family in Philadelphia. There's Phil Lombardo from the Genovese family. I think his underboss, Tony Salerno, may be handling things there now. That's a strong family right now. They got Chin Gigante, the guy who hit Costello, as a right-hand there and Gerry Catena, another strong guy, is the *consigliere*. The Gambinos, they got John Gotti after he killed Paul Castellano. For the Lucchese family, it's this "Tony Ducks" Corallo with this "Christy Tick" as the *consigliere* and Sal Santoro as the underboss. Then in the Colombo family they got Carmine Persico as the boss, Jerry Langella right up there, and Persico's brother, Allie, is the *consigliere*. Then of course, the other family is that prick's, Bonanno. He'll be there himself, don't doubt that. I can see the bastard now with that slick smile on his fucking face!"

The Commission meeting was set up soon. It was held in an old roadhouse over the George Washington Bridge near Fort Lee, New Jersey. Present were Carmine Persico, "Tony Ducks" Corallo, John Gotti, "Fat Tony" Salerno, Joe Bonanno, himself, and Nicky Scarfo. Zerelli had been invited but did not attend.

Tony Accardo got right down to business, as always. "Fellas, first of all I bring Joe Ferriola with me. He is my new boss in Chicago and he will represent Chicago most of the time from now on. Now I want to get down to the serious business that has brought us together today. I want to accuse Joe Bananas here of going into Las Vegas! We all know that's against the rules. Ten years ago we sat down, none of you was here then except Bananas and me but this Commission decided then and it's still the fuckin' rule today that Chicago has got Las Vegas and the rest of you has got Atlantic City. Now if that rule isn't still good, tell me now!"

Nobody said a word. After a few moments, Accardo went on. "Now I think somebody in this room is violatin' that rule. And I'm looking right at him!" He put his steely eyes right on Joe Bonanno.

Bonanno looked him in the eye, but said nothing. By saying nothing, he accomplished two things. He tacitly admitted the accusation and he steadfastly challenged Accardo to continue.

"I want a vote right now. I want to know if this is sanctioned by The Commission. If it is, then I'll know how to deal with it in my own way. If it's not then let's say it's not and order this man to get his ass out of my territory!" Accardo spoke harshly, looked at the group, and sat down.

Bonanno still said nothing. Neither did anyone else. Finally, John

Gotti spoke. "I think both of you's should leave the room while the rest of us discuss this." All approved and the two J. B.'s left the room without so much as looking at each other.

Salerno, Persico, Corallo, Gotti, and Scarfo then conferred. They had all been in on the move of Bonanno heretofore. They had been given to understand that it was in their best interests, financially, if Bonanno was to succeed in taking away a big hunk of what the Chicago family controlled in Las Vegas.

Accardo and Bonanno, who had not spoken to each other, moved back into the room, along with Ferriola.

Again, it was Gotti who spoke. "It is our decision that we table this matter for now. We'll sleep on it. We can't decide right now."

Accardo stood up. Without a word, he motioned to Ferriola, and the Chicago pair moved out. As Ferriola drove him back into Manhattan, Accardo said to him: "This is the same as if they voted for him, against us. We know what we gotta do, Joe."

The fat was in the fire.

13

Jack and Glory Meet and Settle In

JANET Zaleski, now Glory Praise, took to her new job with the enthusiasm she had formerly given to her tennis and basketball. She wasn't much of a dancer but she was a quick study. Thanks to Debbie Lee, who gave her great encouragement and a few tips, she slowly began to get the hang of the kick-line. It wasn't all that hard once you picked it up and, with her physical conditioning and her natural ability, she broadened her talent every day.

She and Betty Bjornson, the other new showgirl, became good friends. Betty had struggled to get a stage name. Finally, with the counsel of Glory and Debbie, she settled on one. Boots Barnes.

Glory and Boots decided to be roommates. They were directed by Debbie to the management of the Alexis Park. The Alexis Park is a resort on Harmon Avenue, a more or less residential area eight blocks or so off the Strip. Harmon Avenue runs between Tropicana Avenue and Flamingo Road up alongside the Aladdin and therefore the Alexis Park is twelve blocks or so from the Tropicana. It is generally for tourists who want to stay someplace quiet, away from the Strip, but don't want to be too far away. In fact, it has what they call an "ESP Membership," for Especially Special Persons, who guarantee to stay twelve times a year for a special lower rate, $85, for each stay. Each suite consists of a small kitchen, a parlor, a bedroom with a fireplace, and a bath with a jacuzzi. Since the Trop kept ten rooms there on a constant basis, the girls were given a special group rate and the right to all the amenities, including a well-equipped health club. Not that Glory and Boots needed to keep in shape, but Glory, especially, felt the need to keep her muscles taut with daily light weight lifting, alternating different sets of muscles every other day.

What got to be a problem was Joe Agosto. He hadn't used the "casting couch" when he approved the audition of Glory but then perhaps because of the presence of Steve North and Mel Greenberg he had been somewhat inhibited. But now he began to make his presence felt. When Glory finished her bit on the line for the Folies, he began to show up. At first she was able to duck behind Boots and protest that they had "other plans." But as the weeks went by, burly Joe became more obtrusive.

Finally, one night in March, he did everything but twist her arm. She finally agreed to a quick dinner down the Strip at Bally's. The spot, called Caruso's, is a favorite of the locals, even though it is located in one of the Strip hotels. It is not as grand as Barrymore's there, and many prefer Gigi's in the same hotel. But, especially for those lovers of Italian cuisine, Caruso's is a fine spot. When they finished, Agosto insisted on "showing" Glory the little suite he maintained in Bally's away from his Tropicana. Defiantly, Glory resisted. She had not come this far in her life to lose her virginity to the likes of a hood like Joe Agosto.

Then into her life came John Holmes. "Jack," as she was soon to call him, had been an agent for the Gaming Control Board. He had been hired by the legendary Tom Carrigan and worked with many of the best agents the GCB ever had, such as Dennis Gomes, Elton Vogel, Larry Whelan, Bob McGuire, Rich Carr, Dennis Healy, and Gary Gleason, and had partnered with Duane Noyes, the former FBI agent who went to work as a gaming investigator when he quit the Bureau. Holmes had learned his trade well. Like Gomes, who had gone into the administrative side of the business as GM at the Aladdin after he quit the Board, Jack Holmes eventually went to work for the casinos. He did a stint in corporate security with Warren Salisbury and Chuck Thomas at Caesars Palace, then in the administrative end with Benny Binion at the Horseshoe, downtown. He had no problem—in view of his background—getting a license from his former colleagues. Thanks to Jim Powers, the director of corporate security at the Golden Nugget's many casinos in Nevada and Atlantic City, Jack was recommended to Steve Wynn, the owner of the Golden Nugget, and groomed for an eventual top spot there after a short apprenticeship at the Four Aces.

Now, however, he was approached by John Walsh who himself was the new owner of the Vegas Star. He asked Jack to dinner.

That night they met at the Golden Steer on Sahara Avenue. While they dined on the specialties of the house, pheasant and guinea hen, John Walsh broached the subject to John Holmes.

"Jack," Walsh told him, "we're looking for just the right man. Now you know I am associated with one of the great prosecutors in our nation's history, Bill Herlands, and he has suggested to me that we look for a man with a law enforcement background but one who has gained considerable experience in the gaming business, especially on the hotel side. We are thinking of you. We have contacted guys like Joe Yablonski and Herb Hawkins, the former FBI chiefs here, Ed Hagerty at Bally's, and Chief Justice John Mowbray of the Nevada Supreme Court. They endorse you highly. We have also gone to your former boss, Tom Carrigan, who is now living in Reno, as you know. We made what you guys call a full field investigation. Now, would you be interested in us?"

Holmes paused for a moment and then said, "If you can offer better than what I have now, I'd check it out."

"What we offer is the top spot, you'd be our GM."

"Fine, I'd be interested. Of course, who wouldn't? Except I don't know anything about you guys," Holmes said.

"Between me and a man named Donald Ford from Detroit we own over forty per cent. We are the prime investors. He also is a former prosecutor, with the Strike Force there, and is a relative of the Ford Motor Company family in Detroit. The other investors number about a dozen and none has more than seven or eight per cent, so I'm the biggest by far and Donald Ford is the only other substantial one."

"Well, sounds very good to me. Let me check with my buddies at the GCB and get back to you. I would imagine the salary and other benefits would be in the seven-figure range, commensurate with what other GM's here make?"

"That is precisely the figure we are discussing," Walsh responded.

When it was all said and done, Holmes had checked out the group with the Gaming Control Board and found no problems. Once his attorneys had examined the contract offered him, Holmes signed and moved his things over to the Vegas Star. He had no idea he was working for Joe Bonanno. Obviously, Walsh and Ford did. And they had slipped a clause in the boiler plate of the contract which got by Holmes and his attorneys. It was not quite as iron-clad a contract as Holmes felt it was. He could lose everything if he got out of control. But he was unaware of that.

The first thing Holmes tried to do—and the first time he began to realize he wasn't in firm control—was to hire a director of security. He had gone to his old boss up in Reno, Tom Carrigan. Carrigan was now retired from the Gaming Control Board but consulting casinos regarding security. As sharp and honest a man as ever had been in Nevada gaming enforcement, Carrigan recommended Al Zimmerman, a former FBI agent in Las Vegas who had done exceptional work in the Bureau's Organized Crime Program. When Zimmerman indicated that he might come out of retirement to become the chief of security at the Vegas Star, Holmes took it up with the board of directors of CamStar, the holding company which owned the Star and the hotel which would soon be built, the Camelot. Walsh was CamStar's chairman of the board. Ford was president, and both were members of the board. There were no outside directors. Obviously, Walsh and Ford ran the holding company. Or so it appeared to Holmes. Joe Bonanno had another idea as to who should be director of security. He had the first vote. And the last vote. And the veto power.

Joe Bonanno's choice was Richard Becker. Dick Becker had been a member of Metro, the combined police department and sheriff's office which enforces the criminal law in Clark County where Las Vegas is located. He had gotten the job thanks to Harry Reid, who at the time was on the Gaming Control Commission and was to become a United States Senator from Nevada. He was known as "Reid's ribbon clerk." Now, in Las Vegas, that is not all that bad. One of the Title III intercepts monitored by Bill Ouseley in the "Strawman Case" in Kansas City, had indicated that Joe Agosto or one of the other people working for Nick Civella in Las Vegas had a "clean face." Some people had uncharitably interpreted that as a reference to Harry Reid, meaning he was "on the pad." But that was never substantiated and in Las Vegas Harry Reid is a powerful political heavyweight. So even if you are known as Harry Reid's "ribbon clerk" there, you have some clout.

The first clash between Holmes and Walsh came over Becker. When the dust had died down, Holmes realized that he might be general manager of the Vegas Star, but that when push came to shove, it was John Walsh who called the shots. And Walsh knew in turn that it was Joe Bonanno who held the rudder.

That night Holmes went for a walk. Since the Star was located far down on the Strip between the Marina and the Tropicana, he quickly came to the Trop and decided to drown his sorrows with a quick libation in the Tropics, the bar and restaurant in the new Island Tower there. It was late at night, early in the morning actually, but Jack was in no hurry to get home to Joyce, his wife, and their two kids.

It just so happened that on that same night Glory Praise and Boots Barnes decided to have a quick drink and a snack in the Tropics after their show on the way back home to the Alexis Park. This was highly unusual for them, but Glory and Boots had just gotten "off probation" at the Folies Bergère and were now given permanent status. They decided that a quiet little celebration was in order.

Jack Holmes observed the pair as they glided into the Tropics and was impressed. But Jack Holmes had seen hundreds of showgirls in his dozen years in the business. In addition, he was a happily married man. Not one to dally. There was something about the blonde, however. She had all the beauty and poise of a showgirl, but she seemed a cut above what Jack had observed in the past. Something set her off from the crowd—not necessarily her physical appearance or how she handled herself. It was something else; something Jack couldn't immediately put his finger on.

As unusual as it was for Glory and Boots to linger at the Trop after their show, it was just as unusual for Jack Holmes to send a drink over to a showgirl. But it must have been an unusual night. Jack waved to the maitre d', not some ordinary waiter. The maitre d', as would almost anyone in his position in Vegas, had recognized Mr. Holmes the moment he walked in. After all, the announcement of his appointment as general manager of the Vegas Star had been front page news in the *Review-Journal* and the *Sun* as well as a lead item on the local TV news. Al Tobin of the *Review-Journal* had done a follow-up feature on Holmes, and Luke Michaels and Richard Urey of Channel 13, the ABC affiliate, had him on their Sunday morning "Newsmakers" interview program. Mike O'Callaghan, the former governor, then a columnist on

Hank Greenspun's Las Vegas *Sun,* had devoted an entire column to Holmes.

So, when the maitre d' himself brought the drinks to Glory and Boots's table, they knew there was something unusual going on. Then he informed them, in his usual solemn manner, that "Mr. Holmes, Mr. Jack Holmes, of the Vegas Star, sends his compliments to the ladies." Ordinarily, Glory, although maybe not Boots, would have graciously declined. In fact, she started to. But when she looked over at her would-be benefactor, she quickly put the name proffered by the maitre d' with the face. She realized that this was no Vegas vagabond hustler, no Strip sharpie, and no tourist from Des Moines on the make. She quickly changed her mind. She returned Jack's smile. Encouraged thusly, Holmes left his seat at the bar and came to their table. "I'm John Holmes, general manager of the Vegas Star, and if I'm not being too forward, I'd like to join you for a few moments before I head home to my family."

Holmes had quickly disarmed himself as was his intention. He wanted these girls, especially the blonde, to know that whatever it was he had on his mind, it wasn't lust. Or, at least not blatant lust. Glory smiled and Boots giggled. Holmes sat down.

Holmes extracted his business card from his card case and gave it to Glory. Now he had made three subliminal moves. First, he had demonstrated he was a man of distinction, not some ordinary customer of the bar. Second, he had indicated that he was a family man, not out on the make. Third, he had clearly made it known that it was Glory, not Boots, in whom he might be interested.

It wasn't as if the thunderbolt struck immediately, but there obviously was a feeling of attraction that emanated from Jack Holmes to Glory Praise and then was reflected back. Whatever it was that Jack had observed from a distance in Glory that set her apart from other showgirls, that same subconscious something mirrored itself in Jack in the estimation of Glory. Their initial meeting lasted about twenty minutes. As he was about to take his leave, Jack looked into Glory's big blue eyes and asked: "May I give you a call sometime?" Glory responded hesitantly, "We live at the Alexis Park."

That was that. Jack soon had other things on his mind, the nagging thoughts that everything at the Vegas Star was not quite what he had expected the position of general manager would be. He motioned to one of the car hikers who quickly drove his car from the nearby parking space to the entry way of the Star. He drove home to Joyce, his good wife, and their lovely kids.

Other events would soon push his thoughts away from Glory. It would be a rough ride for Jack Holmes at the helm of the Vegas Star.

14

Moe Dalitz Comes Out; So Does Glory

IT was time for Moe Dalitz to take hold and do his thing. As Joe Bonanno had recounted to his capos at their sit-down at the Bar Bon, Dalitz had been approached by his longtime associate and ally, Meyer Lansky, before the famed "chairman of the board" of organized crime died in 1983. As a result of the Lansky connection, Dalitz had agreed to meet with Bonanno. After Dalitz was convinced that Bonanno had the motivation, the strength, and the power to do what he intended in Las Vegas and, after meeting with old friend Joe Zerelli and becoming aware that The Commission would secretly back Bonanno's play, Dalitz had decided to throw in with Bonanno. Bonanno's plan, as presented to his capos at the Bar Bon, was in motion.

Dalitz had been with Tony Accardo and his Chicago mob since their meeting at the Stardust and then in the Monte Carlo Room of the Desert Inn in the 1950s. All had gone well for both sides until Sam Giancana, a horse's ass of the first order, had sent his mirror-image to Las Vegas to be his representative. Dalitz never could understand how a man so capable as Joe Batters had given his mantle to one such as Giancana. Was it any wonder that such a man would appoint such a fool as Tony Spilotro to be the "man" in such an important part of the Chicago mob's operation as Las Vegas?

Dalitz had had many clashes with Spilotro since "The Ant" had arrived in Las Vegas in 1971. First, Spilotro had set up at Circus-Circus, where he operated out of the gift shop for which he had been able to obtain a license under the name of his wife, Nancy Stewart. Then he used the poker room at the Dunes and the clubhouse of the Las Vegas Country Club for his sit-downs. Soon he would buy a jewelry store off the Strip and name it the Gold Rush. All of that was well and good, none of those locations represented anything which was of any consequence to Moe Dalitz. Circus-Circus and the Dunes had nothing to do with the operations of the United Hotel Corporation which was the holding company for the hotels under Dalitz's umbrella. At one time or another, well into the early eighties, Dalitz had interests in the Stardust, the Desert Inn, the Riviera, the Hacienda, the Fremont, and, at least to some extent, the new Sundance (he owned the land on which it was built on Fremont Street).

Dalitz had truly become "the godfather of Las Vegas." Without any question he was the most powerful man in the Sin Capital of the U.S.A. Not Paul Laxalt, who would become a power in the United States Senate, trading on his close friendship and access to Ronald Reagan. Not Frank Sinatra or Wayne Newton, although they had great leverage because of their draw to any hotel which could sign them to a contract. Not any of the many mayors, none of whom became a power in his own right. No, whenever it came to any important job in Vegas—whether it was to build a Catholic cathedral such as Guardian Angel or a major hospital such as Sunrise—it was Moe Dalitz who got the call to line up the support needed from anybody who was anybody. Due to the unique nature of Las Vegas—and, for that matter, the entire state of Nevada—there has been no one in its history with the behind-the-scenes power of Moe Dalitz. And obviously not *all* his power was behind the scenes.

It was now time for Dalitz to come out from behind the bushes. Dalitz was the man who would give Bonanno's dream of conquest credibility and who would give Joe Bonanno's operations the expertise it needed to succeed. It was time to lend his expertise to the gaming end of the Vegas Star and then later to set up the casino which would be the ultimate objective of Bonanno's dream, the gigantic Camelot.

John Holmes was the man out front, the man who gave credibility to the Bonanno operations, and the man who had so easily been licensed by his former colleagues in the Gaming Control Commission, but Holmes would be relegated to the management of the hotel side of the operation and, even there, would be kept pretty much in the dark. When push came to shove, it would be John Walsh and Donald Ford, the ostensible owners, who would have the final word on any project Holmes might be prepared to block. Besides, the gaming end of the operation was where Bonanno and Dalitz had all their chips—literally and figuratively. The hotel end of the business should stand on its own feet, possibly make a few bucks, but that wasn't the big concern. There is no great concern even about the bottom line at the casino because the *sine qua non* is the skim. Without the ability to skim properly—to steal the money won by the casino at the tables and machines after it was taken from the "dropboxes" under the tables and before it could be officially counted in the counting room—there would be little or no reason for anyone like Bonanno or Accardo and company to be in the gaming business. Obviously, for the legitimate businessman, though, that position is overstated since gaming stocks such as Aztar, Golden Nugget, Circus-Circus, Caesars World, Bally, Promus, Showboat, and Hilton are favorites on Wall Street. Donald Trump is not into Atlantic City because he is a chump. He has done very well in his hotel-casinos without skimming. At least until recently. So have Steve Wynn, Kirk Kerkorian, the Boyd family, and Howard Hughes. They have run clean operations where the bottom line has not been diminished by skim. They have hired security directors who are tough and honest, people like Jim Powers, Ed Hagerty, Warren Salisbury, Emmett Michaels, John Schrieber, Carl Underhill, and Red Campbell, and given them the wherewithal and the backing to do their jobs properly. In the hotel-casinos run by Moe Dalitz, however, the hidden owners, the mobsters, have been uninterested in the public profit and loss statements. It is the nonpublic, under-the-table skim they have their eyes set on. The "21 holes in the bucket" which skim master Carl Thomas talked about in the basement conference with the Civella family of La Costa Nostra in Kansas City. Carl Thomas may have been the latter-day sultan of skim but Moe Dalitz was the mentor, the man who charted the course, paved the way, the pioneer and still the acknowledged emperor of all he surveyed. If Babe Ruth had been the Sultan of Swat, Moe Dalitz was the King of Skim.

JACK Holmes was sick. As soon as he realized that Moe Dalitz was moving his people into the casino at the Vegas Star, and would be doing the same at Camelot when it was ready, he realized just how much he had been duped. What a chump! Nobody knew better than Jack Holmes what and who Moe Dalitz represented. With his background in the gaming industry Holmes was nobody's fool. He went to John Walsh, his only contact with management. Obviously, he got no solace from Walsh. In his position, Jack was able to learn much of what was going on in "his" casino. He was the general manager, after all, of the entire operation. It didn't take him long to confirm his suspicions that Dalitz had set up a most efficient skim operation.

Holmes found, for instance, that with the connivance of Dick Becker, the chief of security, the "eye in the sky" cameras were not all in the appropriate places. Specifically, he determined that the camera in the counting room itself, where each morning the official tally of the previous day's cash receipts was made, was not recording several of the "dropboxes" there. The cameras were shielded from several of these boxes. Obviously, during the early morning hours it was simple for someone to enter the counting room, with the connivance of Becker, and to skim the dropboxes which were blocked from the view of the security cameras. Later the official count would be made, in the presence of the appropriate authorities representing the Internal Revenue Service and the Gaming Control Board, and those boxes which were shielded from the view of the cameras simply did not contain anywhere near the original amount they had when the security guards brought them there from the casino floor. Holmes also was able to learn that the shift managers were in cahoots with the floor men, the pit bosses, and the dealers, many of whom had been put in place by Dalitz. At appointed times, when assured by Becker that there would be a "malfunction" of the camera recording their every move, these casino employees would filch large numbers of the bills which should have been "dropped" into the boxes and later make them available to Dalitz's operatives who, of course, insured that they never got to the counting room. He further learned that two key security guards who worked for Becker would regularly raid the lock-boxes they were assigned to take from under the tables to be placed in the counting room. All in all, Holmes learned, just about every one of the "21 holes" was being utilized by the operatives of the master mentor, Dalitz. That is what made him sick.

Sicker yet he became when he learned that Dalitz's men were working the "fill slip skim." A "fill slip" is the form a dealer makes out when he or she needs additional cash after taking several "hits" at his black-jack table or crap table. The procedure is that it must be initialed, signifying approval, by the floorman who oversees the dealer and by the pit boss who oversees the floorman. This chain of command is designed to insure that the dealers are not cheating. But, Holmes learned, in certain of the casino pits, all three members of the chain of command were in on the scheme and were conniving to perform the fill slip skim. Of course, this was all done under the command of the Dalitz shift manager and with the ultimate approval of Dominic Lombardi, the casino manager hired over the objections of Holmes, who had been overruled by Walsh.

The night he learned of the fill slip skim, Holmes felt that he had suffered the final blow. There could be no doubt that he was just a front for what was going on at the Vegas Star and would be into the operation at Camelot when that was constructed. His ego was shattered. He had obviously not been hired for his ability. He had been hired as a facade for the CamStar Holding Company and their hotels. What a fool!

What could he do, however? When he had first complained to Walsh, the "hole" in his contract had been pointed out to him. If he resigned he would lose the million-dollar contract he had. He and Joyce had begun to live up to that standard. If he quit he would likely be unemployable in the gaming industry, Dalitz would see to that. He was truly on the horns of the proverbial dilemma.

Rather than go home to Joyce and the kids, he thought of the beautiful blonde showgirl from the Folies. It happened to be a Monday night and the Tropicana showroom was dark. It would be her night off. He recalled that her name was Glory and that she had told him she lived at the Alexis Park. There couldn't be too many "Glorys" at the Alexis Park. He took a chance. Luckily she answered the phone. Or Boots did, and put her on. Would she meet him for a drink? After some hesitation, she agreed. But she didn't care to make it a night out, how about meeting there at the Alexis Park, just for a quick snack and drink, at Pegasus, the resort's own restaurant-bar? There would be a quintet playing and it would be a quiet spot.

As the saying goes, one thing led to another. "A quick drink" led to dinner. That would soon lead to a full evening of dinner and dancing, usually at Pegasus since it was somewhat out of the mainstream. Then it led to the inevitable. Boots had a date one Monday night, and Glory knew her suite mate would not return until the following afternoon for a nap before her show that night. Their suite at the Alexis Park would be Glory's for the next ten hours or so.

Jack had been after her to take the friendly relationship they were enjoying a little bit further. But at this point, Glory Praise was still Janet Zaleski, the same girl she had been when she left South Bend with Steve North to come to Las Vegas several months before. When Holmes repeated his request, at the end of the evening, that they "go someplace else," she shyly took his hand and led him down the resort path along the lighted man-made creek which reminded her of Judie Creek back home in Indiana.

They entered her suite on the second, top floor, overlooking one of the pools at the Alexis Park, and Jack softly took Glory into his arms and kissed her. Long and tenderly. He then gently pulled her into the bedroom. She tried to break the spell by disengaging with the excuse that she wanted to light the gas-fed fireplace in the bedroom. But her heart wasn't in the delay. When Jack persisted, she gave a long sigh and gave in. He gently placed her on the bed and began to undress her.

"Jack," she pleaded, ever so softly, "be gentle, this has never happened to me before."

Jack was startled. He couldn't imagine a Las Vegas showgirl who might possibly be a virgin! All of a sudden he realized what it was that attracted him so much to this beautiful girl. She had all the beauty and charm of the most lovely orchid but that flower had never been crushed! It still had the dew on its petals! No wonder he had caught an underlying mystique about this girl. She might be one of a kind in Las Vegas. The knowledge of her still-in-the-wrapper condition excited him as never before!

Jack was so tender that, for him, it was a magic moment only because he realized that he was the first for the beautiful Glory. For Glory, however painful, it was everything she had dreamed so many times it would be. How many times had she fantasized what it would be with Bobby Doran? Now here with Jack Holmes, a married man in love with his wife and a big time Las Vegas hotel man, it was not the ideal situation. And yet, she enjoyed it. She was not in love, but it was time and Jack had been so nice to her. And he was really a truly nice guy. She took what he gave to her and she enjoyed it.

When it was over, they lay in bed, both totally relaxed before the fireplace. Jack began to talk. He opened himself up to Glory about his problems at the Vegas Star like he never would to Joyce. He told her about Moe Dalitz, about the shielded cameras in the counting room and the "malfunctioning" eye in the sky. He even told her about the fill slip skim being operated at the Star. He told her that he felt he had been duped, that he was undoubtedly fronting for someone with hidden interests in the Star although he did not know who.

When he had exhausted the talk of his situation, he turned back over to Glory. Again, they slowly entwined with each other. Only this time, Jack was more passionate, more unafraid of hurting Glory. And this time, aware of the ambience of the act, Glory was unrestrained. Her natural athletic ability came to the fore and, although she engaged in nothing but the pure basics, she gave great pleasure to Jack and to herself. The transformation of Janet Zaleski into Glory Praise was now complete.

15

Jack and Glory Depart Las Vegas

BILL Richards was then serving as a special consultant on organized crime to the Chicago Crime Commission. While in Chicago on an assignment for the Crime Commission, Richards made contact with Nick Lupresto. Lupresto is a very highly placed member of Tony Accardo's Cosa Nostra family in Chicago. During the twenty-four years Richards had been an FBI agent in Chicago, Lupresto had been developed into what the FBI calls a "CTE," a top echelon criminal informant. For years, while Richards was assigned as an FBI agent in Chicago and even after he left the FBI, Lupresto furnished quality information on a quantity basis to Richards. When Richards was transferred from Chicago, Lupresto ceased to cooperate with the FBI. Although the FBI put extreme pressure on Lupresto to resume his informant status, he steadfastly refused to do so, saying Richards was the only one he trusted. While he continued to talk to Richards, and Richards used his information on behalf of the Chicago Crime Commission and to assist the FBI in their investigations, Lupresto had no contact with any law enforcement agency after Richards left the FBI in 1980.

While in Chicago, Richards met Lupresto at their usual meeting place, the dining room in the Union Railway Station just west of the Loop in Chicago. "None of us guys ever travels by train," Nick had told Richards years ago and they had used a corner booth in the dining room off the main waiting room for over a decade. Both enjoyed cherrystone clams and the ones at the Union Station were fresh and delicious.

On this occasion, Nick had some interesting information for Richards. "Joe Batters is tearing his hair out. That fucking Joe Bananas in New York and Arizona has gone into Las Vegas against the rule giving him and the other eastern mobs Atlantic City and us Las Vegas and he's making big moves out there. He's taken over the Vegas Star and put in a guy named Jack Holmes to run it for him. Joe and Ferriola went to The Commission to stop him but they won't do nothin'. Now we're getting ready to go to the mattresses. If The Commission won't stop Bananas we will. But there'll be blood on the Strip. We don't like that, it scares the tourists away, but Joe means to chop as many of Bananas's guys as he can and throw them out of our territory. It's going to be the bloodiest fight since Prohibition. You watch."

Richards took his information to the Chicago Crime Commission, informing the executive director of the Crime Commission, Pat Healy, of what he had heard. He then walked over to Binyon's, the restaurant just south of the Federal Building on Plymouth Court, and sat down with Pete Wacks and Art Pfizenmayer, the two veteran organized crime agents of the Chicago FBI. He generally apprised them, on a strictly confidential basis, of his information. He didn't have to tell then where he had gotten it—they knew.

It so happens that both the Chicago Crime Commission and the FBI work very closely with the U.S. Senate Permanent Subcommittee on Investigations, occasionally called the "The Rackets Committee." Sen. Bill Roth, Republican of Delaware, was the chairman of the subcommittee, and Sam Nunn, Democrat of Georgia, was the cochairman. Pat Healy felt the information was so sensitive and important that he asked Richards to go to Washington and sit down with Ralph Salerno, who was then working for the committee, and with Jim Mansfield, also with the committee. Salerno, the former chief of detectives on the Intelligence Unit of the New York Police Department, and Mansfield, are both buddies of Richards. In fact, Mansfield had been in the Marine

Corps, at Notre Dame and in the FBI with Richards. You can't get much closer than that.

Mansfield and Salerno recognized the importance of the information as soon as they heard it from Richards over lunch at the Monocle, located just off Capitol Hill on D Street, a favorite watering hole of senators, congressmen, and staffers in Washington. They requested Richards's approval to pass it on to Senators Roth and Nunn. Richards, who had testified before the committee and was acquainted with both, agreed to fill them in.

When he did, the senators made an additional request of Richards. Would he agree to go to work for the Senate committee as a special investigator, and look into the situation in Las Vegas? Since it would obviously take him away from home on a consistent basis, Richards agreed to discuss it with Jeannie, his wife, and get back to the senators. Jeannie agreed with her husband that it would be okay on a temporary basis, so Richards called and accepted the position.

Soon, he was preparing for a trip to Vegas, a town he was most familiar with by this time from his careers as an FBI agent and then as an attorney representing clients who were mostly news organizations being sued for libel by the likes of Sen. Paul Laxalt, who had operated a casino in Carson City—which allegedly was skimmed by the Chicago mob—or by Wayne Newton, the entertainer. In fact, soon after his retirement from the FBI in 1980, Richards had joined the defense team which represented *Penthouse* magazine in the libel suit brought against it by Moe Dalitz. Coupled with his many years in Chicago working against the Chicago mob—up until now at least, the dominant mob in Las Vegas—Richards was well acquainted with Glitter Gulch, the Strip, and the denizens thereof. He knew the territory and the players. He knew where the bodies were buried.

One of the first things he did when he got to Vegas, however, was to hurry up to Reno. He checked in at Bally's, out near the airport, called Tom Carrigan, and made reservations to meet him that night at Gigi's, the fine restaurant in the lobby. (Unfortunately, Caruso's was closed that night.)

"Tommy," Richards said, after he quaffed his first Beck's, "I got a favor to ask of you. You remember you and I once discussed your friendship with Jack Holmes? I need to sit down with him, can you line that up?"

Tom Carrigan could and did. When Richards made contact with

Holmes, however, Jack politely but firmly backed him off. He would not discuss anything to do with his knowledge of what was going on at the Vegas Star, with CamStar, or with Camelot. He knew what had happened to too many people who spilled their guts on what they knew about the mob.

One Monday night soon thereafter, while Richards was dining at the Palace Court at Caesars Palace, he spotted Jack Holmes dining with a beautiful blonde. "Wow, what a figure," Richards thought to himself. He decided to find out who she was, this might lead to something. Richards did not know the maitre d' or the captain of the Palace Court, not being a regular there, since it is one of the most expensive dining spots in Las Vegas. He therefore decided to wait for the couple at the foot of the staircase leading from the ground level up to the restaurant, then tail them out in order to find out the identity of the lovely blonde. In short order, he placed them in a suite at the Alexis Park, a second-floor suite overlooking one of the two pools there. He then walked back to the front of the Alexis Park, facing Harmon Avenue, and, using his credentials as a special investigator for the U. S. Senate, determined that her name was Glory Praise and that her application for a permanent suite indicated that she was employed by Joe Agosto at the Tropicana in the Folies Bergère. Richards found this information very interesting, especially that she worked for the mobster Agosto. But what caught his breath was the location of her most recent previous residence. It showed "422 E. Napoleon, South Bend, Indiana." "My gosh," thought Richards, "that's not far from where Jeannie and I lived when we first got married and I was in school at Notre Dame! In fact, it's not far from where I grew up at 422 East Angela. Boy, I sure know that neighborhood, that's Harder Heights!"

The next night Richards attended the Folies Bergère. He immediately spotted the beautiful blonde he had seen with Jack Holmes the night before at the Palace Court. He intended to intercept her when she left the Trop, but noted that when she did so, she was with another girl he had seen in the Folies. Since the subject he wanted to discuss with Glory Praise was sensitive, he wanted to meet her alone.

The next day he called the Alexis Park. Boots answered the phone, but summoned Glory when Richards asked for her. "Miss Praise," he said, "you won't know me but I'm the uncle of Tim and Pat Richards in South Bend. My name is Bill Richards. They asked me to say hello to you while I was in Las Vegas." Richards had taken a big chance. He knew that his nephews were very popular in their home town, however, and that it was likely Glory would know them. She did. Quite well. "Miss Praise, I'm in the lobby here, I wonder if I might buy you a drink." Now, ordinarily Glory wouldn't think twice about turning down such an invitation in Las Vegas, but she was anxious to hear news of South Bend. She was pretty much estranged from her parents and she thirsted for news of her home town. She also knew Tim and Pat Richards were good friends of Bobby Doran, and she was anxious for news of her old flame.

She agreed to meet Richards in the lobby and when she did, Richards took her by the elbow and graciously escorted her into Pegasus.

"Tell me about Tim and Pat," Glory quickly asked.

"They're both fine. Tim, you know, is in Washington where he is a staffer for a congressman, John Brademas, who you would know, being he's from South Bend. Tim will be running for Congress one of these days. Pat is still at Indiana U., he's one of my real favorites."

"Didn't they have a cousin from Chicago who was the baseball star at Notre Dame, the captain?"

"Hey, Glory," Richard exulted, "you really know how to please a guy. Yes, they sure did. That's my son Bob!"

"I remember one time going up to him at the Capri in South Bend and asking him for his autograph. I was about twelve. He was with his brother, a big, good-looking guy like him."

"Yes," Richards said, "that's my son, Bill. He's a sportscaster in Tucson now."

"What a small world. You are probably related to Greta Richards Lewis. I often competed against her in tennis tournaments."

"She's my niece. She's studying law now," Richards said.

"Do you know Bobby Doran in South Bend?" Glory asked.

"No," Richards replied. "Not *Bobby* Doran, but I sure know the Doran family in South Bend. In fact, Mary Ann married my brother, Joe. I think she may have a nephew named Bobby."

"My real name is Zaleski," Glory told Richards.

"Really? You're no relation to Ernie Zaleski, are you?" Richards asked.

"He's my uncle!" Glory responded.

"My God!" Richards exclaimed. "Ernie is a good friend of mine! Gosh, what a great football player he was! You can be proud of him! He was undoubtedly the finest football player ever to come out of South

Bend. Many times I watched him play for Washington High School and then we went to Notre Dame together. He started off there just like he finished at Washington High. He probably would have been an all-American or maybe even a Heisman Trophy winner if he hadn't torn up his knee so badly. That was the end of his days as a star. He hung on but never really could do the things he used to do. But what a great guy! He's working for the city in South Bend now, isn't he? I saw him in June at a Notre Dame Monogram Club Reunion."

"Yes. He's my favorite," Glory said.

They were off to a great start. Glory had no reason to be threatened by this older man who did not seem to be interested in her physically. Once Richards felt that he had established a rapport with Glory, he suddenly changed the subject. "Glory, I'm going to be very up-front with you. I'm a former FBI agent and now I work for what you might know as the Senate Rackets Committee. I know you are a friend of Jack Holmes. Jack doesn't want to talk to me, but I'd like you to ask him to, just as a favor to you."

Glory went pale. Sharp as she is, she immediately recognized a couple of things. First, that Richards knew that Jack was a married man, with a good reputation, who was dating a showgirl. Although Richards might not know the full extent of the relationship, it wasn't something Jack would want bandied around. Second, she immediately knew what Jack had told her during their pillow talk on their first night in her bed. He had since alluded to the same topic a number of times and it was bothering him considerably. She had an idea why this former FBI agent, now working for whatever this "Rackets Committee" might be, would be interested in talking to Jack.

Richards took it very slowly. He was not about to use his information, what little he had, about the relationship between Jack Holmes and the Folies Bergère dancer as a weapon to influence Holmes to cooperate. But then, on the other hand, these seemed to be two very nice people. They would both immediately grasp the implications. He wouldn't be blunt or vulgar in this situation, but then he probably didn't have to be.

Before they parted, Glory promised she would talk to Holmes and tell him of her meeting with Richards. But she would leave anything further up to Jack. "Fine with me," Richards said, knowing that as soon as Holmes knew that Richards knew even the slightest bit about the relationship, that it would shake him up.

When Richards recontacted Glory, he was told that she had gotten the message to Holmes. Richards then called Holmes who agreed to see him. They agreed to meet in the Regency Room of the Sands Hotel, another of Richards's favorites. At no time did Richard mention his contact with Glory or allude to it. Holmes obviously knew that Richards was aware of her and it influenced him, but there was no need for either party to put it on the table.

Their conversation in the Regency Room was to be the first of many. Soon Holmes was meeting regularly with Richards and soon all of his information was passed to Richards. Richards encouraged Holmes to be alert for further information, but not to do anything to arouse the suspicions of his associates. Holmes was cautioned not to ask any unusual questions or to make any unseemly moves. He was told just to go about his business and to "keep your eyes and ears open." They ceased meeting in restaurants at an early stage in their relationship and instead confined their meetings to Holmes's Lincoln Town Car late at night, not that the late hour made much difference in Las Vegas, but it was much better than meeting in plain sight.

Then one day Glory, who knew of course that Holmes was meeting with Richards, was having a drink at Pegasus with Boots Barnes, her roommate. She frequently confided in Boots about her feelings for Jack Holmes, and Boots knew that the uncle of some of her girlhood friends in South Bend had been in touch with her. On this occasion she idly mentioned to Boots, however, that the uncle "is with the government, some kind of investigator. He's been meeting with Jack."

This was a serious miscalculation, a disastrous slip as it was to turn out. Because Boots was dating a guy named Jim McBride who worked at the Trop as a pit boss—for Joe Agosto. Boots told McBride that she thought it was "very interesting that the uncle of some friends of Glory from her home town is some kind of an investigator and he is a friend of Jack Holmes."

That meant something to McBride, and when he took Boots to Joe Agosto, it meant a lot. Joe was very much aware that the Bonanno family was into the Vegas Star and that Holmes was their front there. A couple days later, while conferring with Moe Dalitz on matters of mutual interest, he brought it up. Dalitz was *extremely* interested.

He looked into it. He had Joe Agosto bring him the personnel file on Glory Praise. In view of McBride's information that the "uncle" is from "Glory's home town," he looked to determine where that might be found. What investigator in Las Vegas was from South Bend? He had Dick Becker, the security chief, find out. None that anybody from the Gaming Control Board or Metro knew of. But when Becker invited an FBI agent to lunch at the Palladium, a run-of-the-mill restaurant at Caesars Palace, he dropped the question into the conversation, as an aside, since the agent certainly wasn't on anybody's pad. The agent knew of no current FBI agent who was from South Bend, but ventured "the only guy I know of from South Bend is Bill Richards. I remember he was a boxing champ at Notre Dame, and his dad was a professor at Notre Dame, that's his home town."

"Bill Richards, who's that?" Becker asked.

"He used to be with us, but he's retired now. Matter of fact, he's in town, working for the Rackets Committee."

Bingo! Becker had it. When he reported to Agosto and Dalitz, Dalitz jumped. "Richards! He's out here? I thought he retired from all of that. He's the guy who was the point man on the *Penthouse* investigation when I sued them over the La Costa story. He's working for who? The Rackets Committee? What are they doing out here?"

Dalitz quickly got hold of Joe Bonanno. He furnished the information he had just received from Becker. The godfather, of course, knew immediately who Richards was—Richards was one of the FBI agents in Tucson who had put him away. "He's with the Rackets Committee now? And he's talking to John Holmes? This is serious business. I'll look into it right away."

That same night when Jack Holmes left the Vegas Star he was followed by Joe Agosto. He was pointed out to two men. One was named "Clean" Immaculata. The other was named "The Ape" Annunciata. They took Jack Holmes to a deserted warehouse off Boulder Highway. They hoisted Jack Holmes onto a meat hook on a wall. They impaled him on it, by slamming him down on it so that it caught him through his rectum. They then questioned Jack Holmes about his relationship with Bill Richards. When Jack would only acknowledge that he had met Richards but had never told him anything, "The Ape" plugged a cattle prod into Jack's penis. Soon Immaculata and Annunciata had the whole story. They let him linger for three days. Then they drove his body to Lake Mead at night. They weighted it with cement blocks, boated out to the middle of the lake, and tossed it in. Holmes's body has not been discovered to this day.

GLORY Praise would remain in Las Vegas for a month. Then, when she finally gave up on her hope that Jack would return—she would never know what had happened to him—she would say goodbye to Boots Barnes and Debbie Lee, and quit her job on the kick-line at the Folies Bergère. She would board American Airlines Flight 248 en route to Chicago O'Hare from McCarran. She would go into the lavatory, take off her makeup, and slip into low-heeled shoes. When she emerged from the lavatory, Glory Praise had died. When she deplaned at O'Hare and switched to an American Eagle flight to South Bend, Janet Zaleski was reborn.

One night a couple of months later, as she was dining at Sunny Italy—called Rosie's by the old timers—with her parents, with whom she had gradually and fully reconciled, her mother hissed: "Glory and Praise to the Lord, there's Bobby Doran over there." Janet shivered for two reasons. She would forever shiver whenever her mother cried her pet phrase. And, at one time, Bobby Doran had *always* caused her to shiver. As if on signal, Bobby saw Janet. He came over. He asked her out. She felt sorry for Bobby. In his sophomore year at I. U. he had wrecked his knee. His football career was prematurely ended just like her uncle's. With it went his fatal attraction to the coeds. He wallowed in alcohol for a while, turned to some fat, and began to lose his hair. He was back in South Bend now, working at L. S. Ayers in University Mall, selling men's clothes. Making a living. Janet's sorrow, however, did not extend to compassion. She very firmly turned down his invitation. With slumped shoulders Bobby went back to his table, to dine alone.

Joyce Holmes waited and waited for Jack to return. She is still waiting. She never remarried—some say because of her devotion, some because she lost her vitality and let herself go.

Boots Barnes stayed on at the Folies and the Alexis Park. She got a new roommate, one with a similar name, Joy Paradise, also a kicker in the Folies. Things turned bad for Boots soon after Glory left, however. It turned out that Jim McBride was not just a pit boss at the Trop. He doubled as a pimp. After he broke Boots in himself, he got her high and turned her on to one of the V.I.P.'s. Soon it became a regular procedure. Soon, Boots got to look forward to it, it sure enhanced her income. Boots began to take uppers to turn on more easily. Uppers led to grass and grass to cocaine. Within a year, Boots was no longer on the kick-line. Within another year she was seen regularly walking the Strip. "You want a party, Mister? Twenty dollars, Mister?" She would never be cognizant of the major role she played in the history of Las Vegas. Nor Glory of her part. But Bill Richards would be.

16

The "Wine Buyer"

BILL Richards would slowly but surely become aware of the disappearance of Jack Holmes. First, it became talk on the Strip that Holmes had "taken off." Then Holmes missed two regularly scheduled meets with Richards in his car. It became obvious to Richards what had happened—at least that he had been the victim of foul play. It wasn't hard for Richards to figure out that it was the Bonanno people who were behind it. But he couldn't be certain.

As chagrined as he was, it did have one benefit from Richards's perspective. He had been through all this before. Years ago he had made an approach to the financier of the Chicago mob, Fred Evans. The first contact was very promising. But there was never a second one. The Chicago mob took Evans out. Another of Richards's sources, Dick Cain, the "made" Chicago mob member, had been shotgunned to death while cooperating with Richards. Although it was the nature of the business, Richards never got used to it. It hurt him deeply when one of his "pals" was killed, very deeply. Until the wound began to heal months later, he would vow never to put a friend or himself through it again. But life, and work, had to go on. The bastards had to be beaten. It was their way of "throwing fear," attempting to deter further incursions within their ranks on the part of Richards and his partners. He couldn't accept that.

The tough part was that there was little he could do. When Cain was murdered, he spent weeks conducting his own personal investigation but had never been able to determine the identity of the killer(s). Years later, the FBI would learn from an informant they developed that the killers were Tony Spilotro and Joe Lombardo. By that time Richards had retired and there was nothing he could do. He was very pleased when Lombardo was convicted in "Pendorf" and looked forward to the day when Spilotro would get his.

The one benefit, however, was that now Richards was freed up to act on some of the information Holmes had given him. None of it would matter to Holmes. It was the time-honored practice of Richards and his associates in the FBI not to utilize intelligence information obtained from any outside source for fear of jeopardizing that source, whether it be a live informant or an elsur, an electronic surveillance device. Now, however, with Holmes presumed to be dead, Richards was free to act on his information and conduct an investigation of the leads presented thereby.

His first thought was to uncover John Walsh. From what Holmes had told him there seemed to be no doubt that Walsh was fronting for someone. But Holmes did not know who. However, Holmes was aware it had to be someone in the mob, high up in the mob, from New York. That was Walsh's background. New York. But who? John Gotti? "Fat Tony" Salerno? Joe Bonanno? Who? In view of Nick Lupresto's information it was probably Bonanno but this was not clear, and Richards needed confirmation.

Networking. As important as it is in business, so it is in law enforcement. The age-old axiom in law enforcement is that no officer or agent is any better than his sources. Richards, after almost four decades in the FBI, with the Chicago Crime Commission and/or the U. S. Senate Rackets Committee, had built up hundreds of contacts inside and outside law enforcement across the country, to say nothing of his scores of contacts in the mob and in other strategic positions in public offices.

If anybody knew anything about John Walsh it would be Richards's many colleagues in the FBI in New York and Ralph Salerno, the former chief of detectives of the Intelligence Unit of the NYPD.

Getting them all together took one phone call. Richards made it to Jimmy Niland. Jimmy at the time was the bartender at T. T.'s Cellar, located at 245 East Fifty-fifth Street, between Lex. and Third Avenues. Before it was gutted by fire in the late 1980s, T. T.'s was the unofficial headquarters of all N.Y.C. FBI agents. Whenever an agent or an ex-agent arrived in New York City, he headed for T. T.'s. There he would meet many of his colleagues, both in the New York office and from any other field office, and catch up on the latest gossip inside the FBI. Who had J. Edgar Hoover just taken a shine to? Or, more often, who had Hoover just dispatched to Butte, Montana, on a disciplinary transfer? Who had just gotten in trouble in Philadelphia? Who had just solved that big bank robbery in Boston? How the SAC in Los Angeles had caught three agents drinking coffee on Bureau time. How the most popular agent in Detroit got caught taking a Bureau car home at night, a strict no-no in those days. How the Chicago office had just planted another bug in the hangout of Joey Aiuppa and was getting good information about his connections with public officials in Cicero. How "New York Bill Richards," not the Chicago one, was ready to march with his bagpipes in the St. Patrick's Day parade in New York. How some New York agents got caught saying goodbye to some female clerks in the New York office who were taking a cruise, a farewell party during the work day when the agents should have been either on a case or on annual leave. Although Binyon's in Chicago would rival it, there was no watering hole in the country like T. T.'s in New York. In fact, it was owned by Tommy Tolan, a former FBI agent—and New York cop—who had been a rookie agent in Baltimore with Richards.

Richards therefore had to make just one call. To Jimmy, the bar-tender. Jim knows them all. Not only the New York agents but many, many across the country. Especially the "heavies," those agents best known to many in the network.

"Jimmy, this is Bill Richards from Chicago. I'm in Vegas but I want to come in on Thursday and I've got to talk to a bunch of the guys who worked O. C. in the NYO. Guys like Jack Danahy, Jim Mansfield, Jim Mulroy, Billy Kane, especially Warren Donovan, Lenny McCoy, Tom Emery, Jimmy Flynn, Bill Beane, Frank Gerrity, Guy Berado, Ted Foley, Max Fritschel, Gus Micek, and Dick Anderson. And if Ralph Salerno is in town, him too. Tell them I'm the 'wine buyer' on this trip. I'll be in there at five o'clock on Thursday. Round up as many of those guys as you can, will you, Jim?"

Jimmy not only could, he did. He got almost all of the old-time NYO agents, those who had worked on organized crime investigations from the early days in 1957 when Hoover first established the Top Hoodlum Program. You could count on Jimmy.

When Richards arrived he checked in at the Waldorf, Frank Costello's old hangout, and then immediately headed uptown to the Cellar. When he arrived he greeted Jimmy and soon found four of the guys he had asked Jim to round up. It wasn't often that Richards was a "wine buyer." It was usually on the other foot. Or to be more exact, in the other pocket. Not Richards's. Soon three other old pals would arrive.

After the usual amenities and after catching up somewhat on what was new in the Bureau—even though, like Richards, they were all retired, once an agent, always an agent—it was down to business.

"Guys, I've got something I want to throw out at you. I hope you can give me this right off the top of your heads," Richards started. "I'm working as an investigator for the Senate Rackets Committee out in Las Vegas as you all know. Now, I developed a source there, Jack Holmes, who was the general manager of the Vegas Star, the place Moe Dalitz moved into a couple months ago. Jack has now disappeared. I'm afraid the mob found out he was talking to me, although I don't know how. It tears me up and I'm determined to find out who was behind him. With Dalitz in there we know it was the mob but we don't know which one, Jack never had an inkling. But here's the clue if I can get you guys to help me. The big man in the holding company which owns the Vegas Star is a guy by the name of John Walsh. He's an attorney from New York with offices in the RCA Building. Do any of you know him? Or anything about him?"

Warren Donovan smiled. Jim Mulroy piped up immediately. Donovan, until his death from lung cancer in 1988, was the Bill Richards of New York. Just as Richards had stayed on the streets of Chicago for decades, so had Donovan in New York—in Brooklyn to be precise. Jim Mulroy was the encyclopedia of the NYO. The book man. Whatever any agent learned, it was given to Mulroy and he correlated it. Put it in its proper perspective and filed it not only in his steel-trap mind but in its proper file in the office. He had become a supervisor of the O. C. Program—the old Top Hood Program—and like Danahy, Mansfield, and Berado, one of the very best.

"Sure, we know John Walsh, don't we, Warren!" Mulroy laughed. "You tell him, Warren, you developed that info."

Warren Donovan took up the story. "First of all, let's order another round on Richards. He can afford it and it's a long story."

When all were settled in and Jimmy had taken care of their needs, Donovan laid it out. This is the way he told it. Donovan was a master story teller and when he had a captive audience he reveled in it. He would cut no corners.

In 1935, Thomas E. Dewey was appointed special prosecutor for New York County, the borough of Manhattan. Office space was leased for Dewey and his staff of twenty assistant prosecutors, ten investigators, ten accountants, several process servers, and many secretaries and clerks in the Woolworth Building in lower Manhattan across the street from Dewey's old location in the U. S. Attorney's office, a block from City Hall and close by the Supreme Court Building.

It was in the latter building where he was soon to impanel a special grand jury to look into the affairs of organized crime in New York City. On July 29, 1935, the jury was selected and assigned to Justice Phillip McCook who turned out to be an honest, capable jurist—just the man to hear the evidence that Dewey was about to present.

What Dewey and his investigators soon began feeding to the grand jury was information concerning the involvement of Lucky Luciano in a major prostitution ring in New York City. When Bonanno heard about that, he cringed. In his Cosa Nostra tradition, involvement in prostitution was forbidden. In the world of Joe Bonanno, of his mentor Salvatore Maranzano, and many other men of respect, the worst thing you could call a man was a "pimp."

On Saturday, February 1, 1936, 160 policemen, assigned to Dewey by NYC Police Commissioner Lewis Valentine, made simultaneous raids on eight houses of prostitution. Hundreds of prostitutes and madams were arrested and taken to Dewey's office for questioning by his assistants. Included were two of the most prominent madams in New York: Florence Brown, the infamous "Cokey Flo," and "Fancy Nancy" Presser.

When Luciano heard about the raid he immediately took off for an area where he knew he would be safe. Years ago, another of his non-Sicilian mob associates, Owen "Owney" Madden, had been dispatched from New York, where he had worked closely with Luciano, Lansky, and Siegel, to Hot Springs, Arkansas. There the mobsters provided him with a budget to corrupt anybody who was anybody in Hot Springs and to make it a sanctuary for wiseguys. Madden also received a mandate to develop the resort community into a gambling den, establishing several casinos to attract the high rollers from the big resort hotels like the Majestic. Owney Madden, for all practical purposes, had become the boss of Hot Springs and controlled anything that moved there. It was his pleasure to harbor his old mentor, *Il Capo di Tutti Capi.*

Joe Bonanno found out where Luciano was hiding. Lucky's location was not supposed to be kept secret from members of The Commission who had business with him. Bonanno devised a scheme. He would manipulate this situation and pilot the demise of the man whose power he wanted to usurp—the man who flouted the traditions he valued so highly and yet still managed to keep the respect of the men whose opinions mattered so much to Bonanno.

Joe searched for the appropriate and propitious manner in which to make his move. After all, he could not afford to reveal his part in what he planned.

In what appeared to be idle conversation with one of his attorneys in Brooklyn, Bonanno learned that one of the young assistants on Dewey's staff was a man named William Herlands. Pressing the matter a bit further, but not tipping his hand, Bonanno learned that Bill Herlands had also been with Dewey in the United States Attorney's office and, that like Dewey, he had returned to private practice in between two stints as a prosecutor. Listening to the gossip of his attorney further, Bonanno learned that when Herlands had been engaged in private practice, he had been associated with another young lawyer, one John Walsh, in lower Manhattan. When Bonanno left his lawyer's office, he consulted the Manhattan phone directory. He discovered that an attorney named John Walsh was located at 290 Broadway, an address in lower Manhattan not far from City Hall and Foley Square, the location of the federal courts.

Not wanting to be identified at any time and yet not trusting any of his lieutenants to do the job, Bonanno lightly disguised himself with a mustache, dark glasses, and a foppish fedora. Bonanno relished this role since he had once taken acting classes when first returning to New York. He secretly considered himself an accomplished actor, and took on different roles and scene-acting when conspiring with his capos.

Bonanno rang for an appointment with Walsh and arrived on March 15, 1936, pursuant to the appointment. When admitted to Walsh's inner office he presented himself as "Mr. Rosenbloom."

"Mr. Walsh," Joe stated, "I have come here to retain you to accomplish something which I understand will be very simple for you to do.

We will never meet again but I may call you. Remember my name, 'Mr. Rosenbloom.' In this envelope is $10,000. It is your retainer for now and for whatever future business we may have." He pushed the envelope across Walsh's desk. "Now, I understand that you have a pleasant relationship with Mr. Herlands of Mr. Dewey's staff. Is that correct?"

Walsh suddenly became wary. He suspected that "Mr. Rosenbloom" might want to put a fix in. He was pleasantly amazed, however, at the next words from his new client who had given him a retainer which would pay his rent and feed his family for the next several months or more.

"I simply want you to pick up the phone and tell Mr. Herlands that Charles Luciano can currently be reached at the Majestic Hotel in Hot Springs, Arkansas, where he is residing in Room 406 under the name of Charles Rosetti."

Walsh waited for the next shoe to drop. There was none. That was it.

On March 20, Herlands and two Dewey investigators travelled to Hot Springs. Without alerting local authorities they registered at the Majestic. Soon they spotted "Charles Rosseti." On April 1 Luciano was arrested on a ninety-count indictment in New York. Although Madden used his influence to delay his extradition to New York, Luciano was eventually escorted back.

The trial started on May 13, 1936. After a few days, "Mr. Rosenbloom" called Walsh. "How is the Luciano trial going?" he inquired. When told that Walsh was unaware of the progress, he was told to make himself aware of the minute details through his association with Bill Herlands, and to make Herlands's interest in furnishing him the details come alive by telling him that the same person who had tipped Walsh off to Luciano's location in Hot Springs might be interested in helping Herlands further through Walsh.

A couple days later, "Mr. Rosenbloom" called again. This time he was informed that one of the key witnesses against Luciano, "Cokey Flo," was being recalcitrant, was very reluctant to extend the cooperation Dewey and his staff needed.

Two days passed. That afternoon Walsh was working in his office when his secretary announced that a Florence Brown was in the outer office, saying that she had been sent by Mr. Rosenbloom. When she was admitted into his office, Ms. Brown immediately informed Walsh that she had been contacted by a representative of Mr. Rosenbloom and that she desired that Mr. Walsh contact Mr. Herlands and ask him to come to Walsh's office so that she could talk to him. When Walsh, unfamiliar with the identity of Florence Brown, seemed somewhat reluctant, Ms. Brown reminded him that she was doing the bidding of "Mr. Rosenbloom." Not realizing the ace he held in his hand, but being well aware of his retainer, Walsh did as requested. He was astounded when Herlands yelped with delight that he would be right over. Herlands recognized Florence Brown immediately as "Cokey Flo."

When Herlands arrived Flo told him: "I know you people been trying to get to me for months and I ain't been polite. But now I have changed my mind. I decided to spill my guts on Lucky Luciano."

Herlands was pleased, to say the least!

"As you know," Flo went on, "I been the girlfriend of Jimmy Frederico who is codefendant of Lucky in your trial. He's also my pimp. And he works for Lucky Luciano."

Herlands continued to be more and more pleased. "Would you testify to that?"

"Under certain conditions. I could also testify that I was present one time when Lucky told Jimmy to close down for awhile because of the heat. Another time I was with Jimmy when Lucky told him that 'I am gonna organize the cathouses like the A & P.' "

"Cokey Flo" had been well briefed. When Herlands ran back to Dewey, Dewey slapped him on the back and told him: "Bill, you've done a great job. That's just what we need. Now I think we've got a chance. Take good care of Flo and make sure she is stashed away. She'll be our key witness." Dewey was unaware that Bill Herlands was not responsible for bringing in "Cokey Flo"—that it was a "Mr. Rosenbloom" who deserved all the credit.

Three or four more days went by. Again "Mr. Rosenbloom" called Walsh. He was told that Dewey's staff greatly appreciated Walsh's help; they had not been told of any "Mr. Rosenbloom," and that they expected that Flo would go a long way towards making the case. But what would really lock up the case, make it airtight, would be corroboration, if they could find somebody else to support her testimony. After all, she was a prominent prostitute, a madam maybe, but still a prostitute.

Two days later, Walsh's secretary announced the arrival of another young lady who had been sent by "Mr. Rosenbloom," one Nancy Presser. "Fancy Nancy" Presser, another madam, was going to be an even better witness than "Cokey Flo." The reason was evident immedi-

Frank Costello

Meyer Lansky

Albert Anastasia

Willie Moretti

Vito Genovese

Charlie "Lucky" Luciano

Tommy "Three-Finger Brown" Lucchese

Joe Adonis

Carlo Gambino

Joe Zerelli

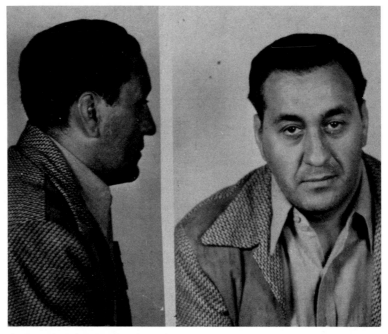

Anthony Joseph Accardo, circa 1935.

Jake "Greasy Thumb" Guzik, treasurer of
Al Capone's mob.

Jake "Greasy Thumb" Guzik

Alphonse Capone

Sam Giancana, circa 1955.

Tony Accardo in the Fifties.

Joe Bonnano

Jackie Cerone, circa 1959.

Pat Marcy

Surveillance photo of Murray Humphreys at Midway Airport, Chicago.

Murray Humphreys, 1958.

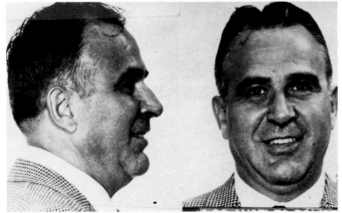

Gus Alex, circa 1958.

 Paul Ricca

 Tony Accardo (left) and Jackie Cerone, circa 1959.

 Murray Humphreys in disguise for testimony before the McClelland Committee, 1959.

Frank Ferraro, 1960.

Paul Ricca, 1960.

John D'Arco, 1960.

Tony Accardo, circa 1961.

"Milwaukee Phil" Alderisio, circa 1969.

Gus Alex in Switzerland, circa 1970.

Dominic Peter Cortina, circa 1970.

Marshall Caifano, circa 1973.

Surveillance photo of Joe Aiuppa (left) and Jimmy "Turk" Torello, 1974.

John Roselli in 1975 after testimony before the Senate.

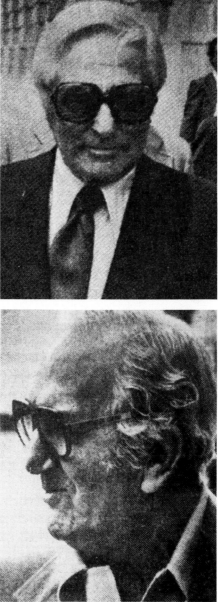

Sam Giancana in 1975 just before his death.

Joe Bonnano, circa 1975.

FBI agents (left to right) Hobie Hart, Dick Held and the author on September 25, 1975 celebrating twenty-five years of FBI service on the part of Hart and the author.

Moe Dalitz, "The Godfather of Las Vegas," receiving the city's "Humanitarian of the Year" award in 1976.

Joe Ferriola, circa 1978.   The author, circa 1978.

The author receives one of many awards from the FBI, 1976.

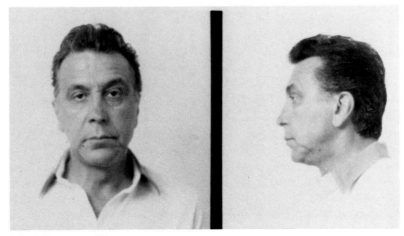

John DiFronzo, 1986.

Sam Carlisi

Joe Bonnano, 1984.

Tony Spilotro, circa 1984.

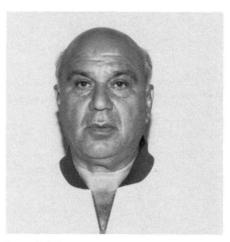

Rocco Infelice, 1990.

Louis Marino, 1990.

Salvatore DeLaurentis, 1990.

The Desert Inn, Las Vegas.

The Stardust, Las Vegas.

The Tropicana, Las Vegas.

The Mirage, Las Vegas.

ately when Bill Herlands rushed over to the office of his colleague Walsh, who was really proving his friendship.

"I not only ran my business under the orders of Lucky Luciano, I divvied up directly with him. And more than that, I fucked him regularly."

Wow, this was getting right down to the nitty gritty! "I used to go up to his suite in the Waldorf Towers where he lived under the name of Charles Ross. Some nights I'd fuck him and sometimes I wouldn't. I guess you know, Lucky can't always get lucky. He can't always get it up."

Holy smoke, this was what you might call the intimate details!

Within the next few days, Lucky was enraged when Cokey Flo did her thing on the stand. "Fuckin' whore," he hissed, not recognizing his redundancy.

But when "Fancy Nancy" got on the stand and testified that the great Lucky had trouble getting a hard-on, he literally flew out of his chair! Could anybody believe he'd have anything to do with this tramp, this broken-down broad, this two-bit whore? He looked at the faces of the jurors. My God, they seemed sympathetic to this poor little ill-treated fallen angel! And when he glanced out over the benches where the court buffs were seated, he immediately was struck by the fact that they had big smiles on their faces. "The great Lucky is a limp dick! Oh, my God, wait until Albert Anastasia and Vito Genovese hear this! It was bad enough that this broad comes in with a story about dividing her trick-take with me or that she says I'd fuck the likes of her, but this is too much, that I can't get on with it."

Luciano hissed at his attorney, Morris Polakoff. "Cross-examine this lying, fucking, no-good cunt!"

Polakoff tried. But the more he did, the more "Fancy Nancy" pressed her case. She knew that "Charles Ross" lived in Suite 39-C in the Waldorf Towers. She knew that to get up there you walked through the entrance by the garage without going into the main lobby of the Waldorf, she knew that the elevator to the Towers was attended, that you rode up to the 39th floor. She foiled Polakoff's attempt to impeach her testimony by accurately describing the couches, the chairs, colors, and the arrangement of the rooms. And then she completely mesmerized the jury when she announced, "Charles was so nice to me, he even let me sleep in his bed when he couldn't get it up and he slept on the couch."

Luciano was now enraged beyond belief! Polakoff lunged at him and tied him down. The more Polakoff tried, the deeper it got. He finally ended his cross in resignation.

How well "Fancy Nancy" had been rehearsed! "Mr. Rosenbloom," who had been to many sit-downs in Suite 39-C, knew it well and spoon-fed her all the details.

It came time for Dewey's summation to the jury. He told them that many of his witnesses had been threatened. He took much of his time reminding the jury of the testimony of Florence Brown. He never referred to her as "Cokey Flo."

Then he came to the testimony of Nancy Presser. He never referred to her as "Fancy Nancy." "For two hours I sat with her, trying to persuade her to testify, that she would not be murdered. If you want to know what responsibility is, try to persuade a witness trembling with terror to go up on the stand. The defense did everything to blast her. They resorted to every device known to break down her story. Why did they try to destroy her by all their evil means, except that they didn't dare face the truth?" Dewey went on for all of seven hours and climaxed by calling Luciano "the greatest gangster in America."

In a charge that lasted two hours and forty-one minutes, Judge McCook made little effort to hide his feelings about what the outcome of the trial should be.

The jury received the case at 10:53 P.M. on Saturday, June 6, 1936. After just ten minutes they took a vote. It was eleven to one for conviction. At 4:30 on Sunday morning they sent word through the bailiff that they had agreed on a verdict. The foreman, Edwin Adrerer, announced it. "Guilty on all counts." Luciano was manacled and immediately taken to the Tombs, the local lockup.

On June 18, Judge McCook pronounced Luciano's sentence. He prefaced it by telling Luciano, "let the record show that should any witness for the people be injured or harassed, the court will request the parole authorities to retain in prison the defendants against whom such witness testified for the maximum terms of the sentence imposed." Luciano got that message. Then he got the next message. Judge McCook sentenced him "to a total of from thirty to fifty years in state's prison." Luciano's luck had run out, and he had just received the longest sentence in history for compulsory prostitution.

"Mr. Rosenbloom" had done the deed just as efficiently as if he had had Lucky Luciano chopped. Luciano would be thereafter confined for years in New York prisons, Dannemora, Great Meadow, and Sing Sing, and then years later after World War II when he had done his part to aid the United States government in deflecting sabotage on the New York and New Jersey waterfronts and, perhaps, in the Allied invasion of Sicily, he was released from prison only to be immediately deported to his native land, never again to return to the United States. Now Joe Bonanno had no de facto *Capo di Tutti Capi* with whom to contend. And, just according to his plan, soon thereafter Joe Bonanno was elected by his peers to chair future meetings of The Commission.

On the evening of July 18, 1936, Thomas E. Dewey met with his staff in celebration of their victory in the Fraunces Tavern in lower Manhattan, the site of some of George Washington's victory parties when our first president was campaigning, both against the British and for the presidency.

Dewey made a toast: "My thanks to all the members of my staff who made this possible. I especially extend my deepest appreciation to Bill Herlands. Due to the highest example of craftsmanship in our profession he was able, after others had failed, to bring in our best witnesses, Florence Brown and Nancy Presser, without whom our success would have been in great doubt."

Bill Herlands took a bow. He secretly gave thanks to his good friend, John Walsh. He gave no thanks to any "Mr. Rosenbloom." After all, he had never heard of him.

Thomas E. Dewey went on to become governor of the state of New York. In 1948, he was the Republican nominee for president of the United States, the odds-on favorite. In the most stunning upset in the history of the United States, he was beaten by Harry S. Truman.

DONOVAN'S story had them spellbound. Mulroy had known it in detail and most of the other NYO ex-agents were familiar with some of the broader strokes but not with the intimate details Donovan provided. They chuckled as "Cokey Flo" did her bit and laughed out loud when Donovan threw in the flourishes provided by "Fancy Nancy." Not only was it a hell of a story, but good for a lot of laughs. They could just see the proud Luciano as he looked out into the courtroom and saw the public grinning as he was described as a limp dick. The Great Lucky!

"Wait, I'm not finished," Donovan exclaimed. "I've got more about the Joe Bonanno–John Walsh connection. But we've got to get paid for this, Richards, you're getting a lot of information for a couple bottles of beer. Let's order dinner—on your credit card—and I'll give you an even better story about Walsh and Bonanno. After all, I'm making a hero out of you. Where else could you get stuff as good as this?"

He was right. Where else would Richards be able to develop just what he was looking for, the underworld connection of John Walsh, the mob he was fronting for, and be entertained at the same time? It would cost the Rackets Committee a couple hundred for drinks and dinner, but it was well worth it!

When Jimmy served up their dinner order—he seemed to do everything but cook at T. T.'s Cellar—Donovan got back to his story. Or at least to another story on the same subject.

IT was after Meyer Lansky had perfected the arrangements for Lucky's mob in Havana through his arrangements with Fulgencio Batista, the president of Cuba. After Luciano had been sentenced, thanks to the testimony of Cokey Flo and Fancy Nancy as arranged by "Mr. Rosenbloom," he was sent to prison for several years but was then paroled and expelled from the United States on the condition that he spend the rest of his life in Italy, the country of his birth. But he sneaked out of Italy in 1946 and travelled to Havana where he was present for the big sit-down of the mobs from all across the United States under the cover of a party for Frank Sinatra. There, at that meeting, Lucky Luciano reestablished himself as the major member of The Commission.

Back in Brooklyn after the confab, Joe Bonanno was back in the same shape he had found himself in during the mid-thirties. Now ten, twelve years later, his peers on The Commission again gave more deference to Charley Luciano than they did to him—even after he had assisted Walsh and Herlands in the conviction of Luciano. It was déjà vu. His efforts to become *the* "man of respect" amongst his colleagues, had had only a temporary effect. He had held "the chair" of The Commission, but as soon as Luciano had reappeared, even in far off Havana, the tide had turned and Luciano was again "the man of honor."

Bonanno decided to do something about it. He decided that "Mr. Rosenbloom" would retain John Walsh once again. When he looked Walsh up in the Yellow Pages under "attorneys," he now found that Walsh had moved up in the world. Literally and figuratively. No longer was his office located at 290 Broadway in lower Manhattan. "Mr.

Rosenbloom" found that Mr. Walsh had his offices high up in the RCA Building at 30 Rockefeller Center. In fact, they were in such a high-rent district that they were located on the floor just below the Rainbow Room, the famous night spot with its elegant ambience and popular dinner-dancing. As he arrived he noticed that Guy Lombardo would be providing the dance music that evening. "Mr. Rosenbloom" decided that in Mr. Walsh's new circumstances, a $10,000 retainer would no longer suffice—even though all he was asking for was a snap of the fingers.

This time, "Mr. Rosenbloom" found a large suite of offices with a dozen secretaries and several associate attorneys. And then he noticed the etching on the door: it was now the law firm of Herlands and Walsh.

"Oh, ho," he thought. "Little did Mr. Walsh suspect that that $10,000 retainer would be the start of all this."

John Walsh was with a client, a good client, when his secretary buzzed him. "A Mr. Rosenbloom is in your outer office, Mr. Walsh," she said. "He said to tell you he would prefer not to be kept waiting. But he doesn't have an appointment and I know he's not a client."

Walsh jumped up like a shot. He shooed his good client out immediately and rushed into his outer office to greet "Mr. Rosenbloom."

"Mr. Rosenbloom, what a pleasant surprise! It's been a long time. Please come right in."

"Mr. Rosenbloom" smiled, once again from behind dark glasses and false mustache. He had expected he would be welcome.

When the door closed behind them, "Mr. Rosenbloom" calmly dropped another envelope on Walsh's desk. This one contained $25,000. Not only had Walsh's circumstances improved since the last meeting but so had "Mr. Rosenbloom's".

"Your retainer, Mr. Walsh. Now, I have another problem for you which I expect you will be able to handle just as expeditiously and just as efficiently as you did many years ago."

"I will do my best, Mr. Rosenbloom."

"Do you have a contact on any of our newspapers?"

"Yes, of course. You may know that Bill Herlands, formerly of Mr. Dewey's staff, is my partner here. As a matter of fact, I should acknowledge to you, Mr. Rosenbloom, that neither Mr. Herlands nor myself would find ourselves in such surroundings if it were not for you. Belatedly, I thank you. And I'd like to introduce you to Bill Herlands. I have never told him the story of how he came to such prominence when

'Cokey Flo' and 'Fancy Nancy' Presser fell into his lap."

"No, Mr. Walsh, I prefer to keep our relationship anonymous. The less Mr. Herlands knows about the source of his fortune, the better."

"Well, then," Walsh said, "yes, Bill has introduced me to a couple of his friends in the local press. Let's see, I could give you one on the *Daily News* or the *Times.* Or maybe the *Brooklyn Eagle.*"

Mr. Rosenbloom gave it a thought. "How about all three." He figured for $25,000 he deserved at least three phone calls, for that would be all it would take.

"You have it. What is it you want?"

"I want you to plant a story. Lucky Luciano is living in Havana contrary to the terms of his parole agreement. In a home in the Miramar section. And he has an interest, financially, on record where it can be found, in the Hotel Nacional."

"Wow! What a story!" exclaimed Walsh. "The papers would pay *me* for a story of that magnitude!"

When "Mr. Rosenbloom" departed, he left a dazed and happy John Walsh. Once again, this man had come into his life to pay him good money when the shoe should have been on the other foot. First, he had earned the undying gratitude of Bill Herlands when he had insured the successful prosecution of the most famous gangster in the gangster era, the thirties. And now he would earn the undying gratitude of three friends in the newspaper business, a debt he could collect on time and again to further his law business. And all he had to do was make three two-minute phone calls, then pocket the $25,000 in cash. Why, he wouldn't even have to declare it. And if he wanted to be really dishonest, how would his partner Herlands find out that someone had dropped into his office for five minutes this afternoon and dropped $25,000 in cash on his desk? What a deal. He hoped it wouldn't be ten or twelve years before "Mr. Rosenbloom" dropped in for a quick chat again. And it wouldn't be until decades later that Joe Bonanno approached Walsh to front for the New York family at the Vegas Star that Walsh would put two and two together and realize that Bonanno and "Mr. Rosenbloom" were one and the same person.

THE story in the three New York City newspapers caused the sensation that Joe Bonanno expected it would. Of all the people it bothered, it bothered Harry Anslinger the most. In 1947, Anslinger was the director of the Federal Bureau of Narcotics, now called the DEA. He made the Luciano situation his war cry. He declared that as long as Luciano remained in the Western Hemisphere he was a threat to the safety of the United States. He sent a formal demand to Cuba. Oust Luciano. Cuba, in the person of President San Martín, but with the corrupt Batista—pulling the strings even from Florida—refused. They acknowledged Luciano's presence but they declined to expel him. In their estimation, he was just another "businessman."

But Anslinger was a tough, persistent man. He obtained an appointment to the White House. Harry Truman was president. He was taking enough heat for what Tom Clark had done in making it possible for Paul Ricca and his underlings to be granted early parole. He wanted no more such heat. Anslinger informed Truman that since Luciano had come to Cuba, narcotics traffic from Havana to the United States had sharply increased. He told Truman that Luciano, arrested years before for involvement in narcotics, was obviously directing the dirty business. Truman backed him and the U. S. government announced that until Luciano was expelled by the Cuban government, it would embargo all shipments of ethical drugs and other medical supplies to Cuba.

That did it. Cuba needed those supplies; it did not manufacture its own. They had no real choice. Several days later, on February 23, 1947, to be exact, as Luciano was having lunch, he was arrested by Juan Hernandez, the assistant chief of police of Havana, and immediately incarcerated at the Tiscoria Immigration Camp, the Cuban equivalent of Ellis Island. Tiscoria is a place not fit for man or beast, being located on a large swamp, infested by mosquitos, with ninety percent humidity. Luciano was then thrown on the first boat out, the S. S. *Bakir,* a rusty old Turkish tub, another place fit for neither man nor beast. Luciano would never again become involved in any material way in Cosa Nostra activities, and he would die of a heart attack at the airport in Naples on January 26, 1962. "Mr. Rosenbloom" had accomplished his purpose; Joe Bonanno was finally rid of Lucky Luciano.

WHEN Donovan finally finished his tale and stopped to swig on the three bottles of Heineken's which Jimmy Niland had brought during his long narration, Richards queried him.

"You certainly answered my question about who John Walsh might be, Warren. Thank you. I'm wondering, how did you get such tight information? It certainly must have been tightly held, not known to almost anyone expect Bonanno."

"You're right. I got it from Bonanno's uncle, Bonventre. You remember when the Bonannos got into what the press called the 'Bananas War'? The house where Bill Bonanno and the other two guys with him were going to the night that war started, when they were ambushed on Troutman Street? Well, it was Bonventre's house where the meeting was supposed to be set up. Joe trusted him completely. Bonanno told him those stories, bragging one night. I developed Bonventre as an informant and he told me. We never did anything with the info, just filed it away. Jimmy Mulroy here did, and sat on it."

"Would the Nevada Gaming Commission have gotten it when they checked on Walsh when he applied for a gaming license?" Richards asked.

Mulroy answered that question. "No, they wouldn't have. It was too tightly held, as you say. If it got out it would have burned Bonventre. So I filed it in a 'June' [secret] file where it wouldn't be disseminated outside the Bureau. When they would have asked for a rundown on John Walsh we wouldn't have given them that."

"That was probably the only piece of information we had on Walsh. If that wasn't disseminated, no wonder he got his license in Vegas," Richards mused.

The evening had been quite a success. Not only had Richards keenly enjoyed getting together with his old associates and had a pleasant evening but he had gained the information he had been seeking. He now knew who John Walsh was and who undoubtedly was behind him.

Now Richards needed another bit of information which would fill out the puzzle he was trying to solve. During the weeks he had been talking to Holmes, Holmes kept mentioning that a shift boss at the Vegas Star seemed to be the man Moe Dalitz was using to perfect his skimming operations. He told Richards that the man's name was Collins. Charles Ross Collins. That meant nothing to Richards. When he checked Collins's application at the Gaming Control Board, he found nothing to indicate that the GCB had been remiss in issuing him a gaming license. Collins had formerly lived on Park Avenue in the seventies, a very good address in New York City. He had attended Culver Military Academy in Culver, Indiana, a very nice school. He had formerly been employed as a captain at the Copacabana in New York, the famous nightclub now no longer in existence. But there was nothing in the files which showed any connection with the mob, no reason why, if Holmes was correct—and he undoubtedly knew whereof he talked—that Collins would be the one being used by Dalitz as his key man to do the all-important skim.

Jack Danahy gave it his consideration. Danahy had been one of the earliest Top Hoodlum Program supervisors in the NYO and had been the director of security for the National Football League after he retired from the FBI.

"Collins. Can't think of anybody by that name except our Pat Collins, the agent who got into the fight with Carlos Marcello in New Orleans. Wait, there was a broad, what was her name, wasn't it Collins, the one who was Luciano's mistress?" He looked again at Mulroy.

Mulroy responded. "Yeah, Marianne Collins. A beautiful blonde. She was a dancer."

Ralph Salerno perked up at that point. "Yeah, when I was with the NYPD, we had a tap on her phone. *She* lived up on Park in the seventies as I recall."

Richards was the first to see the light. "And I suppose you are going to tell me she worked as a dancer at the Copacabana?"

Billy Kane picked it up from there. Billy had the reputation of having more "wine buyers" in his entourage of friends than any other agent in history. He spent more time in cabarets, working at night, with more legitimate businessmen willing to pick up his tabs than any agent. Anywhere. Even more than Chicago agent Ralph Hill. "Yes, she did, as a matter of fact. That's were Lucky met her. You remember Frank Costello had a big piece of the Copa."

Mansfield chimed in next. "What did you say this guy's name is?"

At that point Richards knew. He whispered. "Charles Ross Collins."

Then they all knew. Lucky Luciano lived at the Waldorf Towers, adjacent to the Waldorf-Astoria, under the name of Charles Ross.

Charley Collins *must* be the illegitimate son of Lucky Luciano. There were just too many coincidences. Charles Ross. Collins. It all made too much sense. No wonder Moe Dalitz trusted him to mastermind the skim at the Vegas Star. His pedigree was impeccable!

What a nice evening. Not only jolly but productive!

After Richards said so long to his pals and to Jimmy Niland, thanking him profusely for lining up the evening, he walked down Park Avenue back to his hotel. As he passed the Waldorf Towers just before entering the Waldorf-Astoria itself, he glanced up. "Lucky, you were some piece of work," he thought to himself.

The next day Richards flew from LaGuardia to McCarran. After checking in at the Barbary Coast, he took a cab to the headquarters of the Gaming Control Board. There was no way he could tell the story like Warren Donovan did. The atmosphere just wasn't the same. Nevertheless, without all the frills, he made it quite clear to the GCB that John Walsh and Charles Ross Collins were guys whose supposedly clean backgrounds weren't all that clean. You wouldn't visit the sins of the father on the son—except when the son was closely following in his father's footsteps. Then you closed in.

17

Bonanno Wins a Big Battle

LAS Vegas had been kept clean when Jack Holmes had been killed. No blood had been spilled on the Strip, Glitter Gulch, North Vegas, or anywhere else to scare away the tourists. As far as anybody knew, Holmes had tired of it all, maybe looted the counting room and departed for parts unknown. Phil LaVelle wrote an article about the disappearance for the *Review Journal;* it appeared as three paragraphs on page three of the Metro section. Luke Michaels at Channel 13 thought there might be something to it, but when he went to his executive producer, Richard Urey, the two agreed that there wasn't enough to it. Don Jaye on his "Talk Back" show on KLAV radio, which is broadcast from the Landmark, responded in about ten words to a caller who asked about Holmes, but that was all. The Bonannos had accomplished their purpose. They used torture to find out what they wanted to know—that Holmes had cooperated with Richards. They resorted to murder and achieved their objective—riddance of an employee who had gone sour on them. They disposed of his body and avoided spilling blood in Las Vegas just as they evaded any real law enforcement investigation because the incident would be entered into Metro records as a missing person case, not as a homicide. It was assigned to a rookie officer, Bob Curtin, and quickly put on the back burner.

By May of that year, 1986, however, Joe Batters wanted action. "We haven't done nothin' to show those greaseballs," he said. "I want a hit crew out in Vegas and I want one of the key people at their hotel whacked." Joe Ferriola sent Jerry Scarpelli and three of the best men he had. They selected Dick Becker. It was a well-considered choice. Becker was the chief of security for Dalitz. He was the man responsible for creating the right conditions to ensure the high flow of skim. There was no torture involved with this. Scarpelli and his crew simply curbed Becker's car one day as he left his home near Liberace's Tivoli Gardens Restaurant, in Liberace Plaza on East Tropicana Avenue. They prodded him with ice picks—it wasn't smart in his business to own a convertible—until he got into their car. Then, with two of the crew in a tail car behind in case of a chase, they drove out near the Nellis Air Force Base and dumped him into a ditch. Scarpelli then calmly walked over to Becker and fired two shots point blank into his face. Then one into his heart. The battle was joined. There was no doubt in the minds of Joe Bonanno, Moe Dalitz, or Bill Richards who had ordered the deed.

THEY called him "The Ant." Bill Richards used to taunt him by telling him that it was because of the minuscule size of his brain—and his guts. To say there was bad blood between the two would have been an understatement. Tony Spilotro had gotten his start in Chicago as a juice collector for Sam DeStefano, "Mad Sam," the infamous Chicago torture-murderer. Sam kept a torture chamber down in his basement and was truly in his glory when he could work over a delinquent debtor. If they dropped dead of fright, so what? Sam would just have Spilotro dump 'em in a sewer some place. It became personal between DeStefano and Richards early in the game. One day in the late sixties, Spilotro accompanied DeStefano on an attempted ambush of Richards at the home of one of DeStefano's other collectors whom Richards had targeted as a potential informant. Just by chance, Richards, unaware of the ambush, was detained in the FBI office when his supervisor, Vince

Inserra, called an unscheduled squad conference. Richards never forgot the incident, however, and frequently referred to Spilotro as "You ant!" It soon got to be his media nickname. Spilotro hated it—and hated Richards for coining it.

Joe Bonanno called another sit-down of his *regime.* "My friends, Tony Accardo has called our hand. When he took out Richard Becker, he did what they call throw down the gauntlet. That means he has asked for it. Now, Paulie, I ask you. Who would make what would be a big splash if we clipped him, which one of the Chicago family? I have a good idea, but I want you to tell me."

Paulie Primosa thought for only a second. "Tony Spilotro."

"Why?" Bonanno asked.

"Because he's their man in Vegas. He's been calling the shots out here for ten, fifteen years. And because he is their high-profile guy. You hit Spilotro and it will wake everybody up. You hurt them the most in their family and in their public relations."

"Good thinking, Paulie, I'm proud of you. You studied the situation well. You read my mind." Joe was indeed proud of Primosa. He was handling everything Bonanno could throw at him, both in the brains and the brawn departments.

Joe stood up. The meeting ended when he uttered two words: "Do it!"

Bonanno didn't have to designate who should do it. It would be Primosa, Annunciata, and Immaculata. But it wouldn't be easy. Tony Spilotro lived in a nice section of Las Vegas with his wife, Nancy. A maid came daily. When he went out he was picked up by two of his underlings, Frank Cullotta and Herbie Blitzstein, two old pals from Chicago. Sal Romano, another old Chicago partner, would sometimes replace Blitzstein, and Spilotro's brothers John and Michael seemed always to be around. At the time, Spilotro was headquartered at the Gold Rush, his jewelry store where he was fencing jewelry, furs, and anything else of value, hoping *that* wouldn't come to the attention of Accardo. He had had enough trouble with Joe Batters recently. He was called in to explain why Allen Glick and Carl Thomas had become government witnesses in the Strawman case. He was questioned about his suspected participation in narcotics in Las Vegas. In addition, he himself skated on the Strawman Case only because he came down with one of those all-too-frequent "mob illnesses." He had been indicted in Kansas City with the other top Chicago bosses, Aiuppa, Cerone, Lombardo, and LaPietra, but his case was severed, to be tried later when he recovered.

These were turbulent times for "the Ant." Bonanno wanted Spilotro clipped *in Chicago.* For three reasons. It would keep the bloodshed out of Vegas; it would send a message to Accardo that his men were vulnerable on their home ground; and lastly, it would stir up the press, the FBI, the police, the Chicago Crime Commission, and God knows who else in Chicago—where the immediate suspicion would be that it was Chicago taking care of its own. Accardo, Ferriola, Angelini, Cortina, Infelice, and the rest of the Chicago mob would take the heat. Who would think—other than those guys—that Joe Bonanno would have any hand in it?

On a June night in 1986, June 14 to be precise, the New York hitters got their chance. Tony Spilotro, with his brother Michael acting as bodyguard, left Michael's home in Oak Park, the western suburb of Chicago. (Spilotro maintained a home in Vegas and one in Chicago, and commuted between the two cities, keeping tabs on his "business interests" in Nevada and reporting back to the "home office" in Illinois.) They told their wives, Nancy and Ann, they would be back soon. They weren't. Ever.

The three Bonanno hitters, Primosa, Immaculata, and Annunciata, caught up with the brothers soon after they left Oak Park, heading towards a local night spot, apparently, on Mannheim Road. On a lonely stretch of Mannheim, the terrible trio caught up with the doomed duo. They curbed the Spilotro Caddy, and with .45s pointed straight at them forced Tony and Michael into the station wagon they were driving. The Ape drove his fist into the face of Tony Spilotro while the Clean One did the same to Michael. When Tony attempted to resist, his 5'5" frame was no match for the 5'10", 250-pound Ape. One more fist to the face and Tony was out. Michael saw his big brother go out and decided he had no stomach for any more. He quickly subsided.

Paulie, driving, quickly followed the signs toward Indiana and the Tri-State Tollway. He wasn't sure where he was going but what planning they had done had led them to believe that the best getaway would be out the tollway. When they got out into the farmland, they would use the picks and shovels they had with them to hide the bodies.

First, however, they had another task. To discover as much about the Chicago mob and its situation in Las Vegas as possible. They drove forty miles or so into Indiana and located a desolate farm area. The road signs read "Lowell" and "Enos." Primosa had little idea where they were except that it was a thinly populated area. It would do.

The Spilotro brothers were forced out of the station wagon. Tony had regained consciousness. To intimidate him further, the Ape picked Michael up off his feet and pounded his fist into his face. Then he turned to Tony. It didn't take much. Soon Tony spilled his guts. He was reputed to have killed twenty-five people, and participated in numerous instances of torture with his mentor "Mad Sam." Now he got a little of his own medicine, but not too much, because he caved in very quickly. Apparently he could dish it out, but he couldn't take it.

When Paulie had heard what he wanted, he said to Annunciata and Immaculata, "Let's dig." The trio dug a grave. It wasn't six feet deep like regulation graves, but it wasn't meant to be.

When they finished, they completed their job on the brothers Spilotro. They beat them until there was no life left in their bodies, then tossed them into the shallow grave and covered them lightly.

Primosa, Immaculata, and Annunciata then drove back towards Chicago, hit the Tri-State, and exited at O'Hare Airport. They returned their rental car, hit the washroom to clean up, and flew back to Las Vegas to await the discovery of the bodies, knowing that all hell would break loose. The Chicago mob would realize that their man in Las Vegas had been brutally murdered, with his brother yet, and the Chicago-area authorities would conduct an extensive investigation. They would never suspect a New York gang of hitting a Chicago mob kingpin in Chicago territory. And, of course, the media would make the disappearance a lead story on the front pages of the newspapers and on the TV and radio news. All of it was, of course, highly unwelcome attention to Tony Accardo and his crews.

Bonanno got just what he wanted. And he had a good laugh when he saw that Richards got egg on his face over the matter. Recalling how Bonanno himself had disappeared in the midst of all his troubles in 1965, Richards told the press, "Spilotro pulled a Bonanno." Richards's quotes were all over the Chicago media and they even hit the Associated Press wires as his speculative and inaccurate version of the story was carried all over the country.

Nine days after their abduction, the Spilotros' bodies were discovered by the farmer who owned the cornfield in which the terrible trio had planted them. The farmer called the local sheriff, who called the Indiana State Police, who called the local FBI, who called the Chicago office of the FBI, and Ed Hagerty, then the hands-on Special Agent in Charge of the Chicago office, rushed to the scene. All converged on the cornfield. Soon the press got word, too, and converged en masse on the cornfield—the local reporters from Chicago, Gary, Hammond, Whiting, Crown Point, Valparaiso, Chicago Heights, Joliet, even as far away as Indianapolis, and of course the AP and the UPI. It was a madhouse just as Paulie Primosa had planned it.

"Find the killers," the headlines screamed. "The Chicago mob has killed its man in Las Vegas," the authorities announced. What a mess!

The Chicago mob leaders buried their heads. Whenever they appeared, the FBI was there to interview them about the killing. Pat Healy, the boss of the Chicago Crime Commission, and his consultant, Bill Richards, gave daily bulletins. Richards, of course, had had to quickly alter his tune. Now it was "because Spilotro had developed too high a profile while carrying out his duties as Chicago's representative in Las Vegas." It was not one of Richards's finest hours.

It *was* one of Bonanno's however. "Perfect, perfect, Paulie, you men did it perfectly. I'm proud the three of you are *picciotti* of the Bonanno family! You handled it just right!" Joe couldn't have been happier. Accardo and his family lost face. The Bonanno family had hit the Chicago mob's most public figure in Las Vegas, the blood was not spilled in Las Vegas, the Chicago mob came under extreme pressure from the authorities and the press. Tony Accardo had cause to realize he was up against the strongest of foes. Now, perhaps, he might back down a little, perhaps come to the bargaining table, make a serious compromise and invite Joe Bonanno into Las Vegas to share the wealth.

But if Joe Bonanno seriously contemplated that, he had seriously misjudged his enemy. Rather than putting his tail between his legs and crawling to any bargaining table pleading for a compromise, Joe Batters got *off* his tail. He got to a table, all right, but it wasn't to plead for mercy.

Accardo flew from his home in Indian Wells to his home in Chicago. He now lived part time in a guest home on the property of his daughter, Marie, and her husband, in the Barrington Hills area of Chicago, a wealthy community northwest of the city. The next day he convened the entire leadership of the Chicago mob. The same men who were called before him in January were now called before him in July. It had been ice cold outside during the first meeting. Now the heat was on. Figuratively, literally, and every which way. Inside and out.

"Men, we got our ass handed to us," Accardo began. As usual he wasted no time with pleasantries. "These New York wiseguys have shown us they have some hitters. They have also shown us how they operate. Coming into our city and taking out one of our top people. Sure, that fucking Spilotro had become an asshole, but we needed him in place for a while yet what with all that's going on out there in Vegas. Now, we can pull back and sit down with these greaseballs. Or we can go right after them, show them they ain't the only ones who can pull off jobs like this. They stole the march on us. I admit to you all I had no idea they wanted to go to the mattresses like this. We weren't ready for them. But now we will be. I'm telling you today, I ain't seen nothin' like this since I was with Capone. What we got to do today is what Al had us do when Bugs Moran acted up just like Joe Bonanno is doing today. Bananas thinks he was in a fucking war before, with Masseria during Prohibition. Well, he's started a war to match that. He may not know it now, but he's gonna find out that Chicago fought its own war back then. He may think he's got all the experience in this kind of thing, but he's forgotten that I was in a war like this too. Just like I would have taken Capone over Maranzano in those days, he'll find out that the soldiers in this family are better men any day than those so-called *soldati* he's got. He'll find out all right."

Joe paused and looked around him. He was leaning on his cane with the tuna fish handle. Tony Accardo may have been at an advanced age, an age when most businessmen would be retired, fishing, gardening, and watching TV. But he was still living up to his nickname, Joe Batters, which Capone had fastened on him when he beat an opponent senseless with a baseball bat. Inside, Batters was still the bear he was in the old days. He couldn't get the job done himself, of course; his physical powers would no longer allow that. But the will and the experience and the capability to plan was at least what it had been in prior years. Joe Bonanno would find that out—soon.

Accardo resumed talking. "Men, we got to choose a target from their family, a guy who means a lot to them and who is well known to the public, like they took our guy like that, and chop him. Do it so it attracts the same attention. Now, there's just one guy like that. And he's a fucking turncoat to boot. One guy who means a whole lot to them and who's as high profile, as they say, as you can get. Of course, I'd like to get that cocksucker Bananas himself. But except for him, there is one guy who we could get who would hurt them the most. And the whole world would know it."

Accardo was sure most of those present knew who he was talking

about. It was Moe Dalitz. Joe Batters paused for effect, then asked
Butch Blasi, standing guard inside the door, to go out and bring in Jerry
Scarpelli.

Next, Accardo turned to Joe Ferriola who was officially the boss. In
the Chicago family of La Cosa Nostra, however, there is one above the
boss. Everyone had known that for decades. The Chicago boss runs the
mob on a daily basis. When the crisis comes, however, when the moon
comes over the mountain, there is just one man in Chicago. That man
has been Tony Accardo, seemingly since time immemorial, and he was
demonstrating it now. In spades.

"Joe," Accardo said to Ferriola, "I want you to do this personally.
I know that is unheard of. Heretofore when a man gets to be boss, he
tells his men to do the dirty work. In this case, however, I want those
greaseballs from New York to know that our boss gets his hands dirty.
He don't sit in the fucking sunshine in Arizona and let his men do all
his work for him. He goes out and does it himself! That'll stick it right
up his ass! You have done heavy work yourself. Get yourself three or
four guys and go out there and chop this fucking Dalitz!"

Ferriola was all for it. He had only one question. "What about
spilling blood in Las Vegas? That's against the rules."

"Rules!" Accardo screamed. "Rules? What fucking rules! *They*
threw the rules away when they broke 'em by coming to Las Vegas in
the first place. Fuck the rules! Just get it done!"

Accardo was livid. His men had realized from the beginning of the
sit-down that he meant business today. Now it was ingrained in them.
This was serious, all right. Probably the most serious business since St.
Valentine's Day in 1929!

18

Chicago Shows Its Strength

JOE Ferriola got his ass to Las Vegas in a hurry. He took Jerry Scarpelli and Bruno Banduccioni with him. When they arrived he added some local talent to his crew, Patsy Prestogoni, called Patsy Presto.

Patsy Presto knew the territory and the players. He had been sent out to Las Vegas years before and told to keep his head down. He was given a job in Joe "Pigs" Pignatello's restaurant. "Pigs" was Sam Giancana's old driver-bodyguard in Vegas. Patsy had been a killer in Chicago but he had been kept sub rosa in Las Vegas, only to be surfaced in time of emergency. The time was now.

Patsy Presto knew Moe Dalitz and he knew him well. He knew that every day Moe would have lunch at the Las Vegas Country Club, usually with an old pal, Charley "Babe" Baron, now a general in the Illinois National Guard and the former Chicago man in the Riviera in Havana as well as the former executive host at the Riviera in Vegas.

Ferriola rented a home in west Las Vegas, a couple blocks off I-15 not too far from the Palace Station, which is Frank Fertitta's hotel-casino. Fertitta had friends in Chicago also. He had been associated with Carl Thomas at the Tropicana when it was being skimmed for Kansas City and Chicago. The home Ferriola rented would serve as the command post for his crew.

The crew went to work. They followed Dalitz each morning from the time he arrived at the Vegas Star. Dalitz was surrounded by a complement of four bodyguards, which Bonanno had promised him when he switched sides from Chicago to New York. The boys found that Dalitz had a great interest in following the progress of construction on the Mirage. All that space between Caesars Palace and the Fashion Show Mall on the Strip was being readied for the construction of the hotel itself with its volcanos, waterfalls, aquariums, tigers, dolphins, and hundreds of palm trees. It was to become a magnificent showpiece in a marvelous setting and apparently Dalitz wanted to go to school on it in planning Camelot. After lunch at the Las Vegas Country Club, Dalitz would return to the Star until mid-afternoon. He would then be escorted home by his four bodyguards where he would remain, guarded by a relief shift of two bodyguards. Dalitz was at an advanced age in 1986 and there was no pattern to his very infrequent forays from home after he returned there in mid-afternoon.

The Ferriola crew determined, therefore, that it would not be an easy job. Obviously the guy was on guard. He went from home to the Star, to the country club for lunch, back to the Star, occasionally to the site of the Mirage, and then home—all the time heavily guarded by four bodyguards.

The first thought was to take him at the site of the Vegas Star, which was the Bonanno family's Vegas treasure. The crew worked on that idea for several days, but they had to discard those plans. Dalitz would arrive in mid-morning, with two bodyguards in his car, followed by another car with two more, drive quickly into the underground garage, immediately get into the garage elevator and be whisked straight up to the executive offices. He would reverse the procedure to go to lunch at the country club where he would be dropped off at the door with his four bodyguards, step quickly into the dining room just off the lobby, and join his pal Baron. His bodyguards would sit at tables on each side of him. There seemed to be no way to hit Dalitz and make a clean getaway at the Vegas Country Club. The procedure would then be reversed on the way back to the Star. No way there. From the Star, straight to his home, into his attached garage and into his house for the night without appearing outside. Little chance there.

There seemed to be just one loophole in Dalitz's security, which was on those few occasions when he would visit the site of the Mirage.

In late 1986, the Mirage was not even a hole in the ground. It was barely under construction. The Castaways, which would have to be torn down on the lower end of the property, was still in place. In 1986, the Mirage was still just a twinkle in the eye of Steve Wynn, the owner of the Golden Nugget. But the space was being cleared and Moe Dalitz apparently was most interested in how it was to be built from its inception.

The Ferriola crew waited. Not only were they getting impatient, but they were concerned that if this kept up much longer they were going to be spotted. Then what was now a difficult assignment would become impossible. Bonanno and Dalitz would either have them accosted by their own men or by Metro, where Dalitz had some convenient connections.

Then, one day they got their chance. Ferriola and Patsy Presto were in one car, Jerry Scarpelli and Bruno Banduccioni in the other. Dalitz was observed coming out of the Vegas Country Club after lunch with Baron. Instead of proceeding back to the Star, however, the two-car caravan proceeded to the location of the Mirage. When they arrived at the construction site, Dalitz stepped from the car. He walked onto the grounds, about twenty yards from Las Vegas Boulevard, and began to survey the site, looking towards the adjacent Caesars Palace and across to the Desert Inn, his old spot just up the Strip. He may even have looked down and across the Strip just a little toward the Flamingo, which was the first hotel in that area, the place Bugsy Siegel had built before he got chopped. It was almost the twentieth anniversary of the killing of Siegel.

It wasn't much of an opportunity. The Chicago crew knew that their security would soon be blown if they continued to follow Dalitz around. They knew they would have to make their move under less-than-ideal conditions. Joe Ferriola took the chance even though he realized that there would be blood on the Strip contrary to all the rules of The Commission. He had been ordered by Accardo to chop Dalitz. Accardo wanted it done—and soon—no matter how and where.

Ferriola was in the lead car of the Chicago hit crew with Jerry Scarpelli. They watched as Dalitz surveyed the construction site. He carried with him what appeared to be blueprints of the Mirage and began to study them. His attention was focused. Dalitz's four body-guards remained on the sidewalk some twenty yards from where Dalitz was wandering. They were alert, watching the tourists who were walking on their way to and from the Fashion Show Mall and Caesars Palace.

Ferriola and Scarpelli left their car and joined Banduccioni and Patsy Presto in theirs, across the Strip in front of the Imperial Palace. Ferriola outlined his plan of action.

"We'll pull around to where they are. You see Dalitz out there almost by himself. Patsy and Bruno, you take the bodyguards. We hit them first. Try not to get any of those fuckin' tourists, but we got to take out the guards first. We hit them by surprise, we should be able to take them out. Jerry, you get between the guards and Dalitz. Your job is to help Bruno and Patsy. My job will be to get Dalitz. Jerry, you got to make sure I don't get hit before I get Dalitz. You guys understand what you gotta do?" They did.

The two cars then slowly drove up the Strip, turned left, U-turned at the Fashion Show Mall, and then drove south, down the other side of the Strip. A half block later they pulled up alongside the Dalitz bodyguards. From their car, Banduccioni and Presto leveled their .45s at the four Dalitz bodyguards just as Scarpelli jumped from his car and caught the foursome in a crossfire with a shotgun.

Simultaneously, Ferriola ran from his car to within ten yards of Dalitz. He paused momentarily to aim. The popping sounds of gunfire rocked the Strip. Banduccioni hit the first Dalitz bodyguard and down he went with a .45 slug in his sternum. But Presto was not as accurate. He missed his man. With that the bodyguards sprang into action. One got Presto immediately while Banduccioni was taking care of another. Scarpelli then opened fire. He got a third bodyguard, but as this one went down he had enough life left in his body, from a prone position, to level his gun at Scarpelli and put two quick slugs into his torso. The fourth guard then put two slugs into Presto. Banduccioni turned his gun on this fourth man. They fired at each other simultaneously. Each fell.

At this point, Ferriola fired four shots from his distance at Dalitz. All four ripped into the old man. He fell immediately. Ferriola then turned and saw that he was the only man standing. What a carnage! In the space of about fifteen seconds, eight men were down! Joe Ferriola was the only one left standing! Nobody had gotten off a shot at him, he had been able to walk up to within ten yards of his target while his men had taken out—at great cost—the four obstacles which had stood in his way.

Ferriola quickly threw his weapon away and raced to his car. He left behind the results of the assassination. Where the waterfalls of the Mirage would someday splash, blood had spilled—right on the Strip! Ferriola jumped into his car. He raced down the Strip to Flamingo Road about 500 yards away, hung a right, and raced to the house which had served as his command post.

The ambulances arrived promptly. The bodies were taken to Sunrise Hospital, the hospital, ironically enough, built by Moe Dalitz. Seven of them were DOA, but the old man himself was alive—barely. He was rushed into emergency surgery, then intensive care, and he was hanging on with four bullets in him.

Joe Ferriola quickly packed what he could and got out of town. He drove to Flagstaff, Arizona, where he holed up in a Best Western Motel. He went to a public phone and placed a call to Tony Accardo, giving a glowing report. It was tough that Scarpelli, Banduccioni, and Patsy Presto had been killed. But that was the nature of the game. They were expendable. They had gotten Dalitz!

Accardo, however, by this time knew they hadn't. He had been listening to the news reports from his house along the Indian Wells Country Club fairways. Dalitz was listed in serious condition. But he was not dead. When Accardo reported that to Ferriola, the boss was crushed. The three dead men would not be missed. There were always scores more where they came from in Chicago. But the mission was not an unqualified success. He would lose some face.

"Don't worry about it, Joe," Accardo reassured him. "The prick will probably croak anyway, he's apparently in bad shape from what I hear. And you did the best you could under the circumstances. It's too bad there had to be blood spilled in Las Vegas, and right on the fucking Strip, right down the street from the Stardust, but it had to be done. Now maybe that cocksucker, Joe Bananas, will know he's fucking with a real family!"

Accardo's hopes, at least as far as Dalitz was concerned, would not be realized. The old man would slowly recover. Accardo knew, however, that Joe Bonanno would realize he had a tiger by the tail, that the old Capone mob would not hurry to the bargaining table without bringing some chips of its own. And maybe they would not come at all.

If that's what Tony Accardo thought, he was right. Joe Bonanno now fully realized what he had begun. Bugs Moran had said almost sixty years ago: "Only Capone kills like that." Joe Bonanno might have said: "Only the Capones kill like that." They had struck in broad daylight, right in the heart of the Strip, in the presence of scores of tourists, and they had struck down the key man in Joe Bonanno's organization. Furthermore, the boss of the Chicago family had, in fact, escaped. The three dead bodies were those of supernumeraries, three expendables. For Bonanno, it was a lousy trade.

Now Joe Bonanno was hopping mad! Talk about breaking The Commission's rules! Accardo's animals had shattered two major ones! First, they had hit a major man in the tradition, even though he was not Italian and therefore not a made member of La Cosa Nostra. Moe Dalitz, however, had been a powerful man in the underworld for decades. He had been at or near the top since Prohibition, when he had been the admiral of "the Little Jewish Navy" in Detroit, then later when he headed the Mayfield Road Gang in Cleveland, then became the "godfather of Las Vegas." Nobody hits a man like that without approval from The Commission! The second violation, of course, had been the blood on the streets of Las Vegas. On the streets? On the Strip, for Christ's sake! Right in the heart of the Strip, almost across the street from the Flamingo, just down the Strip from the Desert Inn and the Stardust, all at one time or another lucrative mob casinos. How would the Vegas Star, and in the future Camelot, be affected if tourists became concerned about getting caught in the crossfire of a mob war?

Joe Bonanno put in a call to John Gotti. He considered Gotti the most powerful New York mob figure of the day. Second only to Bonanno himself, of course. Gotti was the boss of the Gambino family, the largest. As always, Bonanno called from one of the public phones he utilized for such a purpose. Not one of those which had been bugged by Richards and his FBI pals in Tucson, but a new one. This particular phone was located just north of the running track at Pima Community College's West Campus, just below the foothills of the Tucson Mountains.

"John," he said—without identifying himself since his Sicilian accent, hardly diminished since he began speaking English when he came to America many years earlier, was readily recognizable to Gotti—"we got to have a sit-down over what this bedbug in Chicago has done in Las Vegas. I want to come in and meet with you first and then present my case to The Commission."

Gotti was hardly enthusiastic. To him it seemed that wherever Bonanno went it meant trouble. But he realized that he and his fellow Commissioners had tacitly endorsed Bonanno's move to Vegas. He knew, therefore, that Bonanno had set the war in motion and had created the problems which now existed. He also knew that it was Bonanno who had hit Spilotro. Who was he to complain now?

"Meet me in Central Park. By Wollman Rink," Bonanno demanded. "At three o'clock on Wednesday."

Gotti reluctantly agreed.

The meet took place as scheduled. Gotti arrived to find Bonanno waiting for him at the ice skating rink inside Central Park, just west of Fifth Avenue and a block north of Central Park South where many of the big hotels are located. When Gotti arrived, he and Bonanno walked toward the Sheep Meadow. "John, I want your support. I want Accardo sanctioned for what he has done. He hit Moe Dalitz without any authority and he did it in Las Vegas. He broke two of our biggest rules. I want to bring him before The Commission and I want it done now!" Bonanno was outraged.

"Joe, let me say somethin' to ya. You are a hell of a guy to complain. I seem to remember years ago when The Commission wanted you to explain whether you were planning to have Joe Columbo hit Carlo Gambino and Tommy Lucchese, you wouldn't show up. Gambino and Lucchese were two of our top men ever. Dalitz is a Jew, for Christ's sake. Now I will agree it shouldn'ta been done without The Commission meeting and agreeing to it. But you're not in much of a position to complain! As for the Las Vegas thing, we shoulda realized Accardo and his bunch in Chicago wasn't gonna take that sittin' down. Especially after you hit Spilotro in their own territory. If anybody should complain it would be Accardo. You went into his town and hit his man without coming to us for approval. You think that wasn't against our rules? To go and hit a top man in somebody else's family, especially in their town? Joe, look at yourself."

They had now traversed the park from east to west. They had come out at the Tavern on the Green, the showcase restaurant located on the western edge of the park.

"I'm gonna get a drink. Joe, I'm sorry, but I can't back you on The

Commission if you decide to go there. You got yourself in this mess, you'll have to get yourself out. The only thing I will do for you is keep Accardo's grievance off our agenda. You want to continue to try to make a thing for yourself and for us in Las Vegas, go ahead. But I can't get behind you if you want to bring Accardo in. I know the rest of the bosses won't back you on that since you got such a lousy track record and since you started the whole fuckin' thing." Gotti had made his point. He was firm. He disappeared into the Tavern on the Green.

Joe hustled up a cab and was taken to Brooklyn. He sat down with Johnny Morales, the man he had left in charge back home while he took off on what now had turned out to be a dangerous journey. After his meet with Morales, he was at least relieved that things were going well in the realm of the Bonanno family in Bensonhurst, Greenpoint, and Williamsburg. He then took another cab to LaGuardia and caught an American Airlines flight back to Tucson. Instead of making the connection in Chicago, he made sure he made it at Dallas/Fort Worth.

BACK along the fairways of the Indian Wells Country Club, Accardo was upset. Joe Ferriola had come in, driving straight from Flagstaff, to give his report to Joe Batters. If Accardo had had veto power over Sam Giancana, he certainly was the power behind the throne of Joe Ferriola. Not that Ferriola was anybody's dummy, he wasn't, but Joe Ferriola was not Tony Accardo.

Accardo wasn't particularly upset with Ferriola. He himself had been involved up close and personal with many a shootout, many an attempted rubout. He remembered his first one, with the Hanlon Hellcats at the Shamrock more than six decades ago. He knew that a lot of things could go wrong. Dalitz was still alive in Vegas (although his condition had not even been upgraded to "stable" yet); blood had been spilled on the Strip, right in front of dozens of tourists; three Chicago hitters were downed. It wasn't exactly the St. Valentine's Day Massacre where everything went off without a hitch. But Joe Batters knew that you had to give credit to the other side occasionally. After all, he had been with Al Capone when Hymie Weiss, Bugs Moran, and their crew had shot up Cicero while Capone and Accardo cowered in their headquarters with machine gun bullets flying over their heads. Weiss and Moran had calmly done their work and then calmly gone on their way. It would be other days then before the retaliation was accomplished.

"You can't be perfect every day, Joe, not in our business," he told Ferriola.

"Now we got to make sure of Dalitz," he continued. "I'm not going to send you back there, you're too hot in Vegas right now. We've got to get somebody else to finish the job. I'll tell you what. Do you remember when we hit Jim Ragen in 1946? No, you were just a kid then. Lenny Patrick and his guys hit him bad, but he was getting well in the hospital. Then we got him while he was still in the hospital. We still got a guy around who worked on that. And he knows his way around Vegas, too. Reach out for Gussie in Florida and sit down with him. Give him the story. Tell him I want Dalitz taken care of just like he did Ragen."

In 1946, Tony Accardo, in his position as boss of the Chicago outfit, had coveted the Continental Press, a race wire owned and operated nationally out of Chicago by James Ragen. Accardo ordered Ragen chopped. Chicago mobsters Lenny Patrick, Davey Yaras, and Willie Block got the job done. They shotgunned Ragen while he was driving in his car on the South Side of Chicago. Gus Alex and Frankie Strongy were in a tail car, just in case. But Ragen refused to die of his wounds. For that reason Murray Humphreys, with Alex assisting him, was commissioned to take Ragen out while he recuperated in his hospital bed, all the while telling the FBI about current mob conditions in Chicago. Since he had a ready fount of information available unsolicited, it was the *one* time prior to 1957 that J. Edgar Hoover evinced any interest in organized crime in Chicago. But when Humphreys and Alex were able to get to Ragen in the hospital, it not only ended the life of an important FBI source, it also terminated the investigation, which was called "Reactivation of the Capone Mob" (CAPGA, for short). So it turned out to be a two-headed victory for the Chicago mob. They captured Continental Press as they intended, and they squelched the only FBI investigation into their efforts up until that time.

Accardo would now reach into his vast experience and attempt to repeat the Ragen success. He would once again call on his old reliable, the guy with the brains *and* the brawn, that deadly combination. And his man was Gussie Alex.

Gussie Alex was not happy when he picked up his phone in Fort Lauderdale and got the word. He enjoys spending as much time as he can walking on the beach alongside his condo on Galt Ocean Mile. Gussie likes to work on his tan. His first wife had once told him he looked so handsome with a tan that it had become a fetish with him. When in Chicago, he spends every afternoon he can at the Riviera Club, swimming under the glass dome along Lake Shore Drive at Randolph, keeping up that tan. In Fort Lauderdale he suns on the beach or alongside his pool. Maybe he could keep it up on this assignment in Las Vegas, but probably not. Besides that, Gussie had been getting a little lazy in his old age. He was approaching seventy, not the age when guys want to get involved in the rough stuff. This job, however, wouldn't call for rough stuff. It would be what the mob calls "heavy work," but there wouldn't be any lifting to it. This job would take sophistication, craft, guile. The dirty work would be done by someone on the inside, not Gussie or any other Chicago gunsel.

So Gussie kissed his wife, "Shatzie," the blonde former Playboy bunny, and took an Eastern Airlines flight to Atlanta. There he switched to United and flew into Vegas after another connecting flight at O'Hare. When he arrived at McCarran, he caught a cab to Sam's Town. He didn't want to be seen on the Strip or downtown so he had decided to stay on the outskirts. Furthermore, Sam's Town caters to the cowboy trade, featuring a decidedly country and western theme. It wasn't a crowd that would recognize the boss of the connection guys from Chicago.

Before he left Fort Lauderdale, Gussie had called Sidney Korshak in Palm Springs. Sidney knew everybody in Las Vegas; he had been operating in and out of there since the days of Bugsy Siegel. He had been the attorney for such entertainers as Dinah Shore. One of the few times he had gotten crosswise with his clients in Chicago was when he placed Dinah at a hotel where Chicago was uninvolved, taking customers away from their joints. Murray "The Camel" Humphreys dressed him down for that. "We built you up, don't ever forget where you come from. We call, you come runnin'," was the gist of what he had told Korshak. Now Gussie called and Korshak came runnin'.

When he arrived, Gussie was jumpy. He was the best at what he did, corrupting public officials, but the stress got to him. He once had to go for treatment at Silver Hill in New Canaan, Connecticut, years before, the same place where Joan Kennedy had been treated, but he had recovered. After many years uninvolved with the "heavy work," this assignment made him just a little uneasy, recalled some of the old-time anxiety.

"Sid, let's take a drive. Let's go out to Red Rock Canyon where we can talk. It's a nice day, the drive out there will be good for us. Maybe I can get some sun."

Gussie likes to drive. It relaxes him. So they picked up a rental car at Sam's Town and drove the twenty miles or so out Charleston Boulevard to the scenic Red Rock Canyon, a rock formation gorged deeply into the sandstone. They took a very short walk. "Sid, I need to get somebody inside Sunrise Hospital. Who do you know can help me?" Gussie said.

Sidney Korshak knew immediately what Gussie had in mind, and he wanted no part of it. Moe Dalitz had been his friend for decades. Besides, this was totally outside his sphere of activity. Say what might be said about Sidney Korshak, he had never been involved in conspiracy to commit murder, nor would he be now.

"Slim," Sidney Korshak said to his long-time friend, using the same nickname that Gussie' first wife, Margaret, used, "don't say a word to me about what you got in mind. I want no part of this. The lawyer in me immediately sees 'conspiracy.' I'm too old and too long in the tooth to go down now on any conspiracy. So I don't know what it is you have in mind. I assume you have an illness. If you do, go see Dr. Rudolph Shultz. He can help you with your health. Let's be clear on that. You asked me for a good doctor and I recommend Dr. Shultz. He's affiliated with Sunrise Hospital. Now, let's take a look at these beautiful rock formations, the lovely flowers, and breathe some fresh air. Then lemme go back to Palm Springs."

The next day, Gussie made an appointment with Dr. Shultz. Gussie was unaware of it, but it was common knowledge in the gaming industry that Dr. Shultz handled the little niceties when they had to be handled. If a showgirl got knocked up by one of the casino executives, it was Dr. Shultz who handled it, long before abortions became legal. He still did his fair share of third-trimester jobs. Not at Sunrise, mind you, which is among the most reputable hospitals in the country, but at a back-alley abortion clinic he operated.

Gussie's problem was that he had to penetrate one of the most renowned hospitals in the world, one of the very best. He was dealing with a major league medical facility.

When Gussie made the appointment with Dr. Shultz, he used Sidney Korshak's name. In Las Vegas, that is a magic name. It opens doors wide. Dr. Shultz recognized it immediately. "Dr. Shultz," Gussie said, "I need some part-time assistance with my wife. It has been recommended to me that you might know an orderly from your association with Sunrise Hospital who might help me part time. I wouldn't want to take him away from his full-time duties, but I need him a couple hours every other day or so. I'll pay very well. I would want one who might keep his eyes away from what he might see in my house, if you catch my meaning."

Dr. Shultz caught Gussie's meaning. He knew of an orderly who worked regularly at Sunrise and who helped him at his back-alley clinic. This guy knew how to "avert his eyes."

The orderly's name was Ben Jackson. Gussie called and made an appointment to see Mr. Jackson. He invited him to dinner at the Sultan's Table at the Dunes. When Gussie arrived, the maitre d' placed him so close to the violin players that Gussie was unable to carry on the conversation. He "toked" the maitre d' and got a table off in a corner. Ben Jackson wasn't used to such treatment. He had never before dined in one of the gourmet dining rooms of one of the large hotels on the Strip. The buffet rooms were more his style. Gussie ordered the best. Since Veal Oscar is a specialty of the Sultan's Table, he recommended it to Ben Jackson. He ordered the rack of lamb, another feature there. He also ordered a bottle of Cuvaison Chardonnay to accompany the meal. Gussie is very familiar with the Dunes since it was owned by Major Riddle of Chicago and then later by Morris Schenker, a friend of Tony Giordano, the mob boss in St. Louis.

When he felt his newfound friend was sufficiently impressed and mellow, Gussie made his move. Soon he and Ben Jackson understood each other. It would take $100,000 but it could be done. Ben Jackson could do the deed easily enough, but he had to think about how to escape detection. Gussie was using an alias with Jackson, and he would never be seen in Las Vegas again. He had no worries about whether Ben got away or not, just that he got the job done.

The next day they met again. Ben had figured out a way, a cash payment of $100,000 delivered all up front, on the spot, engaged his mind. He had it figured out. Gussie thought about giving Jackson half now, half upon completion, but he wanted no further contact with the man. Gussie made sure Jackson was aware of how easy it would be to locate him if there was any double-crossing involved, then gave him the money, checked out of Sam's Town, caught an America West flight to Phoenix, and waited for the news. It came the next day. Moe Dalitz had been poisoned in the intensive care unit at Sunrise Hospital, Las Vegas.

The "Godfather of Las Vegas" was dead. Gussie flew back to Fort Lauderdale. Joe Batters caught the news as soon as Gussie did. There was no reason to be in contact. Gussie had done his job. He hadn't lost his old touch. Now maybe he could retire for good. At least from the "heavy work." The work of his "connection guys" would always be in demand. As long as there was a Chicago mob.

19

The War of the Godfathers in Full Bloom!

WHEN Bonanno returned to Tucson, he summoned his family leaders to another sit-down.

"Men," he said, "we've got to make a great effort. Our enemy has shown his strength and his willpower. We have lost two of our top advisors, two top executives of our hotel. We have destroyed their top family capo in Las Vegas. Let us even up the score. I have decided who our next target should be. It should be one who transcends both facets of their situation in Las Vegas. They have a man there who for decades has been one of their very top people. He was a key figure in their gambling network in Chicago from the early sixties to this day. First in Chicago, then in Miami, then in Las Vegas. Not only that but he has been their key man in their major hotel in Las Vegas. When we get him it will not only deprive them of such a person but it will show the world how strong we are that we can pluck them from a person who is so widely recognized throughout the country."

Bonanno then assigned the terrible trio to do the job. Paulie Primosa,

Michael "The Clean One" Immaculata, and Angelo "The Ape" Annunciata would do Bonanno's dirty work once more.

Their target would be Frank "Lefty" Rosenthal. In the very early 1960s, Lefty had gone to work for the Chicago mob soon after graduating from high school. He had been a boyhood chum of Tony Spilotro at Steinmetz High. Then, without any help from Spilotro, who was nothing but a street punk at the time and who was to make his bones with the demented Sam DeStefano, Rosenthal began his career. He obtained a job through another friend, "Johno" DiDominico. John answered the phones, took the bets, and was otherwise a general factotum at the Angel-Kaplan Sports Service on Clark Street in the Loop, just north of the old Sherman Hotel, then known as the Sherman House, a spot which is now a parking lot. Johno got Lefty a job as his relief. Soon Lefty worked his way up and was sent to Miami by Donald Angelini, the "Angel" of Angel-Kaplan. Donald's boss, as he was for decades, was Joe Ferriola. Ferriola, at the time, worked for Fifi Buccieri and Turk Torello, the capos on the West Side, on his way up to becoming the absolute boss in his own right two decades later. In Miami, Lefty Rosenthal became a major sports-betting force and gained a reputation as one of the best handicappers and gamblers in the United States.

In the early seventies, Lefty was sent to Las Vegas to be Chicago's man at the Stardust, the Capone family's flagship casino. Lefty's old buddy, Spilotro, had been sent to Vegas by Chicago about the same time, 1971, and now the two neighborhood chums were united once again. Spilotro was the "Mr. Outside" for Chicago. He worked outside the casinos, enforcing the rules for Accardo and whoever his "boss of the year" might be. Lefty was "Mr. Inside." He worked inside the Stardust, making sure the skim was sufficient and that it regularly made its way to Accardo and his people in Chicago.

Not that Lefty didn't have his problems in Vegas. He was Mr. High Profile if there ever was one. While working at the Stardust, he also hosted a popular television program, "The Frank Rosenthal Show." He followed the same format as Johnny Carson, Larry King, and the other prominent interview hosts. His guests included almost all the talent who entertained in Las Vegas such as Frank Sinatra, Wayne Newton, Shecky Green, Don Rickles, and Dean Martin. As a result of all this activity, Lefty soon became as well known in Las Vegas as anyone. His Chicago connections were well known, however, and he fought hard but couldn't get a license from the Gaming Control Commission. And the more he fought for a license, the more he promoted his high public profile. In a televised public hearing, he challenged the members of the commission, tried to spill some dirt on them, even going so far as to follow them from the hall after the hearing was over to yell accusations at them.

Lefty fell in love with a showgirl, Geri, but after they were married and had two nice kids, Geri fell in love with another. Who, of all people, but Tony Spilotro. "Mr. Outside" had gotten inside and "Mr. Inside" was outside. What a mess! The police were even called into the situation one night when Geri taunted Lefty that "Tony is my sponsor!"

At the Stardust, Lefty was Chicago's "man." Allen Glick was the owner of record but, as the "Strawman II" tapes would show, Lefty ran the show. Glick was thrown out on orders from Chicago, after the Civellas from Kansas City had travelled to Chicago and met with Joe Aiuppa, Jackie Cerone, and Joey Lombardo. Rosenthal was kept in place. Al Sachs and Herb Tobman then took over the Stardust but Lefty remained "Mr. Inside" for Chicago, not necessarily at the Stardust but wherever their interests were focused.

For all these reasons, Frank "Lefty" Rosenthal was a shining symbol of Chicago's major operation in Las Vegas. If the Bonanno family could chop him, it would be a clear signal to the entire underworld, not to mention the upper world, that the Bonannos were fighting back and, in fact, had regained the upper hand.

Paulie, Clean, and the Ape went back to Vegas. They put a loose tail on Lefty and discovered that he had separated from Geri, who would in fact soon overdose on drugs and die in L.A. They found that Lefty maintained no particular pattern of activity except that he frequented the restaurant of a guy who had a chain of restaurants around the country. He was another guy from Chicago, Tony Roma, one of whose many restaurants was located in Las Vegas and was a favorite hangout of many hoods, including Lefty Rosenthal.

Once the terrible trio established this they devised a plan. The Ape was especially experienced with dynamite. One night when Lefty was entertaining his coterie at Tony Roma's, the Ape wired his car.

The Ape reveled in the art of execution, he had perfected it. Whatever the circumstances demanded, the Ape could handle it. If it took a knife in the back, so be it. If it took a bullet in the kneecap then the *coup de grâce* with another to the head of the now prone target, he could do that too. If it took a rope to garrote his man from behind, Annunciata could perform. If it took a karate chop, the Ape was skilled in that art as well. It was with equal pride that Annunciata had learned the intricacies of bombing. It wasn't all that difficult. Place a stack of some six sticks of dynamite under the hood of the car, up close to the firewall. Then wire a detonator into the dynamite. Wait from a distance of 100 yards until your target is observed entering his car. Then press the remote control to trigger the detonator and watch as the target exploded all over the parking lot.

In this case, however, due to the layout of the parking lot at Tony Roma's, there wasn't enough space to get clear of the explosion and yet be close enough to observe the fireworks. So the Ape went another route. He wired the dynamite directly to the ignition of Rosenthal's car.

When Lefty emerged from Tony Roma's, he stepped into his Cadillac, and, before he closed the door, turned on the ignition. Boom! A shattering explosion rocked the parking lot! Lefty was blown clear away from the car. What a mess!

What saved Lefty was the fact that he had not closed the front door on the driver's side before he turned on the ignition. An old Chicago trick. Therefore, the force of the blast was not confined to the inside of the car; it was diffused so that its effect was not nearly as intense inside the car. Lefty was badly injured, but he was not mortally wounded. Old habits developed in Chicago had stood him in good stead! He would soon recover, although he would never again be a force in Las Vegas. In fact, he would soon leave for Orange County, California, and then for Florida. He is but part of the mob lore on the Strip although in June, 1990 he obtained a reversal of his inclusion in the "Black Book," meaning that he is now once again legally permitted to set foot in a casino.

It was not a major success for the Bonanno family, but it wasn't exactly a failure either. The bombing of Lefty Rosenthal's car sent a very clear signal to the world, and especially to Tony Accardo, that the fight was still on, that the battle was not over, that the war of the godfathers was in full bloom. And finally that the Bonanno family had regained the upper hand.

BACK in Palm Springs, Joe Batters pondered the situation. How to counter Bonanno's latest perfidy? "Let's see, he came right into my territory, in Chicago, and took out one of my top guys. Why not show him he doesn't have a monopoly on that kind of move?"

Accardo summoned Joe Ferriola back to his home by the golf course. "Joe," he told him, "we're gonna demonstrate this Bananas is vulnerable in *his* backyard just like we were. We're going after one of his capos where he lives. Right in Tucson."

The target Accardo had selected was Charlie "Bats" Battaglia, the capo Bonanno had brought with him from Brooklyn when he first moved to Tucson. Along with son, Bill, in fact, Bats was Bonanno's top man in Arizona. Joe had also taken Pete Notaro and "Short Pants" Cacciopo with him when he made his move to the Old Pueblo in the desert, but those two were more or less his handymen, his drivers and gofers. Bats was a capo, a man of substance and ability.

Joe Ferriola returned to Chicago. His best hitters had been killed in Vegas on the Dalitz job, but in Chicago there was a wealth of such soldiers. He selected three more: Nick Nasti, John Sitiani, and Dominic Daddano. Dominic was a nephew of Willie "Potatoes" Daddano, a long-time key man for Sam Giancana and a cousin of Willie, Jr., another up-and-coming Chicago mob figure.

Joe established a command post in a suite of rooms at the posh Arizona Inn, adding insult to injury since it was within three blocks of Joe Bonanno's midtown Tucson home, one that he kept for himself when he was not in residence out at his Bar Bon Ranch. Since Bats's home off Columbus Avenue was not far away, it was a convenient spot.

The fearsome foursome began to stalk their prey. What was Bats's pattern? Where could they grab him? They wanted to take him alive. The plan was to force some secrets from Bats before they killed him, just as had been done with the Spilotro brothers. It was designed to be a signature job, a mirror image of the Spilotro grab. First, to snatch Bats in Bonanno's backyard, just as Spilotro had been grabbed in Batters's backyard. Then to beat him and grill him, then to kill him and dump him. Just like Spilotro.

They got Bats one night as he was driving to a meet with a cohort at the Sheraton El Conquistador Resort about five miles north of Tucson, just below Putsch Ridge on the north side of the Catalina Mountains. As Bats turned east, just off Oracle, onto the long stretch of road which was to take him to the El Conquistador, one of the two cars carrying the Chicago hit crew pulled in front of him and curbed him. Then Daddano and Nasti, in the backup car, smashed the window on the driver's side of Bats's Eldorado and stuck their guns in his face. They shoved him into their car and were joined there by Sitiani. They turned around, drove north into the small town of Red Rock, and then west into the Avra Valley to a remote desert area near the Saguaro National Monument. Bats was hog-tied, with his feet bound to his hands behind his back. Out came the ice picks. Nasti picked up a boulder from the desert and smashed it into Bats's kneecaps. Sitiani pulled out a pair of pliers and applied them to Bats's testicles. Soon they learned all they wanted to know. All about Joe Bonanno, his organization, the identity of his soldiers, his plans and his operations in Las Vegas, Tucson, and Brooklyn. They had a blueprint, a table of organization, and an agenda of the Bonanno family of La Cosa Nostra.

A shallow grave was dug in the desert of Avra Valley similar to Spilotro's temporary resting place in the cornfields of northern Indiana. The only difference was that Bats would never be found. The fearsome foursome were from Chicago. They had not reckoned with coyotes. You don't leave dead bodies in the desert if you want then discovered. Those nocturnal animals, the coyotes, forage in the desert for any food they can get. When they scented Bats's body, they quickly dug it up and howled for their cousins. Soon there was nothing left of Bats but his bones.

JOE Bonanno was sick at heart. The old warrior had had enough. He was a killer, a veteran of the heavy work from "the first days" of the Castellammarese War, the *picciotto,* the musketeer, the rifleman. But these guys were too much. He had found a worthy foe in Joe Batters. These Chicago guys were a match for him and then some. But he would not give up. He had started this war of the godfathers and he would finish it.

Meanwhile Joe Batters was not finished with his agenda of destroying Joe Bonanno and running him out of Las Vegas. Accardo had a bevy of capable lawyers in Chicago. These were reputable attorneys, some of whom had been prosecutors in the United States Attorney's office, the State's Attorney's office and even the Justice Department Strike Force. They learned their trade there, then they quit and entered private practice where they applied the experience gained on behalf of the government to defending clients, some of whom they had previously prosecuted. That is the way the game is played here in the U.S.A. It violates no canon of legal ethics and is accepted practice. A defense attorney stands just as tall before the bench in any courtroom as any other attorney. He gains high positions in his local bar association. He lunches with all of his brethren who practice other kinds of law—personal injury, corporate, negligence, security, or whatever. There is no stigma attached to him. Some, like Pat Tuite, Art Nasser, Sam Betar, and Carl Walsh are among the most intelligent and capable attorneys in Chicago.

On this occasion, however, Accardo needed an attorney knowledgeable about Las Vegas, somebody with contacts there. He considered the old standby, Sidney R. Korshak, but Sid was ill and not up to this task. He considered another, Del Coleman, but Del had broken away from his old associations and was no longer available. Accardo conferred with Art Nasser. Nasser had been an appeals attorney with the Internal Revenue Service in Chicago. He had opened up a practice in Chicago. He had a wide circle of acquaintances, including even the likes of Bill Richards. Nasser recommended Oscar Goodman to Accardo. Oscar is, without question, the most knowledgeable attorney, from the viewpoint of the mob, in Vegas. He has represented just about every mob figure there. He had even been a close friend of Chief Justice John Mowbray of the Nevada Supreme Court and everybody knows Justice Mowbray as the most honest and capable jurist there. When Accardo explained just what he wanted to Nasser, however, Nasser altered his opinion. "If it's the Gaming Control Board you want to reach, Oscar is not the guy. He's got good contacts there, he can get almost anything you want from them. But if the info you want to pass on were to come from him, it would be tainted in their eyes. You want somebody they have a high regard for, somebody who won't be recognized as coming from you."

They decided on Stanley Culbertson. Stan had been the Chief of the Justice Department Strike Force in Las Vegas. He has an outstanding reputation among his peers and is one of the most reputable attorneys in Vegas. He, too, has started his own practice after leaving the government. His contacts with any regulatory and law enforcement agencies are solid and widespread. No information bearing his imprimatur would be questioned.

The information obtained from Bats prior to his demise in the desert was furnished to Sal Solari, a former Chicago burglar who had recently been "made" into the Chicago family of the LCN. Solari had been sent to Vegas in the early eighties and had been assigned to be the eyes and ears of the Chicago mob inside Tony Spilotro's organization. Culbertson would recognize Solari's name quickly and, if he had any doubts as to who he represented, could call his pal, Bill Richards, for confirmation.

Solari made contact with Culbertson. It was the kind of sting Joe Bonanno had pulled on John Walsh and Bill Herlands decades before, but not as highly sophisticated. This time, however, Bonanno would be the victim, not the perpetrator. In a series of meetings held right in Culbertson's office since Solari was not hiding from his people or Culbertson's people, Solari laid out to Culbertson all of the info that had been gained from Charlie Battaglia. Foremost, of course, was that Joe Bonanno was the hidden owner of the Vegas Star, that John Walsh was a front for him as was Donald Ford, that Moe Dalitz had switched sides and had been working for Bonanno before he was killed, that Dick Becker had been Bonanno's man as the chief of security for the Star, that Bonanno was behind the construction of Camelot. Solari also spelled out the identities of the entire skim crew at the Star, the identities of all Bonanno's political contacts in Nevada including such public officials as two city commissioners and a county commissioner, two state legislators, three judges, six members of Metro, a local prosecutor, and, very importantly, a key investigator on the Gaming Control Board itself. As an added bonus, Solari supplied the name of one of the members of the Gaming Control Commission, which made its licensing decisions based on the investigations of the board. Culbertson immediately recognized that commissioner as the one out front in gaining approval of licenses for Bonanno's key employees at the Star. What a bombshell!

Culbertson knew immediately what he must do. He took his information to the Gaming Control Board, particularly to Rich Carr, its chief investigator, and two of his associates. These were people he had worked with while he ran the Las Vegas Justice Department Strike Force; the GCB investigators knew that any information carrying his stamp was accurate. Culbertson honored Solari's request that he not be identified, but vouched that the information came from "a source in a position to know." True enough!

Within days, the information was put to use. It was coupled with the information Richards had obtained at T. T.'s Cellar and given to the GCB. The Gaming Control Commission announced that hearings would be held immediately. Seven key employees at the Star including

Walsh, Ford, the casino manager, the new security chief, and two shift bosses would be given the opportunity "to show cause why their licenses should not be revoked."

Bonanno had been hit right where it hurt. His management team at the Vegas Star had been virtually destroyed!

ACCARDO carried his agenda to the next step. He again summoned Joe Ferriola to his home on the fairways of the Indian Wells Country Club.

"Joe," he said, "I think we got these bastards from New York on the run now. We got to polish them off. We have clipped their first security chief, now I hear the Gaming Control Commission has suspended their new replacement pending hearings. Things should be in a mess there. I also hear they're hiring new security personnel. Either find a guy we can put in there or bribe one of the old ones. They should be all fucked up at this point. I want to put a bomb in their counting room!"

Put a bomb in the counting room! If the Vegas Star hadn't been disrupted by now, this would be the *coup de grâce!*

Joe Ferriola went back to Las Vegas one more time. What the hell, he was supposed to be the boss, he was supposed to be directing things, not getting so close to the action. He had been doing such things for decades, but once you stepped up you were supposed to be able to sit back and assign somebody else to these tasks. In Chicago, however, it was the *consigliere,* old Joe Batters, who was the guy who sat back and gave the orders. And if the boss was the best guy for a job, so be it. Not that Joe Ferriola quarreled with any of that. He had been a young soldier in the family when the only guy who saw fit to operate independently of Accardo, Sam Giancana, was "boss." He knew what had happened to Sam Giancana. First, the government got him, then his own people got him. Ferriola was no Sam Giancana! He did what he was told.

So Ferriola settled back in Las Vegas. He went to see Joe Vasco. Joe Vasco had been a lieutenant when the police department and the sheriff's office in Clark County had been combined to form the single local law enforcement department in Las Vegas, known as Metro. He was on Tony Spilotro's pad. He kept Spilotro and his crew, sometimes called "The Hole in the Wall Gang," informed of what Metro knew and what it was doing about Spilotro and his myriad activities. In fact, when the "Hole in the Wall Gang" went out on burglaries for Spilotro, Vasco went along and operated as a lookout. He was about as bent as any cop could be—anywhere at any time.

Ferriola got a lead from Vasco. Vasco knew Frank Goebbels, a former Metro cop who was now the boss of the night shift on the security detail at the Star. There were dozens of former Metro cops in such positions in many of the Glitter Gulch and Strip hotels. At several casinos, such as the Sahara and the Hacienda, these Metro alums were chiefs of security. So it wasn't unusual to find a guy like Goebbels as chief of a shift at the Vegas Star. The *best* hotels and casinos have former FBI agents as security chiefs, but not the mobbed-up ones.

It wasn't a particularly difficult matter for Goebbels to allow Nick Nasti into the counting room one night. And it wasn't a particularly difficult matter for Nasti to place a bomb on a shelf out of view of the surveillance cameras supposedly recording every movement in the counting room on a twenty-four-hour basis. The bomb was properly prepared by Charles Smith, Accardo's top bomb expert in Chicago, and driven to Las Vegas. It was set to go off at 3:30 in the morning, when the counting room would be empty and the casino itself would be relatively quiet. It was after the "drop" for the previous day had been deposited but before it had been counted and taken away.

The bomb went off as planned. What a mess! It was a miracle nobody was hurt! Hundreds of thousands of dollars went up in the blast and it blew a hole the size of a small house in the Star, which was forced to shut down for a week. Millions more lost.

Joe Ferriola flew back to Chicago. He did not have to report to Tony Accardo in Palm Springs. Every TV and radio station in the country made it their lead item in the early morning news. Tony Accardo thought Joe Ferriola was developing into perhaps the best boss he ever had, maybe even on a par with Jackie Cerone. "Sure as hell better than that fucking Sam Giancana or that slow-witted Joe Aiuppa or guys like Charlie Battaglia or Philly Alderisio, whose regimes had lasted just a year." Maybe this guy would take his place right up there with the best. Accardo sure hoped Ferriola would stay around awhile—preferably for the rest of Accardo's life.

Despite these recent successes, Joe Batters wasn't going to let the pressure off now. He got hold of Ed Donovan, president of the Culinary Union. Donovan had been associated with the Chicago mob for many years. Bill Richards had testified before the Rackets Committee that Donovan was put in place in one of the Culinary Union's Chicago locals by Joey Aiuppa when Aiuppa was responsible for Cicero on behalf of the Chicago mob. Aiuppa took Donovan to Johnny Lardino, the mob's man in the Culinary Union, who put Donovan in place. Eventually, just as Accardo and his pals had installed Willie Bioff and George Browne as leaders of the International Alliance of Theatrical Stage Employees (IATSE), in what became known as the Hollywood Extortion Case, Accardo had made sure Donovan became president of the Culinary Union. Now within days, all the cooks, waiters, waitresses, and bartenders walked out of the Vegas Star on strike. Not only did they strike but their picketing seriously disrupted the flow of players who wanted to gamble or eat at the Vegas Star. Those employees who did not honor the strike by crossing the picket line were harassed. Their cars were scratched and they were bombarded with obscenities. Several fights broke out. It was very damaging, to say the least, to the operation of the Star, just days after it reopened following the bombing of the counting room.

Then Accardo reached out to the president of another labor union where he wielded great influence, the Laborers International Union. For years, Angelo Fosco and Frankie "The X" Esposito were Accardo's men in the national leadership of that union. Once, years before, he had had Jackie Cerone, Fifi Buccieri, Turk Torello, and Skippy Cerone stalk Esposito in the Miami area with a contract to kill him. Only the intervention of the FBI and the Dade County Sheriff's office had prevented bloodshed on that occasion. The FBI listened in on hidden microphones as Cerone and his hit crew made plans to dismember Esposito with an ax and feed him to the fishes in the Atlantic Ocean.

Accardo sent this laborers union local off on another assignment. To strike and picket the construction site of Camelot. The same situation prevailed at Camelot as had at the Vegas Star, the only difference being the identity of the union involved. All work came to a screeching halt.

Then Joe Batters got hold of the president of the Laundry Workers Union. For years, since Murray "The Camel" Humphreys and Gussie Alex had corrupted several of the leaders of this union including Eugene "Jimmy" James and Gus Zapas of New Jersey and Chicago respectively, the Chicago mob has had a hold on it. Soon all the linens and towels needed in the guest rooms and in the restaurants of the Vegas Star went unwashed.

Accardo reached out for the Teamsters union. The Chicago mob had of course maintained a close relationship with the national leadership of the Teamsters since Jimmy Hoffa first came to the attention of Hump through Red Dorfman in the 1950s. They kept up ties through Frank Fitzsimmons, Roy Williams, and then with Jackie Presser, although the latter relationship was not nearly as close. Presser was in power now, and it took but a phone call. All truck deliveries to the Star were halted as the Teamsters struck.

Finally, Joe Batters reached out for the International Brotherhood of Electrical Workers (IBEW). Soon the electricians at the Vegas Star walked out. The IBEW had had ties to the Chicago mob since Hump got next to Mike Kennedy in the thirties. Now the Star was completely shut down, lock, stock, and barrel. Nothing was moving there. Or at Camelot. Joe Bonnano's venture into Las Vegas was obviously in great peril.

JOE Batters then made another move. This time he contacted Jules Cohen, their bag man in Las Vegas, the guy who "carried the stash." Cohen had been given a job years before as a host at the Riviera when it was under the control of the Chicago mob. But his real function was to spread graft for the Chicago mob in Vegas, to develop and maintain the contacts with the public officials, political leaders, law enforcement officers, labor leaders, and especially with the gaming regulators who could look out for mob interests there.

What Accardo needed now was to put a crimp, a big crimp, in Bonnano's plans to build Camelot. He conferred with Sidney Korshak in Palm Springs. What Korshak advised him to do was to attack the "height limitation." Korshak had determined that for Bonnano and his CamStar corporation to build Camelot large enough to fulfil his grandiose dreams, the hotel would have to stand at least fifty stories tall. The piece of property he had acquired along the Strip was simply not wide enough or deep enough to satisfy his requirements unless it was built to fifty stories. Walsh and Ford had gone before the Clark County commissioners and obtained a zoning variance to permit them to build to the necessary height. It was against Clark County ordinances, but Ford and Walsh had spread enough graft from Bonnano's coffers at CamStar to influence a majority of the commissioners to support the variance. It had taken a quarter of a million dollars, but it had been worth it.

Now Accardo used "Chicago tactics" to bring the matter back before the commissioners. Muscle, money, favors, and intimidation. Whatever it took to influence the commissioners. One had had his eye on the hostess at the Bavarian Inn in the Vegas Hilton. He got her. Another wanted an outright bribe of $25,000. He got it. Another was in the meat business. He wanted the contract to supply meat to the Stardust. Done. Another intended to run for Congress in the next election. He would need a campaign contribution much greater than any he had received in the past. He got a promise—from Ed Donovan at the Culinary Union. Another had a son who owned a small dry-cleaning establishment in Minden, a town in northern Nevada, just a few miles from the capital in Carson City. He had nonunion employees, but the Laundry Workers Union was about to organize them. He needed a "sweetheart contract." No problem.

Accardo lined up enough support. One of his commissioners introduced a bill cutting down the county height limitation to thirty-two stories. It was a move aimed directly at Bonanno's balance sheet if he were to go ahead with Camelot. It would effectively nullify the New York family's profits, and Bonanno would be forced to either drop his plans for Camelot or drastically diminish his expectations. Either way it would be another major blow to his dreams of establishing an empire in Las Vegas.

One of the highly influential community newspapers in Las Vegas started a "grass roots" campaign to support the ordinance. "Roll Back" became the byword. "Who are these people behind CamStar? Who are they to come into Las Vegas and destroy our views. A fifty-story height limitation is no limitation at all. Get out the vote, support our Commissioners who support the Roll Back! Roll out the ones who do not support Roll Back!" The local citizenry became aroused, putting substantial pressure on the commissioners. All of a sudden the community newspaper, published by a public relations man who had a contract with the Stardust, began to get considerably more advertising from the hotels. The pressure mounted.

Tony Accardo gloated. He had it "wired" every imaginable way. Came time for the vote and it turned out to be nearly unanimous. The height restriction was rolled back and so were Joe Bonanno's dreams. Camelot would be just half the resort he had planned.

AT that point, Accardo played his trump card. All these niceties were all very well and good, but there was one body, one organization, that wielded more power than any law enforcement agency, any regulatory agency, any court, any prosecutor, any union, or even the Chicago mob. That, of course, was The Commission. In this case, The Commission was the final authority. Only God had more power over Joe Bonanno than The Commission—and Joe didn't recognize Him.

Accardo and Joe Ferriola travelled back to New York and crossed the George Washington Bridge to Fort Lee. Their favorite little road-house there was getting a good workout as the site of The Commission meetings.

Accardo got right to the point, as always. "You guys saw fit to table my request that you keep Joe Bananas out of Las Vegas. Now I want some action on my proposal. I want him ordered out. Now." Joe Batters sat down.

It didn't take long. Bonanno had very little to say. All he could see now was the wreckage of his plan. He tried to plead, but his heart wasn't in it. The Commission members who had shown up for this sit-down—John Gotti, Carmine Persico, "Ducks" Corallo, Tony Salerno, Nicky Scarfo, and Joe Zerelli—didn't even have to ask Bonanno, Accardo, or Ferriola to leave the room. They looked at each other, nodded that they were all in agreement, and left it to Gotti to speak for the group. He stood up.

"Joe," he said, looking at Bonanno, "get out of Vegas. Do it now." It was settled. There was one more item to be settled.

Bonanno stood up. "All right, I accept your decision. I will withdraw my family from Las Vegas. But I want one other order of this body. I want you to insure there will be peace from now on, that the violence of this vicious Accardo will cease here and now, and that my family will be left alone. We will stay in Brooklyn, we will not attempt to infringe on Chicago's territory anywhere, but I want a ruling that we are to be left alone in Brooklyn and in Arizona."

Accardo jumped up. "Bullshit! Not Arizona, he's got no right to Arizona! Chicago owns everything west of Chicago all the way to the fuckin' ocean! And that includes Arizona. He don't get Arizona!"

When Accardo calmed down and sat down, Gotti stood up again. "Joe," he said, "I believe he is right. Your place has always been Brooklyn. I see no reason why that should change. But Arizona has always been 'open territory.' I think it still should be." He looked around the table. Nobody seemed to disagree.

Joe Batters stood up one more time. "Here is what I am willing to propose, and I think we're being kind here. If Joe Bananas wants to live in Arizona, fuck it, let him. But he don't control nothin' there. He lives there, that's all. If we want to do anything in Arizona, Tucson or Phoenix or any other fuckin' place, we got the right to go in there. It stays 'open territory.' We'll leave him alone there but he don't call no shots there. If you guys want to leave him in Brooklyn, that's your problem. We got nothin' to do with Brooklyn. But he can't have Arizona!" Accardo sat down one more time.

The conferees looked at each other again. Nobody seemed to disagree with Accardo. Gotti then spoke: "Let's vote. Joe Bonanno goes back to Brooklyn, he can live wherever he wants, in Arizona or wherever, but he don't control nothin' outside Brooklyn."

The mob bosses all turned the palms of their hands up. That was it. Nobody disagreed. It was over. Obviously, they realized that Tony Accardo was the winner. He played all his cards and came out on top. They knew they had nothing going with Joe Bonanno in Las Vegas. He was the loser. He had nothing to offer them. They voted him down.

Accardo and Ferriola got up without a word. They walked out to the parking lot, got into their rental car, and drove back over the George Washington Bridge. Back into the Volcano. The fire had gone out, however. As far as they were concerned there would be no further eruptions. The lava was already cooling. At least as far as they were concerned. "Let those greaseballs fight among themselves. We're out of it. Our problems are over," Accardo and Ferriola were thinking as they made their way toward La Guardia Airport and the flight home. Little did they know that their problems were really just beginning, that they had yet to reckon with yet another old and very tough enemy.

CHAPTER

20

The Investigation

THE shooting war may have been over, but Bill Richards didn't know that. Even if he had, it wouldn't have made any difference. In his capacity as a consultant for the Chicago Crime Commission and as a special investigator for the Senate Rackets Committee, Richards was working hard to ferret out as much information as he could as to what was going on in Las Vegas involving the Chicago and New York mobs. He was working closely with the Las Vegas and Chicago offices of the FBI and with the two agencies in Las Vegas who had an official investigative interest, the Gaming Control Board and Metro.

When the Top Hoodlum Program was initiated by J. Edgar Hoover in November of 1957 following the Apalachin meeting and Richards was assigned to investigations of organized crime, his first target had been Gussie Alex. He had pursued his target almost continuously for the next twenty years. He bugged the headquarters of the Chicago mob on the Magnificent Mile, listening to Alex and his associates nearly on a daily basis for six years. He developed scores of informants over the years, many of whom were "made" members of the mob. Many of these, including such highly placed members as Dick Cain and one code-named "Sporting Goods," were particularly close to Alex. There wasn't much about Alex that Richards didn't know.

For this reason, when Moe Dalitz was poisoned at Sunrise Hospital in Las Vegas, Richards quickly suspected the work of Gussie Alex. He recalled Alex's involvement in the James Ragen murder in Chicago in 1946. With the aid of the FBI in Las Vegas, the GCB, and Metro, he conducted a full field investigation at Sunrise Hospital. He interviewed all personnel who had been on duty the day and night Dalitz died— every doctor, every intern, every nurse, every orderly, every nurse's aide, every volunteer, every maintenance worker, every visitor to Dalitz's floor. It was a tremendous task for a lone investigator, but Richards was determined to the point of obsession and he knew the Dalitz case could potentially blow the lid off the whole thing. As is true of most good, experienced investigators, Richards had instincts. When one of the nurses told him that an orderly had been lingering in the section of rooms where Dalitz was confined and seemed to have an inordinate interest in the man's condition, Richards zeroed in on that orderly, whose name was Ben Jackson.

Unfortunately for Jackson, he had nobody to lean on, no support line. His only contact with the mob had been Gus Alex and Gussie had met him just two times, then never again. Jackson was a lone wolf, hung out in the wilderness. He began to waver under intense interrogation by Richards.

The break came when Richards discovered that Jackson had been delinquent for several months on his rent payments and on the monthly payments on his car. Just two days after Dalitz died, however, Jackson had very quickly caught up on both accounts. It was an obvious tip-off.

When Richards zeroed in on Jackson as the main suspect, he went to the chief of security at Sunrise Hospital, Gene Stephens, a former sergeant with Metro. A good man. Richards told Stephens that he needed a pressure point on Jackson. Stephens informed Richards that he knew from his years on the force that Ben Jackson had often assisted Dr. Shultz in his illegal abortions at the back-alley clinic. It might be just what Richards was looking for as leverage on Jackson. It would be made clear to Jackson that his job at Sunrise hung in the balance because of his participation in the illegal abortions. Although Jackson's involvement might not be provable in a court of law, enough evidence was available to Stephens through his connections at Metro that Jackson could be terminated at Sunrise. In addition to that, he could be barred from any further employment in the health care community, his only profession, not only in Las Vegas but all over the country. It was a powerful leverage against a player at Jackson's level.

Arrangements were made between Stephens and Richards. Jackson was called into Stephens's office at Sunrise. Stephens let Richards carry the ball from there.

"Mr. Jackson," Richards stated, "you know Sergeant Stephens here. Of course, he's in charge of security at this hospital. Now, Sergeant Stephens is also a former officer at Metro. While he was at Metro, he conducted investigations of illegal abortions. He became very much aware of you and your participation in many such abortions. He has informed me that he does not feel that a person like you deserves to be working in this, one of the very best, hospitals in the world. He has given very serious consideration to terminating you. Now, let me introduce myself. I was an FBI agent for thirty years. I am currently a staff investigator for the Senate Rackets Committee. I am investigating the murder of Moe Dalitz. I believe you know I have focused in on you as the perpetrator of this crime. I want you to know that I am recommending to the Senate Rackets Committee that we hold hearings on the murder of Moe Dalitz and that I am recommending further that you be subpoenaed so that you can be interrogated concerning your role in that. I am also in contact with James Anderson, chief of the Justice Department Strike Force here in Las Vegas. So, Mr. Jackson, what I am saying to you is that, number one, you stand not only to lose your job here but your ability to get a job in any health care unit in the world. Number two, the Senate Rackets Committee is prepared to bring you before it to question you about your role in the killing of Moe Dalitz in the forum of a public hearing, open to the public and the press. You will become quite notorious if that should happen. Number three, the results of our investigation will be made known to the Justice Department with a view toward prosecution. I want you to think about all this. You lose your job and your profession, you become known to the world as a killer, and then you go to prison for murder, perhaps to the electric chair, perhaps just for life. Think about it. We're going to leave you alone for fifteen minutes. When we come back, we will talk."

A lot of what Bill Richards told Ben Jackson was bluff. He was attempting to take advantage of a bit of puffery so that the unsophisticated Jackson would believe he was in a hell of a bad spot. On the other hand, there was a kernel of truth to what Richards was saying. Jackson was not in a good position. He probably *would* lose his job. There *might* be a Senate Rackets Committee hearing involving some embarrassing questions concerning Jackson's role in the poisoning of Dalitz. He probably would *not* be prosecuted if he kept his mouth shut. Unless he confessed, there was no real evidence connecting him with the crime. But many individuals who are not hardened criminals and are not aware of the methods of law enforcement interrogation are not able to think out what is provable and what is not when the wheels of justice roll. Such as the case with Ben Jackson. He had no more than a high school education in Jackson, Mississippi, and had never before encountered a real live federal law enforcement officer. When Richards had mentioned that he was a former FBI agent he purposely garbled the word "former," figuring Jackson would believe he was still with the Bureau while now working with the Rackets Committee. Jackson was sweating; this was a real deep ditch he had been thrown into.

When Richards and Stephens reentered the room they noticed Jackson's fidgeting.

Richards got right to it. "Jackson, here's what we propose to you. You tell us your story, factually and honestly. If you do, I will see that you get into the witness protection program and that you get immunity."

Richards could see this had gone over Jackson's head. "What I am saying to you, Jackson, is that if you honestly tell us what you know and agree to testify to that, we will give you immunity. That means we will not send you to jail. Then we will make sure you are protected and that you will get a job in another area of the country where we will stay in touch with you, help you solve any real problems you have, and be your friend."

"You can promise me all that now?" Jackson asked.

"No, not right now. But if you tell us now off the record what you know, I'll take you to the man who can. In the meantime, Sergeant Stephens here will allow you to keep your job and I will see that you are not called before the Senate. How's that?

"First, I must tell you your Miranda rights. You have the right to remain silent, you have the right to an attorney. If you can't afford one, one will be appointed for you. You don't have to say anything. If you do, anything you say can be used against you. Whatever you might say

can be used against you in a court of law. I want you to know that—
even though I give you my personal promise right now that this is off
the record. I want to stress to you, you have the right to an attorney
and that if you do tell us anything which incriminates you it can be used
against you in court."

Richards did not intend to lose Jackson's testimony because he didn't
read him his rights. He felt he should explain to Jackson, because he
was not technically a lawman and Jackson was not actually under
arrest, that Jackson could not necessarily rely on Richards's promise
of immunity, but that if the promise could not be upheld then Jackson's
statement would certainly be kept off the record. None of this seemed
to make any difference to Jackson. It all seemed to fly right over his
head.

"What if I can't tell you who the man behind it is?"

"We'll show you pictures," Richards said. "I think I know who it
was."

"Well, a man did come to me and ask me to knock off Dalitz in the
I.C.U.," Jackson admitted.

"The intensive care unit," Richards said.

"Yes, but I won't admit I did," Jackson responded.

"Okay, let's leave it at that for the moment," Richards said, not
wanting to take the chance of turning Jackson off by rushing it.

"Without admitting you went along with him, what did he offer
you?" Richards asked.

"Let's say $100,000."

"Do you still have it?" Richards asked quickly, hoping Jackson
would tacitly admit he had taken the money.

At this point, Jackson clammed up. The interview went no further.
Richards tried, but Jackson was adamant. He would make no further
admissions.

When the meeting was about to break up, Richards admonished
Jackson. "Don't try to skip, Jackson," he said. "We'll find you."

Richards then did two things. First, he put together a "spread," a
rogue's gallery of photographs of likely candidates for the role of the
instigator who approached Jackson with the idea of killing Dalitz.
Richards then went to James Anderson, chief of the Justice Department Strike Force in Las Vegas. He suggested that, in return for his
testimony, the government grant Jackson immunity from any prosecution—federal or state. Anderson agreed. On one condition. That the

person identified by Jackson be a major player in organized crime. There was no real reason to grant immunity to someone unless he could produce someone much bigger than himself. The minnow might be traded for the shark, but there is no justification for excusing anyone of a crime, particularly the crime of murder, unless there is a major benefit in doing so.

The next day, Stephens tapped Jackson on the shoulder while he was working in the hospital and brought the orderly into his office. Richards and Anderson were waiting there.

"Jackson, here is the man," Richards said. "This is the man who can make the arrangement for you we discussed the other day. You remember I spelled out for you just how we can take care of you for the rest of your life? Well, this is the man who can make it happen."

Anderson nodded, very seriously. "If you tell us who put you up to this, we will keep our end of the bargain."

"Do I have to admit I did anything?" Jackson asked.

"We'll get to that later. Right now, Mr. Richards has a spread of photos he'd like to show you. You tell us if you see the person who approached you," Anderson said. Then Anderson read Jackson his Miranda rights, just as Richards had done the previous day.

Jackson looked at the spread, quickly spotting the man who had made the arrangement with him after the dinner at the Sultan's Table in the Dunes Hotel. Richards had placed three photos of Gus Alex among the twenty-five in the spread. Jackson hesitated. This was it. It was his moment of truth. Jackson felt that if he declined to pick out the picture he would be hung out to dry, all by himself. It was a tough position to be in. He felt clammy. There was a knot in his stomach. He hesitated.

When Jackson looked up, he gazed into the stern countenances of Richards, Stephens, and Anderson. Nobody smiled. This was *very* serious stuff.

Jackson slowly reached for one of the photos of Gussie Alex, a stand-up mug shot, front view and side view, taken by the Los Angeles Police Department some years ago. He handed it to Richards, who was elated! His old foe! The guy he had battled for years, his first target when J. Edgar Hoover had initiated the Top Hoodlum Program in 1957. A guy who had never been convicted of anything! But Richards said nothing. He didn't want to spook Jackson.

"Do you see any more photos of this fellow?"

As Jackson glanced over the photo spread again, Richards caught Anderson's eye. He winked and smiled broadly. Although Anderson was unfamiliar with Gus Alex's physical appearance, seeing Richards's wink he knew they must have something big. And Anderson would certainly be aware of Alex's odious reputation by name.

Jackson then picked out the other two photos of Gus Alex. Compared to Gus Alex, Ben Jackson was peanuts. It would be like trading a sparrow for a dinosaur if Jackson could be persuaded to agree to testify against the mob kingpin.

Richards took Anderson out into the corridor, and informed Anderson what they had, reinforcing his colleague's sketchy knowledge of just what Alex represented. Richards's enthusiasm bubbled over. "Let's do it!" he shouted as he squeezed Anderson's arm.

They returned to the room. "Mr. Jackson," Anderson said, "if you will tell us all about this situation, from beginning to end—off the record for now, not to be used against you—I will communicate with my superiors in Washington with my recommendation that you be given immunity in return for your testimony. What that means is that you will never be arrested or taken to court with regard to any of this. We will put you in the Witness Protection Program where you will be given a new identity and a new job, probably in a hospital somewhere away from here. Do you understand that?"

Jackson said he did, then told the whole story—how he had been approached by Gus Alex, how they had dinner at the Sultan's Table, how Alex made the $100,000 payment in cash up front, and of how he, Jackson, had poisoned Dalitz in the intensive care unit at Sunrise Hospital. All off the record.

Anderson then communicated with his boss in Washington, who took it to *his* boss, the U. S. Attorney General, Dick Thornburgh. Soon the word came. The deal was approved. With that, Anderson went back to Ben Jackson and recorded the entire story, this time very definitely *on* the record.

Richards and Anderson then went to Chicago, where they conferred with Gary Shapiro, the chief of the Chicago Strike Force and his top assistant, Jeff Johnson. They decided to keep Jackson on ice, to bring him before the federal grand jury in Chicago and obtain his complete testimony, then relocate him in the Witness Protection Program.

The Witness Protection Program is staffed by the U. S. Marshal's Service. When witnesses such as Ben Jackson, Jimmy Fratianno, Joe

Cantalupo, Henry Hill, and Frank Cullotta cooperate with the government by agreeing to testify fully about their coconspirators in the mob, they are given assumed identities, a monthly stipend, expenses for their families, if any, protection when necessary by the marshals, help in obtaining employment, and relocation to an area where they are completely unknown. It's a tough life for a protected witness—not an easy one. The Marshal's Service does all it can to make it as smooth and efficient as possible, but it is a difficult task by its very nature and glitches do occur. The alternatives to the program, however, suffer by comparison. The life of such a witness is in constant danger. If he is left to fend completely for himself, especially in the early stages after leaving the mob and testifying against them, his chances of survival are not good. Furthermore, it is most difficult for former hoods to adapt to an entirely new life style—making an honest and comfortable living for themselves and their families. For Ben Jackson, however, it was not so hard. He was one of the unusual ones in that he had always been able to make an honest living for himself. His problem had been that on just one occasion in his whole life he had succumbed to the pressure of the one big pay day, the $100,000 in cash proffered to him by Gussie Alex. Ben was relocated from Las Vegas to Boston. Especially since he had no family, it wasn't so difficult for him. Two affable marshals drove him to Boston, found him a new job in his chosen profession as hospital orderly, found an apartment in a nice complex, and kept him in close touch with his support line, the Marshal's Service. Any problems he had in his new environment with his new identity were brought to the attention of the marshal assigned to his case and every effort was made to iron them out.

He would be ready to testify against Gus Alex when needed.

WHEN Richards returned to Las Vegas, he began work on another piece of the puzzle: how the Chicago mob had bombed the counting room of the Vegas Star. By this time the Star had been sold by CamStar at a bargain basement price after all that had happened to it, to Tojo Yashudi, a wealthy Japanese industrialist. Yashudi was in the process of reorganizing his staff. When Richards sat down with him he found that Yashudi had wisely retained Tom Carrigan, the former chief investigator for the Gaming Control Board, who had opened his own agency consulting with Nevada, New Jersey, and foreign casino operators as to their business. Richards and Carrigan had been pals for years.

Richards contacted Carrigan and lunched with him at Michael's in the Barbary Coast.

"Tommy," Richards said, "I'm working on the bombing of the counting room at the Star. It's obvious it had to be an inside job. There is somebody probably still working there who had a hand in setting it up. He could lead us to the bomber, who could lead us to his superior, and the chain could reach all the way to Tony Accardo."

"Boy, you're shooting for the moon. I heard Tony Accardo has never spent a night in jail," Carrigan replied.

"Hey, that gives a guy added incentive," Richards said. "All the more reason to work hard on this one. The guy has skated all his life, maybe we can nail him now. I've locked horns with him for over thirty years since I first met him in about 1960. He's an old man now and he's never been successfully prosecuted. The closest was when we convicted him for income tax fraud in 1960 but the mob got to a couple of appeals judges. The conviction was overthrown and he beat the retrial. The top mob boss in America, and he's never been incarcerated."

"How can I help?" Carrigan asked.

"Two ways, Tom. First, let's you and me go over the personnel records at the Star. Then let me sit in with you while you interview them for your reorganization. Just introduce me as your assistant. Let me get a feel for them. Then, if we get lucky we'll see where we go from there."

"Okay, no problem," Carrigan said.

They started. Soon they came to Frank Goebbels. It didn't take a genius to spot it. First of all, he had the strategic position. He was the security chief on the night shift. He was the obvious guy in position to introduce an imposter into the security crew and allow him entrance to the counting room. With the help of Carrigan, Richards brought Goebbels back for a second—and third and fourth—interview. They laid it right on the line. Goebbels was going to be fired if he didn't cooperate. Not only that but he would be blackballed. Not only in the gaming industry but wherever he went looking for future employment in his chosen profession, the only profession he knew, law enforcement. Richards would see to that. Obviously, it was the latter threat which carried the most weight since Goebbels would not be keeping his position at the Star even if he decided to talk. The Star would have no objection, but his life would be in great danger if he talked to Richards. He certainly wouldn't be able to remain in Las Vegas. He was a tough nut to crack, and it eventually became clear that he wouldn't.

Finally, Richards and Goebbels had one last meeting. Carrigan had agreed to retain Goebbels, even consider him for a better job, if he would only tell Richards what he knew on a strictly confidential basis. Hand up the bomber, but off the record without any agreement to testify. It was less than half a loaf as far as Richards was concerned but better than no deal at all.

Richards went back to Chicago where he conferred with his old pal, Pete Wacks, the veteran FBI agent who had been a rookie when Richards was the senior agent on the Organized Crime Squad, C-1, in Chicago. "Who are the most logical Chicago mobsters who might have planted the bomb at the Star?"

Wacks ran down a short list of his suspects. Nick Nasti was on the list.

"Can you give me a couple photos of these guys," Richards asked. Since Richards was operating in his official capacities, Wacks complied. He furnished the shots of the mobsters on his list. Some were surveillance photos, shots of the mobsters taking by the Bureau in their natural habitats on the streets of Chicago or in mob hangouts. Some were "mug shots," taken by the FBI or the Chicago Police Department of the mobsters when they had been arrested. Some were passport photos. There were two of Nasti, one a surveillance photo in company with Joe Ferriola, his boss; the other, several years old, a "mug shot."

Richards took them back to Las Vegas. He sat down with Frank Goebbels one more time and spread the photos out on the table. Goebbels took his time. After a few minutes, he picked up the photo of Nasti with Ferriola. He quietly handed it to Richards.

"Which one?" Richards asked. He was hoping it was Ferriola.

"The one on the left," Goebbels replied. It was Nasti.

"Are you sure? Take a look at the rest of the photos here. Make sure," Richards asked.

Goebbels carefully checked all the photos one more time. He failed to see the mug shot of Nasti as a possibility. When Richards picked it out and handed it to him without a word, he still didn't ID it. It was too old, not a good current likeness of Nasti since he had put on a considerable amount of weight as he advanced up the ladder of the mob. But it didn't make much difference. Goebbels seemed sure of his selection. Richards stood up. He shook hands with Goebbels and said to him: "You'll probably never see me again, but good luck here at the Star, thank you."

THE next day Richards checked out of the Barbary Coast, turned in his rental car at McCarran, and flew American Airlines direct to O'Hare. He took a cab to the Sheraton Plaza where he checked in with Cathy, the world's best concierge. She had him upgraded to a suite, easily done not only because of her influence but because he is a member of the Sheraton Club International. Then he called Pete Wacks. "Pete, can you meet me at Eli's? I've got some news," he said.

Richards walked the three blocks from the Sheraton Plaza to Eli's Place for Steaks. Eli Shulman had been a pal of Richards's before he died and now his wife, Esther, and son, Mark, ran the place. It was usually Richards's first stop in Chicago, a place where he met old pals like Jack and Pat Brickhouse, Judge Abraham Lincoln Marovitz, Bill Hartnett of "Here's Chicago"; Ray Shryock and George Mandich, with whom he had worked in the FBI; Frank Mauro, the car dealer; Miles Cooperman of the Sheriff's Office; Bill Fudala, Richards's old sparring partner; and Bob Lee and Joe Archibald, old pals from Notre Dame.

Richards informed Wacks of Goebbels's identification of Nasti. "I need to know as much as possible about his current activity, his associates, his hangouts, everything, Pete," Richards said. Richards already had one leg up on Nasti. During his twenty-four years with the FBI in Chicago, Richards had met just about every mobster of any stature in Chicago. He had targeted Nasti as a potential criminal informant, what the Bureau calls a PCI, in 1975 when Nasti was first "made" into the Chicago family. He had intercepted Nasti twice as he came out of his home in Melrose Park, a western suburb of Chicago. Nasti, however, turned out to be a particularly tough target. Very few hoodlums had ever told Richards to go fuck himself, but Nasti came close to it. The conversations had been very short and unproductive from Richards's point of view. He knew that his job now would be difficult.

The reason it would be particularly difficult was that he had no evidence against Nasti in the counting room bombing. He had made a deal with Frank Goebbels that he would not give him up as having fingered Nasti nor would Goebbels ever be identified to anyone as the source on Nasti. Carrigan would have a good idea, but he was solid as a rock and would not tell anyone else. So Richards had no evidence to take to the Chicago or Las Vegas Strike Forces and no information he could use as leverage in talking to Nasti. He came into this battle with no ammunition.

When Pete Wacks filled him in, however, he gave Richards his first intimation that it might not be an impossible job. For one of the things

Wacks mentioned was that Nasti's closest associate in the Chicago mob, his running partner, was Peter Castigone.

Peter Castigone! Wow! This gave Richards a real high because he knew Peter Castigone well, very well indeed. Since the mid-Seventies, in fact.

21

A Pal of Richards's

THE year was 1975. Postage stamps cost ten cents. The United States pulled out of Vietnam. Mother Elizabeth Seton became the first U.S.-born saint. Patty Hearst was captured. President Nixon had resigned the previous summer. Bill Richards had just switched from C-1, one of the Chicago FBI-organized crime squads, to C-10, the other, after a personality conflict with Vince Inserra, the fine C-1 supervisor and Richards's old pal.

When he reported to C-10 and to his new supervisor, Bob Dolan, Richards was assigned full time to informant development and was given the job of supervising the Chicago FBI office informant programs. It was his job to target as many potential informants as he could and to oversee other agents who were charged with the responsibility of developing their own informants, a job every FBI agent has if he is working on criminal matters and especially organized crime matters. An FBI agent is judged by his success in developing informants and his success, or lack thereof, is a major part of his annual efficiency report which is submitted every spring.

Richards had had two prime areas of success in the FBI. One was the penetration of mob headquarters where hidden microphones had been planted in order to overhear the conversations of the major mobsters. The other was in the development of informants such as Dick Cain, the "made" member of the Chicago mob who had been assigned to infiltrate law enforcement and then later became the chief confidant of Sam Giancana when Giancana was boss of the Chicago mob. Richards had developed dozens of strategically placed informants inside the mob including two upper echelon leaders, "Sporting Goods" and "Romano." It was therefore a natural for him to be assigned full time to this task although he felt let down since he could no longer devote investigative attention to his longtime foes such as Tony Accardo and Gus Alex or to his favorite interest, the alliance between crime and politics, with Pat Marcy and John D'Arco, Sr. as his special targets.

It wasn't long after Richards received his new assignments on C-10 in 1975 that he targeted Peter Castigone as a potential criminal informant (PCI). Peter had just been "made" into the mob.

Castigone had entered the underworld at the age of twenty-five when he became a "juice" collector for "Mad Sam" DeStefano. Sam was the leading juice guy in Chicago. He had more money "on the street" than any other hoodlum. It was in the form of loans at usurious rates of interest to those high-risk borrowers who were at least temporarily down on their luck, such as gamblers, burglars, and even some businessmen who were not in a position to go to legitimate lending institutions, such as banks or savings and loans. Many of them would come to "Mad Sam." He would lend money to almost anyone, no matter how bad a risk, whereas other Chicago loansharks were much more discriminating. The reason was that Sam loved to torture a delinquent borrower. He would prefer it if a juice victim did not pay him, at least not on time. He could then take him down to the torture chamber he kept in his basement and, with the help of guys like Tony Spilotro, Leo Foreman, Chuckie Crimaldi, Patsy Coletti, and his brother, Mario DeStefano, use his ice pick and his hammer on them.

Peter Castigone entered this world in the early 1970s. Tony Spilotro moved up from DeStefano into the organization itself, eventually to become Chicago's "Mr. Inside" in Las Vegas. DeStefano replaced Spilotro with Castigone and it was Castigone's job to collect the regular payments from Sam's juice borrowers, to locate delinquent borrowers and bring them to Sam, then make sure they were tied securely while Sam tortured them.

After a couple of years of that kind of work, a good breeding ground for outfit recruits, Peter went to work with Felix "Milwaukee Phil" Alderisio. Again Castigone followed "Tony the Ant" on his way up the ranks. Alderisio had been the major hit guy for the Chicago mob, the guy who did the heavy work for Tony Accardo's organization. Alderisio and his partner, Chuckie Nicoletti, were in charge of the heavy work, and they had a small cadre of workers to assist them. Peter Castigone became a member of that cadre. Then when Alderisio moved up in the very late 1960s to become the absolute boss of the Chicago mob, elevated by Accardo, Castigone moved up with him.

For all of the above reasons, Castigone was a natural target for Richards, who was mandated to increase the size and quality of his stable of informants after his move to C-10. Richards intercepted Castigone early one morning after arriving early at his residence in Melrose Park and waiting for him.

Richards introduced himself to Castigone while exhibiting his credentials. "You've probably heard of me but I know we've never met. I'm the senior agent on the FBI organized crime squad in Chicago."

"Yeah, I know who you are, Richards. You're the guy who set up the family pact to keep our families out of the crossfire between you guys and us guys. You're also the guy who 'threw the fear' into Rocky DeGrazia after he beat up one of your agents. Yeah, I know who you are."

Richards knew that Castigone would be aware of his reputation as a "stand-up guy," an FBI agent who had never framed any mobster and who dealt with them straight from the shoulder, using strictly above-board tactics in his investigations. It was this reputation, developed over the course of some two decades, that enabled Richards to influence mobsters to at least sit down with him. Richards played it low key, but he knew, after all these years, that most mobsters were curious about him and his reputation, that his background might influence them to want to talk with him. This was just the edge he needed since it gave him the opportunity to ingratiate himself with his target. He could demonstrate to them that he *was* a decent guy, that although he was on the other side of the law and could not be corrupted, he was a guy who could be interesting and useful to cultivate. Furthermore, in the back of every mobster's mind is the thought that someday he will probably need a friend in court—somebody who might be on his side when he runs afoul of the law. Since most mobsters get in trouble with the law sooner or later in their lives, it didn't hurt to have somebody who just might be sympathetic to their problem. A good example of that was Butch Blasi, the confidant of all the top bosses of the Chicago mob, the driver-bodyguard-appointment secretary of such absolute bosses as Tony Accardo, Sam Giancana, and Joey Aiuppa. Blasi frequently commented to his associates and to the soldiers in the Chicago mob that Richards had kept him out of prison when he testified before a federal grand jury that he did not believe a witness who was implicating Blasi in a series of burglaries. As a result Blasi had not been indicted. He justifiably credited Richards for that. Each time he spread that story it had the serendipitous effect of demonstrating to all those who heard it that Richards was a "stand-up guy" and somebody whose friendship might not be all that bad to enjoy.

This is not to say that most mobsters responded favorably by cooperating with Richards, they didn't, but the longer Richards was able to maintain a relationship with them the better chance he had of turning them. For every twenty PCI's he contacted, perhaps just one was ever developed into a fully cooperative top echelon criminal informant (CTE). But when an agent worked for over two decades on informant development and targeted hundreds of PCI's, he was bound to hit on several even if he had no expertise whatsoever. Even a blind squirrel finds an acorn now and then. And Richards was no "blind squirrel." He knew his targets and he stuck with his personal motto, which he adopted when he was a Golden Gloves boxing champ, "Keep Punchin' and Keep the Faith," applying it particularly to his efforts to develop informants. If only for the reason that for years he had resisted promotion to a desk job, Richards was the one agent who had been able to build a substantial stable of informants inside the mob. As he gained more and more access inside the mob he became more and more adept at addressing the mobster in his own ambience, in his own vernacular and on his own turf. And as the years went by, Richards became well versed in the history and the players in the mob. Whereas a newer agent might turn off a targeted PCI early on when his lack of background knowledge became apparent, Richards could easily discuss mob personalities and history with his contacts.

Richards remembered very well one of his first attempts at informant development. Within a year after the initiation of the Top Hoodlum Program in 1957 he had approached Chuckie Nicoletti, the mob hitman. Nicoletti had agreed to meet him on a snowy weekday morning at a gas station on the corner of California and Lexington Avenues on the West Side of Chicago. When Richards showed up, Nicoletti was waiting for him. He told Richards to follow him. Richards followed him for several miles in his car before Nicoletti led him almost right back to where they had started, to the Cal-Lex Social Club. Richards followed Nicoletti inside. At this point Richards felt he was doing well. Nicoletti obviously had insured that no one on either side of the law had followed them. He had "dry cleaned" himself. It was a sign that he had not informed his associates of his intentions to meet Richards, a sign that he might be receptive to the approach.

The meeting started off well. Nicoletti served Richards coffee and doughnuts. But as they began to discuss the general affairs of the mob, it became obvious to Nicoletti that Richards was unfamiliar with most of the background and history of the Chicago mob and, more to the point, with the nicknames of Chicago mobsters. For instance when Nicoletti began to talk about "the white haired guy," Richards had to ask who the "white haired guy" was. When Nicoletti mentioned "Joe Nick," a reference to Joe Ferriola, Richards again had to demonstrate his ignorance. When Nicoletti made a remark about "the guy on the fifth floor," Richards had to be told that the reference was to Mayor Richard J. Daley, whose office was on the fifth floor of City Hall. It not only impeded the flow of the conversation but it indicated to Nicoletti that he was dealing with one of the uninitiated, a novice in the investigation of the mob. Who needs a friend like that? Who needs a friend inside the FBI who obviously was on the lower rung of the organization? If you might someday need a sympathetic ear, even one which could not be bent, why cultivate the friendship of some supernumerary who would be in no position to help?

Eighteen years later, however, by 1975, Richards had developed the reputation inside the mob of being the "guy out front" for the FBI, what the mob called "the G's heavy." By this time, having been at it since 1957, he had a stable of a dozen informants inside the mob. As each furnished information about their associates it brought Richards more and more into a position where he felt he knew almost all of the active members of the Chicago mob. By 1975 when he made his approach to Peter Castigone, he was polished in dealing with the likes of Castigone. He knew his informants better than he knew most of his FBI associates. Through them he knew the personalities and the idiosyncrasies of most of the Chicago mobsters. From one in particular, one he code-named "Magellan," he knew a lot about Castigone's background.

He knew Castigone's wife's name was Connie, he had children named Peter, Jr., and Frank; that he had attended Fenwick High School, that his wife attended St. Bernadette's, where his kids went to parochial school; that he was a Purdue football fan (even though most mobsters are Notre Dame fans), that he sponsored a Little League team; that he had a mistress named Dolores Plummer who was a cocktail waitress at Rocky's on North Avenue; that Peter had tinnitus. Richards knew the names of all Castigone's mob associates, such as Nick Nasti; the location of all his hangouts, such as Rocky's and the North Avenue Steak House; the fact that two of his brothers worked for the city in the sanitation department and one was a movie projectionist at the United Artists Theatre; that his mother was a daily communicant; that his mob area was bounded by Central Avenue to Harlem Avenue and from Chicago Avenue to North Avenue; and many, many more things about the personal and professional life of Peter Castigone. They would all provide conversation pieces, the material Richards would need to ingratiate himself with Peter as a nice guy, an easy guy to talk to and maybe, just maybe, somebody Peter could trust. Not trust to the point where he would put his life in Richards's hands by talking about things he shouldn't talk about—not yet—but maybe to the point where a tidbit now and then, some not-so-sensitive information, might put him in the good graces of this most respected of G-men, so that someday when Castigone might need a favor, whatever that might be, just maybe this guy would be there for him. When you're violating the law every day of your life, it doesn't hurt to look for an escape hatch. Maybe someday he might have to make a call. After all, many of the guys he associated with had been found in automobile trunks. The world he lived in was a cruel one. Today Peter Castigone was in solid with his people. Tomorrow, who knows? In his milieu, Peter knew there are ups and downs. It didn't take much for some of the unstable guys he knew in the profession to get mad at you. Peter knew that it didn't hurt to have a friend in the right place if he should ever tread on the wrong toe, even inadvertently. And you would be hard pressed to simply call the FBI office and say: "Let me talk to an agent, any agent." But if you can call the FBI and say "Tell Bill Richards it's urgent, he has to get to me right away," then that's a whole new ball of wax.

So, Bill Richards had the leverage it took to make an approach to a guy like Peter Castigone. He got his foot in the door, which was more than most law enforcement agents got. He got many of his targets to sit down with him, at least for a few minutes. After that it was up to him to carry the conversation further. After that it was problematical.

When Bill Richards intercepted Peter Castigone a few blocks away from his home as he drove his Cadillac west on Harlem Avenue, Peter was at least predisposed to be curious about what Richards might want. He agreed to follow him in his car to Columbus Park, located on Central Avenue off the Eisenhower Expressway. Richards then joined Castigone in his car.

The conversation was entirely desultory on this, what Richards hoped would be the first of many such meetings. It was free and easy. Richards deliberately refrained from posing any sensitive questions so as not to make Castigone uncomfortable or to turn him off. At the end of the meeting, which went off nicely, Richards requested that they meet again in a couple of weeks. Castigone hesitated, but agreed. They arranged to meet at the Como Inn on Milwaukee Avenue on the Near Northwest Side of Chicago. The Como Inn has many small dining nooks where private meetings can be held. It is run by the Marchetti family and features fare from all over Italy, with a fine wine list.

Castigone arrived and asked for the reservation in the name of "Mr. Berlin," as Richards had instructed. Richards had already arrived but instead of going to the nook he had reserved, he watched Castigone arrive and then waited to see if anyone followed him or if anyone already there took any notice of where he was headed. When he observed nobody who looked suspicious, Richards then circled the restaurant and entered the nook from the opposite direction from which Castigone had entered.

Again the conversation started out casually. Richards ordered a vodka gimlet while encouraging Castigone to have a martini. They then ordered dinner, Richards requesting his favorite meal anytime at any place, spaghetti with Italian sausage, while Castigone had a veal dish. Richards asked Castigone to order the wine, well aware that Castigone was a wine enthusiast, a member of a wine-tasting club, and that he prided himself on his knowledge of fine wines. Castigone chose a Frascati Superiore, Fontana Candida, which he touted as a moderately priced but enjoyable white Italian dinner wine.

The pair chatted amicably, ordering a second and third round of cocktails before the meal arrived. They developed a mild rapport. Richards told Castigone about his family. His son, Bill, had just graduated from Career Academy in Chicago where he had studied broadcasting and had just gotten a job at WLNR in Lansing, Illinois, where he was a newscaster, disc jockey, and sportscaster, doing live high school basketball and football games. Castigone talked about his sons, who played football in the Catholic League for Fenwick. Richards told of his son, Bob, who played football and baseball at Notre Dame and of his friendship with Johnny Lattner, the Notre Dame all-American who had won the Heisman Trophy and who was a graduate of Fenwick. When Richards mentioned he had been a prizefighter, Castigone said he was a fight fan. The conversation turned to the fighters of the day—Muhammad Ali, George Foreman, Joe Frazier, Ernie Terrell. Richards mentioned he knew Terrell, who was managed by Bernie Glickman.

With the mention of Glickman, Castigone raised his eyebrows. It was well known that Glickman had been a front for the mob. When Richards caught this signal, he asked Castigone, "Did you know Joe Batters called off the contract you guys had on Glickman after he testified before our grand jury?" No, Castigone was not aware. He had not been a made guy when that happened, so Richards told Castigone the whole story of his deal with Accardo to cancel the contract on Glickman's life.

Castigone was aware of Richards's reputation and that he had gone face to face with most of the top men in the Chicago outfit, including Sam Giancana and Castigone's two mentors, Sam DiStefano and "Milwaukee" Phil Alderisio. Both had discussed their trials and tribulations with Richards in the presence of Castigone. But this was a new story to Castigone. He had never met Accardo, who was too far up the hierarchy to be one of Castigone's confidants. He had seen him a couple of times at funerals and many times on TV but had never been introduced to him up to that point. Castigone was impressed. If "the man," the historic Joe Batters, had seen fit to meet with Richards, why couldn't he?

At this time in 1975, Jackie Cerone, the former mob boss, had just come out of prison after being convicted for ITAR-gambling on the testimony of Lou Bombacino, a witness developed by FBI agent Paul Frankfurt with the help of Richards and Pete Wacks, who was a rookie on C-1 at the time. The FBI was eager to learn what role Jackie might play in the mob now that he was back. Richards suspected that Rocky's, the place where Castigone hung out in Melrose Park near his home, was Cerone's headquarters. So he took his first shot at some sensitive information.

"I hear Jackie is back at Rocky's," he mentioned, quite casually.
Castigone looked at Richards and then nodded.

"I hear he's taking over again," Richards affirmed.

"I don't know," Castigone responded.

"He's sitting at the big table again at Rocky's, meeting every noon."
Richards was speculating.

"Yeah, but that don't mean necessarily that he's the cigar again,"
Castigone parried.

"Maybe not. What do you think?" Richards asked.

"Well, you seem to know a lot about him and what he's doin'. Yeah,
he's back in. But O'Brien still wears the hat."

Richards quickly changed the subject. He didn't want to spook Castigone. He had gotten Castigone to acknowledge that Cerone was back
holding court at his old headquarters, Rocky's. He had gotten Castigone to state that Joey "O'Brien" Aiuppa was still the boss even though
Cerone, the old boss, had returned. Knowing what he did about Castigone's background, Richards was able to bring up the subject of Cerone. His knowledge that "O'Brien" was a nickname for Aiuppa spared
him the discomfort of acknowledging to Castigone that he was unfamiliar with that mob moniker, an admission which would ordinarily turn
off the target. Richards would write a report at the office. He would
report that his new PCI, under the confidential number assigned to him
for record purposes, had advised on this date that the former mob boss,
Jackie Cerone, had resumed his leadership role in the Chicago mob but
that Joe Aiuppa still retained the top spot as the boss. Although Peter
Castigone would hardly recall what he had told Richards—he was,
after all, under the influence of a slight buzz and Richards had slipped
it into the conversation obliquely—it was a sensitive piece of information. For the moderate price of a nice meal and some cocktails and wine
at the Como Inn and a couple hours of one agent's time, the Chicago
FBI was now aware that Cerone was using Rocky's as his headquarters
again, and that whatever business would be discussed with him there
would concern the strategic affairs of the Chicago outfit from his perspective as one of its very top bosses, probably the underboss. If the FBI
could place a microphone at Cerone's regular table, it could become a
highly productive bug. Obviously, the development of Peter Castigone
as an informant was off to a good start.

Richards and Castigone met regularly thereafter at the Como Inn.
Richards used it only for his meetings with Peter. They would enter and

leave separately so that no one except one who closely approached their nook could observe them together. That entailed some risk, but nothing undue. It would have been safer to meet in a car, on some lonely road at midnight or dawn. But that same secrecy would probably turn Castigone off. It would make the very nature of the meetings too blatant. This way he could rationalize that he was meeting Richards merely for a nice meal and a few drinks, a social occasion. Since Richards rarely asked him direct questions of a sensitive nature and instead drew him into oblique lines of conversation, he never gave Castigone the feeling that he was a dirty "stoolie" or a "snitch." Richards never used these words when talking about or thinking about his sources. He cringed whenever he heard a fellow law enforcement officer call a source a "snitch," even if it is a familiar term used extensively by many police officers and even some FBI agents: Richards always thought of his informants as friends, his confidants, guys with whom he had a special relationship. In his lexicon there was never a disparaging thought of a source as being a "snitch." No, these guys were his pals, his buddies.

22

Another Pal of Richards's

Now, more than a decade later, when Pete Wacks informed Richards, in his role as a special investigator for the Senate Rackets Committee, that Peter Castigone was Nick Nasti's partner in the mob, it struck Richards with the force of a five iron. What luck! Peter Castigone had been a steady source of information from 1975 to 1978, when Richards left Chicago for Tucson. When he left, Richards suggested to Castigone that he continue to cooperate with the FBI. Richards offered to bring another agent—he had Pete Wacks in mind—to the next meeting and introduce him so that the transition could be made. Castigone refused, however. He trusted Richards as a friend, not as an FBI agent. The relationship which had taken four years to develop would not be turned over to anyone else in the FBI. After all, it was an accepted fact that the FBI is the enemy. It was their job to put guys like Castigone in prison, not treat them to fine meals at the Como Inn. And Richards had never been obtrusive. He had led Castigone into conversations about his mob associates and their activities but he always let Castigone define

217

the parameters. He never attempted to get Castigone to discuss anything he did not feel comfortable with, and he had never asked him to go out of his way to develop information for Richards.

When Richards transferred to Tucson, the informant files on Castigone in the Chicago office and at FBIHQ in Washington were closed, as were the files on some twenty other such "pals" of Richards. It caused a very noticeable gap in the information available to the FBI. Headquarters cajoled the Chicago office. The fact that Richards was no longer in place was no excuse. The proud agents in Chicago were loath to admit that one man had accounted for seventy-five per cent of their informants. So the new coordinator of informant development, Richards's replacement, sent two agents out to see Peter Castigone—and to every other of his sources. They reported back, very perplexed. Yes, Castigone admitted he knew Bill Richards. But he denied he had ever been Richards's informant. He and Richards had a "pleasant" relationship but he was not an informant. Okay, he might have had some long, serious conversations with Richards, after all they were friends, but Richards had never asked him any questions about the mob. "Hell no, I won't answer your questions or 'continue to be an informant,' go fuck yourselves!" That seemed pretty definite. "Are we sure this guy was an informant?"

Richards knew where Castigone was coming from, however. He recalled the code name they had used for each other was "Bob Stupid." When he returned to Chicago from Vegas on his mob war investigation, Richards called Castigone's residence. Castigone's wife, Connie, answered the phone and Richards asked her to have Peter call "Bob Stupid" at the Sheraton Plaza, 787–2900. The next day he got the call.

"Hey, I thought you retired," Castigone said.

"Well, I did and I didn't. I'll tell you about it. Meet me at the same old place. Do you remember the name we used to reserve the nook for?" Richards asked.

"Yeah, but I don't know if I want to meet you. You fucked me up," Castigone stated.

"How did I do that?" Richards asked, not aware that agents had contacted Peter and asked him to "continue to be an informant."

"Well, I want to discuss it with you anyhow," Castigone said. "Okay, I'll meet you. Same spot. Noon tomorrow?"

"Fine. See you then."

When Castigone and Richards took their places in one of the nooks at the Como Inn, Castigone hit him with it.

"What the fuck, Bill," he said. "Did you tell your people I was an 'informant'?"

"Tell me what happened."

"Two fuckin' 'G guys' come to see me. They said was I interested in continuing to be an informant like I was for Bill Richards. I said who the fuck was an informant. For Bill Richards or for any other fuckin' guy. Not me. You got the wrong guy, fellas."

Richards was somewhat prepared for this. One of his other "pals" had come out to Tucson to complain to him about the same type of approach. Another had called him to complain. Another had spent time in the Metropolitan Correctional Center when the Bureau put pressure on him which he resisted. Now he realized that Castigone had been bluntly confronted with the nature of the relationship he had with Richards, one that Castigone, who was no dummy, had never consciously thought out. He had obviously been aware he was supplying information to Richards but he was completely unaware Richards was going back to the office and recording it—to be read by all agents with a need to know.

"Peter, I apologize. I never thought of you as an 'informant' but it's obvious other agents did. Whenever something would come up in our conversation which was pertinent to any of our ongoing investigations I would put it in a report. I had to do that, Peter, to cover my ass. What if I had been observed by another agent or a cop and it got back that I was meeting with you. If I reported information from you from time to time, I was covered. But if I didn't, it was my neck. They would think I was on your pad. I hope you understand."

Castigone didn't all that much, actually. But he soon settled down into the pleasant relationship he had had with Richards. They had developed a nice friendship over the four years they had known each other. Richards told his pal that he had retired from the FBI in 1980 but that he had gone to work for the Chicago Crime Commission and was now also working for the Senate Rackets Committee. Soon Castigone was bringing Richards up to date on his nonprofessional life, his family, even on Dolores Plummer. Richards, although he had no mistress, did likewise. Within a short time it was like old home week. The two old pals slipped into their former relationship. Not as an FBI agent and an "informant," but as two old pals who had not seen each other for several years.

Although Richards had expected to wait for two or three such meetings before he brought up the subject of Nick Nasti, he found Castigone so open and friendly that he decided to get to it late on this, their first meeting. Actually, Richards found that it was a recent phenomenon. During his career in the FBI, it was a very difficult matter to turn a mobster, to get him to sit down and furnish hard-core information. It is still difficult, but not as difficult as it once was. As time has passed, the code of *omertà,* the oath of silence, has eroded even in made members. As one after the other have violated the oath and testified against fellow mobsters, it has become easier for each successive informant to decide to talk. When Jimmy Flynn, the New York agent, first turned Joe Valachi in New York and Bill Richards turned Ricardo Scalzitti, aka Dick Cain, "Sporting Goods," and a couple of other CTE's in Chicago, it had been unique. But as scores of other top echelon informants had been developed, it became easier. Now the climate was such that many had gotten away with it and were fully protected. It was still very unusual for a "made guy" to "turn," but it was not the absolute impossibility it had once seemed.

So Richards, feeling he might better strike while the iron was hot, decided to take advantage of Castigone's amiable and talkative mood: "Hey, I hear you're partnered up with Nicky Nasti now?"

"Yeah, I am. Nick is a good money maker. He and I get along good. We got a territory on the Northwest Side where we got a 'street tax.' We control the offices and we got the wrinkles out of our bellies." What Castigone meant was that Nasti had a way of producing income for the mob, that he and Nasti had been assigned a geographical area on the Northwest Side of Chicago which they controlled exclusively for the mob and where they enforced a fee on anyone who operated on the periphery or outside the law such as burglars, thieves, highjackers, pornographers, strip joints, bars, and taverns, and where they took fifty per cent of the winnings from the bookmakers in their area. It was a blueprint of how the mob operated in Chicago, dividing up each neighborhood and assigning it to a soldier or two. Each soldier reported and paid a percentage of his income to a capo. Each capo then furnished a portion of that to "the West Side," the top leadership of the mob. Each absolute mob boss since Al Capone had lived in the western suburbs of Chicago; hence the term "West Side," meaning the boss.

"I hear Nasti does some heavy work, too."

Castigone drew back at this point. "That's what you hear, huh," he stated without denying or affirming.

Richards said nothing, waiting for Castigone, hoping he would expand. He did. "Actually, Nick is pissed. He did a job out West and it don't seem he got recognized for it by Joe Negall."

Richards was pleasantly surprised. He had not expected when he sat down that the conversation would proceed so quickly and so smoothly to the area of his concern. Times were changing, he thought. Penetration of the mob proceeded more quickly and easily than ever.

"So Negall is not an easy guy to work for?" Richards asked, referring to Joe Ferriola's mob moniker.

"No, it's not that, he's a good guy. But for some reason Nick thought he'd get something out of what he had done right away. It hasn't worked out that way. It's been several months now and we're still where we were on the Northwest Side."

"What was the job?" Richards asked, hopefully.

Castigone just looked at Richards for a few moments. "If I knew, I'd sure keep my trap shut on a question like that," he replied. Richards realized he had pushed to the limit. It wasn't *that* easy.

It didn't matter. Richards knew the answer to his question.

"Do you think Nasti would sit down with me?" Richards asked.

"He told me he already knows you. I told him I know you, too. So you wouldn't be a virgin to him. He told me you are a stand-up guy, you didn't try to hurt him in any way when he didn't sit down with you. Yeah, I think he'd meet with you, but I don't know that he'd talk to you, if you know what I mean? Give him a shot. Tell you what, you'll impress him if you call him at this number, this is the number for the place where we set up. It's a book. Ask for 'Number Twelve,' that's him. But don't ask him to call you back, of course. Call him at eleven o'clock any weekday. We're always there then."

"You'll be there?" Richards asked. When Castigone nodded, Richards told him: "I'll check back with you to see how he reacts to my call. Just call me at the Sheraton Plaza, I'm always back there late at night. Call me after ten or so."

It was settled. Richards stood up and walked out the front door. As if by instinct, Castigone delayed at the table for ten minutes or so and then exited by the other door to the restaurant.

The next day, after Richards checked his little black book and refreshed his memory that he had used the code-name "Mr. Little" with Nasti, he called the "office" that Castigone had identified as their headquarters. He asked for "Number Twelve." When Nasti came to the phone, he informed Nick that "This is Mr. Little. Remember me? I'm back in town." As Castigone had predicted, Nasti agreed to meet with Richards the next day. Slowly, reluctantly, but he agreed. They arranged to meet in the cafeteria of the Museum of Science and Industry on the mid-South Side of Chicago. The museum is one of Chicago's finest tourist attractions, on a par with "Here's Chicago." It features the U-505 German submarine from World War II, Apollo 8, an underground coal mine, and "Yesterday's Main Street." A tourist attraction it is, not a place any self-respecting hoodlum would be expected to visit. It was off the beaten path for mobsters and therefore an ideal place for law enforcement agents to meet with their sources.

That night Richards got a call at the Sheraton Plaza. It was Castigone. He was calling as arranged. "He took it pretty good. I listened when you called him but he didn't say nothin' to me. That's a good sign. If he was gonna slough you off, he woulda told me and then maybe go to Rocky Infelice and try to set you up. No, he clammed up about what that call was, he didn't want me to know that you even called him or that he was gonna meet you. That's a good sign."

At three o'clock the next afternoon, fifteen minutes after Richards had arrived and commandeered a rear booth in the cafeteria, Nasti arrived as scheduled.

"Hey, it's been a long time. Good to see you, Nick," Richards exclaimed.

"Yeah, it has been. Thought you gave this shit up."

"Well, I'm not FBI anymore, but now I'm with the Crime Commission and the Senate Rackets Committee," Richards said, not mentioning that his assignment was Las Vegas.

The conversation then became desultory, two old acquaintances though not really friends, catching up on what the other was doing. Except that one, Richards, was much more open about what he was doing than the other. This wasn't going to be easy. Richards quickly got the feeling that nothing much had changed as regarded Nick Nasti's attitude toward cooperation with "the G." He had agreed to a meeting, though, and that was further than "Mr. Little" had progressed when he had been an FBI agent. His instinct was that it would take time for this relationship to blossom to the point where he could ask any questions even remotely relevant to the fireworks in the counting room at the Vegas Star or, for that matter, anything else. So Richards backed off. He did suggest, however, that they meet again next week. Nasti was noncommittal. All he would say was, "Call me." Nasti left first, Richards fifteen minutes later. Neither had noticed any party interested in their conversation.

It was obvious to Richards that Nasti agreed to talk to him for much the same reasons his partner, Peter Castigone, had agreed—mainly to have established contact with someone who somewhere down the line might be in a position to do him some good should he ever have a big problem on either side of the law. If he was arrested and facing prosecution, it would be good to have a friend in Richards. It is a common position mobsters find themselves in. They want to have an arm's-length acquaintance with somebody in law enforcement they can turn to if it ever comes to the point where such a friend is helpful. On the other hand, that doesn't mean they will become full-fledged informants. They feel a need to make a friend, but not *that* much of a friend. In Bill Richards's case, with thirty years in the FBI, and with his present positions as consultant for the Chicago Crime Commission and staff investigator for the Senate Rackets Committee, he was undoubtedly the best friend any mobster could have. So, for all these reasons, he was not an easy guy to tell to go fuck himself.

A week later, "Mr. Little" called "Number Twelve" again. "Number Twelve" was agreeable and "Little" asked him to meet him at Grassfield's, way up on the North Side. When Nasti showed up, the pair had another amiable, but very general, conversation. When Nasti agreed to yet another meeting the next week, Richards felt he was getting closer to the time when he could expect answers to easy questions. In the meantime, Richards met once more with Castigone.

"Bill, I suggest you talk to Nick about Joe Negall. As time goes by, and Joe isn't doing anything for Nick, Nick's getting more and more upset with him. I don't know exactly what Nick did but it was somethin' very large and he feels he hasn't been rewarded for it," Castigone told Richards.

So at the next meeting at Grassfield's, Richards swung the conversation to Joe Ferriola. But it didn't work, Nasti refused to talk about his boss. Worse yet, Richards had spooked him. Thereafter, he refused to meet. The relationship had come to a halt. Richards figured the Nick Nasti case was just another unsuccessful attempt at informant development. For every one that worked, he had a score that didn't.

RICHARDS then flew to Washington. He contacted Jim Mansfield and Ralph Salerno at Stars, the bar and restaurant on top of the Sheraton National Hotel in Arlington, between Arlington National Cemetery and the Pentagon. "Guys, I think I've done just about all I can for the committee. It seems I'm at a dead end. The FBI will go forward with Ben Jackson and indict Gussie Alex and they have promised that your committee will get first crack at his testimony. That's not much for you, although Gussie is a good catch for the FBI. But I'm anxious to get back to Jeannie and that old Arizona sun. There isn't much left on this case." Salerno and Mansfield agreed.

Richards then flew out of Washington National en route to Tucson by way of a connection in Chicago at O'Hare. From there he placed a call to Pete Wacks to give Wacks an update.

"That's too bad, but I understand your position," Pete said. "It's about time. Settle down, enjoy your retirement, you've earned it. Oh, incidentally, we've got a good case on your two friends, Castigone and Nasti. We've got them dead bang on an ITAR-gambling case. With Nasti's background, he'll go away for ten-fifteen."

Richards jumped at this. "Pete, that might be just the leverage we need. Would you guys mind if I stayed here for a couple of days and discussed it with the prosecutor? We should talk about a plea for those guys. Nasti could hand up Joe Ferriola."

Wacks was noncommittal. "If you want, we can talk. But we've got them dead bang. Title III. They'd have to give us something very good."

What Wacks was saying was that the Chicago office of the FBI had developed an Interstate Travel in Aid of Racketeering case on Castigone and Nasti, based on their gambling activity. The case was solid because the evidence was based on court-ordered wiretaps as authorized under Title III of the 1968 Omnibus Crime Act which had given the FBI authority for the first time to produce the tapes as evidence in court against those monitored or discussed. Although Ramsey Clark, the attorney general at the time, had denied the FBI access to this law, the FBI began to employ it when Clark left in 1970. It has been, along with the RICO Statute, the most powerful legal weapon the FBI has today in its arsenal in the fight against organized crime.

When Richards sat down with Pete Wacks and Bob Long, the FBI case agent on the ITAR-gambling investigation, he found that Jeff Johnson was the Strike Force attorney assigned to the case against

Castigone and Nasti. Johnson was not only the best assistant U. S. attorney in the history of the Strike Force in Chicago, but a good friend of Richards's.

Johnson, Wacks, Long, and Richards got right down to brass tacks. They agreed that Richards could explain to Nasti and Castigone what lay in store for them and offer to bring them to Wacks, Long, and Johnson to discuss a deal. Richards was the logical guy to handle that due to his rapport with the two hoodlums.

They met separately, first Castigone, the less important, then Nasti. Richards delivered to each of them approximately the same message. "Refuse the deal and you're dead-bang gone—for ten-fifteen years with an 'organized crime tab,' meaning you won't see any early parole. It'll be the full sentence. And, Nick, you especially will get a heavy sentence when the judge sees the presentence report on your background. You can kiss your wife and kids goodbye for a substantial portion of the rest of your life. And when you come out the world will have passed you by. On the other hand, if you want a deal, I'm in position to put you in touch with the people who can make it. But you and I have to discuss what you can deal with first. It'll have to be good, starting with the top, Joe Ferriola."

Nick Nasti went home to talk to his wife and think about it. Going into the Witness Protection Program was no snap of the fingers. It was a big decision for the whole family since they all would be affected. But the other alternative was also a big problem for the whole family.

"Number Twelve" called "Mr. Little" the next day. They met once more at the Museum of Science and Industry.

"Bill, my wife and I decided I will deal with your people."

"Fine, Nick, that's great. I think you're doing the right thing. But you know it won't be easy. I never want anybody to think I'm not being completely above-board and candid. It's a hell of a tough life, but as you know from previous experience, so is going to the pen. You're sure you've thought it out completely?"

"Yeah, I've thought it out completely. If your people have got the wiretaps you told me about, and I remember the conversations you described to me, then I'm gone. You couldn't have bullshitted them, I know what I said and what was said to me."

Richards took Nasti to Wacks, Long, and Johnson. They played the tapes for him to authenticate that the evidence was solid and available.

It depended on what he had to deal with and how willing he was to deal at all. After reading Nasti his Miranda rights, Johnson laid out the options.

For openers, Nasti could plea bargain. He could be charged on a lesser charge than ITAR-gambling with the government recommending to the judge a minimal sentence, not the sentence which would ordinarily be recommended (the full sentence would ordinarily be recommended in this case in view of Nasti's previous conviction and his organized crime affiliation). Johnson reiterated to Nasti that an organized crime tab would be placed on him in ordinary circumstances, mandating no parole and the full sentence. Johnson explained the full range of what the plea bargain could entail all the way up to the ultimate—full immunity from prosecution for any and all of his crimes, right up to the present. In the case that Nasti fully cooperated by testifying completely about all of his organized crime associates and assuming that this information was of a magnitude to make the grant worthwhile to the government, he and his family would be placed in the Witness Protection Program.

Nasti was a tough bargainer. He declined the invitation to retain an attorney, feeling he was fully competent to negotiate for himself. He wanted complete immunity and bargained for it by promising complete cooperation once it was granted. He wanted the Witness Protection Program. One more thing he wanted. Once this was all over and he was relocated under the WPP, he wanted to sit down with a writer and author a book on his experiences from the time he was born to the date of the publication of the book. Richards promised he would help Nasti find a coauthor. He even opined that since he was thinking himself of developing a third career—his first being as an FBI agent for thirty years, his second as an attorney representing news organizations being sued for libel, a consultant for the Chicago Crime Commission and an investigator for the Senate—as an author, he might even find it mutually advantageous to work as coauthors. Richards promised to be of assistance in any way possible.

Once Nasti's conditions were bargained for, the FBI agents, the Strike Force attorney, and the Crime Commission/Rackets Committee investigator set out to learn what Nick had. It was time for him to put *his* chips on the table. They had to be blue ones—pertinent and important.

First of all came the bombshell. Right off the top of the deck. Joe Ferriola, under orders from Tony Accardo, had sent Nasti to bomb the counting room of the Vegas Star! Wow! Right off the bat, the two top leaders of the Chicago mob. How could he prove it? He was sent by Ferriola personally, he sat down with Ferriola and received his orders directly from Ferriola. How did he know that Ferriola was ordered by Accardo to do the deed? Ferriola told him so. Right away, the four lawmen cooled off—a little. Clearly, Accardo would have a potentially successful defense in citing the hearsay rule, but perhaps some legal research could be done to find that this was one of the many exceptions to that rule. No, Nasti had never met with Accardo, not over this. Well, that was a problem.

"What do you mean, you never met with Accardo *over this?*" Richards asked. "Have you ever met with Accardo?"

"Yes, I have, on one occasion," Nasti replied.

"When was that?" Johnson queried.

"About two weeks after I returned from Las Vegas. I went to Castigone's daughter's wedding. Joe Ferriola took me over to Joe's table and introduced me as the guy who did the work out West. Joe shook my hand and said 'good job.' "

The lawmen perked up. Hey, that was much better!

"Let me get this straight," Johnson said, very seriously. "Joe Ferriola took you over to Tony Accardo—that's who you're calling 'Joe' for 'Joe Batters'?"

"That's right."

"And he said precisely, what?" Johnson asked.

"As best as I can recall, he said: 'This is our guy who did the work out West,' " Nasti responded.

"Go on."

"And Joe Batters shook my hand and said, 'Good job.' "

"Anything else?"

"No, that was it."

"Um, that's good. We can take that into court and tie it into the conspiracy. We certainly can indict Accardo on that and hopefully we can sell it to the jury."

Pete Wacks, being the sharp agent he is, took it just a bit further.

"Nick, was there anybody else who was there who heard Joe Batters say that?"

Nasti hesitated just a moment. "Sure, Peter was. He was with me when Ferriola took me over, he's my partner."

"Holy Christ!" Johnson was ecstatic. The FBI and the Strike Force had the same leverage on Castigone as they did on Nasti. They were both defendants in the same case, they were partners in the mob, and Castigone had been quite cooperative in the past. He would be the corroborative witness for Nasti's testimony. If he heard Ferriola say *"our* man who did the *work out West"* and heard Accardo respond to that by saying "good job," it would seem to be a situation Johnson could sell to his Strike Force chief, Gary Shapiro, and to their superiors back in Washington. Hopefully, a grand jury and then a trial jury would buy it. It was the truth and although probably not pertinent in a legal sense until tied up with the testimony of Nasti explaining its relevance, it *would* be tied in. In Johnson's estimation as an experienced and capable government attorney and in the much more limited legal mind of Bill Richards, also an attorney, it would be admissible and a good, solid judge would find it so.

The lawmen did not stop there, however. They were interested in putting together a RICO case. If ITAR had been an *important* addition to the government's tools in the fight against the mob when it was passed in 1961 under Bobby Kennedy's Justice Department, RICO was the *major* weapon. It was passed in 1970 after having been drafted by a young Justice Department attorney named G. Robert Blakey, who received his early training as counsel to the same U. S. Senate committee Richards was now working for, the so-called Rackets Committee, when Senator John McClellan was the chairman. It was now the weapon of choice if the facts were such that they fit the RICO Act. In a nutshell, RICO makes it a federal crime to conduct the affairs of an "enterprise" through a "pattern of racketeering." A pattern is said to exist when members of such an enterprise have committed at least two acts of racketeering within ten years of each other. These acts can include murder, robbery, gambling, using the phone or the mail for illegal purposes, and, in the specific case at hand, arson and/or bombing. The act provides for the confiscation of the ill-gotten goods of the enterprise.

Immediately, the lawmen saw the possibilities. This could be the largest case ever brought before a court. It would rival The Commission Case in New York City, which sprung Rudy Giuliani into national prominence and which he used as a springboard for his campaign as mayor of New York City.

This case could conceivably wipe out the Chicago mob! But lawmen saw that Nasti was tiring under the stress. Not that any were exerting any pressure on him; it was just the thought that he would have to get up in front of Accardo, Ferriola and company, point them out, face to face, then testify to their crimes. And then live his life thereafter!

The next day they met with Nasti again. He identified Charles Smith as the man who made the bomb and gave it to him with instructions on how to use the timing device which would detonate it.

When Nasti had made his decision to cooperate with the government, he had decided to say nothing about the Charlie "Bats" Battaglia murder. Now he had decided that "these guys were good people, they were treating me fairly, maybe I'd get further consideration for full immunity if I tell them everything I know." When he did, he stunned them. He named Ferriola as the boss who gave the command, and Dominic Daddano and John Sitiani as having done the job with him. Wow! What a case!

That noon, the five had lunch brought in from the delicatessen on the northeast corner of Plymouth Court and Van Buren. Richards was happy to be the gofer who went out and brought it back. He had been a part of some major investigations and prosecutions in his time, but nothing to equal this!

That afternoon, Nick Nasti added to the reputation he would gain as the best mob witness in the history of mob investigations, surpassing the likes of Jimmy Fratiano, Joe Valachi, Frank Cullotta, Lou Bombacino, Joe Cantalupo, and Vincent Teresa. He quickly, calmly, and quietly identified Ernest "Rocky" Infelice, Sal DeLaurentis, and Lou Marino as the men he and Peter Castigone reported to. "My Lord," thought Richards, "Infelice is the underboss to Ferriola and DeLaurentis and Marino are two of his top guys. This is getting better every moment." Nasti identified Infelice, DeLaurentis, and Marino as not only having directed Nasti and Castigone's bookmaking activity, but as having participated in the profits.

If Richards thought the case had reached its potential heights, it had not. The next day, the four lawmen dug still further into this gold mine. Nasti recalled that on one occasion, just as he and Castigone were getting started in their area, they had gotten word that a rival bookmaker, one Mike Rodino, had not ceased his operations as he had been directed to do. Nasti reported this to the underboss, "Rocky" Infelice. Infelice then ordered John "No Nose" DiFronzo and Sam "Wings" Carlisi to "bust Rodino up." A couple days later Rodino ceased his bookmaking on the Northwest Side of Chicago after he had been kneecapped, shot in the knees and crippled for life. DiFronzo and Carlisi were yet two more Chicago mobsters who had gone on to bigger and better things after they had "made their bones" by breaking the bones of an uncooperative associate.

A big problem with Nasti's testimony, as good as it would be, was corroboration. He was obviously an impeachable witness in view of his long career as a wise guy, and it would seem obvious to a jury that he might just be trying to save his own hide by inventing stories about his fellow travellers. There had to be additional evidence to shore up the case. In fact, it is the law that the testimony of an accomplice, or of an unindicted coconspirator, *must* be supported by corroborative evidence. Castigone's testimony in this respect would be important. It would be up to the FBI, however, to obtain further supportive evidence or testimony of some type to convince a jury that Nasti was not perjuring himself in order to obtain leniency for his own crimes. It was the opinion of all the lawmen involved that Nasti would make an outstanding witness. He was as articulate as you might expect any mobster to be—in the mold of Accardo and Cerone. He was also out of central casting when it came to the role of mobster. That had its good and bad points. As a hood, he lacked some credibility. By the same token one wouldn't expect that Little Lord Fauntleroy would have been in a position to gain the information he was now offering as testimony. For prosecutors, there is a thin line between presenting a witness who obviously had to be a bad guy to be involved to the extent he was with the defendants and one who's just out to save his own hide. The jury has to believe that he has now turned the corner and is on the side of the law. For starters, it is important for the prosecution to be up front about the deal. Since the defense attorneys will bring out on cross-examination that a deal has been made—that in return for his testimony the witness has obtained immunity for his own crimes making it conceivable that he is concocting his testimony to serve his own personal interests—it is best to bring that out on direct examination by the government attorney. "Did you receive this promise only for your truthful and honest and sincere testimony? Isn't it true that you will be prosecuted yourself if you perjure yourself? Wasn't that made absolutely clear to you? Do you understand that if you are not being entirely truthful in what you say that you will be prosecuted to the full extent of the law?" Some jurors will have problems nonetheless with accepting at full face value everything a witness like Nasti says. But then they look at the defendant. If he testifies in his own defense his testimony will be weighed against Nasti's. Most jurors can evaluate and make a decision accurately as to who is lying. On the other hand, few defendants testify in their own defense because any prior conviction can then be used against them on cross-examination to impeach them. Unless they take the stand, prior convictions ordinarily cannot be introduced in evidence. This is one of the very few edges the prosecution has in such a trial. The testimony of the government witness can be challenged on cross-examination and perhaps by independent witnesses, but usually not by the all-important defendant himself. In some trials, such as the John Gotti trials in New York, the jury has not believed some of the government witnesses who were career criminals. But in most they do when supportive evidence is introduced. In this case, Johnson, Richards, and Wacks were willing to bet that Nasti would be believable for a jury and that if they could develop any kind of verification, any supportive evidence at all, then he could convince a jury that what he would testify to was honest and accurate. Primarily, the corroborative witness who would back him up completely to the satisfaction of the jury would be Peter Castigone. It wasn't a slam-dunk, but it was as good a case as most government attorneys are handed by their investigative agencies. It was sure worth a shot!

Wacks and Long went out to see the bombmaker, Smith. Eventually, once he became fully aware that the government had a solid case against him, he caved in. He would testify that he had made the bomb on the orders of Ferriola and given it to Nasti. Castigone would testify that he had heard the conversation between Ferriola, Accardo, and Nasti. He would also verify Nasti's testimony regarding the involvement of Rocky Infelice, Sal DeLaurentis, Lou Marino, "No Nose" DiFronzo, and Wings Carlisi in the criminal acts he had identified. The entire leadership of the Chicago mob was about to be had! From "The Man," the *consigliere* who actually made all the major decisions, to the boss, the underboss, and numerous other top men in the family. The case even gained a major defendant when Jeff Johnson got the bright idea of adding the Gussie Alex killing of Moe Dalitz to the list. Gussie Alex was another top mobster, the leader of the connection guys. Add Ben Jackson to the list of witnesses. Tie it all into one big RICO case!

Assuming that Nasti, Castigone, Smith, and Jackson could be kept alive and true to their commitment to testify fully and truthfully, this would become *the* landmark case which would bring the Chicago mob to its knees. Of course, it had also to be assumed that the Chicago mob would not get to the jury, that an honest judge would preside and that none of the witnesses would be killed or alter their testimony before they were able to testify.

When it all seemed to be wrapped up for presentation to the federal grand jury, Richards walked over to 79 West Monroe, Suite 605, the site of the Chicago Crime Commission. He asked John Jemilo, Jerry Gladden, and Jeanette Callaway to join him in Jemilo's office. Jemilo, the former deputy superintendent of the Chicago Police Department, is the executive director of the Crime Commission. Gladden, a former sergeant in the Intelligence Unit of the Chicago PD, who worked closely with Richards through his years there, is the chief investigator for the CCC, and Jeanette Callaway is the administrative brain, the commission's associate director. Richards gave a full report, on a strictly confidential basis, as to the progress of the investigation and the impending indictment. He had kept them more or less advised all along but now he filled in all the details.

Richards then headed for Washington where he met with Jim Mansfield and Ralph Salerno, the Rackets Committee investigators. With them, he met with Senators Bill Roth and Sam Nunn, the chairman and cochairman of the committee. He also gave them a full report.

As Richards explained to Roth, Nunn, Mansfield, and Salerno, it was his intention, no matter how the RICO trial would turn out, to take the copious notes he had kept and present all the evidence about the Accardo operations in Las Vegas to the Nevada Gaming Commission. He would make sure the commission had the transcript of the testimony and other evidence presented at the trial of the Chicago Ten. He had also obtained the approval of Nick Nasti to make himself available to the Gaming Commission. Nick would be in the Witness Protection Program following the trial but it would be no problem for the U. S. Marshals to take him to some location where he was not living and was not known, for questioning by the commission. Richards had been involved in similar situations before. He had interviewed such major witnesses as Jimmy Fratianno and Joey Cantalupo at neutral locations while they were in the WPP.

The RICO case therefore was the major instrument in Richards's longtime investigation of Joe Batters. In the first instance, it hopefully would send him to prison. But if for some unforeseen reason the trial would not be successful in this regard, then the evidence could be used to destroy what Accardo had built up through the years in Nevada—the major source of the income to the Chicago mob and therefore to him. Richards wielded a two-edged sword. Send Accardo to prison for the first time in his life and/or wipe out his interests in Las Vegas.

With that, Bill Richards packed his bags where he was staying, at the Sheraton Grand on Capitol Hill, taxied to Washington National Airport, and caught an American Airlines flight through O'Hare to Tucson. He wrapped his arms around Jeannie. It was good to be home. It was good to enjoy a job well done.

23

RICO!

BEFORE Nasti and Castigone became known to the mob and to the world as informants, Pete Wacks and Jeff Johnson sat down with them again. "We'd like you guys to carry a wire," they told them. Virtually in unison, they replied, "Bullshit! No way!"

"Carrying a wire" is probably the single most productive method of obtaining evidence of wrongdoing. Wacks, the FBI agent, and Johnson, the Strike Force attorney, wanted Nick Nasti and Peter Castigone to wear concealed microphones whenever they expected to have a serious conversation with their peers and, especially, with the bosses in the Chicago outfit.

Wacks and Johnson worked on the pair, and they finally agreed to do it in selected situations, only when it was as secure as possible and only when the very heart of their business was expected to be under discussion.

One day, when Nasti and Castigone were scheduled to meet with Rocky Infelice, the underboss of the Chicago mob, they first met in a room rented by Wacks at the Hyatt-Regency O'Hare in Rosemont, near O'Hare Airport. Wacks had brought along Jim Schlaker, the "sound man" of the Chicago FBI office, an experienced and capable technician. Schlaker "wired" both mobster-witnesses with Nagra body mikes. As they then proceeded to the meet with Infelice at Giannotti's, a restaurant on Lawrence Avenue in Norridge, a western suburb of Chicago, Wacks and Schlaker followed at a distance of three to four blocks. Nasti and Castigone were able to transmit their conversation over the "wires" they carried concealed on their bodies. When they got to Giannotti's, they were greeted by Donald Angelini, the capo who used the place as his headquarters. He motioned to Rocky Infelice, who sat at a corner table.

"Hey, you guys, I been waitin' for ya!" Infelice said. "Sit down."

"Yeah, we got tied up in traffic," Nasti said. "What do you want to see us for?"

"You were a little short last week, weren't you? I heard you only forked over six grand, that's short. What happened?"

"Had a bigger payout to the new captain in our district. We got to grease him good," Castigone said.

"That's bullshit and you guys know that! Look, I've been spendin' a lot of time on this. I lay out $35,000 a month for the coppers. And that's just the nut. I lay out ten for the sheriff, you know, the Bohemian, and five to another guy," Infelice said.

"I got no right to ask, but what do you get for $10,000 a month?" Nasti asked, performing as coached by Wacks and Johnson, attempting to have Infelice elucidate on his claims.

"Sheriff never bothers us," Infelice responded to Nasti. Then Infelice continued, "Then we got another guy at the States Attorney's office. Then we got another guy downtown. So you guys are supposed to clear with me before you increase your nut to that guy over there, you don't go off half-cocked and do it on your own. You guys are startin' to bother me. I got a good mind to knock you off that spot!"

Nasti got nasty as this point. "You do, huh, Rock. Look, I knew you before you got up to this top spot now, buddy. I knew you when you was foolin' with dope. Don't come on to me!"

"Nick, that's the fuckin' trouble with you. You think you're such a fuckin' hot shot. Just because you did some heavy work out West, now you think we owe you. Fuck you, Nasti, I'm your fuckin' boss now and you do what I say and you like it and you shut up! Now, from now on we take care of your copper through our man downtown and you come up with the full amount every fuckin' week! Do I make myself clear?"

The conversation went on from there, but Wacks and Johnson had heard enough. What they needed from this conversation was corroboration of the racketeering enterprise, one of the key elements of the RICO statute, and of the pattern of activity, at least two acts of racketeering within a ten-year period. Here were three. One, the payoffs to public officials with the reference to the "Bohemian," apparently the number two man in the Cook County Sheriff's Office. Two, the reference to the State's Attorney's office; and three, the reference to the coppers downtown, i.e. the headquarters of the Chicago Police Department, which is located at Eleventh and State, generally considered "downtown." Infelice's remark about his knowledge that Nasti had done "heavy work out West" indicated that he was a coconspirator in the bombing of the counting room at the Vegas Star. Furthermore, from the essence of the conversation, any jury would buy the fact that Rocky Infelice was, in every sense of the word, Nasti and Castigone's superior in this racketeering enterprise.

Johnson and Wacks were ecstatic. If they could just keep Nasti wired with the Nagra for two or three more conversations with the other prospective defendants, his future testimony in the trial would not only be corroborated by Castigone but by these "Title III" recordings, which were evidentiary, having been authorized by Judge Abraham Lincoln Marovitz, senior judge of the U. S. District Court for Northern Illinois, and were therefore completely legal and admissible at the trial.

Within the next month, Nasti, sometimes with Castigone and sometimes alone, met with Wacks and Schlaker and got "wired" prior to meetings with Sal DeLaurentis, Lou Marino, Dominic Daddano, John Sitiani, John DiFronzo, and Sam Carlisi. He led them all into conversations recounting their participation with him in various crimes which would serve as the nexus for the prospective indictments. It was a nervewracking endeavor for Nasti but he executed it well. He was able to obtain incriminating statements on the Nagra body-mike from each of his coconspirators. However, he was *not* able to arrange a sit-down with either Tony Accardo or Gus Alex. He simply was not big enough to reach up for those two. Furthermore, even if he had, Wacks and Johnson doubted he could entice those two experienced and capable hoodlums to make statements to Nasti that would incriminate them. It was one thing to deal with the likes of the underboss Infelice and other top Chicago mobsters like Carlisi and DiFronzo. They would be out-standing catches if they could be snared in Johnson and Wack's net. They were the heart of the Chicago mob in 1990—the three top men in the day-to-day, street-level operation of Chicago's LCN. Great catches! As great as that catch would be, though, Accardo and Alex would make it the greatest ever if they too could be successfully prose-cuted. But there was just no way Nick Nasti had the stature to obtain an audience with either of them. Even if he did it would be highly unlikely he could induce either of them to admit their involvement in such activity as the killing of Dalitz or the bombing of the counting room at the Vegas Star.

So it was, in early 1990, that Wacks, Richards, and Johnson made their decision to "unhook" Nick Nasti and Peter Castigone. Both were greatly relieved. They had not enjoyed going into the lion's den, taking the chance that the Nagra would be discovered and their role as govern-ment informants uncovered.

Arrangements were made to enter both Nasti and Castigone in the Witness Protection Program. They would be relocated from Chicago with their wives and children. They were quickly whisked away by the U. S. Marshal's Service after they had completed liquidation of all their fungible interests, such as winning bets, at the "office," i.e., their book-making operation. They were taken to Oklahoma City. Wacks, in par-ticular, had wanted them separated since if one was recognized, the other could fall into the same trap. But while Castigone and Nasti *wanted* to remain together for company, it was their wives who *insisted* on it. They would share this unique experience together; it would make the difficult life ahead that much more bearable. Not much, but at least some. They were placed in adjoining suites at the Skirvin Plaza, Okla-homa City's best hotel, for a few days. The marshals had made contact with Bob Fitzpatrick, now retired but for years one of the FBI's *very* best organized crime agents, whose work in Detroit is legendary. Fitz-patrick has lived in Oklahoma City for eighteen years and knows the town like the back of his hand. Furthermore, his wife, Alice, is one of Oklahoma City's top real estate brokers. Between them, the Fitzpa-tricks located two pleasant homes in a solid middle-class area near the Greens Country Club and the two mob-witness families were made as comfortable as possible. The marshals gave them fictitious identities including new Social Security cards, driver's licenses, credit cards (with a strict limit), voter registration cards, medical alert I.D., and the other accoutrements of a new identity. Their children were enrolled in good parochial schools in their new neighborhood. A deputy marshal, Jim Corboy, was assigned to assist them in any necessity in their lives.

Oklahoma City was far enough away from Chicago to offer protection but not so far that Pete Wacks and Jeff Johnson could not fly down occasionally to debrief Castigone and Nasti and help prepare their forthcoming testimony. It wasn't easy for the pair but it was as good as possible under the circumstances, a situation they could live with. That was the whole point.

Now Johnson, with the aid of Wacks and under the supervision of Gary Shapiro, began to outline the strategy for the case. And then something else fell into their laps. For the past couple years, the FBI and the Strike Force had been working on "Operation Kaffee Klatsch." It hadn't been assigned either to Wacks in the FBI or Johnson in the Strike Force, and although they had been aware that there was such an investigation going on, they hadn't focused on it.

"Operation Kaffee Klatsch" is an investigation of the corruption in the Regular Democratic Organization of the First Ward in Chicago, known simply as "the First Ward." Years before, Bill Richards and his associates on the "O.C." Squad, C-1, of the Chicago office of the FBI—Marshall Rutland in particular—had installed a hidden microphone in the offices of the First Ward, in Suite 2306 at 100 North LaSalle, on the corner of Washington in the heart of the Loop, right across the street from City Hall. This bug was dubbed "Shade" because the climate in the First Ward was so shady and because it was located in the shade of City Hall, and it had developed reams of information identifying Pat Marcy and John D'Arco, Sr., as the conduits through which orders from the Chicago outfit were passed on to those public officials, police officers, political leaders, labor leaders, and businessmen in a position to provide favorable treatment to the mobsters. Marcy had been identified by Richards when he testified for the Chicago Crime Commission before the Senate Rackets Committee as a "made" member of the Chicago mob whose assignment was to infiltrate politics. D'Arco was the alderman of the First Ward as well as the First Ward Democratic committeeman, a position which gave him authority to dispense the patronage, mostly in the form of jobs. He was the alderman who challenged Richards with the assertion that he, D'Arco, was "too big a man in Chicago to be embarrassed by the FBI." Richards subsequently "embarrassed" D'Arco by interrupting a secret meeting he was having with Sam Giancana, then the absolute boss of the Chicago mob and Accardo's caretaker.

The only problem with the bug placed by Richards and Rutland was that the information obtained therefrom was inadmissible in court. It had been placed in good faith on the part of the agents under the authority of J. Edgar Hoover, who extrapolated the power given him by attorneys general to protect the national security, extending it to investigations under the Top Hoodlum Program. At the time, 1962, there was no "Title III" authority for court-approved eavesdropping. It wasn't until 1968 that this power was established and not until 1970 when Ramsey Clark was replaced as attorney general that the FBI was given authority to place hidden microphones and tap phones under court orders, making the information obtained there from admissible as evidence in court. Therefore, none of the information obtained by Richards and his colleagues from their bug at the First Ward could be used in "Operation Kaffee Klatsch."

"Operation Kaffee Klatsch" is a major investigation by the federal government, as Wacks and Johnson knew. But they had only recently become aware that their investigation could be entwined with "Kaffee Klatsch" and become one gigantic RICO case. What a major blow to organized crime in Chicago if all the defendants could be tried together in one sensational trial! It would be, if successful, the biggest prosecution anywhere at any time! State or federal! Bigger than the Al Capone income-tax fraud trial in 1932. Bigger than Lucky Luciano's trial for prostitution in New York in 1936. Bigger than the Hollywood Extortion Case in 1943. Bigger than the Tony Accardo-Jackie Cerone income-tax evasion case of 1960. Bigger than the grant of immunity to Sam Giancana in 1965. Bigger than the three prosecutions of "the dominoes," the top bosses of the Chicago mob from 1966 to 1971. Bigger than the "Pizza Case" in New York in the mid-1980s. Bigger than the "Commission Case" in New York in the same time frame. Bigger than the "Greylord Cases" in Chicago during the mid- and late 1980s. Bigger than "Pendorf" in 1983. Bigger than "Strawman I" and "Strawman II" in Kansas City in the mid-1980s. Bigger than any of the three Gotti trials in New York during the late 1980s into 1990. Bigger than anything at any time in any place in the history of the United States!

"Operation Kaffee Klatsch" was aimed at determining the extent of corruption in Chicago. It struck right at the heart of what Gussie Alex and his connection guys had been doing for decades in Chicago, paying graft and using whatever other leverage they had to obtain favorable treatment from any public official or private citizen who could provide it. As part of the investigation, a Chicago attorney, Robert Cooley, had carried a wire for three years. His wire, and his testimony in support of it, could be added to the Wacks-Johnson indictment to obtain indictments against his targets—Pat Marcy, John D'Arco, Sr., and several judges and other top public officials. As another prong of "Kaffee Klatsch," the FBI had placed a hidden video camera and a hidden microphone in Booth One at Counsellor's Row Restaurant, located right next to the First Ward headquarters. Booth One was regularly reserved for D'Arco, Marcy, and their new alderman, Fred Roti. This bug had been in place for months and obtained much valuable information about the machinations of Marcy and D'Arco, Sr., in particular while carrying out their orders from the mob, from Gussie Alex in particular. Unfortunately, that phase of "Operation Kaffee Klatsch" had come to a screeching halt in July 1989, when the camera and the bug were discovered by a busboy at the restaurant.

That was what brought it to the attention of Wacks and Johnson. If Gary Shapiro, the Strike Force chief in Chicago, would approve, and if he could obtain the sanction of the acting United States attorney in Chicago, Ira Raphaelson, and if Raphaelson could obtain the authority of the Justice Department in Washington, all of the evidence from both cases could be wrapped together in one enormous case. It would be a tremendous victory over organized crime if successful. It would bring Joe Batters and his Chicago mob truly to their knees.

First, the government representatives would have to confirm that the evidence against all of the defendants could be linked, logically and legally. The case would have to be constructed to withstand the appropriate defense that it was crafted to the legal detriment of any of the singular defendants. It would have to withstand the charge that it had been designed to provide any unfair disadvantage to any of the defendants. The evidence would be forced to show the crimes which constitute the *"pattern* of the *enterprise"* to be within the same framework—as the pattern of a single enterprise—the Chicago family of La Cosa Nostra. It had to establish that all the defendants were engaged in the identical enterprise and that they were overtly engaged in the same pattern or in a conspiracy to violate laws falling within the same pattern. It had to outline clearly the key elements of *pattern* and *enterprise.*

Johnson and Shapiro worked on it. They examined minutely each piece of evidence, each defendant, and each witness. When they concluded their review they were satisfied that there would be no successful legal defense to the effect that the many crimes involved were not part of a pattern on behalf of the Chicago outfit, Tony Accardo's mob.

They took the results of their study, all neatly compiled in their legal brief, to Ira Raphaelson. After careful scrutiny, Raphaelson agreed and authorized that the brief be sent on to Washington to the department for approval. A couple of weeks later, in February of 1990, the word came down. It was a go!

Tony Accardo had won the war of the godfathers, but would he win this war? Or would everything he had worked for since the day he had joined the Capone Mob in the mid-1920s, some seventy years earlier, be destroyed? At his age, he had to win. This would be the last hurrah. There would be no chance for any comeback if he lost this battle.

24

The Trial

THE federal grand jury, sitting in the Northern District of Illinois in the Dirksen Federal Building at 219 South Dearborn in the Loop, returned the indictment on February 14, 1990. How fitting. It was Valentine's Day, exactly sixty-one years after the massacre. The only living participant in the slaughter that day in 1929 was Tony Accardo, aka Joe Batters, who was among the ten top leaders of the Chicago family of La Cosa Nostra who were indicted.

It was a 54-count, 102-page indictment. Count One was a racketeering conspiracy. Count Two charged that some of the defendants conspired to conduct an illegal gambling business consisting of a sports bookmaking operation. It alleged that the gambling business was conducted out of a number of different locations over the years including many "wire rooms." Counts Three, Four, and Five charged several of the defendants with various extortionate credit ("juice") transactions stemming from the gambling business. Counts Six and Seven charged that two other gambling businesses were operated by members of the family enterprise. Count Six charged the defendants with conducting an illegal blackjack game from 1968 to 1988. Count Seven involved an illegal parlay card bookmaking business from 1986 to 1989.

Counts Eight and Nine related to the extortion and murder of Hal Smith, the independent bookmaker whom Accardo had instructed Ferriola to bring into line or "clip." The indictment alleged this was done in aid of the racketeering enterprise and that Smith was murdered on February 7, 1985, in order to maintain the racketeering enterprise. At the time, the indictment charged, Hal Smith was a well-known, large volume bookmaker in the Chicago area who had refused to pay the street tax or protection money to the defendants in connection with his gambling business. Count Nine concerned the shooting of Mike Rodino, charging that this was done to further the goals of the enterprise. Counts Ten through Thirty involved the filing of false and fraudulent income-tax returns for the years 1983 through 1988.

Count Thirty-One charged Tony Accardo with conspiracy in ordering the bombing of the counting room at the Vegas Star. Count Thirty-Two charged Gus Alex with conspiracy in the murder of Moe Dalitz. Count Thirty-Three charged Joe Ferriola with participating in the assault on Moe Dalitz. Count Thirty-Four charged Ferriola with conspiracy to murder Charlie "Bats" Battaglia in Arizona. Counts Thirty-Five and Thirty-Six charged Dominic Daddano and John Sitiani with the Battaglia murder. Count Thirty-Seven charged Rocky Infelice for conspiracy to violate the Interstate Travel in Aid of Racketeering-Gambling Statute. Count Thirty-Eight charged Infelice with bribery based on his conversations with Nick Nasti and Peter Castigone as recorded on their Nagra body-mikes about his payouts to the "Bohemian," on the Cook County Sheriff's Police, and to other Chicago public officials. Count Thirty-Eight charged Sal DeLaurentis with conspiracy to violate the ITAR-gambling statute. Count Thirty-Nine charged Louis Marino with a violation of the same statute. Count Forty charged John "No Nose" DiFronzo with a violation of ITAR-gambling, and Count Forty-One charged him with the shooting of Rodino. Count Forty-Two charged Sam "Wings" Carlisi with the shooting of Rodino and Count Forty-Three charged him with violation of ITAR-gambling.

Counts Forty-Three through Fifty charged the defendants Ferriola, Infelice, DeLaurentis, Marino, DiFronzo, and Carlisi with failure to register as individuals engaged in the business of accepting wagers and to pay the special occupational tax required by Internal Revenue Service regulations.

Counts Fifty through Fifty-Four charged Capt. Gregory Barry, commander of the vice squad in the Central District of the Chicago Police Department; Judge Raymond Boverholzer of the Circuit Court of Cook County, Criminal Division; attorney Boyd Wolferman and Chief Investigator Paul O'Neil of the Cook County Sheriff's Office with bribery, in that they accepted bribes to fix cases. This was all part of the "Kaffee Klatsch" investigation. There was a last-minute decision not to "wrap" the investigation of Pat Marcy and John D'Arco into the RICO trial. They would be dealt with at a later date.

The indictments were announced by U. S. Attorney General Dick Thornburgh, who travelled to Chicago specifically for the purpose. He stressed that the indictments were a major breakthrough in the federal efforts against "The Accardo Family" enterprise, and that it was his expectation that convictions based on the indictment would "bring the Chicago mob to its knees." He announced that "the dogged work of the FBI has paid off in a significant indictment of racketeering activity, including murder, extortion, bribery, financing, and collection of usurious loans and illegal gambling." He was accompanied to the news conference by James D. McKenzie, the SAC (Special Agent in Charge) of the FBI office in Chicago, and by Gary Shapiro, the chief of the Organized Crime Division of the U. S. Attorney's office in Chicago. As is customary, the street agent who developed the case, Pete Wacks, and the assistant U. S. Attorney who formulated the strategy after the evidence had been developed by Wacks, Jeff Johnson, were nowhere near the conference. It was the chiefs who took the credit.

The prime witness before the grand jury had been Nick Nasti, who testified against Accardo, Ferriola, Infelice, DeLaurentis, Marino, DiFronzo, Carlisi, Daddano, and Sitiani. Obviously he was the key. Also testifying in support of Nasti's testimony was his partner, Peter Castigone. Ben Jackson testified against Gus Alex. Charles Smith testified against Joe Ferriola in that Ferriola had ordered Smith to make the bomb used by Nasti at the Vegas Star. Pursuant to the promise made to Frank Goebbels by Bill Richards that he not be identified or called to testify about his role in the bombing of the Vegas Star, Goebbels was not present. All the "Title III" evidence was presented, including all the Nagra evidence against the four "Kaffee Klatsch" defendants.

On February 20, 1990, a special detention hearing was held before

U. S. Magistrate Thomas Rosemond in the Dirksen Federal Building. Jeff Johnson represented the government. Bond was set for Tony Accardo at $2,750,000. Magistrate Rosemond noted that since Accardo would have to put up cash or securities of ten per cent and since that was $275,000, the precise amount found in his residence by the FBI when it executed a search warrant in 1978 after the slaying of six burglars, it was not an unreasonable sum. Ferriola, Infelice, DeLaurentis, Marino, Daddano, Sitiani, DiFronzo, and Carlisi were remanded to the custody of the U. S. Marshal without bail for incarceration in the Metropolitan Correctional Center located at Clark and Van Buren Streets in the Loop. The four "Kaffee Klatsch" defendants were released on bail of $200,000 each. Gus Alex was released on bail of $1,000,000 after he presented affidavits from two personal physicians, corroborated by a government doctor, that his mental and emotional health was such that he could be seriously incapacitated if incarcerated. He signed an agreement that warranted that he would remain in Chicago until after completion of the trial rather than travel elsewhere, including to his Fort Lauderdale home.

The case was assigned to U. S. District Court Judge Abraham Lincoln Marovitz, a senior judge, long noted for his honesty and capability. He excused himself, however, because he is a close personal friend of Bill Richards, one of those involved in the investigation. It was then assigned to Judge John McGrath with a trial date of November 1, 1990.

The defendants retained four of the very best defense attorneys in Chicago. Pat Tuite was selected by Joe Ferriola, Rocky Infelice, Sal DeLaurentis, and Lou Marino. Tuite, a former assistant States Attorney in Cook County, is arguably the very best criminal lawyer in Chicago and has had outstanding success in defending the accused. In fact, in 1984, he had successfully defended three of the same defendants—Infelice, DeLaurentis, and Marino—against a similar ITAR-gambling charge. Tuite had attacked the affidavit showing probable cause prepared by the FBI and was able to show discrepancies in it.

Accardo was defended by Carl Walsh, the attorney who had successfully defended him against charges of contempt when he lied in response to accusations leveled at him during Bill Richards's testimony before the U. S. Permanent Subcommittee on Investigations in 1983. Carl Walsh is the son of Maurice Walsh, who was Accardo's attorney when Accardo beat an income-tax fraud case against him after he successfully appealed his conviction on an earlier trial in the mid-sixties. Carl Walsh was also retained to represent Gus Alex, a longtime client. Whenever Richards had formally interviewed Alex in the past, it was in Carl Walsh's office.

DiFronzo and Carlisi were represented by Art Nasser, a formal appeals attorney for the Internal Revenue Service in Chicago. Nasser is an experienced Chicago attorney, associated in practice with Walsh, and had represented Tony Spilotro in the past. Defendants Daddano and Sitiani were represented by Sam Betar, a former top assistant in the United States Attorney's office in Chicago who had previously represented Jackie Cerone, the former top boss of the Chicago mob. Betar also represented each of the "Kaffee Klatsch" defendants, Captain Barry, Judge Boverholzer, attorney Wolferman, and Chief Investigator O'Neil.

ABOUT five days before the trial started, Bill Richards received a call in Tucson from Nick Lupresto, his longtime CTE (top echelon criminal informant) from his days on the "O.C." squads in Chicago.

"Bill," Lupresto said, after some initial pleasantries, "would it surprise you if I told you the connection guys have gotten hold of the jury panel list and each of us are supposed to find out all we can about the prospective jurors so they can be approached before or during the trial?"

It was no surprise to Richards. It was the same trick Jake "Greasy Thumb" Guzik had used as boss of the connection guys back in 1931 when Al Capone had been indicted and that Murray "The Camel" Humphreys had used in 1960 as boss of the connection guys when Tony Accardo and Jackie Cerone were about to go on trial. Now that Gussie Alex was not only the current boss of the connection guys but a defendant himself, it was only logical that he would go to school on his predecessors.

Richards put in a call to Jeff Johnson. Without disclosing his source, a promise he has kept for years to Lupresto, he tipped Johnson off about the ongoing efforts to get to the jury.

"Bill," Johnson said, "thanks a lot. I'll go to Judge McGrath and make sure he switches jury panels at the last minute. Bill, while I've got you on the phone . . . I'm worried about Nasti and Castigone. They're getting antsy and the trial hasn't even started yet. You know where they are. Why don't you go talk to them? You're the guy who brought them over in the first place and I think you're the guy who can calm them down. It would mean a lot to us."

Richards agreed. Jim Corboy, the deputy U. S. Marshal responsible for the "care and feeding" of Nasti and Castigone in Oklahoma City, made the travel arrangements for Richards. In Oklahoma City he stayed in the home of his old pals, Bob and Alice Fitzpatrick, and visited for two days with Nasti and Castigone. He found that what apparently was bothering them was the natural remorse that might be expected as the moment of truth approached. Like nervous bridegrooms, they were beginning to wonder whether they were doing the right thing. Richards had gone through it before, especially with Lou Bombacino when he was about to testify against Jackie Cerone, Donald Angelini, Dominic Cortina, Frank Aurelli, and others in 1971. Needless to say, it is extremely difficult to get up on the stand in front of a group of killers (and one's former associates), look them in the eye, doom them to a long imprisonment, and then withstand a withering cross-examination by tough, capable, experienced defense attorneys.

Richards spent two days with his pals in Oklahoma City. On the last day he was joined by Pete Wacks who had also developed a good rapport with the pair. Richards and Wacks felt they had alleviated Nasti and Castigone's concerns and offered them the support they needed to brace themselves for their ordeal. Wacks then told Richards that Oliver "Buck" Revell had told him to ask Richards to come to Chicago for the trial and lend his counsel. "Buck" Revell actually runs the Bureau today. He is the Executive Assistant Director in charge of investigations. He and Richards are good friends, having served together in Chicago in the 1970s. When Richards accepted gladly, wanting to remain a part of what figured to be the most sensational trial in the history of organized crime, he was greeted by Jeff Johnson, who invited him, as a fellow attorney, to sit at the government table in the courtroom during the trial and aid in the prosecution of the case. Richards readily accepted the offer, grateful for the recognition it represented.

When the trial commenced on November 1, 1990, the first thing Judge McGrath did was follow the example set for him in the previous major trials of Chicago mob leaders Capone and Accardo. He announced that he was requesting his bailiff to switch jury panels with another judge. Down the drain went all of Gussie Alex & Co.'s homework! They should have expected it. When Richards looked over at

Gussie Alex at one of the defense tables—there was no room for all the defendants and their attorneys at one table—their eyes met. Richards smiled. Gussie did not.

The press table emptied. All the reporters rushed to telephones outside the courtroom to report this development. It became a news flash on all the television and radio stations in Chicago.

Pat Tuite then stepped up. "Your Honor, I move for a change in venue. It is our contention that the outrageous sensationalism practiced by the media prior to this trial, continuing into a crescendo today, has made it impossible for our clients to receive a fair trial in this court."

Jeff Johnson leaped to his feet. "If Your Honor would, please. The defendants made their own publicity. They are all residents of this judicial district. Whatever publicity that may have been engendered is of their own making. I am confident, however, that Mr. Tuite, his associates, and the government can pick a fair and impartial jury. I respectfully request Your Honor to deny Mr. Tuite's motion."

Judge McGrath had expected the motion. He announced that he would take it under advisement pending attempts to impanel the jury. Again, the reporters hurried from the courtroom to file their updates, only to return momentarily. (They didn't want to miss any of the action!) They made quick calls on their cellular phones—a boon in this situation—then returned to the courtroom without having to stand in line before the few pay phones in the corridors of the federal building.

All four of the defense attorneys then made substantially the same motion, i.e., that their clients be severed from the trial. They based their motions on the claim that the crimes charged were all separate and distinct and should not be "lumped" into one charge. Jeff Johnson again sprang to his feet. "Your Honor," he cried, "these defendants have chosen to associate with each other and, as the evidence will show to conspire with each other. The evidence will show, Your Honor, that this indictment has been properly framed and that the RICO statute authorizes what the attorneys for the defense call 'lumping.' "

Judge McGrath also took that motion under advisement and would later rule against it, as he would the motion for change of venue.

The process of jury selection, the "voir dire," began. It was to be a along and tedious episode in this trial. All preemptory challenges on both sides were exhausted. Many were excused for cause when they admitted they were aware of the background of the matter before the court or knew of the reputation of one or more of the defendants.

Several admitted they might be unable to render a just verdict in the event it was shown that any of the defendants might be associated with organized crime.

Finally twelve jurors and two alternates were selected. Jeff Johnson then made a motion to sequester the jury in a hotel. Art Nasser objected for the defense. The motion was denied, Judge McGrath citing that it was expected to be a trial of lengthy duration which would create a hardship for the jurors and their families. He then looked directly into the faces of the defendants and said: "In the event this court receives any information indicating that any objectional contact is made with any of the jurors, you will each be held accountable."

Pat Tuite was on his feet immediately. "Your Honor! I object! To insinuate that any of these defendants would think of such a thing is prejudicial! I demand a mistrial!"

Judge McGrath banged his gavel. "Sit down, Mr. Tuite. I deny your motion. This court will decide what is prejudicial."

Tuite sat down. He motioned to an assistant on the other side of the railing. (There was simply no room for the assistants at the defense tables.) He instructed this lawyer to research the law and quickly give him a brief on Judge McGrath's remarks in front of the jury. He listed it on his legal pad under the heading "Appeal Points."

"Is the government ready to present its case?" Judge McGrath asked.

Jeff Johnson stood. "We are, Your Honor. The government calls Nicholas James Nasti to the stand."

The press and the spectators—those court buffs who were lucky enough to be admitted to the overflowing benches by the U. S. Marshals who were controlling and guarding the courtroom—buzzed and stirred.

Nick Nasti was escorted into the courtroom by the marshals, who then stood in the corners of the room. Nick glanced quickly at the defendants for the first and last time during the trial. On the other hand, they glared at him long and hard for the duration.

Nasti was sworn in. Jeff Johnson approached him and led him through the preliminaries: his name, former residence, his status as a made member of the Chicago Cosa Nostra, and his bookmaking activities. He then identified Tony Accardo as "Joe Batters, the *consigliere* of the Chicago outfit." He said that "outfit" is what the members called the Chicago mob. He then identified Joe Ferriola as the boss, Rocky Infelice as the underboss, Gus Alex as the leader of the connection guys, John "No Nose" DiFronzo as a top capo, and Sam "Wings" Carlisi, also a top capo. He identified Daddano, Sitiani, DeLaurentis, and Marino as "active made guys."

Under questioning by Johnson, Nasti then detailed for the jury how he had been ordered by Ferriola to place the bomb in the counting room by the Vegas Star. He said that Ferriola told him that he had been "ordered by Joe Batters to do this."

This raised a great hue and cry from Carl Walsh, who strongly objected. "That's hearsay. A witness is not allowed to say what somebody else might have said out of his presence!" Since Nasti had volunteered the information before Walsh could realize what he was saying and make this timely objection, Judge McGrath ordered that the jury disregard Nasti's statement regarding Accardo.

Nasti then answered Johnson's questions about Infelice.

"Did there come a time when you had a conversation with Ernest Infelice, whom you know as 'Rocky', at Giannotti's Restaurant in Norridge?"

"Yes, I did," answered Nasti.

"Tell us what was said by Infelice," Johnson asked.

At this point, Pat Tuite, Infelice's attorney, jumped in. "No foundation, a leading question," he shouted. Judge McGrath overruled the objection.

Nasti then detailed the remarks made by Infelice, which indicated his role as Nasti's superior in the "enterprise," his bribery of law enforcement personnel, and his knowledge that Nasti had done some "heavy work out West."

Tuite again objected on the grounds that the comments were pointless and irrelevant. Judge McGrath again overruled him, saying, "That is up to the jury to decide."

Johnson then laid the foundation for the admission of the tape recording from the Nagra body-mike with which Nasti had been wired during the conversation with Infelice. He asked leave of Judge McGrath "to continue the testimony of the witness" after the recording was played for the jury. Transcripts of the conversation were then placed in evidence, marked Government Exhibit A, and the tape was played as each juror scanned his or her own copy of the transcript. In several spots, Tuite objected but was overruled with statements from

Judge McGrath to the effect of, "Let the jury hear it and interpret for themselves."

When Nasti took the stand again following the playing of the tape, Johnson attempted to solidify the recollection of the jury as to what they had just heard. He attempted to ask questions by reviewing the same material that had just been covered by the tape. Tuite was too bright and alert for that, however. He objected, saying "that matter has been covered, he's already answered this line of questioning, this is redundant and wasting the time of this court, Your Honor!" Judge McGrath sustained this objection.

Johnson then led Nasti into the circumstances of the kneecapping of rival bookmaker Mike Rodino, by Infelice, DiFronzo, and Carlisi. When Tuite objected to this line of questioning, again on the basis of the hearsay rule, Johnson was able to overcome the objection by drawing from the witness the fact that he had driven the car on the occasion of the assault on Rodino and had pointed him out to the three shooters. It was not hearsay, therefore, it was the testimony of an eyewitness.

Then Johnson questioned Nasti about his role in the murder of Charlie Battaglia. He incriminated Ferriola, Sitiani, and Daddano in this testimony. Again, however, he ran into trouble, this time from Walsh, when he attempted to testify as to the participation of Accardo in the episode. Judge McGrath sustained Walsh's objections by ruling that such testimony was prohibited by the hearsay rule since it was merely Ferriola's word; the witness had not been present when Accardo had given the order to Ferriola. Johnson had anticipated that Walsh, Accardo's attorney, would object and that the judge would sustain the objection. He knew, however, that the most astute jurors could anticipate Nasti's answer to the question. It wasn't a completely lost effort although it came close to violating the rules of legal ethics.

At this point Johnson concluded his examination-in-chief. He turned Nasti over to Tuite for his cross-examination. Nasti expected a real grilling. And he got it.

What Nasti was prepared for was something he had not prepared his wife and kids for. At the age of eighteen he had raped and sodomized a young girl. The rule of law is that such an event cannot be brought out unless it resulted not only in an arrest but in a conviction. Unfortunately for Nick, then and now, he had been convicted of the crime. Tuite hammered him with questions about it. It was bound to affect Nasti's credibility in the minds of the jury. Johnson just hoped it would not completely impeach his testimony. He could and would attempt to smooth it over during his summation to the jury at the end of the trial by indicating that "no angel could have been present when Nick Nasti did the things he testified to. Nick Nasti may not be an angel and if he had been he wouldn't have been in place to see and hear what he did. Then he wouldn't have been here to testify in order to insure that justice is carried out."

The direct examination had taken a day and a half. Tuite's cross took two days. When it was over Nick Nasti was shaken, as was his testimony, but, in the estimation of Jeff Johnson, it could have been much worse. That evening he would tell Wacks and Richards, "Nick stood up pretty well. We didn't have a virgin on the stand and Pat Tuite was able to bring that out. But, all in all, I think he did just about as well as could be expected. I think the jury bought it. All in all, I think he was a credible witness."

THE next day it was Peter Castigone's turn. It was his function to corroborate Nick Nasti's testimony. Not to add anything new, but just to back Nick up—to add to his credibility in the minds of the jury.

Jeff Johnson led him slowly into the gist of his testimony. His background in Chicago and as Nasti's partner in the bookmaking business, how he had been made into the Chicago outfit. Then Johnson got to the heart of the matter.

"Did there come a point in time when your daughter got married?"

"Yes," answered Castigone.

"At her wedding reception, did you invite Tony Accardo and Joe Ferriola and did they attend?" Johnson asked.

"Yes," answered Castigone.

"And during the reception, did there come a time when you accompanied Joe Ferriola when he led Nick Nasti into the presence of Tony Accardo?" asked Johnson.

"Not that I remember," answered Castigone.

"Oh, my God!" thought Richards. "Not that he remembers? What is that? We went over that time and again for months, what does he mean, not that he remembers?"

"Let me rephrase the question," Johnson said. "At the wedding reception for your daughter, did there come a time when you were in the presence of Nick Nasti, Joe Ferriola, and Tony Accardo at the same time?"

"Not that I remember," Castigone responded.

"Let us try it one more time. At the reception for your daughter did you or did you not overhear a conversation between Joe Ferriola and Tony Accardo when Ferriola introduced Nick Nasti to Accardo?"

"Not that I remember," Castigone answered.

Johnson was stunned. So were Wacks and Richards. This witness, who had been debriefed on this precise topic and for this precise moment, had obviously gone sour. He was no dummy, he had not forgotten. That was impossible. Was it possible he had been reached? Richards looked over at Gussie Alex at the defense table. This time it was Alex who had a slight smile on his face, just before he looked up at the ceiling. It was a very contented look.

"Your Honor, may I have a moment?" Johnson asked. He conferred with Richards and Wacks. "I'm going to try a different tack and then I'm going to ask that he be declared a hostile witness so we can ask him leading questions."

Johnson tried again. "Mr. Castigone, do you recall a time when you were having problems with a Mr. Mike Rodino?"

"Not that I remember," Castigone answered.

"You have no recollection that Mr. Rodino was kneecapped by Rocky Infelice, Sal DeLaurentis, and Louis Marino?"

Same answer. Castigone didn't remember.

"Your Honor, I ask that that witness be considered a hostile witness. May I approach the bench?" Johnson asked.

Johnson and the battery of defense attorneys stepped up to the bench. Tuite, Walsh, Betar, and Nasser all seemed very smug.

"Your Honor," Johnson said quietly, "this witness has informed us on several occasions as to my questions today in a completely opposite manner. He has informed us he was with the witness Nasti on the occasions I asked him about, directly in opposition to the manner in which he is now testifying. I ask that he be considered a hostile witness." Judge McGrath looked at the defense attorneys. He expected vigorous opposition to the plea of Johnson. He got none. The four continued to look smug.

Johnson stepped back in front of Castigone. He asked, "Mr. Castigone, is it not a fact that you and I, and Mr. Richards, have gone over your testimony on several occasions before today?"

"Yes," Castigone answered.

"And isn't it a fact that on each of those occasions you told us you were with Nick Nasti when he was introduced to Accardo by Ferriola and that you were with Nasti when you set up Rodino for Infelice and the others?"

"Not that I remember," answered Castigone.

Try as he may, Johnson was unable to elicit from Castigone anything in support of Nasti's testimony. The more he tried, the more Castigone replied with his now monotonous answer: "Not that I remember."

The mob had gotten to Castigone! When and how, Richards, Johnson, and Wacks did not know. Nasti's testimony had been somewhat shaky. The government had expected that it would be firmed up by Castigone's corroboration. It was not. It was a damaging blow to the government's case—to say the least. When Judge McGrath asked Tuite if he had any questions for Castigone on cross, Tuite answered: "No, Your Honor." Why ruin a good thing? Let the jury's memories of Castigone be his refusal to respond affirmatively to "the one who brung him," in this case the government. He was their witness but he had testified for the defense, which had double the effect it would have had he been "brung" by the defense. It couldn't have worked out better from Tuite's viewpoint.

Johnson conferred with Richards and Wacks. "I could ask for a recess now and we would try to regroup. But I'd like to get right on to our next witness, don't give the jury any time to reflect. Let's get Ben Jackson on, quickly."

Ben Jackson was hurried onto the stand. He testified as to how he had been contacted by Gus Alex and wined and dined at the Sultan's Table at the Dunes in Las Vegas.

"Do you see that man in the courtroom today," Jeff Johnson asked.

"Yes, I do," Ben Jackson replied.

"Would you point him out?"

Ben Jackson pointed directly at Gus Alex. "The man in the dark gray suit with the pin stripes, wearing a maroon tie. With the tan."

"Let the record show," Jeff Johnson said, "that the witness has pointed out the defendant, Gus Alex."

Ben Jackson then testified how he had received $100,000 from Gus Alex to poison Moe Dalitz in Sunrise Hospital in Las Vegas. He made a fine witness for the prosecution.

Then it was time for his ordeal on cross-examination.

"Mr. Jackson, are you testifying for the government in return for any consideration, any promise, any understanding, any agreement from them?" Carl Walsh queried.

"Yes, I am."

"Would you tell this court and this jury just what that promise is?"

"I have been promised immunity."

Carl Walsh let that sink in. "You have been promised immunity. Tell us what you understand that to mean."

"I understand that to mean that I will not be tried for anything I have done."

Walsh let that sink in. Then he thundered, "You will not be tried for *anything* you have ever done! You will not be tried for *anything* you have ever done! My, Mr. Jackson, that is some kind of promise! Everybody should get a promise like that! You have committed murder by your own testimony, and now you receive a promise you will never be prosecuted for it? Or for anything else in your entire life? My God, that's one *hell* of a promise!"

Walsh had made his point.

Jeff Johnson then stepped up for the re-direct examination. "Mr. Jackson, there is one major promise you do not have. And that one is the promise that you *will* be prosecuted if you commit perjury, am I right?"

"That is right."

"Let us make this clear. You have been firmly instructed to tell the truth, the whole truth, and nothing but the truth. If you lie on this stand you will be prosecuted. Let me ask you, have you told the truth, the whole truth, and nothing but the truth when you say you accepted $100,000 from the man you have identified as the defendant Gus Alex to murder Moe Dalitz?"

"Yes, I have not lied. I have told the truth."

With that Judge McGrath halted the proceedings for the day, to be continued at ten o'clock the next morning.

Bill Richards hurried into the marshal's lockup in the Federal Building. He rushed into the cell holding Peter Castigone. "Peter, how could you do this, you double-crossed us! What the hell happened?"

Castigone would not look at Richards. He kept his eyes focused on the cell floor. No matter what Richards said, he would not look up or respond in any fashion. Richards was devastated. In his forty years in law enforcement, ever since his rookie days as an FBI agent in 1950, nothing like this had happened to him. He had been rebuffed by potential informants and told to go to hell, but he had never before been double-crossed. It was a new and terrible experience. He felt responsible for Castigone and his duplicitous conduct. He was the one who had "developed" him, first as an informant and then as a witness. He was the one who had "brung" him, and the result reflected badly on him. He put his hand on Castigone's shoulder. "Peter, you're a sorry specimen. Go back to the assholes. They can have you! But remember, we'll get you some day! You're our number one target from now on!" A year later, Castigone and Richards would meet again, but that's a whole new story.

THE next day it was Charles Smith's turn on the stand. He testified that he had made the bomb at the direction of Joe Ferriola, whom he knew as Joe Negall, the boss of the Chicago mob. He testified he turned the bomb he made over to Nick Nasti on the orders of Negall. When he answered that he knew that it was that bomb which blew up the counting room of the Vegas Star, Judge McGrath sustained the objection of Art Nasser that the answer was based on an assumption and therefore objectionable. Nasser had no luck with Charles Smith on cross. His story was pat. He "remembered" everything.

Jeff Johnson then placed the "Kaffee Klatsch" evidence on the record. It consisted primarily of Title III information obtained by attorney Robert Cooley as he conversed with the defendants Barry, Boverholzer, Wolferman, and O'Neil concerning the fixes they conspired to execute in the cases of several defendants in the Criminal Division of the Cook County Circuit Court. One of these fixes was on behalf of Joe Spadevecchio, a mid-level West Side "made member" who had been charged with bookmaking in the Loop. Another was on behalf of Dominic "Toots" Palermo of South Holland, a rising star in the southern suburbs of Cook County. Barry was linked to the Spadevecchio fix. Judge Boverholzer was linked to both. Wolferman and O'Neil were charged with the Palermo fix. The bribes in the "Kaffee Klatsch" phase of the RICO trial totaled $250,000. The evidence also consisted of the information developed from the video camera and the bug at Counsellor's Row Restaurant across from City Hall.

Jeff Johnson then concluded the government's case. The defense called none of the ten mob defendants to the stand. To do so would have opened them up to cross-examination as to their entire past histories, their whole careers in the mob. Although Accardo and Alex alone of the mobsters had never been convicted of a crime which could be presented in full flower to the jury when they took the stand in their own defense, Johnson would have had the opportunity to question them about everything that had happened. Accardo could have been questioned about his early days in the enterprise, from Al Capone through the St. Valentine's Day Massacre to Nitti, Ricca, to his reign as boss, the reign of Sam Giancana, and the rest of his "career" as *consigliere.* Gus Alex could have been questioned about his role in "the enterprise" which was the *res gestae* of the government's case. From his days as the shotgun slayer of Vince Bozik on the South Side of Chicago, to his role as the bodyguard of Jake "Greasy Thumb" Guzik, to his current role as chief of the connection guys. When they did not take the stand in their defense, however, there was no way for the government to get them there. They stood mute. As did all the other mob defendants. It was textbook tactics. No competent defense attorney would have strategized otherwise.

The defense did present evidence, however. Mostly alibi evidence. Witnesses who observed the defendants in other places at the precise times they were identified by Nasti and the other witnesses putting them at the scene of the acts.

When the defense rested, Judge McGrath dropped a bomb. He ruled that the evidence against Gus Alex did not tie him into the "pattern" necessitated by the RICO statute. "I make no ruling," he announced, "on the merits or the sufficiency of the evidence against this defendant, Gus Alex. My decision is not prejudicial. There is no reason why this defendant cannot be charged with conspiracy to commit murder in a separate prosecution. I leave that up to the appropriate authorities. My ruling today should be no bar to any such consideration. The facts in this case, based on the evidence presented here, however, do not constitute sufficient basis in the law to sustain a charge of a violation of the RICO statute. I order his release."

Wow! What a disappointment for Richards, Wacks, and Johnson. Richards looked over at his longtime adversary, the guy he had pursued for thirty-three years, and this time Gussie had a big smile on his face.

Jeff Johnson's summation for the government took six hours. He went over the entire presentation. He carefully explained how the government's witnesses had testified as to the "pattern of the enterprise," how the individual crimes detailed filled out the pattern, and how the Chicago family of La Cosa Nostra became the "enterprise" defined in the RICO act. He completely skipped over the testimony of Peter

Castigone. It was an impassioned, eloquent summation. Johnson is a most capable attorney and his straightforward presentation impressed Wacks, Richards, and most of the crowd of spectators—and, hopefully, the jury as well.

Each of the four defense attorneys then took a turn. Tuite, especially, was impressive. His defense of Ferriola, especially, was forceful.

The jury retired to consider the verdict. They were out six days. Finally, they informed the bailiff they had a verdict.

Johnson, Richards, and Wacks resumed their places at the government table. At long last, eleven months after the indictment, the trial was about to be concluded. Richards, especially, was on pins and needles. It had been a long, hard road, but it was now coming to an end. Now his work would be judged by a jury of twelve men and women, tried and true.

The jury foreman stood up. He read the verdicts. As to the defendant Joseph Ferriola: "Guilty on all counts!" As to the defendant Ernest "Rocky" Infelice: "Guilty on all counts!" As to the defendant Dominic Daddano: "Guilty on all counts!" As to the defendant John Sitiani: "Guilty on all counts!"

"My God," Richards thought, "get to Accardo!"

The jury foreman continued. As to the defendant Salvatore DeLaurentis: "Guilty on all counts!" As to the defendant Louis Marino: "Guilty on all counts!" As to the defendant John DiFronzo: "Guilty on all counts!" As to the defendant Sam Carlisi: "Guilty on all counts!" As to the defendant Barry: "Guilty!" As to the defendant Boverholzer: "Guilty!" As to the defendant Wolferman: "Guilty!" As to the defendant O'Neil: "Guilty!"

Finally he got to the one he was obviously saving for the last. "As for the defendant Anthony Joseph Accardo, also known as Joe Batters, *"Not* guilty on all counts!"

There it was. Richards slumped back into his chair. It was half a loaf! They had gotten some big fish, but the "Big Tuna" had slipped off the hook once again. He would continue to boast that he had never spent a night in jail in his whole life! From 1923 to 1990, from Capone throughout his own long reign as "the Man," as the venerable godfather of the Chicago family, the most important man ever in the history of the Chicago mob, nobody had ever laid a glove on him. That might well be his epitaph. To be marked on his gravestone. "They never got me." Not the authorities, not his own people. Nobody had ever survived in the crucible which is Chicago—or anywhere else for that matter—for as long as he had. The man proved to be invincible. He could now sit back and watch his sunset from his home on the fairways of the Indian Wells Country Club in Palm Springs or in the guest house of his daughter's beautiful home in Barrington Hills outside the city of Chicago. The city he had conquered and ruled. "They never laid a glove on him."

25

Accardo's Nadir

ALTHOUGH Tony Accardo had won the major war of his life in the battle with fellow godfather Joe Bonanno, then followed that up by beating the government one more time, possibly the last such fight of his life, it did not turn out to be a total victory for him or for his outfit. Not by a long shot!

Before he left Chicago to head for his own spot in the sunshine to write his memories, Bill Richards gave it one more shot. He sat down with Jeff Johnson and Pete Wacks. They did a critique of the case they had presented to the jury—where they had triumphed and where they had failed. They were aware of the problems *ab initio* with the hearsay evidence rule which prevented the admittance of much of Ferriola and Infelice's conversation regarding the role of Joe Batters in Nick Nasti's "work out West." They had realized from the inception of the case that the evidence against the old man Accardo was flimsy. But, knowing that such work couldn't have been done without the sanction and the approval of Accardo and that Nasti's testimony was truthful, accurate, and sincere, they had followed through to the best of their ability to try to make Accardo pay for his prime role in the affair. It was not to be. Accardo kept his record spotless. He had "skated" one more time and had won what was possibly the last court battle of his life. (Maybe and maybe not.)

Richards had one other thought, however; one last weapon in the arsenal to thwart the Chicago mob. He discussed it with Wacks and Johnson and was given *carte blanche* to pursue his course.

Remembering the rules of evidence from his law school days and from the long review he had made of the law when he passed the bar exam in 1958, Richards was aware of the relaxation of the hearsay rule in hearings before administrative boards. He knew that such bodies, in the effort to do the job they are mandated to do, have the discretion to accept *whatever* evidence is available to them and then to assign the proper weight to it.

The Nevada Gaming Control Commission falls into this category of administrative boards. In order to get at the truth and properly regulate the gaming industry in Nevada, the commission is allowed to receive whatever evidence it deems worthwhile, no matter what its sources, then to evaluate it. Naturally, testimony from the horse's mouth subject to cross-examination carries the most weight. But in the absence of such a source, the commission is empowered to hear other evidence and to weigh it in fulfilling its objective of keeping Nevada clean of undesirable elements.

Wacks and Johnson gave Richards their authority to go to Las Vegas and meet with the Gaming Control Board with the objective of winning a recommendation to the parent Gaming Control Commission, that he testify concerning *all* the evidence that had been developed for the trial of the Chicago Fourteen—including that which was properly excluded by Judge McGrath. Not only did he want to present Nasti's testimony—including the hearsay which had been excluded from the hearing of the jury—but also the information gleaned during Peter Castigone's pretrial debriefings before Accardo's people had apparently gotten to Castigone, causing him to "forget" all that he had previously disclosed.

Whereas years ago, Richards would not have had great faith that the Nevada Gaming Control Commission would extend itself and give great weight to his testimony, the climate there was now such that he felt the commission members would listen and take it all into account, to at least hear it and then decide whether it was creditable, pertinent, and trustworthy.

Richards travelled to Las Vegas one more time. He had called ahead and received an appointment with Rich Carr, supervisor of the Intelligence Division of the Gaming Control Board, and Ron Asher, Chief of the Enforcement Division of the GCB. In broad strokes, he outlined all of the information which had been developed against the Chicago Fourteen, hearsay and all. He placed particular emphasis, of course, on the interests of Accardo & Co. in Nevada.

Carr and Asher took Richards to Jerry Cunningham. Cunningham had been a top official of Metro, the combined police department and sheriff's office in Clark County. Cunningham had left Metro and become a Gaming Control Commissioner. He commands a great deal of respect in law enforcement and gaming enforcement. Richards was aware of his reputation and knew whatever he presented to Cunningham would be handled with the attention it deserved—one way or another.

When Cunningham heard Carr, Asher, and Richards's presentation he went to his fellow commissioners. They scheduled a hearing. They requested Richards, under oath, to put it all on the record. They travelled to Salt Lake City to meet with Nasti himself and hear his version.

Then in the late winter of 1990, the commission rendered its decision. It revoked the gaming licenses of all those connected to Accardo and the Chicago outfit. It wiped the slate clean of the unwholesome influence in Nevada of the Chicago mob. All the Chicago fronts were thrown out of the casinos.

Years and years of effort, tons and tons of money the Chicago mob had poured into Nevada to gain its dominance there was down the drain. It was truly a disaster for Accardo. He prided himself in having built the Chicago mob into the richest and best organized in the country during his reign. Now things were falling apart. When he had done the necessary spadework to build Chicago's interests in Las Vegas into their chief income producer, he had taken justifiable credit. Now he must accept a great portion of the blame when, while still "the man" in Chicago, things fell apart so that not only was Vegas no longer the fount of the Chicago mob's greatest income, but the well had almost completely dried up! At the same time, he must also accept the guilt laid at his feet for the destruction of his leadership. Although he had "walked" in the great RICO case, he was the only one of the Chicago

Fourteen who had done so. Even Gus Alex, who had been severed from the trial, would have to undergo the rigors of a separate trial at a later date. When Judge McGrath severed him, he made pointed comments that he was not judging the actual merits of the case and that it was done without "prejudice," meaning that Alex could be brought to trial in the future. Jeff Johnson and Gary Shapiro surely had every intention of insuring that Gus Alex would be tried for his participation in the poisoning of Moe Dalitz.

Accardo's personal victory in the courtroom in Chicago therefore was a Pyrrhic one. His outfit was decapitated. The flow of VEGMON, Vegas Money, no longer found its way straight to Chicago. Two powerful blows to the Chicago godfather. The beat of the Chicago mob goes on. Not nearly as strong and as loud, however, as before. The forces of good are prevailing and there is now a light at the end of the tunnel—getting brighter and nearer all the time.

AND Joe Bonanno, the other great godfather of this tale, is completely out of it. He is retired, living in Tucson, and no longer has any connection whatsoever with "the Bonanno family" either there or in Brooklyn.

The other J. B.—Accardo—still has his finger on the pulse as the *consigliere* in Chicago. But it is a far weaker finger than in days gone by, and the pulse he fingers is considerably muted. It still beats regularly—but not with the great strength it did before. Joe Batters brought it to its zenith—and then guided it to its nadir. The proud godfather has been shorn of his glory.

If the devil lets Salvatore Maranzano look up these days to see what Joe Bonanno has done with the Castellammarese family, Maranzano sighs and whispers: "Giuseppe Bonanno, Giuseppe Bonanno, how you have gone wrong! How you have failed me!"

If the devil lets Al Capone look up these days to see what Tony Accardo has done with his family, Capone, too, sighs and whispers: "Joe Batters, Joe Batters, how you have gone wrong! How you have failed me!"

Joe Bonanno and Tony Accardo never get to Las Vegas these days. If they would they would see the new climate. They would roll their eyes in amazement. The Mirage, Excalibur, and Kirk Kerkorian's proposed MGM, his new dream in the shade of the Tropicana, far surpass the hotels Accardo built and Bonanno dreamed of building. These new hotels would serve as a beacon to the old warriors to remind them of what they had lost.

First, Accardo threw Bonanno off the Strip and then the regulators of that Strip rose up and threw Accardo off. All that bloodshed for nothing! Who said good guys don't win every once in a while?

Epilogue

Tony Accardo is alive and fairly well today at the age of 84, residing on Road Runner Drive in Indian Wells in the Palm Springs area of California. He spends considerable time in the Chicago area, residing in the guest house on his daughter's property in Barrington Hills. He continues to be the "consigliere" of the Chicago family of La Cosa Nostra.

Joe Bonanno is alive and fairly well today at the age of 84, residing on Sierra Vista Avenue in midtown Tucson, five miles from the author. He spends considerable time in the San Jose area, residing at the home of his daughter and son-in-law.

The hotels described herein in Las Vegas as being "mobbed up" by the Chicago Outfit are now clean. These would include the Stardust, the Fremont, the Desert Inn, the Riviera and the Flamingo. The Tropicana is now owned by Aztar, the newly formed gambling operations of Ramada, Inc. and no longer has any mob taint.

Ernest "Rocky" Infelice, John "No Nose" DiFronzo, Sam "Wings"

Carlisi, Sal DeLaurentis and Louis Marino are all continuing to operate as top leaders of the Chicago mob. Infelice, DeLaurentis and Marino were indicted in February, 1990 for violation of RICO.

Pete Wacks is currently serving as an FBI agent in Chicago.

Jeff Johnson is currently serving as an assistant United States Attorney in Chicago, assigned to the Organized Crime Division.

Donald Angelini and Dominic Cortina were convicted of a violation of the Interstate Travel in Aid of Racketeering Statute in late 1989 and, in March, 1990, were sentenced to twenty-one months each.

Joe Agosto died of natural causes in protective custody in 1982. He was a government witness in the "Strawman Case" in Kansas City.

Frank "Lefty" Rosenthal is currently residing in Florida. He recently won a suit taking his name out of the "Black Book" of persons excluded from Nevada casinos. There is a body of opinion in Chicago law enforcement circles that he recently has been named the Chicago mob's representative in Las Vegas.

Allen Glick is living in La Jolla, California under heavy protection after testifying for the government in the "Strawman Case."

Carl Thomas has returned from prison to Las Vegas but has been denied a gaming license in spite of his testimony for the government in the "Strawman Case."

Art Pfizenmayer is the supervisor of the organized crime squad of the FBI in San Diego.

Gary Shapiro became the Chief of the Organized Crime Division of the United States Attorney's Office in Chicago when the Justice Department Strike Forces were merged into the offices of the U.S. Attorneys nationwide by U.S. Attorney General Dick Thornburgh in January, 1990.

Pat Tuite, Carl Walsh, Art Nassar and Sam Betar continue to practice law as defense attorneys in Chicago.

Bob and Alice Fitzpatrick continue to reside in Oklahoma City.

Tom Carrigan continues to reside in Reno.

Sidney Korshak continues to reside in Palm Springs.

Tommy Tolan continues to operate an investigative agency in New York City.

Frank Gerrity continues to operate his polygraph agency in NYC.

Warren Dovovan died of cancer in 1988.

John Bassett is retired and, although owning a howe in Panama City Beach, Florida, travels with his wife, Elaine, in a Winnebago nine months a year.

Marhsall Rutland and Ralph Hill died of natural causes in 1975 and 1985, respectively.

Murray "The Camel" Humpreys died of a heart attack on the evening of November 23, 1965 after having been arrested by the FBI that afternoon.

Jake "Greasy Thumb" Guzik died of a heart attack in 1956.

Frank "The Enforcer" Nitti committed suicide by shooting himself in the head in 1943.

Debbie Lee continues as a "principal" in the Folies Bergere at the Tropicana in Las Vegas.

John Jemilo continues as the Executive Director of the Chicago Crime Commission. Jerry Gladdin continues as Chief Investigator and Jeanette Callaway continues as Associate Director of the Chicago Crime Commission.

Ralph Salerno continues to lecture to police agencies across the country on organized crime.

Sunrise Hospital was sold to Humana several years ago and is now named Humana Hospital Sunrise. It is one of the world's best health care facilities.

Frank Cullotta and Sal Romano remain in the Witness Protection Program after testifying against Tony Spilotro.

Gerry Scarpelli committed suicide while confined in the Metropolitan Correctional Center in Chicago in 1989.

Gus Alex, 74, continues to maintain residences on Lake Shore Drive in Chicago and on Galt Ocean Mile in Fort Lauderdale, Florida. He continues as boss of the "connection guys" in Chicago.

Jackie Cerone is in federal prison in the Austin, Texas area. Joe Aiuppa is in federal prison in Minnesota. Both were convicted in the Strawman II Case.

Pat Marcy and John D'Arco, Sr. continue to serve as functionaries of the Regular Democratic Organization of the First Ward in Chicago. However, they have been identified as targets in the FBI's "Operation Kaffe Klatch," which was expected to produce indictments soon after this book went to press.

Federal Judge Abraham Lincoln Marovitz continues to serve as a senior judge in the U.S. District Court of Northern Illinois.

Oliver "Buck" Revell continues to serve as the Executive Assistant Director in charge of all investigations of the FBI.

Into 1990, Las Vegas business was growing 8% to 10% per year. It is the fastest growing city in the United States. With the addition of the

Mirage and Excalibur, capacity in 1990 has increased to 75,000 rooms from about 61,000 in 1988. In its first month of operation, December of 1989, the Mirage set a record $58 million in revenue ($40 million from the casino and $18 million from rooms). It had a 10.8 market share. When you consider that Las Vegas now has some 70 casinos, it's easy to see how far it has come since Bugsy Siegel opened the Flamingo!

Appendix A

TESTIMONY OF WILLIAM F. ROEMER, JR.
SPECIAL CONSULTANT ON ORGANIZED
CRIME, CHICAGO CRIME COMMISSION,
BEFORE THE U.S. SENATE PERMANENT
SUBCOMMITTEE ON INVESTIGATIONS
HEARING ON ORGANIZED CRIME

MARCH 4, 1983

SECTION I

History of Organized Crime
in Chicago

THIS statement was prepared by William F. Roemer, Jr., special consultant to the Chicago Crime Commission, from a variety of sources including his personal knowledge, public records, and the files of the Chicago Crime Commission. Mr. Roemer was a special agent of the FBI for thirty years; assigned to the Chicago office of the FBI for twenty-three years, the period 1957 to 1978 having been spent on the organized crime squads where he was the senior agent during most of the 1970s.

The origin of what has become known as organized crime began in Chicago in the World War I era when Jim Colosimo, in order to eliminate competition for his nightspots and houses of prostitution, put together a very loose, poorly disciplined group of thugs and thieves of Italian and Sicilian extraction.

Matters continued in this way until Johnny Torrio, who had joined Colosimo in 1910, and who had made some efforts to organize along the lines of the Sicilian organization known as the Mafia which many of his underlings had membership in, brought in a young New Yorker named Al "Scarface" Capone. Capone had done some "heavy work" for the mob in New York and had a reputation there for being a resourceful, aggressive young gunman with a future.

Torrio had come to the conclusion that Colosimo did not realize the potential of what he had and was an overly cautious leader whose lack of aggressiveness was holding back the opportunity which Torrio and the others had in Chicago. He, therefore, commissioned Capone to execute Colosimo which Capone did with quick dispatch in 1920.

Torrio then succeeded to the leadership of the motley crew left him by Colosimo, and with the aid of Capone, began to do two basic things. First, he began to enforce a tight discipline and, second, enlarged the membership. Although the members of the organization who were responsible directly to him were of Italian and Sicilian derivation, he worked very closely with other groups of non-Italians who were working in Chicago. Sometimes the distinctions between who were actually members of the Torrio mob and who were on the fringes were so blurred that it amounted to the same thing.

With the advent of Prohibition, Torrio and Capone, with the counsel of their old associates in New York, were made aware of the enormous potential for gain from bootlegging and from the speakeasies which could be set up.

At this point, organized crime in Chicago became big business as it did all over the country. The membership was greatly enlarged and although, strictly speaking, Italian or Sicilian descent was a requirement for a "made" member of the group, many individuals who worked on the fringes of the organization and many who belonged to groups who made agreements with the Torrio group to operate were not of such descent. As a result of this history, many of the people who actually became upper echelon leaders of organized crime in Chicago have not been Italians or Sicilians, a situation which is almost unique in Chicago.

Things continued along during the early 1920s until Capone got greedy. Mainly for the same reason that Torrio wanted Colosimo out of the way, Capone, seeing even more wealth available, had an attempt made on the life of Torrio. Although not successful in killing Torrio, it caused Torrio to decide he had had enough and he turned over the leadership of the mob to Capone as soon as he was able to leave the hospital.

Under Capone the Chicago mob became perhaps the most disciplined and the most wealthy group of organized crime in the country.

At this point, perhaps, it might be well to discuss the alliance Capone and his successors had with groups of organized crime elsewhere. It should be understood up front that there is no type of national organization where a leader, say in New York, can issue an order to the leader of the Chicago group as to how he should run his outfit. However, there is a grouping of the heads of "the families" in the major sections of the country who have formed what in effect is a "board of directors" of organized crime which they call "The Commission." Capone, as top boss in Chicago, represented Chicago. The leaders of the five New York City families, the Buffalo family, the New

England family, the Pittsburgh and Philadelphia families, the Detroit and the Cleveland families, have traditionally had membership on The Commission. Membership has varied from nine to twelve throughout the years and The Commission continues to be a highly structured, tightly disciplined group to date.

Actually, the primary purpose of The Commission is to enforce the boundaries of organized crime. It is the current consensus of knowledgeable sources and informants that the Chicago family of organized crime controls all areas west of Chicago as of 1983. This would include the Kansas City, Milwaukee, St. Louis, Denver, Los Angeles, San Diego, and San Francisco (actually San Jose) areas where organized crime is controlled by established groups inasmuch as these groups are actually subservient to the ultimate authority of the Chicago mob. As a matter of fact, the Chicago family has made a substantial drive in recent years to solidify its hold on the West Coast and the mountain states. Certain areas such as Las Vegas and Miami are "open territories" where families from all over the country are allowed investments. For instance, for years The Stardust in Las Vegas was a Chicago investment while the Sands was a New York operation.

Returning to the Capone era, the membership of organized crime mushroomed during the Prohibition era and almost the entire membership reaped tremendous profits from the various enterprises the mob participated in.

These enterprises included illegal whiskey and beer, the speakeasies in which they were sold, night spots where prostitution flourished, gambling, "juice" (the extortionate lending of money at usurious rates which is known as "loan sharking" and "shylocking" elsewhere) and labor racketeering.

At about the same time the Prohibition Amendment was repealed, Capone was convicted in federal court in Chicago of income tax evasion. This ended his reign, as it turned out, since he was never to return to Chicago.

Taking over for Capone, was his top lieutenant, Frank Nitti. Nitti, known as "The Enforcer," was Capone's muscle man and the obvious choice to succeed him.

However, Nitti encountered an overwhelming problem immediately.

The proceeds from the Prohibition-related activity had been staggering. But Prohibition was over. How could organized crime make up the loss? In fact, there was no way it could. However, Nitti was very fortunate that a man named Jake "Greasy Thumb" Guzik had been brought into the organization. Guzik became, under Nitti, a mastermind who showed the mob how to invest the millions garnered from Prohibition and trickling in from gambling. Gambling became the lifeblood of the outfit, but investments in legitimate businesses primarily through front men not only multiplied the profits but gave the mobsters a method by which they could evade the efforts of the government to do with them what it did with Capone.

Parenthetically, it is of interest to note that Guzik, a Jew, was the forerunner of several non-Italian successors to him. Murray "The Camel" Humphreys succeeded Guzik when Guzik died in the 1950s and promptly enlarged the functions of this faction of organized crime to become "the fixers" who built and maintained contacts with public officials, law enforcement officers, labor leaders, the judiciary and businessmen who could be influenced or controlled to provide favorable treatment to organized crime. As a matter of fact, to show how this nonethnic feature progressed through the years, when Humphreys, a Welshman, died in November, 1965, his functions were taken over by Gus Alex, a Greek, who in turn, in the mid-1970s, was to become one of the members of the three-man leadership team, the triumverate, in charge of the affairs of organized crime in Chicago in the early 1970s.

Aided by the expertise of Guzik, Nitti rebuilt organized crime in Chicago to the point where, although obviously not producing the income available during the Capone era, it remained a viable, tightly structured organization able to support its members.

In the early 1940s, Nitti, along with several other top leaders of the mob in Chicago, including Paul Ricca, Louis Campagna, Ralph Pierce and others, was indicted for the million dollar extortion of the Hollywood movie industry through the use of labor unions controlled by the Chicago mob along the guidelines set up by Guzik, now assisted materially by Humphreys. Shortly following the indictment, Nitti committed suicide in 1943.

Succeeding Nitti was Ricca, also known as Paul "The Waiter" DeLucia. Ricca, a very capable leader, had his own troubles since he was soon to be convicted in the Hollywood Extortion Case, but his leadership was noted for something which is very unusual in organized crime families. Ricca had a son who was a drug addict. He, therefore, observed firsthand what drug addiction can do to society. During his reign, he decreed that no member of Chicago organized crime could have anything to do with narcotics trafficking. Actually, his decision was not strictly humanitarian, but also allowed for the fact that drug trafficking alienated the contacts set up by the Guzik-Humphreys-Alex faction. The influence of the mob would wane, according to the Ricca theory, if the heinous crime of dealing in narcotics was associated with them. According to his thought, as long as "victimless" crimes such as gambling were the sole support of the mob, their contacts outside the organization could be maintained.

Ricca continued as the boss even while he spent three years or so in federal prison after his conviction, with Anthony J. Accardo as his caretaker chieftain. Ricca was paroled in the late 1940s in a scandal which engulfed the Truman administration since he was turned loose long before his sentence expired.

Following Ricca as boss, and as the Chicago representative on The Commission, was Accardo, another in the long line of capable leaders. Accardo, perhaps, has been the most capable leader in the history of the Chicago group. With the aid of the Guzik-Humphreys faction which was able to expand the number of contacts providing favorable treatment to the mob, Accardo had a most successful rule. The membership expanded and income flourished, primarily from the wide-open gambling then allowed by the Guzik-Humphreys contacts in Chicago and its environs.

In 1957 Accardo had enough and handed over the reins to Sam "Mooney" Giancana. Giancana, a tough, swaggering, flamboyant murderer who had long served Accardo, was a natural for the spot, but it was not long before he, and later his associates, was sorry he found himself where he was at that particular time in the history of Chicago organized crime. Because the federal government was about to become directly involved for the first time in the investigation of the day-to-day operations of organized crime in the United States.

The seeds of Giancana's destruction were sown in a set of circumstances set in motion in November, 1957, when scores of the top bosses of organized crime throughout the United States were summoned to a meeting at the home of Joseph Barbara in the small, quiet upstate New York community of Apalachin. The meeting came to the attention of a lone New York state trooper. The bulk of the attendees scattered wildly through the woods when several troopers investigated but several were gathered in. Giancana had been there, but was one of the successful escapees.

No law enforcement agency in the country had been aware of the proposed meeting and none was able to satisfy the outcry which followed as to how scores of the top leaders of organized crime were able to move so freely around the country without attracting the notice of authorities.

As a direct result of the Apalachin meeting, J. Edgar Hoover initiated what in 1957 was called the Top Hoodlum Program but which is now called the Organized Crime Program. Never before had the FBI been involved in a strict intelligence type investigation of organized crime. Heretofore, the FBI would investigate organized crime members if they became involved in a violation within the jurisdiction of the Bureau, but not until then. Inasmuch as the hierarchy seldom violated federal statutes defining federal crimes existing in 1957, very little was known to the FBI or any other agency about the identities, background, associates, activity, personal habits or of the residences of even the upper echelon leaders.

This quickly changed in early 1958 when Mr. Hoover ordered the intensification of Top Hoodlum investigations and volumes of information were developed by the FBI.

Up until this time Colosimo, Torrio, Capone, Nitti, Ricca, Accardo, and Giancana and their underlings had more to worry about with internecine combat rather than from law enforcement, or at least federal law enforcement.

But organized crime soon became aware in the late 1950s that a new force must be reckoned with. In 1961 the federal government was given a series of three laws as new weapons to fight with: Interstate Travel in Aid of Racketeering, Interstate Transportation of Wagering Information, and Interstate Transportation of Gambling Paraphernalia. The first weapon in particular proved to be a formidable one.

Giancana, an old alley fighter, decided in 1963 that the best defense is a good offense. He took unprecedented action when he brought a civil suit against the SAC and the Chicago office of the FBI to obtain an injunction prohibiting the "lock step" surveillance which the FBI maintained on him in the summer of 1963. He produced movies of FBI agent Roemer, whom he knew personally from confrontations he had previously had with him. These movies, produced in court, showed Roemer and others following Giancana. When the SAC declined to identify the agent or to acknowledge Giancana's claim as to his identity, the SAC was found in contempt of court and fined. Restrictions were placed on the surveillances of Giancana by the FBI. For example, the FBI was ordered to allow one foursome between its agents and Giancana's group on the golf course. Although the restrictions were relaxed somewhat by the appellate court, Giancana had clearly won a round in the battle.

But the fight was not over. In 1965 Giancana was subpoenaed before the federal grand jury in Chicago and asked scores of questions based on the intensified investigation of him since 1957. Obviously recognizing that he could not truthfully answer these questions without exposing himself and practically all of his associates in organized crime, Giancana refused to accept an offer of immunity and then was sentenced to a year in jail for contempt of the order of the court to testify.

Giancana spent his year in jail and, convinced that he would again be hauled before the federal grand jury with similar results, he fled the United States and toured the world, headquartering in Mexico until he was expelled from there in July, 1974. A lot of water passed over the dam between his departure in 1966 and his return in 1974 which will be discussed hereinafter, but the Giancana saga picked up almost where it left off when Giancana was again subpoenaed before the federal grand jury. This time, however, justice was cheated when Giancana was executed in gangland style in his residence in Oak Park, Illinois, late on the night of June 19, 1975. As will be explained later, his handling, or rather his mishandling of the leadership of the Chicago mob undoubtedly played a big part in his slaying.

To return to the days of the 1960s, however, when Giancana voluntarily exiled himself from the country, his job went to Sam "Teets" Battaglia. Now, Battaglia was a leader in the mold of his predecessors. Strong, aggressive and capable. But he did not last long. Taking over for Giancana in 1966, he was convicted the same year in federal court and sentenced to federal prison where he was to die.

Still stocked with a pool of capable leaders who had the ambition to succeed to the mantle of Capone, the mob simply reached out for the likes of Jackie Cerone. Cerone ruled well and his decisions were immediately obeyed. For three years. Then the federal government caught up with Cerone. He was convicted with the weapon given the FBI, ITAR, and sent to prison.

Now the organization had a problem. Since the FBI was injected into the fight, every top boss was sent packing off to federal prison. Now it was found that the intelligent, capable leader was just smart enough to recognize that taking over the top job was hazardous duty. Especially when the experienced leader had been able to put away more than enough money from the long, lucrative years he had toiled in organized crime, he was most reluctant to jeopardize the last decades of his life when the example set by Giancana, Battaglia, and Cerone in the immediate past three years was fresh in his mind.

But there was a man on the scene who campaigned for the job and who was successful. This was Felix "Milwaukee Phil" Alderisio. Alderisio, one of the worst in a long line of Chicago torpedoes, for years had done the "heavy work" for the organization, the torturing, killing, and intimidating necessary for the successful operation. A man in this position was used to getting what he wanted and since he wanted to be boss and few who were qualified did, Alderisio got it. However, Milwaukee Phil was no Accardo—and not even a Giancana. For the first time, the membership became aware that policy decisions were being made based on something other than good sense. But it made little difference. Because the same fate that befell those before him came to Alderisio. In 1970, after about a year in the spotlight, he was convicted of bank fraud and sentenced to federal prison where he died in 1971.

Now the organization was really in trouble. First, they ran out of brains. Now they ran out of brawn. The intelligent leaders saw no reason to change their minds about accepting the crown and now even the unintelligent leader had gotten the message.

Eventually, after the organization floundered for a while, a solution of sorts was found. Accardo, who had been spending most of his time fishing in Bimini and travelling, was prevailed upon to agree to spend some time in Chicago where his counsel would be available, at least on major policy matters if not on the day-to-day operations. Gus Alex, the heir to the Guzik-Humphreys line, a most intelligent but highly nervous, cautious person with a history of confinement for depression in the renowned Silver Hill Sanitarium in New Canaan, Connecticut, reluctantly agreed to be available to maintain contact with the remaining associates of Guzik and Humphreys. Alex insisted, however, that he, like Accardo, should be able to spend the bulk of his time out of Chicago, in his case at his condominium in Fort Lauderdale, Florida, where he still spends half his time. But with Accardo and Alex having agreed to be part-time bosses, there was a need for an operations manager, a man with some authority who would be available on a continuous basis. Finally, this spot was given to Joseph "O'Brien" Aiuppa. Aiuppa is an elderly man whose expertise heretofore had been confined to gambling and strip joints in Cicero. It was not expected by law enforcement agents that Aiuppa had the potential to be an effective leader. However, he appears to have grown in the position and at this point in time, in 1983, some dozen years later, history has been kind to Aiuppa and due to the fact that he has been fortunate enough to have survived those years it can be seen from this viewpoint that he has served his organization creditably.

In 1978, Alex eased himself out of the leadership role and since that time he has confined himself primarily to the role which will be discussed hereinafter, that of the leader of the "corruption squad" of organized crime.

At this time, in 1978, Jackie Cerone, back from prison in 1974 and relatively inactive due to the fact that he realized that he was a "sitting duck" for law enforcement and not desiring to be in prison again, was importuned to once again assume a leadership role. In 1978, Cerone assumed the role of "underboss" to Aiuppa with the feeling that Aiuppa, then in his early seventies and in ill health, would soon step down and give the leadership reins to Cerone.

At the present time Cerone is, for all intents and purposes, the leader of the Chicago family of organized crime. A very strong, aggressive and forceful underboss has been appointed to assist Cerone in the person of Joseph Ferriola, also known as Joe Negall. Cerone, now sixty-eight years of age and with a history of a reluctance to lead, is grooming Negall for the top job somewhere, apparently, in the mid-1980s.

Current Status and Structure of Organized Crime in Chicago

THE foregoing is not to be taken to say that Tony Accardo and Joseph Aiuppa are no longer active leaders. Both, however, prefer to keep a distance from Chicago and an insulation between themselves and the day-to-day operations. Accardo, who spends niney per cent of his time at his Palm Springs area residence on Roadrunner Drive in Indian Wells, California, is still called upon when matters of high policy are to be determined and for this reason he still maintains a Chicago area condo. After all, he was the best leader the Chicago mob has ever had and his experience goes back to the days when he was a muscle man for Capone in the 1920s. He is truly the elder statesman of the mob.

Aiuppa likewise is trying to keep a distance between himself and the daily routine. Although he continues to spend a great deal of his time at his residence in Oak Brook, a southwestern suburb of Chicago, he spends a large amount of his time in Palm Springs and on Bimini. There is a body of opinion among law enforcement people in Chicago that Aiuppa continues to be the boss. It is our best information that for all practical purposes Cerone is, but it is clear that Aiuppa still wields a great deal of power and that Cerone clears the more important decisions with him.

Another shadowy figure in a key position of leadership is Gus Alex. Alex is also one who has served his organization well and now desires to put some distance between himself and the ordinary problems of his group. Alex still maintains his condominium on Lake Shore Drive in Chicago, but spends most of his time at his other condo on Galt Ocean Mile in Fort Lauderdale, Florida. There is really no way the mob is going to let Alex simply fade away. His contacts among politicians, public officials, labor leaders and members of the judiciary are simply too valuable to waste.

The Chicago capo who has been undoubtedly the most important mid-level leader in recent years is Joe Lombardo. However, as we meet today, Lombardo's star is fading, if not faded. For the past several years Lombardo was responsible to the mob for two of their uppermost interests: (1) The control and maintenance of their many and varied interests in Las Vegas and the continued spread of their empire westward from Chicago, and (2) The control and maintenance of their influence with the Teamsters and particularly that union's Central States Pension Fund.

Lombardo has had nothing but troubles in recent years. In 1979, the Chicago office of the FBI penetrated the offices of Lombardo's chief contact in relation to the Teamsters, Allen Dorfman. Dorfman for decades had been the liaison between the mob in Chicago and the Teamsters union. In fact, it was his father, Paul "Red" Dorfman, who had initiated such contacts. The elder Dorfman was a pal of James Riddle Hoffa and when Hoffa became president of the IBT (International Brotherhood of Teamsters) in the late 1950s, it was Red Dorfman who brought Murray Humphreys and Gus Alex to Hoffa for what was to become a longtime and close relationship between the Teamsters and the mob, not only in Chicago but all over the country. The younger Dorfman had a great influence on Central States Pension loans and, as a consequence, many high risk loans were made from the fund to businesses and associates affiliated with the Chicago crime syndicate. It was the responsibility of Lombardo to control and manage Dorfman and, through Dorfman, the assets of the Teamsters.

But when the FBI in Chicago penetrated Dorfman in their investigation code-named "Pendorf" (penetration of Dorfman) they penetrated a lot more than Dorfman. They penetrated the entire Lombardo echelon of organized crime. For Lombardo was almost a daily visitor to the Dorfman offices where the microphones were planted under Title III (court ordered) authority. This exposed both functions of Lombardo to almost complete FBI scrutiny. It resulted in the recent conviction of Lombardo, Dorfman, and Roy Williams, president of the IBT. But, almost as important, it gave the FBI in Chicago a great wealth of intelligence concerning the machinations of the Chicago Cosa Nostra in general and the Lombardo faction in particular. This, presumably, will be dealt with in greater deal in the statement being made to this committee by the FBI.

For many years, the first function of Lombardo, the control of Chicago mob interests in Las Vegas, has been spearheaded for him by Tony Spilotro. Spilotro not only was the overseer of Las Vegas interests but also of the continuing spread of the Chicago group westward, to California in particular. Spilotro came up through the ranks of the Chicago gang just like everybody else, through the use of heavy work: the arm and the gun. He became the extension of Chicago in Las Vegas and for years served his bosses in a satisfactory fashion. Recently, however, his affairs and his function have come more and more into the glare of the media and he lost some favor with his superiors. Now, in February, 1983, he was arrested by the FBI in Las Vegas on an Unlawful Flight to Avoid Prosecution warrant, the result primarily of testimony of Frank Cullota, one of his former lieutenants, who has implicated him in two murders in Chicago several years ago. This arrest was assisted by Ray I. Shryock, chief of the Organized Crime Division of the Cook County State's Attorney, who expedited the process in Chicago leading to the arrest of Spilotro in Las Vegas, a good example of cooperation of local and federal law enforcement officials here.

It, therefore, is obvious that the career of Spilotro, like that of his immediate superior, Lombardo, is in serious jeopardy at this point in time.

The most active capo in the Chicago LCN as of March, 1983, is undoubtedly Joseph Ferriola, better known to his associates as Joe Negall. For years Negall was a top henchman of the notorious Fiore "Fifi" Buccieri and then of James "Turk" Torello, when those two had responsibility under Giancana for the lucrative West Side of Chicago and then, after Giancana, had complete responsibility to oversee the prime source of income to the Chicago group, gambling. Negall is considered to have the most potential to become the successor to Cerone some years down the line.

Negall's top lieutenant right now is Dominic Cortina. Cortina knows as much about the operation of a handbook as perhaps anyone in the country, certainly in Chicago. His sidekick, a pal since boyhood, Donald Angelini, aka Don Angel, is also a Negall top kick. Ernest "Rocky" Infelice, like many of his associates, a former burglar and thief but in the case of Infelice one with a much longer history of imprisonment, ranks among the top Negall cohorts. Louis Marino, Sal Bastone, and Sal DeLaurentis are mid-level Negall lieutenants. Joe Spa, true name Joseph Spadevecchio, has long been a close associate of Negall and worked well and long for Buccieri and Torello. However, his recent assignments seem to indicate he is not as highly regarded as in the past. Joseph Grieco, Wayne Bock, John Varelli, Arnold Garris, and Americo "Pete" DePietto are also highly regarded Negall soldiers. Bock is a former pro football player and provides muscle for Negall and the mob. Garris is a veteran bookmaker who has great expertise in this area. DePietto has a long history of confinement for such crimes as burglary and robbery.

Though not as productive for the Chicago LCN as fellow capos Lombardo and Negall, the prime money makers, another experienced Chicago boss is Vincent Solano, president of a local of the Laborers union in Chicago. It was a surprise when Solano succeeded Dominick DiBella as the capo in charge of the North Side of Chicago in the late 1970s. Many had expected that Joseph "Caesar" DiVarco, the cocky little boss of Rush Street, Chicago's nightclub district, would succeed to the mantle of DiBella. However, at the time, DiVarco was under prosecution and it is felt that this was the prevailing factor in Solano's selection. Solano, for years, had been the chauffeur and bodyguard of Ross Prio when that capo had ruled the North Side. Prio was the North Side capo from the 1950s into the 1970s. DiVarco, while serving under Solano, also has capo status, something which is very unusual, an indication the mob puts a high emphasis on its interests on Rush Street.

Working right under Solano and DiVarco is "Big Joe" Arnold, a longtime companion of DiVarco. His interests are centered on Rush Street. Working with them under Solano, until about 8:30 P.M. on February 10, 1983, was Ken Eto, who ran the bolita gambling for the mob, a venture estimated from his records to garner some $20,000,000 annually for the Chicago LCN.

However, on February 10, 1983, Eto was shot three times in the head at contact range by two Solano-DiVarco soldiers: Jasper Campise and Frank Gattuso. Surprisingly, Eto survived this attack and is currently cooperating with the Chicago FBI. He has implicated at least DiVarco and Arnold along with Campise and Gattuso in the conspiracy to kill him and, if fully coopera- tive, his revelations would be catastrophic to the mob.

Mike Glitta is the "street boss" of Rush Street under the aegis of DiVarco.

Working under Solano in the Rogers Park area of the North Side, an area where gambling flourishes, are Lenny Patrick and Len Yaras. However, it is believed that Patrick is relatively inactive at this time. For years, from the 1940s until the mid-1970s, Patrick was a valuable upper echelon gambling boss. At first his domain was Lawndale, a predominately Jewish community on the West Side of Chicago. But as that neighborhood changed and much of his clientele moved to the Rogers Park area, Patrick moved with them. After his imprisonment in the early 1970s, however, Patrick seemingly has not regained his lofty position and, although seen from time to time in activity which indicates that he still has some mob capacity, it appears that Patrick is not a force to be concerned about. His spot has been taken, ironically enough, by Yaras. Yaras is the son of Patrick's longtime partner, Davey Yaras who moved to Florida when Lawndale diminished as a source of revenue to his faction. Patrick and Yaras were so close for so many years that it is almost as if Patrick was succeeded by his own son.

Proceeding down the line of important capos we get to Al Tocco. Tocco is the successor to the most productive Frank LaPorte and then to the less capable Al Pilotto as the capos in charge of southern Cook County, an area headquartered in Chicago Heights and including Will County, with Joliet as the county seat. Whereas LaPorte, in particular, was a highly valued capo in the Chicago scheme of things, Tocco has not yet made his bones in this area. The best information indicates that since there has to be a boss in southern Cook County, Tocco is the best of what is available, a rather poor lot. When United States Attorney for the Northern District of Illinois, Dan Webb, characterizes the Chicago mob as a bunch of "street punks," he would place Tocco at the head of the bunch, along with LaPietra, a capo discussed hereinafter.

As would be expected after the description of Tocco, his crew is a motley one. Joe Barrett, Tony Berretoni, and Chris Messino are his top lieutenants and they are a poor group compared, for instance, to Negall's crew.

The remaining capo is Angelo LaPietra who controls the South Side of Chicago. However, the South Side of Chicago is a relatively unproductive area for the Chicago Cosa Nostra and for this reason, although he is at least as capable as Tocco, LaPietra's seat at the table of capos is the last one.

LaPietra succeeds Ralph Pierce who died in July, 1975. Pierce was a Murray Humphreys protégé and, when the South Side was productive, he had a key role in organized crime in Chicago. However, when Pierce died of a heart attack, the prime source of income on the South Side, as on any Side, was gambling and this was given to Negall. LaPietra has some interest in a relatively new income producer, chop shops, but he shares this with Tocco. The term chop shop refers to the chopping up of stolen autos and the resale of the parts. This racket, taken over by the syndicate only some dozen years or so ago, has become productive although it has never begun to rival such traditional income producers as gambling or juice.

Working under LaPietra are Frank Calabrese, John Monteleone, John Fecarotta, his brother Jimmy LaPietra and Frank "Skid" Caruso. Caruso for decades has run the gambling activity in the predominately Italian neighborhood on the Near South Side, in the area which is known as The Patch. Also soldiering for LaPietra are such familiar names as Charles "Specs" DiCaro, Nick Montos, Vince Inserra, and Angelo Imparato. DiCaro is virtually retired. Joe Lamantia is another active LaPietra soldier.

There are others whose responsibilities are not clearly defined, at least in the mind of this consultant. One would be Chuckie English, true name Charles Englisi. English was the top lieutenant of Giancana during Giancana's reign as the top boss from 1957 to 1966. However, he is now aging, and although seen from time to time in the company of some prominent LCN members, particularly at Bruno's Service Station, a mob hangout and meeting place on the West Side, it is not clear that he is currently active. The Pettit brothers, Joe and Larry, while active, seem to sometimes serve Lombardo and sometimes Negall.

Another outfit member who deserves some mention is Frank "The Horse"

Buccieri. Buccieri is the brother of the deceased capo, Fiore "Fifi" Buccieri. Frank was slated to take over his brother's slot in the outfit when Fifi died. However, he did not have the ambition to become a capo. He desired the easy life. He, therefore, negotiated for concessions wherein he has a certain status in Chicago which gains him the income he needs to maintain a high life style with a residence in Palm Springs, California, where he is able to spend most of his time, something he would not be able to do if he was the capo of a crew here in Chicago.

Others would be Frankie Schweihs, perhaps the leading "hit man" of today. Schweihs, a big, tough, thug has been used extensively in the past ten years or so for the heavy work. He continues to be used in this capacity, especially since Wayne Bock, mentioned above, is seriously ill at present.

Two other individuals who should be identified are Anthony "Bucky" Ortenzi and Sam Carlisi. They are the bodyguard-drivers-errand boys for Aiuppa. For many years it has been Ortenzi who must be contacted if another mobster wants to see Aiuppa. Dominic "Butch" Blasi is another appointment secretary of Aiuppa, just as he was with Accardo and Giancana for decades. However, he has health problems at present which seriously hamper his availability and he is virtually retired.

The heavy work of the outfit, the violence, has been handled in recent years by several people, whereas years ago they were commanded by Alderisio and by Chuckie Nicoletti and all hits were supervised very closely if not actually committed by this pair. However, in recent years this appears to be a function of the ubiquitous Lombardo. He apparently has directly participated in some of these himself. One of these was the shotgun killing of Richard Cain, true name Ricardo Scalzitti, on December 20, 1973. Cain was a made member of the LCN in Chicago whose function was to infiltrate law enforcement. After a career of moderate length in the Chicago Police Department, Cain became the chief investigator of the Cook County Sheriff's Office. After a short tenure there, ending in controversy, Cain became the confidant and trusted lieutenant of Giancana. After travelling extensively with Giancana all over the world with a home base in Mexico, Cain returned to the United States in the early 1970s. He attempted to manipulate his way into the rackets assigned to capos, using his clout with Giancana as a lever. However, since Giancana was in self-imposed exile, as detailed hereinabove, his clout was insufficient to protect the loose cannon which was Cain. Hence Cain's slaying.

There is a small body of authority linking Lombardo to the killing of Giancana himself. Giancana had returned to the country after being expelled from Mexico in the summer of 1974. Within a year he had worn out his welcome and he was quickly dispatched with the favorite weapon of the mob today, a .22 caliber revolver with a silencer. Most authorities believe this was accomplished by Dominic "Butch" Blasi, Giancana's most trusted aide and his bodyguard-driver-appointment secretary. It is an accepted fact that Blasi was on the scene of the crime, Giancana's home at 1147 S. Wenonah in suburban Oak Park, at or very close to the time of the act. However, it is not the opinion of this consultant that Blasi committed the deed.

Violence has certainly become an accepted practice in Chicago today. It appears to be much more common and life appears to be much more cheap than heretofore. The reasons appear to go hand in hand with the content of what is to appear hereinafter in an examination of the alliance between crime and politics. The hoodlums obviously believe they are better protected from surveillances and from ultimate prosecution than they have been in the past. This certainly does not appear to be a fact on the federal level. The FBI, the U.S. Justice Department Strike Force and the U.S. Attorney's office have recorded significant accomplishments in the very recent past. The Pendorf investigation of the FBI and the subsequent prosecution by the strike force, for instance, as described above, are accomplishments certainly equal to, and perhaps surpassing, anything done in the past years on any level.

However, it also appears to be true that no body of law enforcement in Chicago today has an active and frequent surveillance function. Whereas years ago the FBI and the Chicago Police Department, during the period when William J. Duffy was deputy superintendent in charge of the organized crime function, regularly surveilled most of the leaders and many of the prominent members. It is certainly accepted by knowledgeable law enforcement people that surveillance for the sake of surveillance is pointless. However, there are many selective occasions when it is most productive and it does not appear that at present law enforcement in Chicago is utilizing this technique except on the most selective of occasions.

It would seem entirely possible that should a hit man feel that he is the possible subject of a surveillance or that perhaps his victim is, he is going to be much more circumspect before attempting this assignment. Furthermore, it would appear that should the leader who sanctions the hit feel that there is a good possibility that his meeting with the capo who in turn orders the hit might be under surveillance, he will not open himself to a conspiracy charge by such a meeting.

This may seem to be a simplistic approach and in no way is it meant to be the all-inclusive answer to the problem. It appears to have merit, however, and is a suggestion respectfully forwarded.

The above represents a serious attempt to identify the individuals and functions of the leading LCN members in Chicago as of the date of this hearing. No attempt has been made to identify each and every soldier who is currently working for the Chicago mob. It is felt that for the purposes of this hearing it is sufficient to point out just those leaders and prominent members whose activities make a significant impact on the citizenry of Chicago. That there are others who represent a danger is certainly true. However, it is felt that to dilute this narrative by an endless identification of each and every common ordinary soldier in the Chicago LCN would diminish the impact of those so spotlighted. However, in the event this committee would desire that this be done, it can be accomplished in the future.

The umbrella which protects the Chicago mob and the linchpin which holds it together, enabling it to function, is its alliance with politics.

Nowhere can organized crime operate effectively without the connivance of public officials. This would include law enforcement officers, legislators, judges, and key public officials.

We believe that nowhere in the country has this been truer than in Chicago.

It has been widely reported that the FBI engaged in extensive electronic and other surveillance beginning in 1959 and continuing until about July, 1965. Information gathered during that period was spectacularly revealing information, especially concerning the links between organized crime and this city's elected officials. Some of this story has been told, some has not. But, in any case, it needs to be recited today to alert the citizens of this city to the kinds of things that have gone on in the past and will probably be repeated in the future.

In 1959 the headquarters of the Chicago Cosa Nostra was in a luxurious custom tailor shop located on the Magnificent Mile on North Michigan Avenue in Chicago. There daily meetings took place of the upper echelon leaders of that era. Tony Accardo, Sam Giancana, Murray Humphreys, Gus Alex, Ralph Pierce, Les Kruse, and Frank Ferraro, Giancana's underboss, were the prime movers who visited almost daily.

Frank LaPorte, the capo in southern Cook County, would come in and give a long report on his territory, with particular emphasis on the identities of those law enforcement officials and public officials who were on his payroll. It was a revelation because some of these people were officials who were most trusted and cooperated with.

We became aware of an association between Murray Humphreys and John D'Arco, then the alderman and Democratic ward committeeman of the First Ward, the ward which encompasses Chicago's Loop and its Near South and West Sides. It soon became apparent to us that (1) Humphreys had a long acquaintance with D'Arco and (2) that he occupied a domineering role over D'Arco.

We learned that Humphreys was upset with D'Arco because D'Arco had influenced the Chicago mob to back Richard J. Daley when Daley ran against the incumbent Martin Kennelly for mayor of Chicago in 1955. It was clear that, much to its surprise, the mob had little influence on Daley.

At this time I want to point out that Capt. Joseph Morris had been in charge of the Scotland Yard unit of the Chicago Police Department and Sgt. William

J. Duffy had been his protégé there. However, their unit had been disbanded in the mid-50s. Humphreys wanted to be sure that Morris and Duffy were not put back in charge of organized crime investigations. Unfortunately for him, Orlando W. Wilson was named superintendent of the Chicago Police Department and he soon named Morris deputy superintendant in charge of a newly created Bureau of Inspectional Services which housed the organized crime function. Morris promptly named Duffy the director of the intelligence unit, the unit which had the primary responsibility for investigation of the mob.

In early 1960, however, Humphreys and D'Arco had better luck. Together they decided that a particular friend of theirs, a police official who had a glorious reputation in Chicago as a hoodlum fighter but who was actually in the pocket of the mob, should be selected as the commander of a police district, a choice assignment and a strategic one for the outfit. Soon after they made their decision the announcement of the appointment of their man was made.

At about that time I had my first confrontation with D'Arco. Giancana, then the boss of Chicago LCN, had returned from a trip he made to Mexico. Customs officials, recognizing him, had searched him and found a list of the code names of all the top hoodlums in Chicago together with a figure after each name. On the list was the name of D'Arco. We suspected that it was a list of the number of points each hoodlum was to get in a race track in Mexico which we knew Giancana had been negotiating for. So I went to D'Arco in his office across from City Hall and said, "Alderman, you are a public official of the city of Chicago and being public-spirited I am sure that you desire to help the FBI determine the significance of this list. Why would your name be on such a list when all the others are the top gangsters in Chicago?"

This raised the ire of D'Arco and he shortly informed me that although he grew up in the same neighborhood as did Giancana and most of the other people named on the list, he did not have an understanding of the nature of the list. When he asked me why I would come to him with such a question, I told him that the FBI had no desire to embarrass him by asking such a question about him or anyone else.

D'Arco then became quite angry and he told me, "Roemer, the FBI cannot embarrass me in this town. You go throw your best shot. I am too big a man in this town to be embarrassed by the FBI. As long as my constituents elect me nobody can embarrass me."

I was hard pressed to forget those words as the years went by. Soon after, I began to concentrate on Sam Giancana and we learned that John D'Arco was not the only First Ward official working under the control and domination of the mob. In fact, we found something much more sinister than that in the First Ward. We found that an actual made member of the Chicago Cosa Nostra was running the First Ward and giving orders to D'Arco. This man was under the discipline of Giancana and the mob and was the sub rosa director of the affairs of the regular Democratic organization of the First Ward. He kept a very low profile, as ordered, and his title has been actually "Administrative Assistant," but from our coverage of Giancana, there was no room for doubt that Pat Marcy was the real boss of the First Ward. Not only of the Democratic First Ward but a man who exercised the same domineering control over the committeeman of the regular Republican organization of the First Ward, in those days Pete Granata, then a highly placed Illinois legislator. Of course, Marcy is still there today.

In fact it became so evident to us that the regular Democratic organization of the First Ward was but an extension of organized crime in Chicago that we documented our case to J. Edgar Hoover and the rest of the leadership of the FBI in Washington, and began work on the First Ward itself at 100 N. LaSalle, across the street from City Hall. We were not surprised to find that Marcy and D'Arco were merely conduits for the orders which flowed from the mob, usually in the person then of Giancana, to those politicians and public officials including law enforcement officers and members of the judiciary, who were under their control.

Marcy, like Dick Cain, identified hereinabove, is an actual member of the mob. Whereas Cain had been groomed from an early age to infiltrate law enforcement, Marcy had been groomed to infiltrate politics. His true name is not Marcy. It took us a long time to determine his actual name, which I recall as Pasqualino Marchone.

During our investigation we learned that Marcy was close to a police officer assigned to the First District of the Chicago Police Department. A bribe had been offered through Marcy and the police officer to a particular officer who was assigned to the First District vice squad and who would not overlook violations at the bars and strip joints then on South State Street in the Loop in the First Ward. He would not accept the bribes and he kept on enforcing the law. Marcy and the police officer actually made plans to kill the recalcitrant officer.

I remember that we advised Robert F. Kennedy of this shortly after he left this committee and became the attorney general. He was appalled.

Another recollection of mine about this period concerned a time when a former boss of mine in the FBI, Roswell T. Spencer, retired from the FBI and became the chief investigator for the Cook County State's Attorney. He told his boss, Dan Ward, "Watch out for John D'Arco." Ward replied, "That's the first thing Mayor Daley told me."

Marcy, being the power behind the First Ward throne, frequently met with Giancana. Not in the First Ward headquarters but instead the usual procedure was for Dominic "Butch" Blasi, Giancana's bodyguard-driver-appointment secretary to pick Marcy up and take him to the meeting place.

Marcy also had another set of bosses. These were Humphreys, Alex, and

Ferraro, Giancana's underboss. The "corruptors" as we called them. Alex was the mob boss of the Loop. He controlled the gambling and the take from the nightclubs and strip joints which existed, particularly on South State Street during the 1950s and 1960s.

Humphreys during this period of time was the master fixer of the mob. Alex, Ferraro, Ralph Pierce, and Les "Killer Kane" Kruse were members of his group. Their responsibility was to work through Marcy and others to insure that organized crime in Chicago got favorable treatment from labor leaders, businessmen, law enforcement, public officials, and members of the judiciary.

I remember one time in May of 1960 when we followed Humphreys on a trip he made to Washington, D.C. After he arrived there he made a visit to a congressman representing a district of Illinois. When he went in he was carrying a package. When he left an hour or so later he was not carrying a package. He then went to the Hamilton Hotel in Washington. There he met a congressman representing another district of Illinois. When he went in he was carrying a package. When he came out an hour or so later he was not carrying a package.

It was the practice of the hoodlums not to allow anything to expose the officials working with them. For example, Humphreys would encourage a judge to be a "hanging judge" and to get himself a reputation as a tough judge, on the side of the prosecution. Then he could do a favor for the mob and if someone criticized him, he could just say, "Look at my record; look at my statistics. You can't just pick out this one case."

Pat Marcy occasionally met with Gussie Alex. I remember one time we had an informant who was being called on the carpet because he had violated one of the mob tenets. He was called to the Normandy Lounge, in the same building but around the corner from the First Ward headquarters. There he met both Marcy and Alex since his problem involved gambling in the Loop, the domain of both Marcy and Alex.

I had other contacts with John D'Arco as matters came up. I remember on one occasion he told me that he knew that I was a member of the bar and a graduate of Notre Dame Law School. Although I discussed it with my superiors later as a possible attempt to bribe me, we agreed that he had not gone that far when he told me that he was sure that with his help I could make "twice as much money the first year as you make in the FBI" if I were to quit the FBI and open up a law office in Chicago.

I also had contacts with Pat Marcy. However, whereas D'Arco would submit to interviews, Marcy would not. He constantly refused to answer any questions and routinely referred me to his attorney.

Now there came a time when we learned that Giancana had become disenchanted with D'Arco. He apparently felt that D'Arco was a liability in the city council. He, therefore, was considering ordering D'Arco not to run for reelection for either of his posts in the First Ward and even stripping him of his post with Arco Insurance Company. This action was opposed, however, by Humphreys, Alex, and by Accardo. Marcy was playing both sides by letting D'Arco think that he was supporting him but instead telling Giancana to replace D'Arco.

We in the FBI also consulted about it. Was the situation enhanced or worsened with D'Arco aboard? Would a new face be better or worse? We agreed between ourselves that D'Arco, even with his shortcomings, was an effective tool of the syndicate and that it would be much better if he were replaced by somebody who would be bound to have fewer contacts, less experience and might not have the blind discipline to the commands of Giancana, Humphreys, Alex and the rest of organized crime. We therefore agreed to wait for the right opportunity and, if it presented itself, to make a move enabling Giancana to see fit to ignore the advice of what we considered to be the real political experts in the outfit, Humphreys and Alex.

Soon the right opportunity presented itself. We found that Giancana had agreed to a sit-down with D'Arco to allow D'Arco to plead his case. "Mo", as Giancana was known to his associates from his true name, Momo, would meet with D'Arco at two o'clock in the afternoon in a private room at the Czech Lodge in North Riverside, a remote southwestern suburb of Chicago.

Three of us FBI agents went out to the Czech Lodge. Since we did not know which of the several private dining rooms there was to be used for the sit-down, we split up. I spotted Buddy Jacobson, an aide of D'Arco who had worked for Jake Guzik since the 1920s or 1930s in the First Ward, acting as a lookout outside one of the private rooms. I knew, therefore, that this must be the site of the sit-down.

I brushed past Jacobson, no problem because by 1962 Buddy was elderly. Alone in the room, I spotted Giancana and D'Arco hunched towards each other over a small table, obviously engaged in a most serious conversation.

"Ho, ho, ho, it's Mo," I shouted. Giancana recognized me from many confrontations and glared. I turned to D'Arco. Thinking to myself, I wonder who might be embarrassed now, I put out my hand and said, "Hello, John." D'Arco, apparently with the reflex action of a politician, returned my handshake and smiled.

Giancana, still sitting, struck out under the table and kicked D'Arco. "This is Roemer, you [obscene]," he shouted to D'Arco.

D'Arco turned ashen, quickly disengaged his hand and sat down. He looked at me and he looked at Mo. And back to each of us again. I think then he realized for the first time that perhaps, in fact, the FBI did have the ability to embarrass him.

The next day it was announced that D'Arco had suffered a heart attack and was taken to a hospital. He then announced that he would not run for reelection as alderman.

However, it turned out to be a Pyrrhic victory for us and for Chicago. Ultimately, it was decided that D'Arco, although he would give up his seat on the city council, would retain his interest in Arco Insurance and his post as Democratic ward committeeman. This being an elective post, he would have to run for election but that was the least of his concerns.

As a result, John D'Arco is still with us today.

Many machinations took place before a successor to the alderman's post was elected in the First Ward. But first Giancana chose his nephew, Anthony "Busy Busy" DeTolve.

When it turned out on the eve of the election that DeTolve was a bumbling idiot, Giancana told him to get lost and replaced him as a write-in candidate with a personable, capable attorney named Michael Fio Rito. However, we knew that Fio Rito was a suburbanite and not eligible for election in the First Ward of Chicago. Dick Ogilvie and his men conducted an investigation showing that Fio Rito could not have been living at a Loop area hotel as he claimed.

I met with the intelligent Fio Rito and explained to him the many problems ahead for him which included the investigation of his apparent fraud in his residency and the fact that he would have to live under the domination of Pat Marcy, Sam Giancana, Murray Humphreys, Gussie Alex et al.

I could not properly explain this in a first meeting with Fio Rito because he came accompanied by a close ally of Marcy, but in a second secret meeting I believe I got my point across to Fio Rito.

Ultimately, Fio Rito announced that he was resigning his newly won alderman seat.

Now the First Ward and the outfit were doubly embarrassed. First, they had to replace their candidate just days before the election, after the ballots had already been printed. Then, after their candidate prevailed, he withdrew.

The next in the line of First Ward aldermen was Donald Parrillo. Parrillo was the son of a former Republican official from the West Side. Parrillo served on the city council for several years, as I recall, and then he was replaced by Fred Roti. Roti is the son of Bruno Roti who was before my time. But as I understand it, Bruno Roti had a very important leadership position in the Cosa Nostra in Chicago, on the Near South Side, probably under Frank Nitti in the 1930s.

By the time Roti was selected, our surveillance was less intense. However, as the years went by, we continued to develop information indicating to us that Pat Marcy continued to call the shots which his superiors in the mob commanded and that he continued to be the conduit through which the orders from the leadership of organized crime passed to those politicians and public officials who were under the control of the Chicago Cosa Nostra.

Informants continued to advise us through the years that D'Arco and Roti were the front men for Marcy and for the mob. They continued to have the same success, or lack thereof, with Mayor Daley and the same general type of success with Michael Bilandic when Bilandic succeeded Daley in the mid-1970s. By this I mean that Mayor Bilandic treated the First Ward at arm's length and did not accede to their every wish although he did not take any action to expose or curtail the First Ward in their dealings with other public officials.

IT would be an overstatement to say that I am appalled but it would conversely be an understatement to say that I am merely surprised to find that the Chicago mob seems to be better entrenched and more active and more powerful than they were in years past.

I have heard Dan Webb, the U. S. Attorney, say recently that he considers the mobsters just a "bunch of street punks." I agree with him to some extent. If he means that the average rank and file soldier is just a punk, I have no argument. I agree. They are the dregs of society.

However, if Dan is talking about Accardo and Cerone, for instance, I would respectfully disagree. I have met frequently with them, particularly Cerone. I know neither has a Harvard or Yale education, but they are wise, streetwise.

Jackie is an avid reader of best sellers. Even though he suffered a heart attack some time ago, he is apparently fully recovered and keeps himself in top condition at the age of sixty-eight by working out daily. He is a strong force to be reckoned with, both mentally and physically. A worthy foe for any law enforcement officer. Accardo the same. This man has been a force in the Chicago Cosa Nostra for some seven decades! He is the most respected boss the outfit here ever had. How can a man like that be underestimated? Aiuppa is not in the same class in my opinion with Accardo and Cerone, and from my brief encounters with him I would say he would know that. But he has his own qualities and anybody who has survived some dozen years as the top boss here has to have the experience, knowledge and contacts to be a worthy adversary of law enforcement.

The heir apparent, Joe Ferriola, aka Negall, is from the same mold. This man is also a force and so is Donald Angelini whom I've talked to on many occasions. Another definite force. I have the same feeling about Dominic Cortina.

Therefore, at least as far as the leadership is concerned, I would not want to be guilty of any underestimation.

Turning to a discussion of the political arm of the mob, the same things I say about Cerone, Accardo et al., can be said about Pat Marcy. The man is probably seventy now. Chicago crime and politics have been his life. I would venture to say that he might be the most knowledgeable politician in Chicago today. The mayor, the chairman of the county board, the party chairman are all far less experienced in terms of years spent on the political scene in Chicago. (Or more precisely behind the political scene in Chicago.)

Having said that, let me address the current political situation in Chicago today as it pertains to infiltration by the outfit.

My sources in the mob, in politics and in law enforcement tell me that at no time has the First Ward been so close to the power in Chicago. By the First Ward they indicate Marcy, D'Arco, and Roti. What we are really talking about when we refer to the First Ward in this context is organized crime. Any Chicago administration which fails to recognize the place organized crime plays in the First Ward is at least naïve if not worse.

As I near the conclusion of this statement to this committee, I would like to pick a somewhat more recent example of what I have been trying to say concerning the obvious current power of LCN in Chicago.

Keep in mind that way back in 1959, when this committee was sitting with similar hearings on the mob in Chicago, Murray Humphreys, then the master fixer of the mob, told John D'Arco, then and now the figurehead out front in the First Ward, his minimum desire. He told D'Arco that under no circumstances did he want Joe Morris or Bill Duffy put back in any position of power to investigate organized crime in the Chicago Police Department.

Talk about going full circle. Nothing changes in Chicago.

In 1980, Joseph DiLeonardi was the superintendent of police in Chicago. Jane Byrne was the mayor. According to quotes attributed to DiLeonardi in the public press at the time, he was approached in his office by two of Mayor Byrne's top aides, William Griffin and Michael Brady. Griffin was to become deputy mayor and was Mayor Byrne's recent campaign manager. According to DiLeonardi, these top aides told DiLeonardi that she wanted Bill Duffy "chased"; demoted out of his position as deputy superintendant of the Bureau of Inspectional Services where he had the ultimate responsibility for the investigation of organized crime.

DiLeonardi states that when he asked Griffin and Brady why Mayor Byrne wanted Duffy replaced, Griffin and Brady replied that it was at the behest of John D'Arco!

DiLeonardi refused to chase Duffy. Two weeks later he was demoted by Mayor Byrne. Shortly afterwards, a new superintendent was appointed. Deputy Superintendent Duffy was demoted to a watch commander in a Far North Side district where he remains today, far from the fight against organized crime.

It will be interesting to see how the election of a new mayor and the concomitant new administration will affect the outfit. In analyzing their situation, attention could be invited to the fact that they have existed with some eight or nine Chicago mayors since Colosimo. Under some, such as "Big Bill" Thompson and Jane Byrne, they have thrived. Under some, such as Tony Cermak, they have been hard hit. Under some, such as Kennelly and Daley, they were treated with a benign neglect. And yet, as of the date of this hearing, they are as strong as ever.

Appendix B

"HOODS WHO"-WHO'S WHO IN ORGANIZED
CRIME IN METROPOLITAN CHICAGO

JULY 1, 1990

PREPARED BY THE CHICAGO CRIME
COMMISSION
JOHN J. JEMILO, EXECUTIVE DIRECTOR
JERRY GLADDEN, CHIEF INVESTIGATOR
JEANNETE CALLAWAY, ASSOCIATE
DIRECTOR

ACCARDO, ANTHONY

DOB: 04-28-06
DL #: A263-0100-6121
Vehicles: Olds - 736
HT: 5'11" **WT:** 180 lbs.
Eyes: Brn **Hair:** Gray
Criminal history: FBI# 1410106
Convictions: Tax case reversed

AIUPPA, JOSEPH

DOB: 12-01-07
DL #: A100-4900-7342
HT: 5'6" **WT:** 180 lbs.
Eyes: Brn **Hair:** Gray
Criminal history: IR# 17860
    FBI# 951184
Convictions: 1986 Las Vegas skim-
    ming case 28 years, presently in
    Federal prison

ALEMAN, HARRY

DOB: 01-19-39
DL #: A455-3773-9019
Vehicles: Mercedes - RA3277
HT: 5'8" **WT:** 160 lbs.
Eyes: Brn **Hair:** Brn
Hangouts: Race tracks
Criminal history: IR# 12312
    FBI# 711489D
Convictions: RICO 1980 30 years.
    Out in 1989.

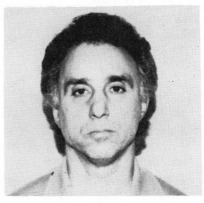

ALEX, GUS

DOB: 04-01-16
DL #: A420-2801-6094
HT: 5'11" **WT:** 175 lbs.
Eyes: Brn **Hair:** Gray
Hangouts: Health Club, 400 E. Randolph
Criminal history: FBI# 4144200

ANDRIACCI, JOSEPH

DOB: 10-20-32
DL #: A536-4333-2299
HT: 5'8" **WT:** 160 lbs.
Eyes: Brn **Hair:** Blk
Hangouts: 1500 W. Taylor, Rosebud Cafe
Criminal history: IR# 70064 FBI# 52158F ISB# 10083960
Convictions: 1965 Burglary (Michigan) 3–10 yrs.

ANGELINI, DONALD

DOB: 09-30-26
DL #: A524-1902-6278
Vehicles: Cad. lic# AIR 1511
HT: 5'10" **WT:** 165 lbs.
Eyes: Brn **Hair:** White
Hangouts: Gianotti's Rest. 8422 W. Lawrence
Criminal history: IR# 42277 FBI# 39024F ISB#927135
Convictions: 1970 Fed. gambling 5 years & $10,000, 1989 Fed. gambling 21 months & $75,000 fine

BASSO, DOMINICK J.

DOB: 02-15-38
DL #: B200-1703-8046
HT: 5'10" **WT:** 233 lbs.
Eyes: Brn **Hair:** Brn
Criminal history: Dupage IR#
  71527
Convictions: 1-7-88, Syndicated
  gambling

BASTONE, CARMEN PETER

DOB: 04-25-31
DL #: B235-1153-1118
Vehicles: Leased
HT: 5'10" **WT:** 210 lbs.
Eyes: Brn **Hair:** Brn
Criminal history: IR# 55356
  FBI# 731629E
Convictions: 1975 False statements
  to FHA

BASTONE, SALVATORE

DOB: 08-09-35
DL #: B235-7853-5226
Vehicles: Leased
HT: 6'1" **WT:** 250 lbs.
Eyes: Brn **Hair:** Blk
Criminal history: FBI#
  369832M8
Convictions: 1987 Fed. racketeer-
  ing 18 months

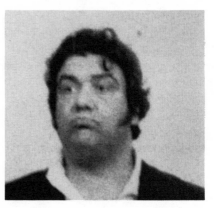

BELLAVIA, ROBERT

DOB: 10-21-39
DL #: B410-7603-9300
Vehicles: DL-1278G
HT: 5′7″ **WT:** 220 lbs.
Eyes: Brn **Hair:** Brn
Criminal history: IR# 160739
   FBI# 791221D ISB# 1224395
Convictions: 1963 Arm. robbery 1
   to 3 years.

BIANCOFIORE, MICHAEL

DOB: 10-02-25
DL #: B521-5522-5281
Vehicles:
HT: 5′9″ **WT:** 210 lbs.
Eyes: Brn **Hair:** Blk
Criminal history: IR# 218078
   FBI# 4575351 ISB# 331004
Convictions: 1969 Extortion/rack-
   eteering 7 years.

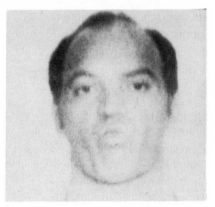

BILLS, SAMUEL

DOB: 07-28-44
DL #: B420-7964-4214
Vehicles: XP9155
HT: 5′7″ **WT:** 150 lbs.
Eyes: Hazel **Hair:** Brn
Criminal history: IR# 115719
   FBI# 391983F ISB# 840571
Convictions: 1972 Burglary, 7 years

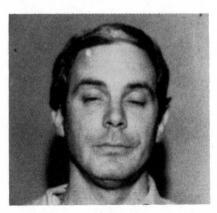

BOCK, WAYNE

DOB: 05-28-35
DL #: B200-8963-5152
Vehicles: PC6664
HT: 6'4" **WT:** 240 lbs.
Eyes: Brn **Hair:** Gray
Criminal history: IR# 38606
  FBI# 267318F ISB# 930153
Convictions: 1967 Possession hijacked $50,000 silver, 7 years.

CALABRESE, FRANK

DOB: 03-17-34
DL #: C416-2703-4079
HT: 5'10" **WT:** 210 lbs.
Eyes: Brn **Hair:** Brn
Criminal history: IR# 32295
  FBI# 702188B ISB# 570248
Convictions: 1954 Interstate auto
  theft

CARIOSCIA, MICHAEL

DOB: 03-18-33
DL #: C620-5413-3113
Vehicles: HA5953
HT: 6'0" **WT:** 185 lbs.
Eyes: Brn **Hair:** Blk
Criminal history: IR# 149726
  FBI# 622871A
Convictions: 1972 Narcotics 10
  years

CARLISI, SAM

DOB: 12-15-21
DL #: C642-7812-1356
Vehicles: Cad lic# EK5085
HT: 5'9" **WT:** 195 lbs.
Eyes: Brn glasses **Hair:** Blk thin
Criminal history: FBI#
882656V3
Convictions: Tax case 6 months
1985

CASTALDO, MIKE

DOB: 08-08-29
DL #: C234-5572-9225
Vehicles: 86 Buick - DZB255
HT: 5'10" **WT:** 190 lbs.
Eyes: Brn **Hair:** Blk
Hangouts: Gene's Deli, 2202 N.
Harlem
Criminal history: IR# 16095
FBI# 984574B
Convictions: 1956 Extortion, 4 to 7
years

CERONE, JOHN P. SR.

DOB: 07-07-14
DL #: C650-4351-4193
HT: 5'7" **WT:** 160 lbs.
Eyes: Brn **Hair:** Bald
Criminal history: FBI# 627727A
Convictions: 1970 Federal gam-
bling conspiracy, 5 years, 1986
federal casino skimming case, 28
years. Presently in federal prison

CIMINO, VIRGIL

DOB: 06-19-43
DL #: C550-8604-3174
Vehicles: EJ8762
HT: 5'8" **WT:** 190 lbs.
Eyes: Brn **Hair:** Brn
Criminal history: IR# 110892
  FBI# 353371F
Convictions: 1971 Fed. drug violation

CORTINA, DOMINIC

DOB: 01-28-25
DL #: C635-1602-5028
Vehicles: RNR 578
HT: 6'2" **WT:** 210 lbs.
Eyes: Brn **Hair:** Brn
Hangouts: Onion Roll Rest. 6935
  W. North Ave
Criminal history: FBI# 338524G
Convictions: 1970 Fed. gambling 5
  years, 1989 pled guilty Fed. gambling 21 months, $75,000 fine

COZZO, VINCENT JAMES

DOB: 01-15-36
DL #: C200-8703-6015
Vehicles: CH 9525
HT: 5'8" **WT:** 200 lbs.
Eyes: Brn **Hair:** Brn
Criminal history: IR# 17020
  ISB# 560729 FBI# 1686126
Convictions: 1964 Poss. of stolen
  goods 3 years

D'Amico, Marco

DOB: 01-01-36
DL #: D520-5403-6001
Vehicles: LNA 606
HT: 5'8" **WT:** 190 lbs.
Eyes: Blue **Hair:** Brn
Hangouts: Elmwood Pk. Social
  Club 7520 W. Diversey
Criminal history: IR# 460096
  ISB# 1241674 FBI#
  484765L8

D'Antonio, James

DOB: 02-26-28
DL #: D535-4502-8057
Vehicles: CE9817
HT: 6'3" **WT:** 190 lbs.
Eyes: Brn **Hair:** Gray
Criminal history: IR# 20989
  ISB# 310371 FBI# 4274659
Convictions: 1945 Burglary 2 years,
  1968 10 years

DeLaurentis, Salvatore

DOB: 08-20-38
DL #: D465-7983-8237
Vehicles: MKB 240
HT: 5'9" **WT:** 160 lbs.
Eyes: Brn **Hair:** Blk
Criminal history: FBI# 112469H
  ISB# 0592290
Convictions: 1965 Gambling

DEMONTE, FRANK

DOB: 12-20-27
DL #: D553-2502-7361
Vehicles: 602091
HT: 5'11" **WT:** 180 lbs.
Eyes: Brn **Hair:** Gray (balding)
Hangouts: Union Hall, 6121 W.
  Diversey
Criminal history: IR# 94618
  ISB# 1086720 FBI# 480181F
Convictions: 1983 18 months Federal contempt

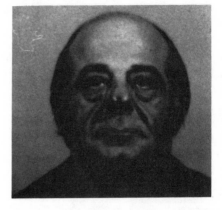

DEROSA, FRANK

DOB: 10-05-43
DL #: D620-2614-3284
Vehicles: BA5716
HT: 5'10" **WT:** 190 lbs.
Eyes: Brn **Hair:** Brn
Criminal history: IR# 25115
  FBI# 222091F
Convictions: 1974 5 years for interstate theft

DIFRONZO, JOHN SR.

DOB: 12-13-28
DL #: D165-4602-8354
Vehicles: DL 633N
HT: 5'10" **WT:** 170 lbs.
Eyes: Brn **Hair:** Brn
Hangouts: Gene's Deli, 2202 N.
  Harlem
Criminal history: IR# 53127
  FBI# 65585
Convictions: 1950 Burglary 2 years

DIFRONZO, JOSEPH

DOB: 10-25-34
DL #: D165-4803-4304
Vehicles: MY 266
HT: 5'9" **WT:** 175 lbs.
Eyes: Brn **Hair:** Brn
Hangouts: Valentino's Cafe, 3410
  N. Harlem
Criminal history: IR# 222216
  ISB# 550364 FBI# 245009C
Convictions: 5 years for burglary

DIFRONZO, PETER

DOB: 5-13-33
DL #: D165-6603-3137
Vehicles: CCY 911
HT: 5'8" **WT:** 185 lbs.
Eyes: Brn **Hair:** Brn
Hangouts: Gene's Deli, 2202 N.
  Harlem
Criminal history: IR# 258821
  FBI# 392342B
Convictions: 1965 Interstate stolen
  prop. 10 years

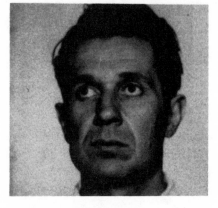

FORLIANO, THOMAS

DOB: 10-01-49
DL #: F645-8384-9280
Vehicles: FZP913
HT: 5'7" **WT:** 180 lbs.
Eyes: Brn **Hair:** Brn
Criminal history: IR# 181267
  FBI# 512 749G
Convictions: Burglary

GAGLIANO, GARY

DOB: 12-27-43
DL #: G245-2934-3368
Vehicles: IZ 590
HT: 5'11" **WT:** 190 lbs.
Eyes: Brn **Hair:** Blk
Criminal history: IR# 271297
  FBI# 26330E
Convictions: Bank robbery

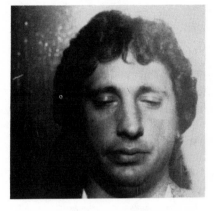

GRIECO, JOSEPH

DOB: 12-23-27
DL #: G628-4852-7364
HT: 5'11" **WT:** 190 lbs.
Eyes: Brn **Hair:** Brn-Gry
Hangouts: Majestic Eagle
  Investments, 6300 N. River Rd.,
  Rosemont
Criminal history: IR# 60391
  FBI# 367272C
Convictions: 1985 Federal obstruc-
tion of justice 5 years.

GURGONE, MICHAEL

DOB: 08-31-37
DL #: G625-5413-7248
Vehicles: RYH 234
HT: 5'11" **WT:** 225 lbs.
Eyes: Brn **Hair:** Blk-Gry
Criminal history: IR# 204180
  ISB# 389170 FBI# 28637D
Convictions: Robbery 1989

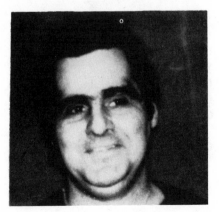

IGNOFFO, ROLAND

DOB: 05-27-49
DL #: I251-7304-9151
Vehicles:
HT: 5'10" **WT:** 185 lbs.
Eyes: Brn **Hair:** Brn
Criminal history: IR# 177481
  ISB# 1625874 FBI# 749207G
Convictions: 1985 Syndicated gambling 5 years prob.

INENDINO, JAMES

DOB: 12-14-42
DL #: I553-4404-2355
Vehicles:
HT: 5'7" **WT:** 160 lbs.
Eyes: Brn **Hair:** Brn
Criminal history: IR# 461084
  FBI# 371131
Convictions: 1978 Dangerous offender 20 years out in 1989.

INFELICE, ERNEST "ROCKY"

DOB: 03-16-22
DL #: I514-7252-2078
Vehicles: OF7241
HT: 5'11" **WT:** 200 lbs.
Eyes: Brn **Hair:** Bald-Gray
Criminal history: IR# 100891
  ISB# 489576 FBI# 308006B
Convictions: 1973 Sale of narcotics 10 years; presently in Federal custody (MCC)

LAMANTIA, JOSEPH

DOB: 02-01-34
DL #: L553-4863-4032
Vehicles: 383923
HT: 5'7" **WT:** 225 lbs.
Eyes: Brn **Hair:** Brn-Gray
Hangouts: Ital. Amer. Club 268
   W. 26th St.
Criminal history: IR# 26316
   ISB# 452341 FBI# 677113A
Convictions: 1951 Burglary 2 to 5
   years

LaPIETRA, ANGELO

DOB: 10-30-20
DL #: L136-0002-0309
HT: 5'5" **WT:** 180 lbs.
Eyes: Blu **Hair:** Bald
Criminal history: IR# 394436
   FBI# 1777460
Convictions: 1942 Sale of narcotics,
   1986 Federal skimming case, 16
   years, presently in Federal prison

LaPIETRA, JAMES

DOB: 03-28-27
DL #: L136-4402-7090
Vehicles: DXD969
HT: 5'11" **WT:** 215 lbs.
Eyes: Brn-gls **Hair:** Blk-balding
Hangouts: Ital. Amer Club, 266
   W. 26th St.
Criminal history: FBI# 4484680

LAVALLEY, JAMES F.

DOB: 04-29-44
DL #: L140-4464-4122
HT: 6'0" **WT:** 220 lbs.
Eyes: Blu **Hair:** Brn
Criminal history: IR# 57500 -
Enforcer FBI# 741789E
Convictions: 16 Arrests, 4 convictions, 1 assault, 2 burglary, 1 larceny

LOMBARDO, JOSEPH

DOB: 01-01-29
DL #: L516-4802-9001
HT: 6'9" **WT:** 175 lbs.
Eyes: Brn **Hair:** Blk
Criminal history: IR# 592124
FBI# A1313042
Convictions: 1983 Conspiracy to bribe U.S. senator, 15 years, 1986 Las Vegas casino skim case, 15 years. Presently in Federal prison

MALMENATO, MICHAEL

DOB: 10-01-31
DL #: M455-5583-1280
Vehicles: EV 7149
HT: 5'9" **WT:** 185 lbs.
Eyes: Brn **Hair:** Sandy
Criminal history: IR# 63903
ISB# 450131 FBI# 779700A
Convictions: 1961 Burglary 2 years

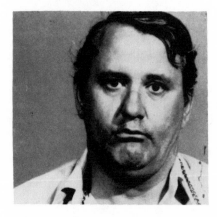

MARCELLO, JAMES
DOB: 12-13-41
DL #: M624-4504-1354
Vehicles: DV3237
HT: 5'8" **WT:** 158 lbs.
Eyes: Brn **Hair:** Brn

MARINO, LOUIS
DOB: 03-14-32
DL #: M650-5383-2076
Vehicles: FS 8607
HT: 5'11" **WT:** 200 lbs.
Eyes: Brn **Hair:** Brn-Gray
Hangouts: Marano Produce 15
  South Water Mkt.
Criminal history: FBI# 635608F

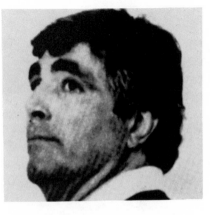

MARTIN, GINO "BLACKIE"
DOB: 09-29-22
DL #: M635-2802-2277
HT: 5'10" **WT:** 160 lbs.
Eyes: Brn **Hair:** Balding-Blk
Criminal history: IR# 44770
  FBI# 824944C
Convictions: 1959 Mail fraud 1
  year 1964 Grand theft

MESSINO, WILLIE
DOB: 01-07-17
DL #: M250-9201-7007
Vehicles: FYD 192
HT: 5'7" **WT:** 190 lbs.
Eyes: Brn-gls **Hair:** Brn
Hangouts: Gene's Deli, 2202 N.
  Harlem
Criminal history: IR# 55433
  FBI# 922367
Convictions: 1967 Kidnapping 7
  extortion, 10 years.

MIGLIORE, CARMEN
DOB: 08-04-36
DL #: M246-1163-6221
HT: 5'8" **WT:** 195 lbs.
Eyes: Brn **Hair:** Brn
Criminal history: IR#202269
  ISB#A0085840
Convictions: 1961 Mail fraud 1 to 3
  years

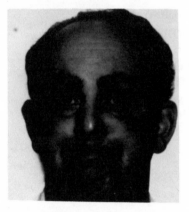

MONTELEONE, JOHN
DOB: 01-29-24
DL #: M534-4602-4029
HT: 5'11" **WT:** 240 lbs.
Eyes: Brn-gls **Hair:** Brn-bald
Criminal history: IR# 180489
  FBI# 835775E
Convictions: 1986 Criminal con-
  tempt 4 years released January
  1990

PANNO, FRANK

DOB: 03-21-33
DL #: P550-1653-3065
HT: 5'4" **WT:** 160 lbs.
Eyes: Brn **Hair:** Brn
Criminal history: IR# 305943
FBI# 641878S1
Convictions: Prostitution 1986
presently in Federal prison

PARRILLI, CHARLES

DOB: 08-28-28
DL #: P640-1502-8245
Vehicles: 89 Lincoln - LP2159
HT: 5'10" **WT:** 175 lbs.
Eyes: Brn **Hair:** Brn
Hangouts: West Suburban Loan
Co. 507 S. Oak Park Ave., Oak
Park
Criminal history: IR# 174406
Convictions: Pled guilty Fed. gam-
bling 1989

PARRILLI, LOUIS

DOB: 12-15-13
DL #: P640-5331-3356
Vehicles: 85 Chrys. - SGR397
HT: 5'10" **WT:** 185 lbs.
Eyes: Brn **Hair:** Brn
Hangouts: West Suburban Loan
507 S. Oak Park Ave., Oak
Park
Criminal history: IR# 21201
Convictions: Pled guilty Fed. gam-
bling 1989

PASCUCCI, JOSEPH
DOB: 10-12-32
DL #: P220-4843-2291
HT: 5'7" **WT:** 185 lbs.
Eyes: Brn **Hair:** Brn
Criminal history: IR# 56914
    FBI# 398584F
Convictions: 1987 2½ years Fed.
    gambling violations

PATRICK, LEONARD
DOB: 10-06-13
DL #: P362-5201-3285
Vehicles: 206861
HT: 5'11" **WT:** 200 lbs.
Eyes: Blue **Hair:** White-balding
Criminal history: IR# 289608
    ISB# 54942 FBI# 635564
Convictions: 1933 Bank robbery,
    10 years Federal criminal con-
    tempt 4 years

PETITT, JOSEPH
DOB: 11-21-24
DL #: P330-4942-4331
Vehicles: BTK 737
HT: 5'9" **WT:** 160 lbs.
Eyes: Blu-gls **Hair:** Brn-Gray
Hangouts: Northbrook &
    Highland Pk Golf Club
Criminal history: IR# 322084
    ISB# 2044141 FBI# 4936094
Convictions: 1947 Passing counter-
    feit notes, 2 years.

PETITT, LARRY

DOB: 09-16-28
DL #: P330-5202-8264
Vehicles: FVW 497
HT: 5'8" **WT:** 170 lbs.
Eyes: Brn-gls **Hair:** Gray
Criminal history: IR# 17643
ISB# 2044156 FBI# 105986A
Convictions: 1981 Battery, 1 year.

PETTI, CHRIS

DOB: 04-01-27
HT: 5'8" **WT:** 170 lbs.
Eyes: Brn **Hair:** Brn
Criminal history: FBI#
F573617G
Convictions: Racketeering 1990 -
awaiting trial

PILOTTO, ALFRED

DOB: 01-06-11
DL #: P430-0001-1006
HT: 6'1" **WT:** 200 lbs.
Eyes: Brn **Hair:** Bald
Criminal history: FBI# 636588
Convictions: 1982 Labor racketeer-
ing, 20 years presently in Federal
prison

Posner, Michael
DOB: 01-01-42
DL #: P256-5594-2001
HT: 5'10" **WT:** 200 lbs.
Eyes: Brn **Hair:** Brn
Criminal history: IR# 102297
ISB# 1092487 FBI# 412158F
Convictions: 1986 Prostitution
"Roman House" Lake Cty. Presently in Federal prison

Rainone, John "Mario"
DOB: 12-16-52
DL #: R550-5505-2357
Vehicles: GE 4277
HT: 5'8" **WT:** 160 lbs.
Eyes: Brn **Hair:** Blk
Criminal history: IR# 508897
ISB# 1876554 FBI#
839072R11
Convictions: 1978 Burglary & conspiracy to bomb 5 years.

Salerno, Robert C.
DOB: 07-13-34
DL #: S465-7733-4199
HT: 5'8" **WT:** 160 lbs.
Eyes: Brn **Hair:** Brn-balding
Hangouts: Race tracks
Criminal history: IR# 119235
ISB# 1132695 FBI# 435936F
Convictions: 1985 Fed. racketeering & extortion

SCHWEIHS, FRANK

DOB: 02-07-30
DL #: S200-2703-0038
HT: 6'0" **WT:** 180 lbs.
Eyes: Grn **Hair:** Grey-Blk
Criminal history: IR# 20146
  ISB# 427869 FBI# 345162A
Convictions: 1989 Extortion, 13
  years presently in Federal prison

SOLANO, VINCENT I.

DOB: 10-12-19
DL #: S450-8601-9291
Vehicles: LU 7188
HT: 5'9" **WT:** 200 lbs.
Eyes: Brn **Hair:** Gray-balding
Hangouts: Union Hall 6121 W.
  Diversey
Criminal history: FBI# 1995439
Convictions: 1940 Con game, 1
  year.

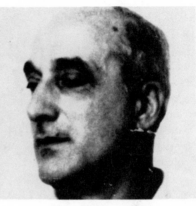

SPADAVECCHIO, JOSEPH

DOB: 02-17-28
DL #: S131-4842-8048
Vehicles: AIR 305
HT: 5'10" **WT:** 170 lbs.
Eyes: Brn **Hair:** Gray
Hangouts: Onion Roll Rest. 6935
  W. North, Oak Pk.
Criminal history: FBI# 599164P5
Convictions: 1979 Fed. gambling
  violation 1989 Fed. gambling vio-
  lation 18 months, $50,000 fine

TOCCO, ALBERT
DOB: 08-09-29
DL #: T200-0202-9226
HT: 5'11" **WT:** 200 lbs.
Eyes: Brn **Hair:** Blk
Criminal history: IR# 398601
　FBI# 296484A
Convictions: Fed. racketeering
　1989, 200 years presently in Fed-
　eral prison

TOMINELLO, RAYMOND
DOB: 06-05-40
DL #: T554-7304-0160
Vehicles: EK7202
HT: 5'8" **WT:** 170 lbs.
Eyes: Brn **Hair:** Blk
Criminal history: IR# 204186
　ISB# 1279932 FBI# 969932H
Convictions: 1989 Fed. gambling, 8
　months, $5,000 fine

VENA, ALBERT
DOB: 06-03-48
DL #: V500-0324-8158
HT: 5'2" **WT:** 145 lbs.
Eyes: Blu **Hair:** Brn
Criminal history: IR# 118902
　FBI# 956792F
Convictions: 1974 Robbery-kid-
　napping, 8 years

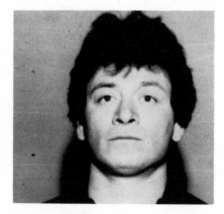

Glossary

Apalachin The meeting of some seventy prominent members and leaders of La Cosa Nostra from all over the country, in 1957 in the village of Apalachin in central New York State. After it was interrupted by Sergeant Edgar Croswell of the New York State Police and agents of the Alcohol, Tobacco and Firearms Unit of the Treasury Department, it led J. Edgar Hoover to institute the Top Hoodlum Program, bringing the FBI into the investigation of organized crime for the first time in its history.

ASAC Assistant Special Agent in Charge of an FBI field office.

AUSA Assistant United States Attorney.

The Black Book A listing by the Nevada Gaming Control Commission of those persons banned from the premises of hotels and casinos in Nevada. Murray "The Camel" Humphreys, Sam Giancana, and Marshall Caifano were among the first so listed.

The Bureau Short for the FBI. Also used within the FBI to identify FBIHQ in Washington, D.C.

Book A bookmaking establishment; in Chicago called an "office."

Bug A microphone surreptitiously placed in a premises—not to be confused with a "tap," a wiretap on a telephone.

C-1 The squad of agents in the Chicago Field Office of the FBI which was mandated to investigate organized crime. The "O.C. Squad" in Chicago.

Capo A high level position in a Cosa Nostra family. A captain. Short for "caporegime" (captain of a regime, a crew) or "capodecima" (captain of ten). In rank, just below the boss, the underboss and the *consigliere*.

Casino Control Commission In New Jersey, the agency mandated to regulate gaming in Atlantic City—to license key employees, hotel-casinos and to oversee the Division of Gaming Enforcement, its investigative arm.

Castellammarese War The war between the forces of Joe "The Boss" Masseria and Salvatore Maranzano for control of New York City, 1930–31. Won by Maranzano, originally from Castellammare del Golfo in Sicily. Led to the formation of The Commission, the ruling body of La Cosa Nostra.

Central States Pension and Welfare Fund The Central States, Southeast and Southwest Areas Pension Fund of the International Brotherhood of the Teamsters; the Teamsters union. Used for many years as the "bank" of the Chicago mob and to a lesser extent by other mob families, particularly in New York, Milwaukee, Cleveland, and Kansas City. Used extensively in the 1960s and 1970s to finance loans to the fronts for mobs in Las Vegas hotel-casinos.

Chicago Crime Commission A private agency, financed by public spirited private citizens concerned with organized crime, inefficiency in government and corruption in politics. Formed in 1919. Offices at 79 West Monroe in Chicago. John Jemilo, former deputy superintendent of the Chicago Police Department, is the current executive director and the board is made up of many of the leading citizens of Chicago and suburbs. The author is a special consultant on organized crime to the commission.

Chop To murder in gangland style.

CIP The Criminal Intelligence Program of the FBI. No longer in usage. Now called the Organized Crime Program. Initially called the Top Hoodlum Program. Nomenclature in use in the 1960s.

The Circus Gang Sometimes called the Circus Cafe Gang. In existence in the period approximately 1912–1925. A group of young toughs and hoodlums, many of whom were recruited by Al Capone into his mob. Tony Accardo, Machine Gun Jack McGurn and Tough Tony Capezio were graduates of the Circus Gang which headquartered at a tavern called the Circus Cafe on North Avenue in Chicago, hence its name.

Clip To murder in gangland style.

The Commission The national ruling body of La Cosa Nostra. Consists of nine to twelve of the bosses of LCN families. New York, with five members, and Chicago with one, are always represented on The Commission. Detroit, New England, New Jersey, Philadelphia are generally represented and Pittsburgh, Cleveland and Buffalo are sometimes represented. The Commission arbitrates disputes between families. It has no right to interfere with the internal affairs of an individual family.

Comp Complimentary services rendered to a "high roller" or a V.I.P. by Nevada and Atlantic City gaming casinos. Such as free rooms, drinks, and meals. Sometimes extended to include escorts.

Con As in "con game" or confidence man. Duplicity; deception.

Connection Guys Called "the corruption squad" by the FBI. A faction of a Cosa Nostra family mandated to corrupt political leaders, public officials, law enforcement members, labor leaders and anyone in a position to provide favorable treatment to the mob. Frank Costello in New York and Jake Guzik, Murray Humphreys, and Gus Alex in Chicago have been leaders of connection guys with Alex currently the leader in Chicago.

Consigliere One of the very top positions in a Cosa Nostra family. The advisor or counselor. Usually a very experienced and capable leader. The consummate *consigliere* is Tony Accardo in Chicago. He has been the *consigliere* in Chicago—except for a brief period in the early 1970s when he resumed his position as boss—from 1957 into the 1990s.

Consuliere Terminology used interchangeably with *"consigliere"* but not as common.

Counter Surveillance The method of insuring against surveillance. The precautions utilized to determine whether one is being tailed. Usually with the use of a "follow car" or person.

Division of Gaming Enforcement The enforcement arm of the Casino Control Commission in New Jersey. Mandated to investigate applicants for licenses in Atlantic City and to police the casinos.

Dry Clean To take precautionary measures to evade surveillance by law enforcement agencies.

Elsur An electronic surveillance. A "bug." A hidden microphone in a strategic premises.

Family A branch of a Cosa Nostra organization. There are currently twenty-four LCN families in the United States. Always named for whoever was the boss in the early 1960s. Examples are the "Genovese Family" or the "Giancana Family."

FBIHQ FBI Headquarters located in the J. Edgar Hoover Building, also known as the FBI Building, between 9th and 10th Streets on Pennsylvania Avenue, NW, in Washington, D.C.

Fisur A physical surveillance, a "tail."

Five Points Gang The gang of young hoodlums in Brooklyn, N.Y. during the 1920s, from which many recruits to the Cosa Nostra emanated. Such as Johnny Torrio.

Forty-Two Gang The gang of young thieves and hoodlums who emanated from The Patch, the area in Chicago centered at Taylor and Halsted Streets in the Italian immigrant area. Many recruits to the Chicago Cosa Nostra were spawned from the Forty-Two Gang such as Sam Giancana and Sam Battaglia. "Mad Sam" DeStefano also was a number of the Forty-Two Gang.

The G Terminology used by the mobsters to refer to federal law enforcement agents, particularly to FBI agents.

Glitter Gulch The downtown area of Las Vegas; Fremont Street.

The Greylord Case One of the great successes of the FBI and the Justice Department. The investigation by the FBI and the United States Attorney's office in Chicago leading to the successful prosecution of some eighty different defendants including Cook County judges, bailiffs, attorneys, and police officers. Investigation was developed primarily by undercover FBI agents posing as local attorneys in the late 1970s and early to mid-1980s. Exposed extent of corruption in judicial system in Chicago.

Grind Joint A casino which is known to "grind" gamblers in and out in a hurry with the intent to win the patrons' money quickly in order to make room for new customers.

High Roller A gambler in a casino who bets large amounts. He is therefore given preferential treatment including comping.

The Hollywood Extortion Case Extortion by Chicago mob of the Hollywood movie studios who paid almost two million dollars in the late 1930s for labor peace. The Chicago mob's control of the International Alliance of Theatrical Stage Employees, IATSE, was the lever utilized by the Chicago mob. Every studio in Hollywood contributed.

ITAR The Interstate Travel in Aid of Racketeering Statute passed in 1961 making it a federal crime to travel to commit a category of crime, particularly gambling. Passed under the auspices of Robert Kennedy when he became attorney general in his brother's administration.

ITWI The Interstate Transportation of Wagering Information Statute, making it a federal crime to pass wagering information across state lines. Little used.

ITWP The Interstate Transportation of Wagering Paraphernalia Statute making it a federal crime to transport gambling devices across state lines. ITAR is used extensively but ITWI and ITWP are seldom used in the fight against organized crime. All three were passed at the same time in 1961.

Juice Loan sharking; shylocking. Used in Chicago to define loans to high risk borrowers such as gamblers, thieves, burglars, and to businessmen unable to obtain loans from commercial sources such as banks or savings and loans. A loan made with the knowledge that extreme physical violence will be used to recover it. Next to gambling the most prevalent source of income to a Cosa Nostra family. Noted for the usurious and exorbitant rate of interest demanded weekly. Usually "six for five," six dollars for every five dollars borrowed.

Kaffee Klatsch The name of the investigation of the FBI and of the Justice Department Strike Force in Chicago to determine the extent of corruption in Chicago. Focused primarily but not exclusively on the machinations of officals of the Regular Democratic Organization of the First Ward of Chicago, such as Pat Marcy, John D'Arco, Sr. and Fred Roti. As part of Kaffee Klatsch, a hidden video camera and an "elsur," a bug, was secreted in the Counsellor's Row Restaurant across from City Hall and adjacent to 100 North LaSalle, the building which houses the headquarters of the regular Democratic organization of the First Ward. Booth One in the restaurant was regularly reserved in the late 1980s by First Ward officials such as Marcy and Roti. Also as part of Kaffee Klatsch, attorney Robert Cooley wore a "body-mike" for some three years to record conversations he had with subjects of the operation. As of the writing of this work, no indictments had been handed down but were expected at any time. Kaffee Klatsch has the potential of being one of the outstanding examples of good law enforcement in the United States in our history.

Kefauver Committee The U.S. Senate Committee chaired by Sen. Estes Kefauver (D-Tenn.) which held hearings on organized crime across the country in the early 1950s.

La Cosa Nostra (LCN) What is known as "traditional organized crime" in the United States. Italian for "our thing." The name of the national organization of organized crime when it was formed in 1931. Used extensively by families in eastern U.S. and by the FBI but almost never by the Chicago family.

The Loop The downtown area of Chicago. Formed by "the loop" of the Chicago Transit Authority's elevated trains. From Wabash to Wells, east to west, and from Lake to Van Buren, north to south, although in general practice it extends from Wacker to Congress and from Michigan to Wacker.

Made Guy An indoctrinated, actual, initiated member of a Cosa Nostra family. Used extensively in Chicago, not so much in New York, where the terminology is "good fellow" or "wiseguy."

Mafia In precise terminology, the Sicilian organization of criminals and hoodlums. As utilized herein, however, it is used interchangeably with La Cosa Nostra, the outfit, the mob, the crime syndicate, the underworld and organized crime. Technically, however, the Mafia and La Cosa Nostra are two separate and distinct organizations with the latter being the American branch of organized crime. For instance, the "Pizza Case" prosecuted in Manhattan in the late 1980s was a prosecution of Sicilians who had migrated to the United States and were actual Mafia members who had no formal connection with the LCN.

The Magnificent Mile That stretch of Michigan Avenue in Chicago noted for its luxurious shops and highrise buildings. Corresponds to New York's Fifth Avenue or Park Avenue or to Beverly Hills's Rodeo Drive. Extends from the Chicago River and the Wrigley Building north to Lake Shore Drive and the Drake Hotel.

Marker An I.O.U. in gaming parlance. The documentation of a debt owed to a casino by a gambler.

The Mayfield Road Gang A group of Jewish organized crime figures who organized gambling activity in Cleveland in the 1930s, spread to southern Ohio and northern Kentucky in the 1940s and to Las Vegas in the very late 1950s. Headed by Moe Dalitz who fronted for the New York and Chicago mobs in hotel-casinos in Nevada.

The McClellan Committee The select committee of the U.S. Senate chaired by Sen. John L. McClellan (D-Arkansas) which investigated and held public and closed hearings on organized crime throughout the country in the late 1950s and early 1960s. Commonly referred to as the "Rackets Committee." Robert Kennedy was its general counsel and John Kennedy was a member.

M.O. Modus Operandi. The method of operation of a mob in ordinary affairs. Or of a law enforcement agency to conduct its routine investigations.

Nagra The make of the body recorder used by undercover operatives. A "body-mike" secreted on the person of a "U.C." operative to record personal conversations with the subject of an investigation.

Omertà The oath of secrecy taken by "made" members or "good fellows" of La Cosa Nostra and of the Mafia not to reveal secrets, not to inform on members and associates and not to covet the wives and girlfriends of fellow members. To be loyal.

On the Arm To extort, to muscle, to intimidate.

On the Pad On the payroll of the mob. Usually refers to a law enforcement officer, political leader or public official who accepts the graft of a mobster in return for favorable treatment.

The Outfit The Chicago mob.

To Pack To carry a weapon, usually a gun.

The Pendorf Case "Penetration of Dorfman." The investigation conducted by the Chicago FBI and the Justice Department Strike Force there which resulted in the convictions of Allen Dorfman of the Central States Pension Fund of the Teamsters, Roy Williams, President of the Teamsters and Joe "The Clown" Lombardo, a Chicago capo. A major accomplishment. The case agent was Pete Wacks, the veteran Chicago FBI agent.

The Red Book A lengthy listing by Metro, the law enforcement agency in Las Vegas, of those persons associated with organized crime in Nevada. Confidential, for the exclusive use of Metro to aid its investigators. Not available to the public; not to be confused with the BLACK BOOK, above.

Resident Agent An FBI agent assigned to a resident agency of the FBI; a smaller office which reports to a headquarters city. For instance, Tucson to Phoenix, or Waukegan to Chicago.

RICO The Racketeer Influenced and Corrupt Organizations Act. Drafted by G. Robert Blakey of the Justice Department, now a law professor at the University of Notre Dame. It makes it a federal crime to conduct the affairs of an enterprise through a "pattern of racketeering." A pattern is said to exist when members of such an enterprise commit at least two acts of racketeering within ten years of each other. These acts include murder, gambling, securities fraud, mail fraud, extortion, robbery and other crimes. Can be prosecuted criminally or civilly and can result in confiscation of the ill gotten goods even before trial. In a civil RICO case, plaintiffs can collect triple damages.

Rush Street The nightclub area on the Near North Side of Chicago.

SAC The Special Agent in Charge of an FBI field office. Except in New York where an assistant director is in charge, such as Jim Fox at present.

Saint Valentine's Day Massacre The infamous killing of seven members of the Bugs Moran gang in Chicago by members of the Al Capone mob including Tony Accardo, the former absolute boss of the Chicago mob and the current *consigliere.* On February 14, 1929.

Scam A scheme designed to defraud the victim.

Sit-Down A meeting between mobsters with each other or with outsiders.

The Strawman Case A two-phased investigation by the Kansas City office of the FBI and the Kansas City Justice Department Strike Force into skimming activities of Las Vegas casinos by mobs in Chicago, Kansas City, Cleveland, and Milwaukee. The first part of the Strawman prosecution concerned skimming at the Tropicana in Las Vegas and the second part, skimming of Argent Corporation Hotels in Las Vegas, particularly at the Stardust. It resulted in the conviction of top leaders of the Chicago, Kansas City, and Milwaukee mobs such as Jackie Cerone, Joe Aiuppa, Frank Balistrieri, Carl DeLuna and Carl Civella. Tony Spilotro was indicted but severed. Before he could be tried he was murdered in Chicago in June 1986. The FBI case agent was William Ouseley.

Society of Former Agents of the FBI Most former FBI agents are members of this organization. It has chapters in major cities and holds annual national and regional conventions (Honolulu in 1990). It also holds monthly luncheons in its scores of local chapters. Bill Beane is the national chairman in 1989–90 and Ted Foley will be the chairman for 1990–91.

Soldier An actual member of an LCN family. Its lowest rung.

SOG The Seat of Government. Now called the FBIHQ. Terminology for headquarters of the FBI in Washington during the reign of J. Edgar Hoover until he died in May, 1972.

Sting Used by law enforcement to "set up" a victim who is already predisposed to commit a crime. An investigative technique. A typical example is when an investigative agency provides a setting where thieves can fence their stolen property. The agency must insure that no entrapment occurs wherein the criminal is enticed to commit the crime by the agency.

Street Agent The front line of combat of the FBI against lawbreakers. The action agent or the brick agent who carries out the work of the FBI. Officially called a field agent. All investigation, arrests, surveillances, undercover work, counter intelligence work, antiterrorist work and installation of ELSURS is done by street agents. The backbone of the FBI.

Street Crew A group of soldiers in a family of La Cosa Nostra. For instance, the Ferriola Street Crew, the largest and most aggressive faction of the Chicago LCN which controlled gambling throughout Chicago in the 1970s and 1980s until Ferriola became the absolute boss of Chicago in 1986.

Street Tax A fee imposed by the Chicago mob on persons who operate on the fringe of or outside the law such as burglars, thieves, highjackers, chop shop operators, pornographers, prostitutes, pimps and X rated movie house operators. A prime source of income to the Chicago mob.

The Strip Las Vegas Boulevard in Las Vegas; the location of most of the biggest hotels in Nevada although there are two or three large ones downtown on Fremont Street. Formerly known as Highway 91. Most of the seventy or so hotels in Las Vegas are located on the Strip.

Tail A physical surveillance.

Tap Wire tapping; monitoring telephone calls. Differentiated from "bugging," planting a hidden microphone in a premises.

The THP The Top Hoodlum Program.

Title III Authority Title III of the 1968 Omnibus Crime and Safe Streets Act which gives authority to federal courts to authorize law enforcement agencies of the federal government, such as the FBI, to wiretap and eavesdrop. The evidence obtained thereby is admissible in court. This authority was granted in 1968 but was not utilized until after Ramsey Clark was replaced as Attorney General in 1970. It is now a major instrument in organized crime investigations.

To Throw Fear Intimidate. The practice of mobsters to place fear in a victim. Usually meant to indicate that the mob does not intend to kill their victim but instead to take what physical action it takes to deter the victim from whatever action he might be taking contrary to what the mob perceives as their best interests.

Tommy Gun, Chicago Chopper The Thompson submachine gun, the weapon of choice of the Chicago mob in the 1920s and 1930s.

Top Ten Program The listing of the ten most wanted FBI fugitives. Designed to make the public aware of the most wanted fugitives.

VEGMON The name given the operation of the FBI in the 1970s in following the skim from Nevada casinos to the mob recipients throughout the country but especially in Chicago, New York, Miami, Cleveland, Kansas City, and Milwaukee. An acronym for "Vegas Money."

VIG Vigorish. The rate at which bets on sporting events is made. Usually $11 for $10, meaning that at a Vegas sports book it takes an $11 wager to win $10.

Wanted Poster Officially called an Identification Order by the FBI. A cardboard poster, publicly displayed, such as in a post office, of a badly wanted fugitive.

West Side Bloc The group of political leaders and public officials in Chicago, generally from the West Side, who are under the influence and/or control of the Chicago mob, primarily under the influence of the Regular Democratic Organization of the First Ward. Now somewhat passé since the West Side has changed its ethnic and racial nature.

Whack To kill.

Wiseguy Used to designate an actual member of a family of La Cosa Nostra in the eastern United States, particularly in New York City. Never used to refer to a "made" member of the Chicago LCN. Practically synonymous with "good fellow."

Work Car An automobile generally souped up and reinforced, used by burglars and thieves to perpetrate a crime and by mobsters when carrying out a hit.

Underboss The number two man in a family of La Cosa Nostra. Responsible only to the boss and level with the *consigliere.* Called a *sotto capo* on occasion in the East.

USA The United States Attorney, the principal federal prosecutor in a federal judicial district.

Index